NEW YORK REVIEW
CLASSICS

THE CRISIS OF THE
EUROPEAN MIND

PAUL HAZARD (1878–1944) was an eminent French historian of ideas and a pioneering scholar of comparative literature. After teaching at the University of Lyon and the Sorbonne, he was appointed to the chair of comparative literature at the Collège de France in 1925 and in 1940 was elected to the French Academy. From 1932 on Hazard also taught at regular intervals at Columbia University, and he was in New York when the Nazis occupied France in 1941. He immediately returned to France to assume the rectorship of the University of Paris but was rejected for the position by the Nazis. Hazard's reputation rests on two major works of intellectual history: *The Crisis of the European Mind*, from 1935, and its sequel, *European Thought in the Eighteenth Century: From Montesquieu to Lessing*, published posthumously in 1946.

JAMES LEWIS MAY (b. 1873) was a British critic and translator, best known as a translator and biographer of Anatole France. His 1928 translation of *Madame Bovary* for The Bodley Head was for many years the standard edition. In addition to translating *The Crisis of the European Mind*, May translated its sequel, *European Thought in the Eighteenth Century*.

ANTHONY GRAFTON is Henry Putnam University Professor of History and the Humanities at Princeton University. His most recent book is *The Culture of Correction in Renaissance Europe*.

THE CRISIS OF THE EUROPEAN MIND

1680–1715

PAUL HAZARD

Translated from the French by
J. LEWIS MAY

Introduction by
ANTHONY GRAFTON

NEW YORK REVIEW BOOKS

New York

THIS IS A NEW YORK REVIEW BOOK
PUBLISHED BY THE NEW YORK REVIEW OF BOOKS
435 Hudson Street, New York, NY 10014
www.nyrb.com

First published in France as *La Crise de la conscience européenne* in 1935
This translation first published in England by Hollis & Carter in 1953

Library of Congress Cataloging-in-Publication Data
Hazard, Paul, 1878–1944.
[Crise de la conscience européenne. English]
The crisis of the European mind / by Paul Hazard ; introduction by Anthony
Grafton ; translated from the French by J. Lewis May.
    p. cm. — (New York Review books classics)
 Original English translation published as: The European mind. New Haven :
Yale University Press, c1953.
 Includes index.
 ISBN 978-1-59017-619-1 (alk. paper)
 1. Europe—Intellectual life. 2. Philosophy, Modern—History. 3. Literature,
Modern—18th century—History and criticism. I. Title.
 D273.5.H313 2012
 940.2'525—dc23

                    2012036638

ISBN 978-1-59017-619-1
Available as an electronic book; ISBN 978-1-59017-639-9

Printed in the United States of America on acid-free paper.
10 9 8 7 6 5 4 3 2 1

CONTENTS

INTRODUCTION

IN THE 1920s and 1930s, French scholars created new ways to do social, cultural, and economic history. First at Strasbourg and then at Paris, Marc Bloch and Lucien Febvre showed students how to free themselves from the tyranny of the "Sorbonnistes" and re-create a past that did not have high politics as its core. They pieced varied forms of evidence—archaeological and literary, legal and religious—together into unforgettably colorful mosaics. Their re-creations of the practices of medieval farmers and craftsmen, the rituals of French kingship, and the religious lives of sixteenth-century intellectuals became models that were imitated for generations. Their journal, the *Annales*, provided a new space for intellectual explorers and a bully pulpit from which to denounce reactionaries. And their disciples—above all Fernand Braudel, who spent the 1930s exploring the archives of the sixteenth-century Mediterranean world—became the most influential historians in the world in the 1950s and 1960s.

The accomplishments of the *Annales* school have cast the other kinds of history practiced in France in the same years into the shade. And that's a pity. For French historians of literature—including a number who held chairs at the Sorbonne and the other bastions of high academic culture—also crafted new kinds of history. Gustave Lanson—a prominent Sorbonniste—argued that the historical study of literature needed to rest on a sociological framework. The historian must tease out both the ways in which social and cultural environments shaped texts and the ways in which texts in turn transformed the social and political world. Lanson became something of a figure of fun, but he helped to inspire some great enterprises. In 1933, for example, another Sorbonne professor, Daniel Mornet, offered a rich account of *The Intellectual Origins of the French Revolution*. The philosophes, he argued—Voltaire and Diderot, d'Alembert and Montesquieu—developed a new "critical spirit." And in the last decades of the eighteenth century, social and political changes transmuted these ideas into the program of modern Europe's first great revolution. Ideas, Mornet held, destroyed the ancien régime. Historians of the French Revolution still contend with his theory.

No one did more to develop the methods of Lanson and other French critics than Paul Hazard. Almost eighty years after it first appeared, his *Crisis of the European Mind* remains one of the most readable, and one of the most revealing, works of intellectual history ever written. Hazard took aim—as is clear from the first pages of his book—not at the eighteenth-century Enlightenment itself but at the decades just before and after 1700. As he surveyed field after field, from history to physics and travel writing to opera, he became convinced that European thought turned critical and modern in these years: "One day, the French people, almost to a man, were thinking like Bossuet. The day after, they were thinking like Voltaire. No ordinary swing of the pendulum, that. It was a revolution." Mornet, and many others after him, argued that the Enlightenment provided the dynamite and matches that exploded Europe's old regime. Hazard, by contrast, insisted that the Enlightenment itself drew more from older traditions than the philosophes (or their historians) liked to admit. Eight decades on, some of the most learned historians at work—John Pocock, Jonathan Israel, Margaret Jacob—continue to debate about the issues that he raised, and to support, as well as to modify, parts of his thesis.

Like Bloch and Febvre, Hazard had to leap every hurdle that the French system of elite education could put in his way before he found a path of his own. Born in 1898, he was, like Marcel Pagnol, the son of one of the Third Republic's industrious and committed elementary-school teachers. Studies at a series of lycées, each more illustrious than the last, brought him to the green quadrangle of the École Normale Supérieure, France's great forcing house of academic talent, where he excelled (he was ranked second in the nation in the agrégation, the competitive examination for secondary-school posts). A scholarship took him to the Villa Medici in Rome, where he spent three years soaking up Italian literature and culture. He taught at lycées and wrote a massive thesis on Italian responses to the French Revolution, which won him a doctorate and a chair at Lyons. Though World War I interrupted Hazard's academic career, he moved to the Sorbonne in 1919 and received a chair at the Collège de France in 1925. With Ferdinand Baldensperger he founded a pioneering journal of comparative literature, the *Revue de littérature comparée,* while producing studies of French, Spanish, and Italian writers. A charismatic lecturer, generous with his time and attention, Hazard attracted crowds at the Collège de France, where attendance was purely voluntary, and as a professor at Columbia, where he taught every other year from 1932 to 1940. In January 1940 he was elected to the French Academy. When France fell, Hazard was in the United States, where he could have stayed. Instead, he returned to Paris, where he taught, in very difficult conditions, until he died in 1944.

The Crisis of the European Mind marked a return to the erudite and wide-ranging scholarship that Hazard had practiced when young but largely abandoned in his middle years. It was an astounding accomplishment. Hazard traced the contours of European intellectual and cultural life in what he identified as its crucial decades: the years when classicism and orthodox theology collapsed, as suddenly and completely as Oliver Wendell Holmes's "wonderful one-hoss shay." He seems to have read everything relevant, from Bayle to Vico, in the original languages. And his choice of themes to emphasize was always intelligent and often prescient. Hazard recognized that late seventeenth-century intellectuals debated the value of historical sources and traditions, such as the ancient narratives of the founding of Rome, in ways so radical that they fascinated and horrified readers across Europe. He placed these apparently obscure arguments, and related ones about the character of the biblical text, at the start of his work—and by doing so made clear that, as historians like Dan Edelstein and Jacob Soll have argued very recently in more detail, the critical culture of the Enlightenment really was born in the learned world of late-Renaissance humanism.

Intellectual history can be dry. Hazard, however, infused his complex and potentially difficult subject matter with rich human interest. Though he believed that a new, critical habit of mind took shape between 1685 and 1715, he knew that this was not the only, or the dominant, note of intellectual life. John Locke, for example, described the creative value of human emotions in a new way—one that Hazard connected, ingeniously, with everything from the rise of a taste for the passionate imaginary world of Italian opera to the spread of new forms of religious sentiment in German Pietism. He also enlivened and enriched his accounts of individual thinkers with vivid pen portraits that showed them thinking and working. Here he describes the indefatigable lexicographer and polemicist, Pierre Bayle, at work on his great *Dictionary* in Rotterdam, where he could write in French without being censored: "He wrote the 'copy,' he corrected the proofs, but he did not mind that; printer's ink smelt sweet in his nostrils. No; but those captious readers, with their finicking objections, each believing that he had the whole truth on his side, gave one a pretty good idea of the depths to which human stupidity could sink; the endless correspondence he had to enter into—that was what wore him down." Few historians of ideas have shared Hazard's gift for showing the reader how past intellectuals actually lived and worked.

The book is astonishingly cosmopolitan. Though Hazard believed that the northern nations, especially England, seized the intellectual leadership of Europe in these years, he also made clear that Italian freethinkers and Spanish moralists did their bit to tear down the enchanted castles of traditional dogma. And though many of his protagonists wrote more than any modern scholar can read, he showed again and again that he had mastered not only the great syntheses of international law and planetary theory but also the pamphlets and plays in which these new ideas reached the larger public.

The larger webs of interpretation that Hazard spun were weaker than his readings of individual texts and traditions. At the start of his work, he proclaimed that the few decades on which he concentrated witnessed a great rupture in human thought. At the end, he admitted that the new "critical urge" of the seventeenth-century thinkers had originated in the Renaissance, where he detected "the same refusal on the part of the more daring spirits to subordinate the human to the divine." Yet he nowhere explained how to reconcile what look like two very different theses. He was also less at home in some areas—such as the history of the physical sciences—than he was in the humanities. And he could not know what more recent scholars have discovered about—for example—the Enlightenment in Iberia, which he did not discuss.

The greatness of *The Crisis* resides elsewhere: in Hazard's astonishing command of materials from many countries and traditions; in the dexterity with which he orchestrated so many different stories; and, above all, in the passion that animated the whole enterprise. Hazard researched and wrote his account of early modern Europe's intellectual crisis as famine gripped the Ukraine, the great corruption scandal known as the Stavisky affair shook the foundations of France's government, and the Nazis took command of Germany—and as Roosevelt and the New Deal restored hope to the United States.

In these dark years, Hazard found in the rowdy, critical thinkers of the seventeenth and eighteenth centuries, as he found in America, sources of hope and models for emulation. In investigating the origins of Enlightenment, he told his readers, he hoped to understand how philosophers had created "a civilization founded on the idea of rights—rights of the individual, freedom of speech and opinion, the prerogatives of man as man and citizen." After Hazard finished *The Crisis*, he continued to study its eighteenth-century aftermath, the high Enlightenment, to which he devoted a three-volume work that appeared after his death. He also attracted and helped to form such gifted students as the brilliant anti-fascist exile Franco Venturi, who after the war would dedicate his life to the study of the Enlightenment in Italy. When Hazard was elected rector of the University of Paris, the Nazis refused him permission to serve. They saw what he stood for. To read *The Crisis* is to learn an enormous amount about a crucial period in Europe's past. But it is also to come into contact with the mind of a great European humanist—one who, like Marc Bloch, found in history not only a refuge from the smelly little orthodoxies of his time but also the arms with which to resist them.

—Anthony Grafton

PREFACE

NEVER was there a greater contrast, never a more sudden transition than this! An hierarchical system ensured by authority; life firmly based on dogmatic principle—such were the things held dear by the people of the seventeenth century; but these—controls, authority, dogmas and the like—were the very things that their immediate successors of the eighteenth held in cordial detestation. The former were upholders of Christianity; the latter were its foes. The former believed in the laws of God; the latter in the laws of Nature; the former lived contentedly enough in a world composed of unequal social grades; of the latter the one absorbing dream was Equality.

Of course the younger generation are always critical of their elders. They always imagine that the world has only been awaiting their arrival and intervention to become a better and a happier place. But it needs a great deal more than that, a great deal more than such a mild troubling of the waters, to account for a change so abrupt and so decisive as that we are now considering. One day, the French people, almost to a man, were thinking like Bossuet. The day after, they were thinking like Voltaire. No ordinary swing of the pendulum, that. It was a revolution.

To account for it, to see how it all came about, we have had to explore some rather unfamiliar country. Time was when the seventeenth century was the favourite field of study. To-day it is the eighteenth. Between the two lies a vague tract, a sort of dubious no-man's-land, in which all kinds of discoveries and unlooked-for adventures may await the explorer. We have made a survey of this territory, selecting as landmarks two dates more or less approximate, starting with the year 1680, or thereabouts,

and ending with the year 1715. In the course of our journey we
encountered Spinoza, whose influence was just then beginnning
to make itself felt. Then we fell in with Malebranche, Fontenelle,
Locke, Leibniz, Bossuet, Fénelon, Bayle, to name but the most
illustrious, to say nothing of Descartes, whose shade still haunted
those regions. These intellectual giants were busy, each as his
genius and his character inspired him, examining, as though they
had just arisen, those problems by which the mind of man is
everlastingly beset, the problem of the existence and nature of
God, of reality and appearances, of free will and predestination,
of the divine right of kings, of the formation of the social state.
Vital problems, every one of them. What was man to believe?
What should be his code of conduct? And, once again, the age-
old question—albeit man had deemed it settled long ago—rose
up anew, the question *Quid est Veritas?* What is Truth?

To outward seeming, the *Grand Siècle* still lived on in all its
sovereign majesty. Thinkers and writers for the most part
deemed that what they had to do was to imitate, to reproduce,
so far as in them lay, the masterpieces which yesterday had
blossomed in such rich profusion. What more could they do,
what more could be expected of them, than to write, or strive
to write, tragedies like Racine's, comedies like Molière's, and
fables like La Fontaine's?

The critics discussed at great length the morality of the Epic,
the propriety of introducing the Christian miracles into the
world of Art. They never wearied of extolling the virtues of that
most resplendent jewel in Art's crown, the three unities. But
meanwhile, in the *Tractatus Theologico-politicus*, in the *Ethics*, in the
Essay concerning Human Understanding, in the *Histoire des Variations
des Églises Protestantes*, in the *Dictionnaire Historique*, in the *Réponse
aux Questions d'un Provincial*, questions were being debated compared with which these paltry matters seemed like the diversions
of doddering old men, or pastimes for little children.

What men craved to know was what they were to believe, and
what they were not to believe. Was tradition still to command
their allegiance, or was it to go by the board? Were they to
continue plodding along the same old road, trusting to the same
old guides, or were they to obey new leaders who bade them
turn their backs on all those outworn things, and follow them to
other lands of promise? The champions of Reason and the

champions of Religion were, in the words of Pierre Bayle, fighting desperately for the possession of men's souls, confronting each other in a contest at which the whole of thoughtful Europe was looking on.

Inch by inch the assailants gained ground. Heresy was no longer a solitary, hole-and-corner thing. It made conquests, it gained disciples. Flown with insolence and pride, it came out into the open, it flaunted itself for all to see. Reason was no longer synonymous with sober good sense, with serene and benevolent wisdom. It became critical, aggressive. The most widely accepted notions, such as deriving proof of God's existence from universal consent, the historical basis of miracles, were openly called in question. The Divine was relegated to a vague and impenetrable heaven, somewhere up in the skies. Man and man alone was the standard by which all things were measured. He was his own *raison d'être*. His interests were paramount. Long, too long, had power been wielded by the pastors of the peoples. They had promised that goodwill, justice and brotherly love should reign on earth. They had not kept their promise. In the great contest where Truth and Happiness were the prizes to be won, they had been the losers. There was nothing for them now but to quit the field. If they went with a good grace, so much the better. If not, well, they would go perforce. The ancient fabric which had provided such indifferent shelter for the great human family, would have to come down. The first task was one of demolition. That well and truly completed, the next thing was reconstruction. Foundations must be laid for the City of the Future. Nevertheless it was equally important, equally urgent, that man should be preserved from falling into scepticism, the precursor of Death, equally important that, to that end, a philosophy should be constructed which, while discarding those metaphysical chimeras that had always led mankind astray, should concentrate on those appearances which are within man's limited grasp and with which, seeing they are all he can ever hope to attain, he should learn to rest content. A political system without divine sanction, a religion without mystery, a morality without dogma, such was the edifice man had now to erect. Science would have to become something more than an intellectual pastime; it would have to develop into a power capable of harnessing the forces of nature

to the service of mankind. Science—who could doubt it?—was
the key to happiness. The material world once in his power, man
could order it for his own benefit and his own glory, and for the
happiness of future generations.

Such are the "notes" by which the eighteenth century is
readily recognizable. What, however, we have made it our
endeavour to bring out is that its essential characteristics were
discernible much earlier than is commonly supposed, that they
were identifiable in a complete state of development while
Louis XIV was still at the zenith of his power and glory, and that
virtually all those ideas which were called revolutionary round
about 1760, or, for the matter of that, 1789, were already current
as early as 1680. Then it was that a sort of moral clash took place
in Europe. The interval between the Renaissance, of which it is
the lineal descendant, and the French Revolution for which it was
forging the weapons, constitutes an epoch which yields to none
in historical importance. For a civilization founded on Duty—
duty towards God, duty towards the sovereign, the new school of
philosophers were fain to substitute a civilization founded on
the idea of rights—rights of the individual, freedom of speech
and opinion, the prerogatives of man as man and citizen.

Five and thirty years of the intellectual life of Europe; a slice
of history impossible to carve out and isolate in time without
having regard to the years which followed, and, more important
still, to the years which preceded it; a tribunal before which Man
himself is arraigned in order that he may declare whether he was
born innocent or stained with sin; whether his hopes of happiness
were centred mainly on this world, or on the world to come;
ideas so pregnant with life, so rich in power whether for attack
or defence, that even now the force of that movement is far from
spent, so far, indeed, that when to-day we deal with our present
problems—religious, philosophical, political, social—we are but
continuing in a measure the great and unresolved disputes of an
earlier day; massive, close-packed works produced in singular
profusion by men concerned less with perfection of form than
with the abundance and cogency of their arguments; recondite
treatises on theology and philosophy; the varied intercourse of
country with country, interfusions, permeations, contacts of
every sort, phenomena which, inexplicable when viewed apart,

and in their own *milieu*, have to be integrated into the atmosphere
of Europe as a whole before they can be readily understood;
routes to be discovered across this mountainous country, bearings to be taken, the lie of the land to be ascertained, pathways
and passes to be explored; people to be portrayed in their habit
as they lived, countenances, some frowning and sombre, some
amiable and benign—such is our material. To essay to deal with
so complex and multifarious a collection as this was doubtless a
formidable undertaking.   We make no apology for having
attempted it; but neither are we under any illusions as to what we
have left in our wake either not done at all, or demanding to be
done anew. And while, of course, we are well aware that one can
only learn all there is to be known about a tree by a careful study
of its roots and branches, we deem that sometimes it may not be
unprofitable to blaze a trail, however tentative and experimental,
across such bewildering and trackless forest mazes.[1]

But there were interludes, lyrical interludes, when works of
poetic beauty were given to the world; and how delightful, as
one cons their pages, to breathe in the exhalations of their per-
fumed harmonies, to suffer oneself to be wafted on the waves
of their subtle music to the empyrean of ineffable beauty.   At
moments such as these, the earth is one great song of enchantment. There were such interludes; but the period we have set
ourselves to explore was not one of them; it made light of such
things as rhythm and cadence; it misconceived the very nature of
poetry; it never knew the incantatory charm that may be born of
words. Not that all feeling for the sensuous and the imaginative
had suddenly disappeared from the world, or that men, for a time,
had ceased to be swayed by their pleasures and their passions.
On the contrary, we have noted how, side by side with works of
pure understanding, considerations of form and colour still
counted in the scheme of things, and how the human heart would
still demand a hearing.

Here it is Pietism, and there Quietism that discover to us the
aspirations of those lofty spirits for whom Reason sufficed not,

[1] In the *Revue des Deux Mondes* of 15th August, the 1st and 15th September,
1932, in the *Revue de littérature comparée* of October-December, 1932, in
L'Europe centrale of the 21st October and the 25th November, 1933, several
fragments of the present work have already appeared. They will be found here
in a greatly modified form.

and who, with hungry heart, yearned for a God of Love. But this very mysticism contributed its quota to the crisis, intellectual and moral, that marks the epoch with which we are to deal. It disavowed the alliance between religion and authority, and, throwing off the bonds of orthodoxy and regarding religion as the spontaneous uplifting of the individual soul to God, it too played, on its own account, the part of innovator. While all this was going on in select religious circles, another parallel process was at work in the world at large. The door had been opened to anarchy by those who held up to contrast the virtues of the primitive, untutored savage on the one hand, and the errors and crimes of civilization on the other.

These years, so rude and unpolished, so crowded with events, with quarrels and calls to arms, so prolific of ideas, are, nevertheless, not without a beauty of their own. As we contemplate those vast movements and watch the great systems of ideas slowly disintegrating, dissolving, to group themselves anew in fresh patterns and obeying different laws; when we look back on our brothers of those days dauntlessly striking out along new paths towards some distant and uncertain goal, yet never faltering, never losing heart, we cannot but feel, as we contemplate them and their struggles, a thrill of mingled admiration and compassion. There was a touch of grandeur in that stubbornness of theirs, in their grim, invincible determination, and if it is, as we shall presently make clear, an inalienable characteristic of Europe never to rest content, but always to be setting forth anew on the immemorial quest for Truth and Happiness, there is a beauty tinged with pathos about that unwearying effort which compels our admiration. Nor is that all. As we study the birth of their ideas, or at least their changing forms; as we follow them along their road, noting how feebly they began but how they gathered strength and boldness as they went along; as we note their successive victories and their crowning triumph we are forced to the conviction that it is not material advantages, but moral and intellectual forces that govern and direct the life of man.

THE CRISIS OF THE
EUROPEAN MIND

ACKNOWLEDGEMENTS

The translator wishes to record his grateful indebtedness to Mr. J. E. Walker, Chief Librarian of the Hendon Public Libraries, for obtaining for him, from sources all over the country, the loan of a number of not easily accessible philosophical and theological works, so that passages from them, quoted in French, might be given in the *ipsissima verba* of the several English authors. For similar services, also most generously rendered, the translator tenders his thanks to his friend Mr. Stephen K. Jones, lately Librarian of Dr. Williams's Library, Gordon Square, London.

January, 1952.

PART ONE

Changing Psychologies

I

THE FERMENT BEGINS

TO preserve existing conditions, to keep things firm and steady, to avoid any change that might disturb an equilibrium so miraculously attained—such was the paramount preoccupation of the Classical Age. There was peril in those questionings that vex the restless spirit. And not only peril, but folly to boot. For let a man rush off to the utmost limits of the globe, what will he find there but what he brings, that is to say, *himself*? And even if he found anything else, would he not have wasted his mental and spiritual riches in the effort? Far better that he should concentrate his powers, and focus them on those eternal questions which are certainly not to be solved by aimlessly flitting about from place to place. Seneca has it that the hall-mark of a well-regulated mind is that it can call a halt when it will, and dwell at peace within itself; while Pascal lays it down that all the ills that afflict a man proceed from one sole cause, namely, that he has not learnt to sit quietly and contentedly in a room.

The classical mind, with the consciousness of its strength, loves stability, nay, if it could, it would *be* stability. Now that the Renaissance and the Reformation—big adventures these!—were over, the time had come for a mental stocktaking, for an intellectual "retreat." Politics, religion, society, art—all had been rescued from the clutches of the ravening critics. Humanity's storm-tossed barque had made port at last. Long might it stay there! Long! Nay, let it stay there for ever! Life was now a regular, well-ordered affair. Why, then, go outside this happy pale, to risk encounters that might unsettle everything? The Great Beyond was viewed with apprehension; it might contain some uncomfortable surprises. Nay, Time itself they would have made stand still, could they have stayed its flight. At Versailles, the visitor got the impression that the very waters had been arrested in their course, caught and controlled as they were, and sent skywards again, and yet again, as though destined to do duty forever.

In Part II of *Don Quixote*, Cervantes presents to us a gentleman in a green cloth riding-coat whom the Knight of the Rueful Countenance encounters on the road. The gentleman in question is making his way towards home, where comfort and good cheer, on a modest scale, await him. He is of some estate, though possessed of no great wealth. He spends his time with his wife, his children and his friends. His favourite diversions are shooting and fishing, but he keeps neither hawks nor greyhounds, only some decoy partridges and a stout ferret. His library consists of some six dozen books, which are sufficient for his needs. Sometimes he dines with his neighbours and friends, and often invites them in return. His table is neat and clean, and not parsimoniously furnished. He likes freedom within limits, and just-dealing, and good fellowship. He shares his substance with the poor, making no parade of his good works. He always endeavours to make peace between those that are at variance. He is devoted to Our Lady, and ever trusts in the infinite mercy of God. Such is how he portrays himself, and Sancho, whose feelings completely carry him away, leaps off his ass and falls to covering the gentleman's feet with kisses. "What mean you by this, brother?" said the gentleman; "why these embraces?" "Suffer me to kiss your feet", cries Sancho, "for verily your worship is the first saint on horseback I ever saw in all my life."

Don Diego de Miranda, he of the green cloth riding-coat, was not a saint. He was merely a preliminary adumbration, dating back to 1615, of the classical ideal of wisdom and moderation. He does not despise the Knight Errant; indeed, he has a secret admiration for heroes and deeds of derring-do, but he draws the line at taking the road himself. He knows that a man is never so happy as when his mind, his senses, and his heart are all working harmoniously together; and having discovered that recipe for a contented life, he clings to it, and will do so till his dying day.

But times change, and fashions with them. That precious recipe of his won't count for much with the next generation, and, when his grandsons arrive at man's estate, they will regard the Knight of the Green Coat as a very out-of-date old gentleman indeed. They will despise his placid, contented outlook on life. No more, for them, of that spell of calm, when a man might go about his lawful occasions with a tranquil mind. Giving vent at last to desires so long repressed, off they will hie them, up and down the world, looking for trouble. If, as time goes on, we see the itch for travel wax stronger, more widespread; if, quitting village, or town, or mother-land, explorers sally forth to learn how others live and have their being, we must recognize in this the first, faint hint of a change already brewing, a change that, later on, will transform the whole complexion of society.[1]

When Boileau was at Bourbon taking the waters, he felt as if he was at the other end of the earth; Auteuil was world enough for him. So was Paris, for Racine; and both of them, Racine and Boileau, were terribly put about when they had to accompany the King on one of his expeditions. Bossuet never went to Rome; nor did Fénelon. Nor did Molière ever revisit that barber's shop at Pézenas. The great classics were not given to moving about; for the wanderers, we must wait for Voltaire, Montesquieu, Rousseau. But, in between, some obscure forces had been at work, preparing the way for the impending change.

The fact is that by the end of the seventeenth century and the beginning of the eighteenth, the Italians had revived their taste for travel; and that the French were as mobile as quicksilver. If a contemporary observer speaks the truth about them, they were so enamoured of novelty that they even took care not to keep a friend too long. According to the same authority, they brought out some new fashion every day, and finding nothing but drabness and boredom at home, packed up their traps and set out for Asia, or it might be Africa, to get a little change of scene, and something to break the monotony.[2] The Germans travelled as a matter of habit; indeed the thing was in their blood; it was a sort of mania with them. There was no keeping them at home. "We are born travellers, every mother's son of us, like our fathers before us, and nothing, no business, however urgent, ever keeps

[1]Trotti de la Chétardie, *Instructions pour un jeune Seigneur, ou l'idée du galant homme*, Paris, 1683, p. 68.
[2]Giovanni Paolo Marana, *Lettre d'un Sicilien à l'un de ses amis, concernant une agréable critique de Paris et des Français*, 1700 et 1710.

us back." So says the German that Saint-Évremond brings on in that amusing comedy of his, *Sir Politick Would-be.* "As soon as we have got hold of a bit of Latin, we prepare to start on our travels. The first thing we do is to procure an Itinerary, showing the various routes we have to take; next, a handbook mentioning all the things that ought to be seen in the different countries. When our travellers are of a literary turn of mind, they invariably take with them a book consisting solely of blank pages, nicely bound, which they call an *Album Amicorum.* Armed with this, they make a point of calling on the various learned men of the locality they happen to be visiting, and beg them to inscribe their names in it." This German of ours is not afraid of hard work. He must needs scale the highest peaks; track the course of the rivers, from their source to the sea, carefully noting down all the fords, ferries and bridges; explore the ruins of amphitheatres and temples, and, notebook in hand, visit all the churches, abbeys, convents, public buildings, town-halls, aqueducts, forts, arsenals; he must make copies of the epitaphs on the tombs; he must not omit belfries, chimes, church-clocks from his purview. Yet he will not hesitate to turn his back on it all, and rush off post-haste, at the first hint that the coronation of the King of France is about to take place, or that a new Emperor is to be elected.

The English travelled as a way of putting the finishing touch on their education. Young gentlemen just down from Oxford or Cambridge, liberally furnished with funds, and attended by a staid and sober-minded tutor, crossed the Straits and set out to make the *grand tour.* They were birds of every feather, these young men. Some thought they had done all that was expected of them when they had sampled the wines of Frontignan and Montefiascone, of Ay and Arbois, of Bordeaux and Xeres. Others, bent on self-improvement, conscientiously examined every cabinet of natural history specimens, every collection of antiques. Every man to his taste! "The French usually travel to save money, so that they sometimes leave the places where they sojourn worse off than they found them. The English, on the other hand, come over with plenty of cash, plenty of gear, and servants to wait on them. They throw their money about like lords. It is reckoned that in Rome alone there are, in the ordinary way, upwards of six hundred English gentlemen, all with people in their pay, and that, taking everything into account, they spend at least two thousand crowns per head every year, so that Rome alone derives from England a yearly revenue of thirty thousand pistoles, good and sound." And in Paris, too, "where there is never any lack of English visitors; an English business man assured me the other day that he had paid out to Englishmen in France a hundred and thirty thousand crowns in a single year, and he was by no means one of the biggest bankers either." It is Gregorio Leti who tells us that, Gregorio Leti,[1] adventurer and globe-trotter, who had at least five countries he could call his own. Born at Milan, he turned Calvinist at Geneva, became Louis XIV's panegyrist in Paris, England's historian in London, and government pamphleteer in Holland, where he died in 1701. Men of learning added to their stores of erudition, as they journeyed from city to city, like that Antonio Conti, for example, a native of Padua, who, in 1713, was in Paris, and two years later in London, where he took part in the controversy concerning the infinitesimal calculus. After that, he went to Hanover to confer with Leibniz, and on his way through Holland, did not fail to pay a visit to Leuwenhoeck. Philosophers went abroad, not to go and meditate in peace in some quiet retreat, but to see the wonders of the world. Such were Locke and Leibniz. Monarchs, too, indulged in foreign travel; Christina of Sweden died at Rome in 1689; and Peter the Great set out for Europe in 1696.

Travel literature, with its indeterminate frontiers, provided a convenient reservoir for the most diverse material, from the dissertations of the learned, to museum-catalogues and love-stories, and so it came to the fore. It might take the shape of a weighty discourse chock-full of the most erudite matter; it might be a study in psychology; it might be a plain, straightforward novel; or it might be a combination of all three. It had its eulogists; it had its detractors. But, praise or blame, both made clear the important place it had come to occupy, and indicated that it was not a thing to be ignored. The same tendencies that fostered its popularity necessarily entailed the production of guide-books, itineraries and the like. There was a large assortment to choose from: *Le Gentilhomme étranger voyageur en France*, *Il Burattino veridico, ovvero Istruzione generale per chi viaggia, Guia de*

[1] Gregorio Leti, *Historia e memorie sopra la vita di O.Cromvele*, Amsterdam, 1692. French translation 1694; reprinted 1793, p. 46.

los caminos para ir por todas las provincias de España, Francia, Italia y Alemania. Cities and towns of outstanding historic importance are treated in separate volumes, e.g., *The City and Republic of Venice*; *Description of Rome for the use of foreigners*; *A guide for the use of foreigners desirous of seeing and understanding the most notable things in the royal city of Naples*; *An up-to-date description of all the most remarkable features of the City of Paris.* There is one alluring title that makes you feel as if you were already glimpsing the fair scenes which it promises and that you really must book your seat on the coach. "Delight" is the operative word: The "Delights", or the "Charms", of this country and of that—of Italy, of Denmark and Norway, of Great Britain and Ireland, of Switzerland. Finally, when all these "Delights" are rolled into one, we have "The Wonders of Europe"!

Attractive as these things were, the "Wonders of the World" outdid them. Indeed, from this time forth, Europe never ceased to explore and exploit the world at large; the seventeenth century thus resuming the task which the sixteenth had bequeathed it. As far back as 1619, an obscure writer, P. Bergeron by name, and a little later, in 1636, Tomasso Campanella, were putting forth this sort of thing: "The exploration of the globe having resulted in discoveries that have destroyed many of the *data* on which ancient philosophy reposed, a new conception of things will inevitably be called for."[1] This idea, which at first gained ground but slowly, received a marked impetus when the Dutch not only opened up trade with the East Indies, but gave picturesque accounts of the strange things they found there; when the English not only displayed their flag in all the oceans of the globe, but described their voyages in the most marvellously circumstantial literature of the kind the world had ever seen; when Colbert told the French people of rich territories and treasures in lands beyond the seas, and recommended them as fitting fields for enterprise. How many were the glowing reports and stirring tales, compiled by order of the king, that came to France from "over yonder"! How little did His Majesty dream that from those very tales would spring ideas calculated to unsettle some of the

[1]For the effects of travel on the mind in the times immediately preceding those with which we are here concerned, see Henri Busson's *La pensée religieuse française de Charron à Pascal*, 1933, p. 284.

beliefs he held most dear, beliefs essential to the maintenance of his royal authority.

Thus the spate of travel-books, Narratives, Descriptions, Reports, Collections, Series, Miscellanea, continued to swell till it overflowed all reasonable limits. Gentlemen sitting comfortably at home by the fireside learnt all there was to know about the Great American Lakes, the Gardens of Malabar, the Pagodas of China and a host of things they would never behold at first hand. The good fathers of the Foreign Missions, Capuchins, Franciscans, Recollets, Jesuits, told of the conversion of the heathen; escaped captives from Tunis, Algiers, or Morocco gave harrowing descriptions of the tortures they had suffered for their faith. Medical men in the service of the trading companies duly reported the results of their scientific observations. Navigators gave the most vivid accounts of their voyages round the world, and the names of Dampier, Gemelli Carreri, Woodes-Rogers were household words for all. It was a sign of the times when that adventurous band of Protestant refugees embarked at Amsterdam that 10th day of July in the year 1690 and, bidding farewell to a thankless Europe, set sail for the East Indies in search of an Eden where they might begin a new life. They never found that Eden.

Minds and consciences were deeply stirred by this startling influx of new ideas, and, by the time the century was drawing to its close, the effect of it was plainly visible. Sir William Temple, having relinquished the cares and preoccupations of political life, was free now to devote himself to the cultivation of his beautiful gardens at Moor Park, and also of his mind. Let us follow him into his study, and essay to catch the trend of his meditations. "What countries", we can imagine him saying to himself, "what countries hitherto unknown to us, or looked upon as rude and barbarous, are now revealed as they really are in the accounts of them brought home by traders, seafarers and pioneers. In those regions that have recently been brought within our ken, and are now the subject of discussion among men of learning, discoveries have been made no less fruitful, deeds have been wrought no less remarkable, than those on which our minds have traditionally been nourished. It is not only their vast extent, the peculiar qualities of their soil, their various climates, their divers products, which engage our interest and

compel our attention, but their laws, their systems of government, their empires." And so Sir William betakes himself to
studying the moral and political history of China, Peru, Tartary
and Arabia. With an eye on a map of the New World, he examines once again the principles that governed and directed the
Old.[1]

Often enough, if truth be told, the traveller who came back
with an idea he took to be new, had really had it already packed
up in his baggage when he went away. But if he was mistaken
about its novelty, he was perfectly right about its impressiveness.
For when he brought it back again to Amsterdam, or London, or
Paris, or wherever it might be, the "sea-change" had made it a
much more imposing thing, far more telling than it had been to
begin with. It is perfectly correct to say that all the fundamental
concepts, such as Property, Freedom, Justice and so on, were
brought under discussion again as a result of the conditions in
which they were seen to operate in far-off countries, in the first
place because, instead of all differences being referred to one
universal archetype, the emphasis was now on the particular, the
irreducible, the individual; in the second, because notions hitherto
taken for granted could now be checked in the light of facts
ascertained by actual experience, facts readily available to all
enquiring minds. Proofs, for which an opponent of this dogma
or of that had had laboriously to rummage about in the store-
houses of antiquity, were now reinforced by additional ones,
brand-new and highly coloured. See them just arrived from
abroad, all ready for use! Pierre Bayle is constantly adducing as
evidence the statements of these up-to-date authorities: "M.
Bernier, in his interesting account of the territory of the Great
Mogul . . .". "We learn from M. Tavernier's description of his
travels . . .". "What we read about China makes it clear . . .".
"*Vide* what the Dutch Trading Company has to say about
Japan . . .". As touching that business about delivering the
moon from bondage, he says, "The Persians still observe this
preposterous custom, if we are to credit the report of Pietro
della Valle. It is also practised in the kingdom of Tonkin, where
the moon is supposed to struggle with a dragon; see recent
accounts by M. Tavernier." "The observations I have just made
regarding the prevalence of immodesty among Christians,

[1] *Essay upon Heroick Virtue*. In the *Miscellanea* of 1690.

reminds me of something I recently came across in M. Rycaut's work" . . . "M. Rycaut's book has created too much stir to have escaped your notice". And when he desires to show—a matter of first-rate importance, this—that the existence of God is not a matter of universal consent, it is travel literature again that obligingly supplies him with his argument. "What, I wonder, would you say if I cited to you the various atheistic races of which Strabo makes mention, and those others which recent explorers have discovered in Africa and America?"[1]

Of all the lessons derived from the idea of space, perhaps the latest had to do with relativity. Perspectives changed. Concepts which had occupied the lofty sphere of the transcendental were brought down to the level of things governed by circumstance. Practices deemed to be based on reason were found to be mere matters of custom, and, inversely, certain habits which, at a distance, had appeared preposterous and absurd, took on an apparently logical aspect once they were examined in the light of their origin and local circumstances. We let our hair grow and shave our faces. The Turks shave their heads and grow beards on their faces. We offer our *right* hand to a friend; a Turk, his *left*. There's no arguing about the right or the wrong of these opposing customs. We simply have to accept them. A Siamese turns his back to a woman as he passes her. He thinks he is showing his respect by not allowing his gaze to fall on her. We think otherwise. Who is right? Who wrong? When the Chinese judge our manners and customs according to their ideas, ideas which took shape four thousand years ago, what wonder if they look on us as barbarians? And what wonder if we, when we judge the ways of the Chinese, look on them as fantastic and absurd? Father le Comte who thus expresses himself in his book *On the Ceremonies of the Chinese*, draws this philosophical conclusion: "We, too, deceive ourselves, because the prejudices of our childhood prevent us from realizing that the majority of human actions are indifferent in themselves, and that they only derive their significance from the meaning the various races of people arbitrarily attached to them when they were first instituted." Maxims such as that take us a long way, take us, indeed, to nothing short of universal relativity. "There is nothing", says

[1] *Pensées sur la Comète*, 1683, ch. XIV, LXXIII, LXXXIX, CXXIX, CLXV; and *passim*.

Bernier, "that opinion, prejudice, custom, hope, a sense of honour cannot do." "Climate", says Chardin, "the climate of each particular race is, in my judgment, always the primary cause of the inclinations and customs of its people." "Doubt", he goes on, "is the beginning of science; he who doubts nothing, examines nothing; he who examines nothing, discovers nothing; he who discovers nothing is blind and remains blind." As we read these highly pregnant remarks, we realize the force of what La Bruyère says in his chapter on the Free-thinkers: "Some complete their demoralization by extensive travel, and lose whatever shreds of religion remained to them. Every day they see a new religion, new customs, new rites."

They arrived, these apostles from distant lands with their strange beliefs and customs, their laws, their own peculiar sense of values. They made a deep impression on a Europe only too eager to question them on their history and their religion. They made answer, each for himself.

The aboriginal American was a problem. Lost to sight in the midst of his continent, a continent so long undiscovered, he was the son not of Shem, nor of Ham, nor of Japheth. Then whose son *was* he? That was the question. Pagans born before the coming of Christ at least had their share of original sin, since they were all descended from Adam. But these Americans? And here is another mystery. How did they escape the Flood? Nor was that all. The Americans, of course, were savages as everyone was aware. When people wanted to give you an idea of what man was like before he acquired the habit of living in community with his fellows, they took these Americans, a horde of creatures wandering about stark-naked, as their examples. But now a very different possibility was beginning to take shape. *Was* a savage necessarily such an inferior and pitiable sort of creature after all? Weren't there savages who were happy enough?

Just as the old-fashioned cartographers used to embellish their maps with pictures of plants, and animals, and natives, so on the intellectual map of the world, we must give a place to the Happy Savage. Not that he is so absolutely new, either. We have met him before. Nevertheless, it was about now, about the period we have selected for this study, between the two centuries, that he took definite shape and determined to stand up for himself. A lot of preliminary work had been done already. The missionaries of the various religious orders, extolling merits in him which were calculated to set him off to advantage, had not paused to ask themselves whether the virtues which they praised so highly were, or were not, the mark of a Christian. With a somewhat impetuous zeal, they belauded the simplicity of these savages, declaring that they derived it from nature; they spoke of their kindliness, their generosity, virtues not invariably conspicuous among Europeans. When these ideas had well sunk in, there came on the scene, as is so often the case, a man who found that all he had to do was to drive them home, and to do so with spirit, with vehemence and, most important of all, with talent. The individual in question was a born rebel, by name the Baron de Lahontan. Having somehow or other found his way into the King's forces, where he was a very square peg in a round hole, he landed, in the year 1683, on the shores of Quebec. His first idea was to carve out a career for himself in Canada, for he lacked neither brains nor courage. He took part in the expedition against the Iroquois; but, impatient of discipline, disgruntled, and forever getting into scrapes, he finally deserted, and came back to Europe where he dragged out the existence of a man who had missed his vocation. When, however, in 1703 he published his *Travels*, his *Mémoires* and his *Dialogues*, he left behind him a monument far more enduring than he can have supposed, although he thought no small beer of himself.

Adario the savage is having an argument with Lahontan the civilized man, and the civilized man has decidedly the worst of it. As against the Gospel, Adario triumphantly sings the praises of Natural Religion. As against European laws, which only aim at keeping a man on the right path by fear of the punishment he will incur if he transgresses, the savage belauds what he calls Natural Morality. As against Society, he puts forward a sort of primitive Communism, of which the certain fruits are Justice and a happy life. So, "Hurrah for the Huron!" He looks with compassion on poor civilized man—no courage, no strength, incapable of providing himself with food and shelter; a degenerate, a moral *crétin*, a figure of fun in his blue coat, his red hose, his black hat, his white plume and his green ribands. He never really lives because he is always torturing the life out of himself to clutch at wealth and honours which, even if he wins them, will prove to be but glittering illusions. Sturdy, untiring on his feet, skilled in the chase, inured to fatigue and privation, what a magnificent fellow is your savage! How noble in comparison! His very ignorance is an asset. Unable either to read or write, what a host of evils he escapes! For science and the arts are the parents of corruption. The savage obeys the will of Nature, his kindly mother, therefore he is happy. It is the civilized folk who are the real barbarians. Let them profit by the example of the savage and so regain man's birthright of dignity and freedom.

But now, alongside the Good Savage, the Wise Egyptian claims his place. But he is not yet quite ready to come on; he is still putting a few finishing touches to his make-up. One might imagine oneself looking on at the piecing-together of a mosaic: a few bits from Herodotus, a few more from Strabo; bits well-worn, but not worn-out; flattering testimony offered by the chronologists,[1] which tends to deprive the Hebrew of his halo and confer it on the Egyptian; narratives brought home by travellers. These latter call to mind that it was on the ancient soil of Egypt that music and geometry were born into the world; that it was on an Egyptian sky that the pathways of the stars had first been charted. Some magnificent passages from Bossuet, from his *Discours sur l'Histoire Universelle*, come readily to mind. The Scythians and the Ethiopians were rude and barbarous races. It was left for Egypt to provide the pattern of a perfect civilization. The Egyptians were a grave and thoughtful people. The glorious tribute rendered them, the tribute which described them as being the most grateful people in the world, implied that they were also the most friendly. Egypt had not only made known the law; she had also kept it, which is far less common. She had called up the dead to judgment; according to the sentence passed on them by that august Assize she had separated the worthy from the unworthy, assigning to the former the honour of stately tombs, casting the latter into a nameless and unhonoured grave. She had suffered the waters of the Nile to flow over the land in order that it might bring forth fruit in abundance; she had built the Pyramids.

Now if Bossuet was carried away like that, the reason was that

[1] See below, Part I, chap. II.

his imagination had been fired by memories of the past, and still more, perhaps, that he had read, pen in hand, the narrative of those lowly Capuchin missionaries who had journeyed deep into Upper Egypt. Aglow with enthusiasm, he hoped, on the strength of what they reported, that the day would come when the fair city of Thebes, Thebes with her Hundred Gates, would rise again in all her ancient glory. Was there not here an enterprise worthy of the Great King? "Had our travellers but pursued their way as far as the spot whereon the city stood of old, they would surely have found some priceless treasure amid the ruins there, for the works of the Egyptians were wrought to defy the ravages of time. Now that the King's name is penetrating into the remotest corners of the earth, and that His Majesty is extending far and wide the researches he has ordered to be made for all that is fairest in Nature and in Art, would it not be a worthy object of this lofty curiosity to seek to lay bare the beauties which lie buried in the deserts of the Thebaid and to enrich the splendours of our buildings with all that ancient Egypt can supply?"

But what he was not so willing to countenance was that a search should be made in those regions for a philosophy remarkable alike for its venerable antiquity and for its astounding novelty. There was a man of pregnant parts and quick, inventive brain, an adventurer, a free lance, one Giovanni Paolo Marana by name, a native of Genoa who, having quarrelled with the city of his birth, had come and taken service under Louis XIV, not, be it remarked, without a wary eye to his own advancement. Among other products of his enterprising imagination, this gentleman brought out, in the year 1696, a curious romance entitled *Conversations of a Philosopher with a Solitary about divers matters appertaining to Morals and Erudition*. This work depicts an aged man of ninety years who boasted a complexion more delicately pink and white than that of a young and comely maiden. What was the secret of this strangely youthful bloom? How was it thus preserved? The answer was that he had dwelt long years in Egypt. There, in Egypt, you may learn the secret of those magic potions which prolong a man's life far beyond the ordinary span. And there, above all, you may acquire the true philosophy, which philosophy, be it noted, has nothing to do with Christianity. In this same romance, moreover, there figures a youthful Egyptian who is the very embodiment of virtue and of knowledge and is able to improvise on the spur of the moment the most marvellous dissertations on themes the most recondite and profound. Such is the wondrous quality of this pagan yet most favoured land.

Here let us skip a few years. We shall now find the figures on the stage more clearly defined, more richly caparisoned, the scenery and accessories more elaborate—sistra, papyrus, ibis, lotus—and now at last behold the Wise Man of Egypt, the *Sethos* of the Abbé Terrasson, the destined idol of the eighteenth century! Sethos will not turn out to be a hero, but a philosopher; not a king, but a guardian of tradition and the things of the past; not a Christian, but an adept deeply versed in the mysteries of Eleusis; a pattern for rulers and all men to follow.

The Mohammedan Arab did not seem destined to enjoy a like good fortune, and Mohammed heard himself called by some rather ugly names: rogue; base impostor; barbarian, who had laid waste the land with fire and sword; heaven's sword of vengeance. But at this point, the men of learning arrived and brought their contribution, wherewith to supplement the tales of the explorers. These erudite gentlemen were particularly concerned with the science of chronology. To shedding a clearer light on the civilization of the East various men of eminence now devoted themselves; for example, M. d'Herbelot, professor at the Collège Royal, and his pupil M. Galland, who succeeded him in the professorial chair; Mr. Pococke, professor of Arabian studies at Oxford; M. Reland, professor of Oriental languages and ecclesiastical archaeology at Utrecht; Mr. Ockley, professor of Arabic at Cambridge. They studied the original texts and the result was that the Arab emerged in a completely new light.

They pointed out, these learned men, that so vast a section of the human race would never have followed in the footsteps of Mohammed if he had been no more than a dreamer and an epileptic. Never would a religion, so crude and childish as his was reputed to be, have exhibited such vitality and have made such progress. If, instead of giving currency to the falsest and most misleading stories, people would go to the Arabs themselves for information, they would perceive that Mohammed and his followers were endowed with qualities of heart and mind that rendered them not a whit inferior to the most illustrious heroes of the other races of the world. Look at the evil things the Gentiles had reported of the Christian religion! Look at the absurdities that were promulgated concerning it! So it is always when things are judged solely from the outside. Doctrines which the Mohammedans never professed were triumphantly refuted, errors they never committed were exposed and condemned. But this sort of victory was too facile by half. In point of fact, their religion was as coherent as it was lofty and full of beauty. Nay more, their whole civilization was admirable. When the tide of barbarism swept over the face of the earth, who was it that had championed the cause of the mind and its culture? The Arabs . . .

The change-over from repulsion to sympathy was the work of but a few years. By 1708, the process was complete. Then it was that Simon Ockley gave utterance to an opinion which, whether it was true or whether it was false, was, two hundred years later, still regarded as a matter for debate. Ockley denied that the West was to be regarded as superior to the East. The East has witnessed the birth of as many men of genius as the West; conditions of life are better in the East. "So far as the fear of God is concerned, the control of the appetites, prudence and sobriety in the conduct of life, decency and moderation in all circumstances—in regard to all these things (and, after all, they yield to none in importance) I declare that if the West has added one single *iota* to the accumulated wisdom of the East, my powers of perception have been strangely in abeyance." This sort of thing gained ground. The Comte de Boulainvilliers, with due acknowledgements to Herbelot, Pococke, Reland and Ockley, compiled a Life of Mahomet in which the change of attitude is seen to be complete. "Every nation," he says, "has its own peculiar type of wisdom. Mahomet symbolizes the wisdom of the Arabs. Christ symbolizes the wisdom of the Jews."

The satirical observer of our national foibles, shortcomings and vices; the curious foreigner who saunters about our streets noting and criticizing everything he sees; the "quiz," at once amusing and exasperating, whose mission it is to remind a self-complacent nation that it does not monopolize the whole of truth nor enshrine all possible perfections, this character—indispensable apparently to European authors, since they adopt him as one of their favourite types and make him do duty again and again ere they finally discard him—in what country are they now going to look for him? Will it be Turkey? or will it be Persia?

It looked as if the choice was going to light on Turkey. One side of it looked towards Europe, and it was more familiarly known. An Englishman, an ambassador's secretary, Sir Paul Rycaut, had written such a vivid account of it that by 1666 his book had become a classic in the literature of travel. There was a constant stream of new editions. Everybody was devouring it. Rycaut's book was followed by a number of others. That same Marana who had been so interested in Egypt, next turned his attention to Turkey. In 1684 he started bringing out what he called *L'Espion du Grand Seigneur*, which had a tremendous success. It was the parent of a numerous progeny of children and grandchildren. Memet the Spy, who took the name of Titus of Moldavia, was a squat, ungainly individual, ill-favoured and niggard of speech. Retiring, unobtrusive, he attracted no particular attention and lived forty-five years in Paris without exciting suspicion. In the daytime he went about out of doors. When darkness came he retired to his room, and there busied himself with writing to the Divan of Constantinople, his chief; or to Haznabardassy, head, and chief curator, of His Highness's Treasury; or to the Agha of the Janissaries; or to Mehemet, eunuch-in-waiting to the dowager Sultana; or else to the invincible Vizir Azem. His letters were full of scurrilous remarks, either about political persons and affairs, or about the Army, or the Church. Nothing escaped his ribald observations.

Nevertheless, the Persian turned the tables on his rival. He regained the laurels, and he kept them. The reason for this was twofold. In the first place, nowhere are there to be found records of travel more engrossing, despite their leisurely style, than the narratives of Chardin. This man, a jeweller and the son of a jeweller, who went to Persia to look for a market for his watches, his bracelets, his necklaces and his rings, this Protestant who found himself an exile from France as a consequence of the Revocation of the Edict of Nantes, was by Nature of a roving disposition. He knew Ispahan better than he knew Paris, and, what was more, he liked it better. The upshot of it all was that any man, however narrow and unimaginative, must have had it borne in upon him from his narrative that far away in distant Asia there were human beings in no way inferior to himself, however widely their mode of life might differ from his own. The notion of "superiority" on which he had hitherto been brought up, as it were, was now no longer valid. Henceforth he must think in other terms. "Difference" not "superiority" was now the appropriate word; a striking psychological readjustment. Yes, in Persia everything is different; those meals you take by the roadside, the strange remedies prescribed by the native physician, the caravansary where you put up for the night, everything is different—clothes, festivals, funerals, religion, justice, laws, all different! Now, these Persians are not barbarians. On the contrary, they are people of extreme refinement, civilized, perhaps almost over-civilized, and, maybe, a little weary of having been so for so long. Chardin underlines the reality, the genuine character of this "other world". He acquaints his reader "with everything that merits the attention of this Europe of ours concerning a country which we might well call another world, not only because it is so far away, but also because its customs, its standards of life, are so different from our own."[1]

The second reason which enabled the Persian to oust the Turk is so obviously sufficient that the mere mention of it renders any further explanation superfluous: after a number of "try outs," of preliminary sketches by various hands, there appeared on the scene, in order to work on material that was now ripe for development, not a man of talent merely, but a man of genius. His name was Montesquieu!

The Siamese, too, came very near to being added to the motley Oriental throng. Louis XIV was very anxious to open up trade relations with Siam and to encourage the spread of the true religion in that country. Feelers, *pourparlers*, were put out to that end. In 1684, the people of Paris beheld the arrival of a deputation of Siamese mandarins. A marvellous sight! In 1685, a French mission proceeded to Siam. A year later, a second Siamese mission came to France. Finally, in 1687, yet another French delegation visited Siam. Then came a number of narratives written by learned clerics and sundry diplomats engaged on the affair. Public curiosity was thus brought to boiling point; and now, by a psychological process which always functions with the regularity of clockwork, a highly advantageous presentment of the Siamese gained general currency: they were a

[1]Preface to *Journal du Voyage du chevalier Chardin en Perse*, 1686.

god-fearing, wisdom-loving, enlightened people, every one of
them! It was given out, for example, that when the King of
Siam was exhorted to become a convert to Christianity, his
answer was that had it been the will of Divine Providence that a
single religion should prevail in the world, nothing could have
been easier for Divine Providence than to execute its design.
Inasmuch, however, as it had pleased the Almighty to suffer a
host of dissimilar religions to flourish simultaneously, it was
obvious that he preferred to be glorified by a prodigious number
of his creatures, each worshipping him in his own way. When
they heard this, men were filled with astonishment. What! had this
Siamese, completely ignorant as he was of European science—
had he thus clearly and forcibly expressed the most telling
argument against the One True Faith that was to be found in the
whole Pagan armoury?

The conclusions which flow from things of that sort create an
atmosphere highly favourable to the spread of heterodoxy.
These Siamese allow a free field to all manner of religions, and
their king gives Christian missionaries full leave to preach in all
the towns and cities of his dominions. Are Europeans as
generous and as tolerant as that? What would *they* say if the
Talapoins (such is the name they give their priests) were to take
it into their heads to come and preach their religion in France?
The Siamese religion is, of course, quite preposterous; they
worship an absurd deity called Sommonokhodom; yet their
morals are strict to the point of austerity. A Christian would
discover nothing to find fault with in their way of life. Whence
it may be inferred—may it not?—that morals and religion are by
no means necessarily connected.

Unfortunately, changes in Siamese government circles frustrated the efforts of the French envoys. The King of Siam was
not converted; the enterprise was abandoned; the Talapoins
were eclipsed by the Chinese Sage.

For in this panoramic survey of ideas, China holds the most
conspicuous place.

Because they had the most far-reaching ambitions, and because
they hoped, by attenuating points of difference and smoothing
away obstacles, to bring into the Christian fold—who could
tell?—perhaps the whole mighty continent of Asia, those

intrepid and learned Jesuits, who, in Pekin, had won the esteem
of the Emperor himself, were doing their best to make the
philosophy of China look so much like Catholicism that only a
a little goodwill would be needed to bring the two together.
According to their accounts, Confucius, who had moulded the
spirit of his country, professed a doctrine so pure that one felt it
was constantly informed by the breath of divine inspiration. He
held that human nature had come from its heavenly home pure
and unsullied, but that, from this state of perfection, it had afterwards declined, and that the task now was to restore to it the
beauty it had lost; wherefore the Chinese, his disciples, should
render obedience to God, and in all things act according to His
will, loving their neighbours as themselves. Reading the precepts of Confucius, one might imagine oneself to have fallen in
with a preacher of the new faith, rather than with one reared
amid the corrupting influences of a state of nature; with a St.
Paul born before his appointed time; with a St. Paul of China.
Clearly, China had drawn her principles from the very fountain
of Truth; the children of Noah, who had spread out over the
eastern parts of Asia, had brought with them the seed which
Confucius had had but to feed and water. Born 478 years before
Christ, he was often heard to proclaim, as with the voice of a
prophet: It is in the West that the true Holy One has His dwelling! Sixty-five years after the birth of Christ, the Emperor
Mimti, interpreting this utterance of the Master, and urged on
by a dream, sent forth into the West certain ambassadors from
his court, commanding them to hold on their way until they
should come face to face with this same saint. Now, it was at that
time that St. Thomas was preaching the Gospel in the Indies;
and if these mandarins had persevered in their mission, instead
of halting at the first island they came to, by reason of their sore
dread of the sea and its perils, it might well have come to pass
that China would have been incorporated into the Church of
Rome.

So too, if the Jesuits had succeeded in their efforts of assimilation, the Far East might not have displayed so strange and outlandish an aspect to European eyes. It was in the year 1697 that
the Jesuits made their last, their supreme, attempt. Then it was
that they gave to the world that great work of theirs, *Confucius
Sinarum Philosophus*. It was a work concerned less with science

than with doctrine, less with facts, as such, than with the interpretation of facts, for it was intended, first and foremost, for the use of young missionaries who, being enlightened by it as to the points of possible agreement, might spread their nets to good advantage. Thus, then, were these soldiers of Christ armed with weapons calculated to serve them in good stead in the battles that lay before them.

But it was not to be. Failure was their portion; and the year 1700 marked the epoch when it became clear that there was to be no fitting of these eastern novelties into the established Christian framework. The dispute regarding Chinese ceremonial lit up and defined two distinct attitudes of mind, and made it inevitable to choose between them. That quarrel was as old as the earliest missions to China, the other religious orders having ceaselessly reproached the Jesuits for their indulgence, their partiality, their over-readiness to minimize difficulties. When, however, these rival orders perceived how the Jesuits succeeded, how in the end they contrived to make the Chinese look like semi-Christians, nay, like Christians indeed, such was the vehemence of their protests that they drew not only the attention of the authorities, but also that of the general public, to the matter in dispute. And everyone knows the virulence which theological controversies assume when the public take them up. Do not be deceived, they cried, the Jesuits are throwing dust in your eyes. The Chinese are idolaters. The Chinese worship their ancestors. The Chinese worship Confucius. The Jesuits in China allow their neophytes to bow down before the altar of Chinoam, to pay honour to their dead with rites of the grossest superstition, to offer sacrifices to their teacher Cun-fu-zu. They veil from them the mystery of the Cross of the Redeemer; they forbear to administer to them the sacrament of Extreme Unction; they make light of the baptismal ceremonies. And in terms like these, the Fathers of the Foreign Missions denounce the writings of Fr. Le Comte and Fr. Le Gobien before the authorities at the Sorbonne and at Rome, accusing them, as the head and front of their offending, of selling the pass, of betraying the fundamentals of the Christian Faith.

The battle was fierce—no quarter given, or taken. Rome decided to send a legate to China to open a fresh enquiry, but, before this could be done, the blow fell, the Sorbonne pronounced its condemnation of the Jesuits. No chance now of adjusting the unknown to the known, the religion of China to the Catholic Faith, or China itself to Christendom. Nothing now remained but to acknowledge the existence of an entity with which no terms could be made, yet an entity at once strange and majestic.

Free-thinkers—and free-livers—betrayed a marked predilection for China:

> Vossius apportait un traité de la Chine
> Où cette nation paraît plus que divine.

In it he said that the only aristocracy recognized by the Chinese was the aristocracy of letters; that they cherished the memory only of those princes who had been lovers of justice and of peace; that the Emperor's counsellors and favourites, philosophers all of them, reproved their master with as much freedom as that with which the prophets of old had been wont to admonish the Kings of Judaea. Had they neglected to do so they would have incurred the censure and indignation of the people. La Mothe Le Vayer is reported to have refrained with the utmost difficulty from crying, *Sancte Confuci, ora pro nobis!* but that was before he had read the works of the Chinese philosopher. When they got to know him better, when they came to take part in the dispute about ceremonies, two points clearly emerged: one was that the Chinese civilization was admirable, the other was that it was fundamentally pagan. What a windfall for the freethinkers, and how they made the most of it!

In the political sphere, for example: The Chinese know nothing of Revelation; they assign to the intrinsic power of matter everything that we attribute to the power of the spirit, the existence of which they deny, as something beyond the limits of possibility. They are blind, and perhaps stubborn. But this they have been for four or five thousand years, and neither their ignorance nor their stubbornness has robbed their political organization of a single one of those wonderful benefits which every reasonable man looks for, and should naturally derive, from a human society: amenities, plenty, the practice of the useful arts, the pursuit of learning, peace and security.[1]

[1] Boulainvilliers, *La Vie de Mahomed*, 1730, p. 180-181.

In matters of religion: it is a matter for astonishment that, among the divers religions of the world, only a single one has been found which, rejecting alike the supernatural and the bugbears of superstitious terror, which are supposed to be such powerful agents in regulating human conduct, only one, I repeat, has been found whose principles are based solely on the necessity of man's obedience to nature.[1]

The Chinese are atheists, not in a negative sense, after the manner of the savage races of America, but conscious, deliberate atheists. They are pious—and they are Spinozists!

So far as I can judge the sentiments of the educated Chinese, in the light of accounts brought home by travellers, and parti-cularly by Fr. Gobien in his *Histoire de l'Edit de l'Empereur de la Chine en faveur de la religion chrétienne*, it appears to me that they are all in agreement with Spinoza in holding that there is no other reality in the universe save that Matter to which Spinoza applies the name of God, and Straton that of Nature.[2]

The Kindly Savage, the Wise Egyptian, the Mohammedan Arab, the Turkish, or the Persian, Satirist—all these were highly diverting and most welcome to those who were looking for a new order of things. But still more popular than any of these was the Chinese sage.

Those who travel in European countries are for the most part sober-minded observers enough; travellers in America, Africa or Asia, fired by the spirit of adventure, or by greed, or by zeal, are considerably more excitable; while those who travel in the Land of Make-Believe know no restraint at all.

There are plenty of these latter, and the difficulty is to know which to choose. Are we to accompany Jacques Sadeur to those far-off lands in the South where he dwelt for five-and-thirty years or more? Shall we set sail with Captain Siden to the land where the Severambes dwell? Shall we fare to that island of Calejava where the inhabitants are all models of good sense? Or shall we land on that other isle, the isle of Naudeley, where they are all models of good behaviour? Shall we entertain ourselves with the story of the adventures of Jacques Massé? They are a long way from being works of art, these imaginary narratives.

[1]Boulainvilliers, *Réfutation des erreurs de Spinoza*, 1731, p. 303.
[2]Collins, *Letter to Dodwell on the immortality of the soul*, London, 1769, p. 289.

The heroes we are invited to meet are appallingly long-winded gentlemen, who are not shy of treating you to elaborate harangues and ponderous digressions. Their style is lumbering and pedestrian. Wrapt up in themselves, they inflict on you the most minutely detailed catalogue of all the knowledge they possess, the relentless recital of all their virtues. The authors of these works are usually just rolling-stones, or deserters from another camp, who load their pages with statements of the views and opinions which have earned them the reprobation of their former comrades. As for the rest, they are ordinary, bourgeois folk endeavouring to escape from their repressions and indulging in visions of the might-have-been.

The recipe is always the same. It invariably begins with a reference to some manuscript which has been carefully handed down, or else miraculously brought to light. How is it that this sort of thing never loses its fascination for story-writers? They all use it unblushingly, one after another, as if they had each hit on something entirely new. This precious document relates the adventures of some enterprising hero who braves the perils of the deep, suffers shipwreck, is washed ashore, and finds himself in some quite unknown land, preferably in the southern hemisphere. Now comes the main point, the real business of the whole affair, which is a voluminous account of the land on which he finds himself, a land never before heard of, a land of which the geographers had no inkling. The author borrows freely from previous Utopias, as well as from the narratives of those who have travelled in distant countries. Some further touches, generally rather absurd, and a few bordering on the indecent, are dragged in. For example, Jacques Seden is a hermaphrodite, which is just as well for him, because the country in which he finds himself is inhabited exclusively by hermaphrodites who look on normally formed people as monstrosities and forthwith put them to death. But such tit-bits are merely frills, embroidery; the essential part of the scheme is to get oneself transported by some means or other to an imaginary land, and there to hold an enquiry into the religious, political and social conditions of the old world; to demonstrate that Christianity in general, and Catholicism in particular, are barbarous and irrational; that governments in general and monarchical governments in particular are iniquitous and hateful; that society ought to be rebuilt from top to bottom. When all this has been duly performed, it only remains for the hero to get himself back to Europe, and there give up the ghost.

What is particularly noticeable in these tales is the passion for destruction that runs through them all. Not a tradition which escapes challenge, not an idea, however familiar, which is not assailed; not an authority that is allowed to stand. Institutions of every kind are demolished, and negation is the order of the day. Elderly sages put in an appearance at convenient junctures to preach lay sermons, in place of duly ordained ministers of religion. They descant in glowing terms of incorruptible re-publics, of tolerant oligarchies, of peace induced by persuasion, of religion without a priesthood, without churches, and of work so innocent of drudgery that it becomes a pleasure. They hold forth about the wisdom that prevails in their land, admirable land, where the very name and notion of sin are forgotten. They dogmatize against dogma. There comes a flash of the imaginative here and there to bring back the atmosphere of adventure, or a "spicy" jest to put the reader in a cheerful frame of mind; so, at least, the author hopes. Then, off he starts again, showing how weary, stale, flat and irrational is our ordinary, work-aday mode of life, following up all this with a dazzling account of the happy times enjoyed by the people of that Never-never Land.

Still more striking is the ascendancy of the geometrical spirit. Everything must be tape-measured. Everything must be arranged according to number and dimension, codified and card-indexed. Authors catch the craze. It enters into their dreams and colours their wildest imaginings. Fearsome and tyrannical is this mania for uniformity. It affects every department of life; even language, everyday speech, feels the effects of its influence. We must speak by the card, or equivocation will undo us. Housing, too, must be strictly rationalized. There are groups called *Sézains*. Each *sézain* comprises sixteen districts, each district contains twenty-five houses; there are four rooms to each house; each room holds four people; that's how a State should be run. That's organization. Streets laid out on a regular, uniform plan; big square buildings, all of a size, all of a pattern. That's town planning, if you like! Gardens all the same size, and all perfect rectangles, with trees planted in rows arranged according to the relative beauty or utility of the trees themselves. Ah, what heavenly gardens! With figures you can prove anything, even the impossibility of the resurrection of the body. Imagine a country with 41,600 villages; each village contains 22 families, and each family consists of 9 persons; total, 8,236,000 inhabitants, representing 10,400,000 cubic feet of flesh. This formidable mass doubles itself every sixty years. Calculate what that would come to in ten thousand years: a mountain immeasurably bigger than the earth itself; therefore the resurrection of the body is impossible. Mountains are irritating, irregular things to look at, and irregularity offends the eye. So what do these southerners do? They level them.

When the mind has drunk deep of that sort of thing, the awakening, the return to concrete reality, is a rude experience. Perhaps, however, we ought to have put it that it was concrete reality that was forced willy-nilly into a sort of geometrical strait-jacket. The coming of Christ, because it staggered the reason, was pronounced a myth; similarly the Bible, because it sometimes puzzled the mind, was declared to be untrue. Real wisdom rejects all but the self-evident. Of all the inventors of Utopias, the one who thought the deepest and searched the longest, Tyssot de Patot, the author of *Voyages et Aventures de Jacques Massé* (1710), writes in his letters: "For so many years now I have been treading the broad, well-lit thoroughfares of geometry, that it pains me to think of the dark and narrow alley-ways of religion. . . . I must insist, everywhere and always, that a thing should be evident, or at least possible."[1]

These are the kind of books in which you will find a deal of rubbish mixed up with a number of miscellaneous but useful odds and ends; in which you will find some ideas very rough-hewn, but very vehement; and sentiments clumsily stated but dynamic. They presage the coming not only of Swift, Voltaire, Rousseau, but of the Jacobins, of Robespierre.

Travel: that did not as yet connote the sensitive soul setting forth in search of dazzling scenes of beauty, wandering under the varying skies of divers lands, essaying to record its own sensations. If it was not that, it meant at all events comparing manners and customs, rules of life, philosophies, religions; arriving at

[1] Tyssot de Patot, *Lettres choisies*, 1727, L. 67.

some notion of the relative; discussing; doubting. Among those who wandered up and down the earth in order to bring home tidings of the great unknown, there was more than one free-thinker.

To read these travellers' tales was a form of escapism. It took one away from a world of intellectual stability into a world of movement and flux. What a host of ideas, hesitant, tentative, were evoked by getting to know something about the Empire of China or the Kingdom of the Great Mogul. As one pondered on these warring dogmas, every one of which claimed to be the vehicle of the one and only Truth; on these divers civilizations, each one of which boasted that it, and it alone, was perfect—what a School for Sceptics was there! "Blind are they, and ignorant of life, who suppose that Europe is self-sufficing; that she has nothing to ask from her neighbours. . . . There is no doubt that if she could open up communications with the Australians she would become a vastly different place from what she is to-day." Europe did not open up communications with the Australians; but, of all those regions which competed for her attention, she responded most readily to the East. It was an East gravely distorted by the European view of it; nevertheless, it retained enough of its original impressiveness to loom forth as a vast agglomeration of non-Christian values, a huge block of humanity which had constructed its moral system, its concept of truth, on lines peculiarly its own. This was one of the reasons why the conscience of the old Europe was stirred and per-plexed, and why, seeking to be thrown into confusion, it ob-tained what it sought.[1]

[1]Gabriel de Foigny, *La Terre austra e connue*, 1676, chap XI.

II

THE OLD ORDER CHANGETH

THOSE writers of the old school, those beloved Classics! What wonderful models they were! Whenever they took it upon them to write, and whatever they wrote, the result was always some work of outstanding nobility. In the sphere of philosophy, they had bequeathed to the world a moral system to which Christianity had but to add the crowning touches. On the field of battle, they had borne themselves like heroes; not story-book heroes, such as Roland and Amadis, but heroes of real flesh and blood. And so, in literature, in philosophy, and in the art of life, we could scarcely do other than mould ourselves on their example.

Then all of a sudden (so, at least, the thing appeared) a number of impious creatures arrived on the scene, uttering the rankest blasphemies; these were "the Moderns", who overturned the altars of the ancient gods. And behold! the word itself, the mere word *modern*, had suddenly become a sort of wonder-working shibboleth, a magic formula which robbed the past of all its power. At first, people were "modern" timidly, half-heartedly. After a while, they came to look on it as a feather in their cap, and bragged about it, trailing their coats. The past, with all its mighty dead, was set at nought. The great thing now was to feel the insolent rapture of youth, to drink deep of its vivifying spirit, to make the most of the day while the day lasted, though the night was bound to come. Better stake all on the present, and leave eternity to take care of itself. Like Marivaux's Trivelin, people came to think that to have four thousand years on your shoulders was nothing to be proud of, but, on the contrary, an intolerable burden. A new superstition, a new fetish, came into being, and we have not rid ourselves of it even yet. Novelty, which in the nature of things must be perishable, fleeting, has assumed such overwhelming importance in our eyes, that, if it is absent, nothing else avails; if it is present, nothing else is needed. If we would escape the reproach of nullity, if we would avoid being objects of ridicule, if we would save ourselves from utter boredom, we have to be constantly more and more *advanced*, in art, in morals, in politics, in ideas, and now, such is our nature, all we care about, all that matters to us, is the shock of wonderment and surprise.[1]

The Past abandoned; the Present enthroned in its place! Yet another transition! How are we to account for it? How came it that a whole section of Europe's *intelligentsia* suddenly dropped the cult of antiquity, which the Renaissance and the classical age had so consistently professed? The famous battle between the Ancients and the Moderns, which is commonly advanced in explanation of the phenomenon, is, in fact, but a symptom of it. Its root-cause is for us to discover.

In their inmost consciousness, men had come to look on history as a very broken reed. The very notion of historicity was tending to disappear. If, now, men turned their backs on the past, it was because they thought it something evanescent, Protean, something impossible to grasp and retain, something inherently and inveterately deceptive. People no longer trusted those who professed to understand and interpret it. Those who pretended to do so deceived either themselves or their readers. A sort of landslide had taken place, and in its track, in what remained after its passage, nothing was to be seen for certain but what immediately confronted the eye, that is to say the "here and now"—in other words, the Present. Henceforth, all the alluring visions lay in front, and not behind.

It was the modern historians who first came under the suspicion of not being the surest of guides. There were a good many of them: Mézeray, Fr. Maimbourg, Varillas, Vertot, Saint-Réal, Fr. Daniel, and that Fr. Buffier who packed up kings, queens, treaties, battles, empires, provinces, cities, in little tuneful rhymes, for people to learn by heart. And Laurence Eachard; Edward Hyde, Earl of Clarendon; Abel Boyer; and, best known

[1]Paul Valéry, *Regards sur le monde actuel*, 1931, p. 161.

of them all, Gilbert Burnet. There was Antonio de Solis who, in 1684, enriched the literature of Spain with a brilliant History of the Conquest of Mexico. And many others besides these, who yearn to be called back from the world of shadows, but who cannot, in common fairness, be adjudged worthy of that privilege. Differ as they might among themselves, there were, nevertheless, some points on which they were all agreed: History is a school of morals, a sovereign court of justice, a stage of honour for good rulers, a place of retribution for bad ones. She enables you to gain an insight into the human character, for she is "a spiritual anatomy of human action". But first and foremost, history is an art. To quote the words of M. Cordemoy, tutor to the Dauphin, "A man is far better employed in effectively displaying the facts of history, than in digging out the evidence for them. It is better for him to aim at infusing beauty, power, precision and brevity into his composition, than at acquiring a reputation for factual infallibility in everything he writes".

Drama, pathos—these things are of the stuff of History; therefore she must be allowed a sumptuous setting. Battles, conspiracies, revolutions, schisms—first-rate material, fine subjects, these! With her taste for rhetoric, she is akin to poetry, for what is poetry but a form of eloquence, an eloquence controlled by rhyme? Noble herself, she breathes the sublime as her native air. She must, of course, provide a rich assortment of speeches, descriptions, maxims, analyses, parallels—as this, for example: Charles V and François Ier are standing before us: "Not content with bringing them into the world at the same time, and in the same kingdom, and with uniting them in a close bond of blood relationship, Providence further decreed that each should derive from the other his principal title-deed to fame. So true is this that, when one of them was called upon to make his exit from the stage, the powers of the other declined, and, from that moment, all his fortunes went awry. . . . Let us then begin this famous parallel with that which is least familiar in the story of our great heroes, and continue it, so far as in us lies, with all the scrupulous accuracy that Aristotle and Plutarch, pastmasters in this kind of composition, would demand of us."[1]

[1]Varillas, *Histoire de François Ier; à laquelle est jointe la comparaison de François Ier avec Charles-Quint par le même auteur,* 1684.

In a word, what every historian of that period was fain to prove himself was just another Livy, only even more eloquent, more ornate than his prototype. All would freely have subscribed the formula elaborated by one of the practitioners of the *genre*, Père Le Moyne. "History", says he, "is a sustained account of things that are true, outstanding, and of public import, written, with ability, eloquence and judgment, for the instruction of princes and their subjects, and for the edification of the commonalty as a whole".[1]

They composed fine prefaces. They protested that their most anxious care would be to observe the strictest impartiality. However, as they also pointed out that it behoved them to champion the cause of their king, their country and their creed, it was clear that they would have to take sides in every discussion, and that their main object would be, not so much to discover the truth, as to ensure the triumph of their version of it. Catholics and Protestants confronted one another, armed with the pen. One extolled the virtues of Louis XIV, another sang the praises of William of Orange. Thus began endless debates, of which the most clamorous were those that raged about *The History of the Reformation of the Church of England* (1679—1715) by Gilbert Burnet; *The History of Lutheranism* (1680), and *The History of Calvinism* (1682) by Père Maimbourg, *The History of the Revolutions that have taken place in Europe in the matter of religion* (1686—1689) by Varillas.

They allowed themselves a free hand. Saint Réal's account of the life and character of Don Carlos, and of the outstanding events of the Spanish conspiracy against the Republic of Venice, reads with all the glamour of a romance. And, indeed, if the novelists draw freely on history for the matter of their romances, why should not an historian return the compliment and make his history as romantic as a novel, as romantic, and hardly less wide of the truth? Varillas, when, in his old age, his eyesight began to fail, dictated to an amanuensis for several hours a day, never troubling to verify a single reference. But he did not wait till he was a dim-sighted old man to begin inventing his facts. One of his critics charges him with fabricating, besides many other fanciful tales, the tragic circumstances alleged to have marked the end of the love-affair of François Ier and Madame de

[1] Le P. Le Moyne, *De L'Histoire*, 1670, pp. 76-77.

Chateaubriand. Varillas' story is that M. de Chateaubriand, on his return from Pavia in 1526, had ordered his faithlesss consort to be shut up in a room entirely hung with black. In order to add relish to his vengeance, he devised a means by which, without being seen himself, he could watch her giving way to transports of despair. In the end, he caused her to be bled to death by a couple of surgeons. That is Varillas' account of the matter, but, in point of fact, in the year 1532, while he was making a journey through Brittany, François Ier made over to the lady in question the rent of a number of manors, and, after her demise in 1537, permitted the husband to enjoy the usufruct of her estate.

Laurence Eachard, who had set himself the task of writing the history of England from the time of Julius Caesar onwards, deems that, in an age of refinement like his own, it would ill become him to go rummaging about among a lot of crude monkish records, and says that he has therefore contented himself with remoulding, and sometimes with merely copying, whatever had struck him as worthy of preservation in the works of his predecessors, ancient as well as modern; thus making open confession of a practice which others followed without so frank an avowal. Some of the stories told about these historians impose no great strain on our credulity. Here is one: Vertot had just finished writing his account of the siege of Malta when someone drew his attention to the existence of some highly important documents bearing on the subject. Vertot told him he was too late, he had finished his siege! Père Daniel went to inspect the works in the royal library, spent an hour there, and declared he was perfectly satisfied. Lucky man! He himself said that a thoroughly well-documented piece of work is a credit to its author; all the same he had examined a fair number of original manuscripts and found the process more painful than profitable. We can well believe it.

This building, with its imposing façade, was majestic to look at, but it was built on sand. The lightest touch would bring it toppling to the ground. Already doubts, misgivings were knocking at the heart of these historians. For they were humanists albeit belated, a tardiness of which they seemed vaguely conscious. Even in the hour of their greatest triumph, there was something that haunted them, that marred their peace of mind. For all their *brio*, for all the *bravura* of their public performances

all was not well within. Something was whispering to them. . . .
Quid est veritas?

Truth. . . . Is truth just a matter of arranging problematic
data, of getting things to fit into a pattern of apparent verisimilitude? Is it just the sort of logical cohesion that a little
thought and ingenuity enables one to impart to things? Is it a
mental concept, a factitious harmony resulting from a process of
skilful composition, a piece of artistry? How difficult it is to
get at it! How far does it become us to pursue our search for it?
Are we to be allowed to invade people's privacy? To go poking
our noses into their houses, sneaking into inner apartments,
tearing off the veils, dragging aside the curtains that conceal the
family secrets? How often has it not happened that two writers,
or three, or four, all describing the same siege, the same battle,
have given widely divergent accounts of it. Which are we to
choose? How is it that events as soon as they come under the
pen, take on, as if by magic, an air of romance? These were the
sort of questions that were disturbing the writers of history.
And who can gainsay that they *are* superficial, that they are incapable of sustained and systematic research, that they are at
once verbose and in a hurry, that they slur over difficulties,
that they are poor hands at tracking down origins, at penetrating
through successive layers of paint till they get to the original
coat? They lack the critical sense; yet not so utterly as to be
wholly impervious to a secret misgiving. In fact we find an open
expression of it in a work entitled *Une Méthode pour étudier
l' Histoire* brought out in 1713 by Lenglet Dufresnoy, an independent, but not conspicuously clear-headed, thinker. "Be on your
guard", said this writer, "nothing is harder than to steer clear
of error. You cannot be too careful; keep to well-tried rules;
don't swallow everything you are told; examine things for
yourself; sift them to the bottom. If a thing strikes you as
singular, out of the ordinary, be all the more suspicious of it;
find out if there was anything that might have misled the writer,
or have tempted him to mislead *you*. Be on the watch; keep a
wary eye. If you don't, the upshot will be that truth and falsehood will have the like dominion over you." That is the danger,
and the danger is recognized. It is revealed by an expression
which is frequently cropping up; an expression which, though
frowned upon, declines to be silenced. To the word Pyrrhonism,

which had created such a commotion in Pascal's bosom, another
was now added, the word *historical*.

In the year 1702, a very distinguished professor, Jacob
Perizonius by name, who, at the time, was teaching Greek and
Roman history at the University of Leyden, was invited to deliver
a course of lectures on the history of the United Provinces. In
accordance with traditional usage, he had to deliver an inaugural
address before the civic authorities, his professional colleagues,
and the students; and the subject he chose for his lecture was
Historical Pyrrhonism. In sonorous Latin phrases, he proclaimed to his audience that society had reached an age when
everything was a target for criticism, and when people were only
too ready to rush to extremes; history, he said, was confronted
with a grave crisis. While some, like ninnies, swallowed the
various fairy tales by which it was distorted, others went to the
opposite extreme and denied that history, in whatever shape or
form, had any validity at all. This latter attitude, he went on,
was gaining ground and was the more dangerous because it was
the more showy, the more likely to attract attention. If it carried
the day, disaster would ensue. The world would relapse into
universal scepticism. And so the speaker affirmed that historic
certitude *was* attainable, and, emboldened by this belief, exclaimed, *Valeat tandem Pyrrhonismus*, to hell with Pyrrhonism!

But the task was beyond him. The adversaries of history were
advancing in three separate columns; three, if not more. There
were the Cartesians following the lead of their master, who said
that a man was no more likely to be a better member of society
because he knew Latin and Greek rather than Swiss or lowland
Breton, or because he knew the history of the Roman or Germanic empire rather than that of the most insignificant little state
in Europe. Malebranche went one better. Historians, he said,
tell us what other people thought, without troubling to think for
themselves. Adam in the Garden of Eden was possessed of
perfect knowledge. Did Adam know history? Obviously he did
not. Therefore perfect knowledge was not history. For his own
part, he, Malebranche, was content to know what Adam knew.
Truth, for such minds as that, is not something which one must
go out and seek in the high-ways and by-ways, it comes to a man
from within, from meditation. Truth is not a matter of history,
but of metaphysics. The Jansenists, too, rigorous moralists as

they were, mistrusted this manifestation of the *libido sciendi*, this everlasting itch for knowledge. But history's bitterest foes of all were the freethinkers.

They looked on history as a sort of personal enemy. They went about complaining that she was as untrustworthy as she was untruthful; that she was a despicable lick-spittle, a base fawner upon the great and powerful. History was like those dishes compounded in the kitchen to suit the different tastes of the diners. The same meat was served up with as many different sauces as there were countries in the world. If read it you must, then remember that you are reading, not to learn the facts, but merely to learn the interpretation that each individual, party, or people put upon the facts, and that, from start to finish, history is one everlasting note of interrogation.

The French were conspicuous for the vivacity of their attack, but there were others no less vigorous. From Leipzig, J. B. Mencken, son of the founder of the *Acta Eruditorum*, launched his thunders against the historians, whom he included, without exception, in a sort of ignoble army of charlatans. Charlatans they were, some of them because, wishing to emulate the splendours of Livy, they strew their narratives with long and tedious declamations, putting into the mouths of rude and uncultivated boors the subtlest and most polished of discourses, and others because, thinking it useless to look for readers unless they gave them something to enchant the eye, they bedizened their pages with all manner of tawdry, secondhand adornments; while others yet again, in order to flatter the Mæcenases to whom they owed their livelihood, embellished their family trees with many a flower of fancy, or invented wholly imaginary ones. But the arch-charlatan, the charlatan *par excellence*, was the Frenchman Varillas. Speaking generally, and taking them as a whole, all historians were charlatans, all of them prefaced their works with the under-taking that they were going to give the truth to the world; and that truth . . . never came!

Yes, thought the wiseacres, there's something in that. In spite of all the "Histories of France" that we have had, not one of them could be trusted. Nor, in the strict sense of the word, is there a history, a real authentic "History of England," nor, indeed, of any country at all. Time was when men swallowed blindly anything they were told. But now, they ask questions.

"Would it not be correct to say that the age of historical pyrrhon-ism began in our time?"[1]

But that the history of Rome should similarly be called in question; to arrive at the conclusion that the ancient writers were not a whit less one-sided, not a whit less irresponsible, not a whit less hollow and pretentious, than these of our own day, would be more painful still. Romulus, and the heroes that preceded him, had come to be looked upon by all educated men as old friends, almost as members of the family. They had known them since their schooldays; they wrote their language, they even composed their letters and their speeches for them. How well it hung together, the venerable old tale! So serene, so stately was it in the telling, that to associate with it the faintest suggestion of un-truth seemed utterly preposterous. It was an epic of real life; nothing less. Once upon a time, or, if you must needs be precise, in the *annus mundi* 2824, four hundred years before Rome was founded, Aeneas set foot on the shores of Latium, accompanied by that scanty band of Trojans who had escaped from the tempest of fire that had reduced Ilion to ashes. For three years now he had been driven a homeless wanderer from sea to sea. At the time of his arrival, Latinus was king. This warm-hearted, hospitable monarch, moved by compassion for the sufferings of Aeneas, received him with great friendliness and, to retain him at his side by bonds as sweet as they were powerful, bestowed on him the hand of his daughter, Lavinia, in marriage. Thereupon Turnus, King of the Rutulians, stung by jealousy, made war upon the Trojans. But he was overcome and slain in battle. Peace being thus restored to Latium, Aeneas was henceforth enabled to wield unmolested the sceptre which Latinus had bequeathed to him on his death-bed, as an heritage which rightfully belonged to him as the husband of his daughter.[2] The whole story hung together like the successive scenes of some stately drama. These Romans were real flesh and blood; as real as any of those whom admiring spectators applauded on the stage with their plumed helmets and abbreviated tunics.

[1] Paulian, *Critique des Lettres pastorales de M. Jurieu*, 1689, pp. 78-80.
[2] As stated by Laurence Echard, *The Roman History from the building of the City* ... 1694. Vertot, in his *Histoire des Révolutions arrivés dans le gouvernement de la République romaine* (1719), though he varies a little as regards the facts, says more or less the same thing.

But no; though it went terribly against the grain, there was nothing for it but to re-portray and gravely alter, the unfaithful pictures of those beloved friends. Nay, it might have to be accepted that they were not portraits at all, but mere phantoms, conjured up from the land of dreams. Dawn was approaching and they would soon be melting into air, into thin air. A voice, a voice which never yet had spoken in vain, had already declared them devoid of substance. That same voice had not hesitated to assert that men were always the same everywhere, childish, vain-glorious, credulous, and particularly sensitive when the matter of their origin was under discussion. As they have always been, he said, so they are to-day, claiming for the race to which they belong an origin reaching back to some remote and mythical past. The Romans invented fables which we accepted as true and took to our hearts:

The Romans were not exempt from this vanity. Not content with trying to establish a kinship with Venus through Aeneas, who led the Trojans into Italy, they must further buttress up their connection with the gods with the story of Romulus who, they gave out, was the son of Mars, and whom, after his death, they made a god in his own right. His successor, Numa, had no celestial family connections to boast of, but the saintly character of his life earned him the rare privilege of holding confidential communication with the goddess Egeria, a privilege which proved of no small assistance to him in the inauguration of his ceremonies. It would appear, in short, that the powers who have the moulding of our destinies had then no other concern than the founding of the city of Rome, and that, even after that event, an industrious Providence took it upon itself to adjust the different characters of her successive rulers to the changing requirements of her people.

I hate admiring references which repose on mere fables, or which are bolstered up by false and misleading judgments. There is so much that is real to admire in the Roman people, that we do them a disservice in flattering them with fairy-tales.[1]

This voice so clear, so peremptory, these daring ideas, came as a rude shock to people who all their lives had clung to their beliefs in undisturbed security. Those "true things" which Saint-Évremond wanted people to admire, how were they to be distinguished from the things that were not true? More than

[1]Saint-Évremond, *Réflexions sur les divers génies du peuple romain, dans les différents temps de la République.*

that, how could people be expected to discard a finished whole, a thing complete and perfect in all its parts, for a conception based on the theory of evolution, an idea hardly comprehensible in those days? Were the frontiers of history to be pushed ever farther and farther back? Were we to ante-date the ages? Were we to play fast and loose with time, on the ground, forsooth, that it is only when it is viewed from afar, and in the shadows, that we can form an idea of what the past really was?

At Leyden Jacob Gronovius asserts that there never was any such person as Romulus. Henry Dodwell, at Oxford, also expresses grave doubts about him. For nearly two thousand five hundred years, countless pens have recorded that the Vestal Virgin, Rhea Sylvia, having given birth to two male children as a result of her amorous intercourse with Mars, these twins, Romulus and Remus, were exposed on the Capitol, where they were suckled by a wolf. That story is so patently absurd that it is hardly necessary to refute it. *Certe nulla est, praeter sacram, historia quae non primas suas origines fabulis immixtas habeat. Historia Romana ante Romulum nulla fide digna. Vel Romuli ipsius fortasse dubia.* It is certain that, with the exception of Holy Writ, there is no history which does not partake of the fabulous in its earliest beginnings. The history of Rome before the time of Romulus is unworthy of credit, and even the story of Romulus is perhaps open to doubt. That was the sort of thing men were beginning to say. Later on it was shown how completely the first four centuries of Roman history were enveloped in doubt and obscurity.

As for the history of Greece, that need not detain us long. It was even more untrustworthy than the Roman. Were people to believe that the Athenians, albeit the most cultivated of men, had no authentic records until quite late on in their history, and that that is why their source and remote origin were completely hidden from them? All their dates and periods are a hopeless tangle. They are very hazy even about the correct dates of their national festivals. Aristophanes brings the gods on to his stage grumbling that the moon gives them no really accurate notion as to when these auspicious events are due to take place. The result is that the gods arrive too late for these public feasts and have to go back with empty stomachs to heaven. Who's going to put any faith in the Greek chroniclers after that?

What is clear is that not only we have not got at the truth in regard to ancient history, but that we have no means of doing so. How did the ancients measure things? What was their system of notation? Those are the kind of things you have got to know before you can speak with any certainty about the practical side of their life. If you don't know them, you can never be absolutely sure about anything, you are merely talking in the air. Points like that are brought up for discussion at the meetings of learned societies such as the Académie Royale des Inscriptions et Belles Lettres. Admittedly, there is no lack of the raw material of knowledge; what *is* lacking is any idea of how to handle it methodically. Men search here and enquire there, but without ever getting any definite response. We hunger for knowledge, and depart unsatisfied. And so we arrive at this melancholy conclusion, that the only really wise man is the man who knows that he knows nothing.

Well then, let us put profane history aside and let us concentrate on the one history that really matters, the history dictated by God. Here all is plain sailing; from the creation of the world to the coming of Christ there is an interval of 4,000 years, or, to be quite precise, 4,004. By the year 129 the population of the earth had considerably increased, and so had evil-doing. In the year 1656, came the Flood; in 1757, men set to work to build the Tower of Babel. The vocation of Abraham dates from 2083. The written law was entrusted to Moses 430 years after the vocation of Abraham, 856 years after the Deluge and the same year that the Hebrew people were delivered out of Egypt. Thanks to these firmly established landmarks, Bossuet, composing his noble *Discours sur l'Histoire Universelle,* beholds a succession of epochs which automatically fall into their appointed places in the great scheme of things. Beneath harmonious and majestic porticoes winds the triumphal road which leads to the Messiah. So delightful was it to fare along that road that minds innocent and quiet furnished their whole lives with memories of its milestones, recalling not only the year, but the month, nay, the exact day, on which occurred this or that memorable event recorded by Holy Writ. The faithful opened their books of devotion: on the 18th February in the year 2305 before the birth of Our Lord, Noah sent forth a dove from the Ark. On the 10th

March, Jesus received tidings of the sickness of Lazarus; on the 21st March, Jesus cursed the fig-tree; on the 20th August, in the *annus mundi* 930, died Adam, the first man.[1]

And then, over against these innocent beliefs, this tranquil peace of mind, loomed up the figure of Chronology. At first sight, it seemed no more than a mild discipline, a salutary exercise designed to train the memory of school-children and to prevent them from getting mixed up about the sequence of events; a dry, rigid sort of thing; a gaunt framework, all bones and ligaments. However, in proportion as the suspicion of confusion in the records of humanity gained ground, so also did the status and reputation of chronology. It was recognized as an indispensable branch of knowledge; in short as a science. It became known as the doctrine of times and epochs. Just as the art of navigation furnishes pilots with rules for sailing the sea without wandering from their course, however long the voyage, so are we indebted to chronology for the skill to find our way with certainty over the vast and shadowy realms of the past. A great undertaking in very truth, that pilgrimage down the long vista of generations dead and gone, peoples and nations that had long since had their day. If chronology was not quite accurately aware of the nature and scope of her laws, this did not hinder her from applying them. She appraised the genuineness of a document, not in the light of the authority behind it, but simply as a matter of pure arithmetic. Chronology pays little heed to the language in which the document is written—French, Latin, Greek, Hebrew or whatever it may be, she is indifferent to its origin or its character. Her nature enables her to flit with ease from the profane to the sacred, for she is, and professes to be, no more than an abstract mathematical device. One thing she knows, however, and knows full well, and that is that it would never do for her to make a mistake in addition.

In some dim recess, at the far end of their libraries, poring over their books, cogitating, comparing, and collating, special-ists, investigators, experts, auditing the account-books of History, pursue their thankless and seemingly innocuous task. If they like it, and they say they love it, then by all means let them get on with it. Pin-pointing a date here, and another one

[1]Quoted by Henri Bremond, *Histoire littéraire du sentiment religieux en France*, Vol. X, 1930, c. VI.

there, totting up the tale of years, how they squabble among themselves! When ordinary folk heard the din of their wrangles, they just laughed. A lot of dryasdusts at their futile games again, they said. But when these learned gentlemen finish their task, or rather their instalment of it (for they began it long ago, as far back as the Renaissance, and finish it they never will), they will have sown more seeds of unrest in quiet minds, and done more to undermine faith in history, than all your open scoffers and anti-religious fanatics ever succeeded in doing. Not that they are all unbelievers; they are not, and some of them go over their sums again and again in the hope of protecting the old beliefs against the encroachments of these new chronologists. The result was that a confused and bitter struggle went on between them. Leibniz joined in the fray; and so did Newton. The currently-received figures seemed pretty easy to add up: Adam lived an hundred and thirty years, and begat a son in his own likeness, after his image; and called his name Seth: and the days of Adam after he had begotten Seth were eight hundred years; and he begat sons and daughters. And all the days that Adam lived were nine hundred and thirty years: and he died. And Seth lived an hundred and five years, and begat Enos. And Seth lived after he begat Enos eight hundred and seven years, and begat sons and daughters. . . . The grand total of all these successive generations shows four thousand years as separating the creation of the world from the birth of Christ. But it looked as if there were some links missing, as if the chain were not complete, for that total is certainly not big enough. Quite possibly, however, the Hebrews had their own special way of counting. But, if with a view to solving their problems, the chronologists adopt the comparative method and seek for dates and figures in the records of the races bordering on the Jews, what abysmal discrepancies they will encounter! It is confusion worse confounded. More and more difficulties come crowding in upon them, till they find themselves at last in a deeper than Cimmerian darkness.

Two races, to come at once to the essentials of the problem, looked like bursting the old framework into fragments when they claimed that they had existed, not for four thousand years— a very pale glory, that—but for tens, nay, for hundreds of thousands. Those Egyptians, reputed so wise, so just, who in other matters had been awarded so many marks of esteem, seemed to go completely crazy when it came to the question of dates. Taking a measureless and invincible pride in the glory and antiquity of their race, they traced their origin back to a past so remote, to an abysm of time so unfathomable, that it seemed to merge them with eternity. However, it was no easy matter to refute them. They were accomplished mathematicians, and their records were clear and unequivocal. In the third century before Christ, "the illustrious Manethon, priest or sacrificer of the city of Heliopolis", had, in obedience to the command of Ptolemy Philadelphus, recorded in writing the history of Egypt. In this chronicle, he enumerated a series of royal dynasties which began before the date traditionally assigned to the Deluge and, uninterrupted by that event, continued long after it. A record more ancient still, written long before the times of the Ptolemies, had it that kings had reigned in Egypt for a space of 36,525 years, even to the time of Mectanebes, the last of them all, who was driven from the throne by Ochus, king of the Persians, nineteen years before the reign of Alexander the Great.[1]

Then again there were the Chinese, learned astronomers, men of sagacity and judgment, abundantly furnished with calendars and almanacs. They claimed, and wanted people to believe, that they had existed from a time so remote as to have been anterior to the date when God created light. Was there ever such barefaced impudence! Compared with the Emperors of China, Adam was but a creature of yesterday. "Yam-Guam-Siem has it that, from the beginning of the world down to the reign of the Emperor Tienski, who came to the throne in the year 1620, there is represented a period of not less than nineteen million, three hundred and sixty-nine thousand and ninety-six years."[2] A formidable problem, there, for the serious-minded folk of those days; a problem which learned men throughout Europe set out to solve, bit by bit, inch by painful inch. In 1672, an Englishman, a student of chronology, John Marsham by name, thought he had found the key to the riddle. Yes, it was true that the Egyptians had had thirty royal dynasties which, if taken end to end, one after another, would exceed the age of the world. But that was the crux of the matter—they must *not* be put end to end, for there

[1] Le P. Paul Pezron, *L'antiquité des temps rétablie*, 1687, chap. XV.
[2] Le P. Greslon, *Histoire de la Chine sous la domination des Tartares*, 1671, I, chap. IX, p. 42.

were dynasties that were not consecutive but collateral, and these dynasties had held sway in their respective parts of the country at one and the same time. . . . In 1687, Père Paul Pezron, a monk of the rigid Cistercian rule, put forward a different explanation: four thousand years, he freely agreed, were inadequate to accommodate the ancient Egyptians. Four thousand years, however, is the period given in the Hebrew version of the Bible. But now take the Septuagint reading; there you will get roughly five thousand five hundred years. With those fifteen extra centuries, those dynasties can be housed comfortably enough. That was a victory for Père Pezron, but his triumph was short-lived. It was not merely that even these additional years were not enough to satisfy the arithmeticians, but it was considered a very rash proceeding to go picking and choosing between the different versions of the Scriptures just to suit the convenience of the Egyptians and the Chinese, and Père Pezron was given to understand that he was slipping from chronology and landing himself in impiety. There was an exchange—not at all a courteous one—of treatises and dissertations. From Italy, Fr. Astorini gave currency to a conjecture which Père Tournemine took up again in 1703. In the ordinary way, when some date is mentioned, say, for example, 1600, and then, when it is desired to refer to some subsequent year within the same century, it is customary, not to repeat the entire number, but to say 610, for instance, when the date you really mean is 1610. Who knows but that the Jews did likewise? Perhaps, not realising this, and taking their figures exactly as they stand, we have understated the total by several thousands of years. That was all very well, but how in the world was one to prove that this mode of notation, which was peculiar to the Italians, had also been in operation among the Hebrews? The whole thing was merely substituting one uncertainty for another.

This difficulty gave rise to another, no less tormenting. Listen yet again to the words of Bossuet: "Thus God, having delivered his people out of the hands of the Egyptians, that he might bring them into the land where he intended them to serve him, made known to them, before establishing them therein, the laws by which they were to order their lives. He wrote, with his own hand, on two tables which he gave to Moses, on Mount Sinai, the foundations of this law, that is to say, the Decalogue, or the Ten

Commandments, which contain the first principles of man's duty towards God and towards his fellow-men. To Moses he also gave other precepts." But some there were who considered that, if the Egyptians were a people of such ancient origin and such profound wisdom, and if the Hebrews dwelt for many years under the domination of the Egyptians, it was logical, indeed necessary, to conclude that the superior civilization would have left its mark on the inferior, and that therefore the Egyptians must have moulded the Hebrews, rather than the other way about. Such was the thesis advanced in the first place by John Marsham, and, later on, in a more strictly scientific form, by John Spencer, of Corpus Christi College, Cambridge. Both of them ascribed to the Egyptians, whom they greatly admired, a decisive influence in the matter of laws, precepts, religious rites—circumcision, baptism, temples, the priesthood, sacrifices, ceremonies—all these came from the Egyptians. When, in order that he might save his people who had fallen victims to the serpents, Moses set up a brazen serpent which healed all those who gazed upon it, it was no miracle that he wrought; he was but repeating an ancient Egyptian incantation. But if that were so, the chosen people would have been, in their essential beliefs, subservient to a pagan race. No longer could it be held that God gave the law to Moses on Mount Sinai; Moses would have merely copied the Egyptians, his lords and masters.

The worthy, the painstaking, Huet, Bishop of Avranches, who, the story went, crammed his house so full of books that one day the place came toppling down about his ears, and who was for ever reading, reading, had a praiseworthy object in view. It was nothing less than to restore Moses to his rightful place, namely, the *first* place. He set out to show that the whole of Pagan theology derived from the acts, or the writings, of Moses; that the gods of the Phoenicians, the Egyptians, the Persians, as well as those of the Thracians, the Germans, the Gauls, the Bretons and the Romans, all proceeded from Moses. Such was the theme of his *Demonstratio evangelica*, 1672; and again of his *Quaestiones alnetanae de concordia rationis et fidei*, 1690. What, however, he failed to perceive was that his argument was double-edged, that it cut both ways, that it could be turned no less effectively against himself. If there were all those resemblances between the Mosaic beliefs and those of Pagan antiquity, was it Moses who inspired the others, or did those other more ancient races hand on their traditions to Moses? Poor Huet! His very success was his undoing, landing the unhappy man in the ranks of the unbelievers. "My father", Louis Racine mildly observed, "did not at all approve of this learned man making use of profane learning to buttress up religion". Antoine Arnauld was less delicate but more direct in what he said: "It would be difficult to imagine a book more fundamentally irreligious; or one better fitted to persuade the budding free-thinker that, although one ought to have a religion, it did not greatly matter which, seeing there was good in all of them, and that even Paganism could stand comparison with Christianity".

That was where the best intentions in the world might bring one. Well; it was a case of one difficulty after another, of doubt piled on doubt. It was a crucial phase in that unending battle which goes on from generation to generation, only its aspect varying according to the fashion of the day, the battle, that is to say, of Science *versus* Religion. Listen to the Abbé Renaudot, who, in the year 1702, was giving his views on John Marsham's book at a meeting of the *Académie des Inscriptions*: his words are vibrant alike with admiration and distress: "In its own particular line, this book is perfect; perfect in respect of the orderliness, the method, the precision, the conciseness and the profound scholarship which distinguish it throughout. At the same time, it is difficult not to animadvert on an author, who, either because he has a special leaning towards Egypt, and its antiquities, or for some other reason best known to himself, has so attenuated everything that lends dignity to the Scriptures and their ancient origin, that he has provided the free-thinker with more food for scepticism than the majority of the declared opponents of religion ever did".

People hesitated; they did not know what to think. Of course one might bolt and bar oneself up within the fortress and hurl back the arguments of the chronologists, telling them that these Chaldaeans, these Babylonians, with their demands for myriads of years to satisfy their claims to racial antiquity, were nothing more or less than a pack of liars; that St. Augustine had said the last word in the matter when he spoke as follows: If the profane authors tell us things contrary to what is set down in the Bible, we should regard them as untrue.

But when they ventured out into the open, ill-equipped as they were to defend themselves against weapons which religious apologetics had so far done nothing to neutralize, the combatants were involved in some very perilous adventures indeed. Figures, as vertiginous as they were vague, lingered on in people's minds: 23,000 years; 49,000 years; 100,000 years; 170,000 years; should one follow the example of Father Antonio Foresti who selected his dates because they were convenient rather than because they were correct? Between the two extremes, one claiming that it was 6,984 years and the other that it was 3,740, since the world began, he counted no less than seventy intermediate opinions. Impossible to accept or verify them all. However, he had to make up his mind, and he made it up in the light of practical considerations quite unconnected with science. Foresti picked his authors on the same lines. These authors, no matter how many you take, all tell different stories. Who's right and who's wrong? If you choose one, you are bound to give the lie to the others. Still, one of them had to be chosen; unless one took a leaf out of the book of the cautious Perizonius who, addressing his students at Leyden, had repudiated the encroachments of Pyrrhonism. Nine years after his inaugural lecture, he said what *he* thought about this chronological controversy. He said it with his customary terseness and with sound, if somewhat chastened, common sense. Demolishing the arguments of one's predecessors was a comparatively simple matter. The constructive part of the business was *not* so easy. The Egyptians themselves had nothing really certain to offer. The most one could do was to establish a few time-relationships in the history of the various ancient peoples, without attempting to pin them down to any definite date. In this way, Perizonius hoped to salvage something at least from the great shipwreck. What was happening now to those ideas which at one time had seemed so stable and so sure? To those tenets at once so simple and so imposing? Where now were those calm and confident affirmations, those ever-fixed marks, those ever constant dates? What *was* one to believe? How could we discern the hand of Providence in what was now a welter of confusion? How were we to assess the value of this or that fact in the field of knowledge, when the facts themselves looked like slipping through our fingers? The new arrivals bade fair to sap the foundations of History, of Providence and of

48   CHANGING PSYCHOLOGIES

Authority alike. The outlook at last became agonising in the extreme. What! The more one searched, the less one found? Was that the measure of the thing? The past became more and more shrouded in mist, and all attempts to dispel it did but render it the more opaque. Time the all-devourer, Time which tends to envelop all things in endless oblivion, has all but hidden from man the date of his creation, the knowledge of how long he has dwelt upon the earth. So true is this that, in spite of all the efforts that have been made in our day to discover the number of years that intervene between the creation of the world and the coming of the Messiah, not only have we failed to reach the truth; we have wandered yet farther from it.[1]

There was, however, a way of reconstructing the past, and that was by archaeological research. A whole tribe of learned men were hard at work undertaking the most dryasdust tasks, digging out original texts, deciphering manuscripts, scraping stones, rubbing coins, a whole little tribe, full of zeal and courage, as busy as an ants' nest, with its artizans, and even its warriors. Sound workmen, with a taste for tackling big jobs, what they intended to do was to make sure of every step they took. Whatever its importance, great or small, they were determined to be completely and irresistibly sure about it. What they aimed at doing was to dig up solid material out of the past, something concrete and perdurable, something that should remain as a permanent possession. There was Francesco Bianchini who sought in archaeological exploration the sure *data* that no documents could give him; Richard Bentley, the Master of Trinity, curator of the Royal Library, a most eminent classical scholar and a man of incomparable intellectual vigour; Pufendorf, a great believer in ancient records; and there was Leibniz. Leibniz went and buried himself in libraries, grubbed about among old documents, amusing himself with copying them with his own hand—royal edicts, diplomatists' dispatches, or whatever they might be. He deemed that a code of international relations should be based on authentic documents, declarations of war, peace-treaties and other similar written evidence, and not on mere words. As librarian to the Duke of Brunswick, he undertook to write the history of the reigning house. After a

[1]Le P. Paul Pezron, *L'antiquité des temps rétablie*, 1687, p. 8.

considerable time had elapsed, he brought out a bulky volume, which was followed sometime later by two others. These did not conform to the fashionable taste in the least, crammed as they were with quotations from original sources. When people expressed amazement at the sort of work he had turned out, he retorted that he had done something a great deal more useful than if he had employed himself in producing resounding phrases, swelling periods, rhetorical flourishes. He told them that his work was something absolutely unique, that the like of it had never been seen before, that he had shed a new light on centuries that had hitherto been shrouded in terrible obscurity, that he had settled a number of disputed points, and rectified a number of errors.

How they laboured at their task! And in every country! Henri Meibom devoted himself to German archaeology; Thomas Gale and Thomas Rymer to the study of English documents; Nicolas Antonio to the beginnings of Spain's literary history. How they toiled, too, in that vast workshop organized by the Jesuits, in which the Bollandists gained particular distinction. How they laboured, those Benedictines, winning for themselves their reputation, their afterwards proverbial reputation, for steady, unremitting toil. So great was their zeal that the impetuous Rancé, the reformer of La Trappe, reproached these industrious brethren with devoting to the pursuit of secular knowledge the hours and the ardour which should have been consecrated to God. Dom Mabillon took up the challenge, whence there arose a long and lofty war of words, in which the question at issue was the nature of the *summum bonum*.

Benedictine lay-brothers toiled with equal zest, as well as Étienne Baluze, and Charles Du Cange, and their combined efforts resulted in research scoring some of its greatest victories. We may call to mind that it was in 1678 that Du Cange published his *Glossarium mediae et infimae latinitatis*; that in 1681 Mabillon published his *De re diplomatica libri V*; and that in 1708, Montfaucon brought out his *Palaeographica graeca*. But if we had to select one example, and one only, from the ranks of those who devoted their lives to research, it would, perhaps, be Antonio Muratori on whom our choice would light. His whole life was devoted to the task of rescuing from oblivion the titles in use among the human race. Shut up from morning till night in his library at Modena, which he scarcely ever left save to make a journey of learned research through the archives of his native Italy, Muratori piled up folio upon folio. His literary, philosophical and polemical writings which alone would have sufficed to establish the reputation of any other man, were really but the products of his leisure moments, *parerga*, which offered him a little relaxation from his main task, the task which he so stubbornly pursued and which involved, as a preliminary, the gathering together of all the documents he could unearth that related to Italy, not so much to the Italy of Roman times as to the Italy of the Middle Ages, till then so utterly neglected. After that, he would essay to bring ten dead centuries back to life.

In England, perhaps the main emphasis was on Greek studies; in Holland, on Latin; in France, on ecclesiastical history and hagiography; in Italy, on her own past. However, there were no watertight compartments; work went on in every country with a common aim. When treasure of undisputed value had at last been brought together; when the junior sciences, such, for example, as numismatics, had delved deep into the earth to lay bare the relics of vanished civilizations; when the salutary lessons of patience and humility provided by those labours had had their effect, and corrected the general view of things, then would the days of historical scepticism at last be over.

Quite so; but when *would* the work be done? How many years, decades, centuries would be needed before one would be able to say, "I know", instead of "I think"; when one could say that such a such a thing *was* so, without fear of misrepresenting the truth? It is a desperate business to find even a piece or two of the vast mosaic, and then no sooner have the finders set to work to fit the pieces into their proper places, than they, too, are called away to the land of shadows, and they and their labours become things of the past, that past which, stealing stealthily upon them, envelops them, too, in its dark embrace. Even supposing they could perform the miracle of coming back to life again, those to whom they offered their little portions and parcels of the vanished past, and whose task it should be to restore to these dead things the form, the hue, the breath of life, would have no use for them, so true is it that archaeologists and historians worked side by side each in complete ignorance of what the other was doing. Soon these paths themselves began to diverge more and more. A new generation was now appearing on the scene, a comfort-loving, care-free generation that fought shy of anything that called for effort. On the one hand were the drudges, people that did the spade-work, who wrote ill, who lumbered up the margins of their books with references, who were heavy, obscure, willing galley-slaves, self-condemned to inglorious labours. On the other side, were the historians, men of soaring genius who disdained to descend to *minutiae*, leaving to second-rate minds the exacting labours of pettifogging research, and carefully avoiding any discussions or arguments which might have tended to dim the fire within them. The slaves got together piles of material, which the great lords of language disdained to look at.

What, when all is said and done, is history? A collection of fairy-tales, when it treats of the origin of nations; and, thereafter, a conglomeration of errors. We fancy we detect in the man who is generally regarded as the typical sceptic, in Fontenelle, a note of sadness bordering on despair when this view of the matter is borne in upon him.

What a prodigious time it takes for man to arrive at any sort of sound conclusion, no matter how plain and straightforward the question at issue may be. To preserve a record of events as they actually happened—there does not seem anything particularly out of the way about that; yet many centuries had to elapse before the power to perform that simple task was mastered. Before then, the things with which men stored their memory turned out to be but dreams and fantastic imaginings.

As children, we are taught so much about Greek myths, and get so accustomed to them that when we grow up we do not recognise how extravagant they really are; but if we could disabuse our minds of our ingrained idea of them, if we could see them with fresh eyes, we should realize with amazement that what is called a nation's early history is in reality nothing but a phantasmagoria, a string of childish tales. Can it really be, we ask ourselves, that such things were ever given out as truth? If those who passed them on did not believe them, what was their motive for deceiving us? How was it that men were attracted to tales so manifestly absurd? And if they were drawn to them then, how is it they are not drawn to them still?

That way of recording history was succeeded by a newer method, which obtained among the more cultivated and disciplined races. It consisted in scrutinizing the motives behind the various actions, and in examining the character of those who wrought them. It proved no less fallacious than its forerunner. For man is bound to be passionate, or credulous, or ill-informed, or careless. "What you would have to discover would be one who had observed things with perfect attentiveness and, at the same time, with perfect impartiality. You would never succeed. At best the historian elaborates an *a priori* plan in which all the parts are dove-tailed together to form a complete whole; the sort of thing the metaphysician does with regard to his theories. He takes certain given facts and then assigns them causes of his own imagining. His work is still less sure, of still more doubtful validity, than the speculations of a philosophical theorist. The only really useful sort of history would be made up of an account of the passions and the errors of man:

Madmen we are, but not quite on the pattern of those who are shut up in a madhouse. It does not concern any of them to discover what sort of madness afflicts his neighbour, or the previous occupants of his cell; but it matters very much to us. The human mind is less prone to go astray when it gets to know to what extent, and in how many directions, it is itself liable to err, and we can never devote too much time to the study of our aberrations.

That, according to this very modern champion of the Moderns in their famous quarrel with the Ancients, is all that history can do for us. Let the present concern itself with the present. Many years are taken up in our schools in compelling young folk to read the works of the Roman historians. How far more profitable it would be to tell them about the times in which they themselves are called upon to live! Really it is difficult to see what light is shed on the affairs of our own day by anything we may glean from Cornelius Nepos, Quintus Curtius, or the first ten books of Livy. And that would be true even if you got the whole thing up by heart, or made a detailed abstract of all the notable thoughts and sayings contained in those authors. It profits little to know the exact number of cows and sheep the Romans carried off with them when they defeated the Aequiculani, the Hernici and the Volscians.[1] But what is going on to-day, our own lives and what the future promises—*that* is what appeals to us, *that* is what bears us away on the wings of enchantment! *Ratio vicit, vetustas cessit* . . .

[1] S. von Pufendorf, *Einleitung zu der Historie der vornehmsten Reiche und Staaten . . . in Europa*, 1682, Preface. See also Malebranche, *De la Recherche de la vérité*, 1674, II, chap. IV, V, VI.

III

THE LIGHT FROM THE NORTH

EUROPE looked as if it had taken permanent shape. The several nations composing it had each such familiar and decided characteristics that the mere mention of any one of them sufficed to call up a whole string of stock-epithets, each the inalienable property of that particular country, just as "white" is of snow, or "scorching" of the sun. Is it the Swiss we are thinking of? Well, they are sincere, level-headed, loyal, unaffected, open-hearted. They possess courage and resolution, and if they are attacked by their foes, they are prompt to hit back at them; they are steady-going, staunch, bold, and of good physique. They make good soldiers and most of them take service in France. However, they must have good pay: *point d'argent, point de Suisse*—no pay, no piper! The Germans? They are warlike and make first-rate fighting men, once they have been licked into shape. They have good heads for business and display aptitude in all such callings. They are not easily incited to sedition and like to keep to the sort of government they have been accustomed to. They constitute a large *bloc*, but unfortunately they are a prey to a whole host of internal divisions, religious and political. . . ."The Poles are brave, with a taste for letters and the fine-arts, rather prone to inebriety, and Catholics to a man." So, in the year 1708, declared the worthy Nicolas de Fer, geographer to His Most Catholic Majesty and to Monseigneur the Dauphin. "The Hungarians are a sturdy race, fond of war and of horses, daring, uncouth and notable toss-pots. Their nobles live in sumptuous style; their womankind are comely and sedate of mien." "The Swedes are an honest and courageous folk and fond of the arts and sciences. The air of their country is clear, keen and salubrious; their forests are the haunt of numerous wild and ferocious animals. The Danes are more or less the same in their manners and customs as the Swedes. The Norwegians appear to be of a simpler type, and are very frank and ingenuous."

When an author was looking about him for a stock character, the various countries thus labelled offered him a convenient field of selection. Anyone thinking of composing a ballet, or an entertainment for royalty had no need to cudgel his brains unduly; there were plenty of foreigners to choose from—Neapolitans, Croats, characters as well-worn as the heavy-fathers, or the lackeys, of the traditional comic stage—maybe even more so. In 1697, Houdar de la Motte prevailed on the *Académie royale de Musique* to perform a ballet entitled *"l'Europe galante"*. "From the various European countries those characters were drawn which offered the most striking contrast one with another and were thus calculated to prove 'good theatre': France, Spain, Italy, Turkey. The authors kept to the notions commonly current regarding their respective national characteristics. The Frenchman was fickle, impulsive, dandified. The Spaniard was true-hearted and sentimental; the Italian jealous, subtle, hot-tempered; and, lastly, the high-and-mighty aloofness of the Sultans and the passionate tantrums of the Sultanas were presented with all the realism that the resources of theatrical production would permit."

Now let us take the same clichés and swing them over to the black, the opprobrious, side. These wishy-washy adjectives then become part of the vocabulary of invective, but the process is the same in either case. In 1700, Daniel Defoe wrote a political lampoon which made a great stir. It was entitled *The True-born Englishman*. Every country gets its compliment. It is all quite plain-sailing:

Pride, the First Peer, and President of Hell,
To his share Spain, the largest province fell . . .

Lust chose the torrid zone of Italy,
Where Blood ferments in Rapes and Sodomy . . .

Drunkness, the darling favourite of Hell,
Chose Germany to rule . . .

Ungovern'd Passion settled first in France,
Where mankind lives in haste, and thrives by chance.
A dancing nation, fickle and untrue . . .

They had been through so many clashes, all these bickering brethren, they had so often made it up, shaken hands and embraced, they had been through so many trials and tribulations that they thought they knew one another, and the notions they then formed, each one of all the rest, never changed any more. How wrong they were. In the western sky, some constellations began to pale, while others were waxing brighter. The light came no longer from the same quarter. It was not only frontiers, rendered fluid by incessant wars, that changed, but the intellectual forces and the collective spirit of Europe. But this change was not effected without a struggle, without suffering, nor was it accomplished without another revolution.

The intellectual hegemony of Europe had always been a family heritage, as it were; a sort of heirloom confined to the Latin races. In the days of the Renaissance, Italy was the tenant-in-tail. Then it was Spain's turn to have her golden age. Finally, France succeeded to the heritage. Any suggestion that the barbarous northerners should ever presume to dispute the sceptre with these queenly races would have seemed both impertinent and absurd. What, forsooth, had they to offer? The monstrous Shakespeare? Or, if they were Germans, the uncouth runes of rugged and untutored bards? People like these did not seriously count. Though they quarrelled fiercely enough among themselves, glowering darkly at one another, playing on one another the most unhandsome tricks, Italy, Spain and France had still their royal descent to boast of, to support their claim; all three of them were daughters of Rome. Spain alone had dimmed her radiance. We will not say that even now she did not fling over Europe some rays of a light that could not be extinguished; but it is a hard task for a nation to go on indefinitely keeping ahead of her rivals. It means she must never falter, never exhaust her strength, never cease to keep bright, and to diffuse around her far and wide the radiance of her pristine glory. But by this time Spain had ceased to live in the present. The last thirty years of the seventeenth century, and, for the matter of that, the first thirty of the eighteenth, were with her well-nigh completely barren. Never before, throughout her whole intellectual history, says Ortega y Gasset, had her heart beat so feebly. Wrapt up in herself, she presented an attitude of lofty indifference towards the rest of the world. Travellers continued to visit her, but they did not conceal the disdain with which she inspired them. They harped on her defects—a populace wallowing in superstition, a court sunk in ignorance. They enlarged on the decay of her commerce and spoke contemptuously of the sloth and vain-glory of her people. As for her writers, her foreign critics re-peatedly gave instances of their pretentious and affected style, and of the eccentricities and irregularities of her stage plays, things calculated to outrage the feelings of all who were con-versant with such matters. People were beginning to say, not only that Spain had lost her power and influence, but that she was a traitor to her own genius. Her romantic spirit, her national pride, her nice sense of honour, her love of justice, her complete unselfishness—all those qualities which had been her particular pride and glory, Cervantes in his *Don Quixote* had held up to ridicule. And the Spaniards by applauding *Don Quixote* had belied their nature and disowned their birthright. Absurd as it was, this idea was not more absurd than a host of other re-proaches with which nations competing for leadership have sought to give the *coup de grâce* to their already weakening rivals.

If Italy retained her vitality, she also evinced a suppleness, an adaptability, which enabled her to change the character of her exports and to seek in other domains, and particularly in the domain of Science, the renown which literature denied her. Abroad, in the world at large, her predominant asset was Rome, the prestige attaching to the Roman name. Never throughout her history did she cease to invoke it; it was the foundation of all her aspirations. Then again there was her language, so melodious, so soft, the very idiom of love. There were her singers, her dancers, her librettists, her musicians, her opera which was the delight of all civilized peoples. It was to the East rather than to the West that her influence spread, to the shores of Dalmatia, to Austria and Poland. Well; when all was said and done, these gains were not to be despised. But the time had now come when there was a call for ideas, and of these she had none to offer. Her sun was setting. Still, even now, what hosts of travellers came crowding to her shores. To name a few of the best known, Gilbert Burnet; Misson, a Huguenot refugee who acted as companion to a young nobleman making his *grand tour*; William Bromley; Montfaucon and Dom Briois his *confrère*; Addison. From what we read of their travel notes, their letters, their stories, one thing constantly emerges and that is an unfading admiration for the Past and an ever-increasing disdain for the Present; that, and the decadence—political, moral and intellectual—of an Italy which, beneath their very eyes, was relapsing into a land of orange groves and ancient ruins, a land of shadows, a land of the dead.

Now it was France's turn. For forty years or more she had played a predominant rôle in European affairs. Friends and foes alike agreed on what Horace Walpole was later to describe as the astounding progress her power made from the Treaty of Munster in 1648 down to the Revolution in England and the first beginnings of the Grand Alliance in 1689. This expansion, this vigour, this glory are the signs of an intense vitality. France is an entity, a person, a moral whole. Her will to unity, her will to expand, follow one another like the steps in a logical process growing increasingly aware of itself. By unity, her ardours are not damped down but directed into a fitting channel. She was ready and eager to deploy outside her own frontiers a force which for a long time to come was not to be turned aside. Her king favoured an active policy, a policy of expansion. He was to be its luminary, its sun. He would create a solar system with Versailles as its centre and of which the countries of Europe should be the satellites. He was the originator of a systematic attempt to produce the pleasing spectacle of an intellectual order in the world.[1]

France is richly populated; richly studded with towns and villages; versed in the arts of war; teeming with an aristocracy always ready to take up arms. Her people are vivacious, witty, adaptable, and full of charm. They are active, skilful, endowed with qualities which ensure success in the most diverse undertakings, particularly in those which call for intuition rather than for prolonged and patient application; on the other hand, they are fickle, volatile and rather apt to brag about their breaches of the moral law; so much so, in fact, that sometimes they boast of

[1]Salvador de Madariaga, *Englishmen, Frenchmen, Spaniards*. London, 1928. Spanish edition, 1929. French edition, 1931.

misdeeds they have never committed . . . . Such is the stereotyped portrait; some of the traits are true enough and have stood
the test of time. But now the idea of gaining a signal success, of
establishing a prodigious supremacy arose, and endowed these
characteristics with a fresh *éclat*. France is *par excellence* the home
of polished manners, good breeding, intellectual refinement, of
the art of living, of courtesy, culture, and all the social graces.
France is the recognized rendezvous for foreigners of distinction
who come from all parts of Europe to seek knowledge and
culture from the various Academies, or to acquire ease and
grace of bearing at the Court. Fascinated by French urbanity,
these foreigners put themselves to school, the school of refinement, of the art of living gracefully. Paris, as being the centre of
this concourse, took precedence over all other cities. Her charm
derived from the freedom and ease which characterized her mode
of life. In Paris no one calls on you to give an account of your
behaviour. If you want to change your habits, you have but to
change your neighbourhood. If someone takes it into his head
to appear one day resplendent with gold adornments and the
next day clad in homely fustian, what concern is that of anyone? In Paris you can get what you want, and you can get it for
the asking. No sooner does some new invention designed to
facilitate the conditions of life come into existence, than it is
immediately adopted there. Time was when Rome towered
above all the cities of the world; now it is Paris.

Whereas her rivals seemed to be suffering from a barrenness
bred of exhaustion, France, as by a miracle, poured forth a
continuous stream of masterpieces, of works of genius, not the
kind of masterpiece adjudged to be so by this or that nation,
desirous of administering a little flattering unction to its own
pride, but masterpieces acknowledged to be such by the world at
large. In the wake of Descartes and Corneille, came Molière,
Racine, La Fontaine, Bossuet, and that generation had not passed
away when Massillon, Regnard, Lesage come to take up the tale.
This exuberant fertility continues for three-quarters of a century.
While the tragedies, comedies, fables, sermons of writers promptly
crowned as classics are constantly being reprinted, yet other
works appear which, added to the existing mass, augment its
power and accelerate its momentum. How could Europe fail
to be enriched by this massive cultural contribution? Thus, the

tradition of supremacy was maintained, and waxed stronger and stronger every day. Imagine what the propaganda value of the very greatest authors must have been; add thereto the effect of those of lesser calibre who followed in the wake of their illustrious leaders; lastly, take into account the third- or even the fourth-raters, the small fry of talent, long since forgotten, but who, in their day, spread abroad and percolated everywhere, people like Bouhours, Rapin, Fleury, and a host of others; taking them all in all, we shall get some faint idea of the extent, the depth, and the infinite variety of France's contribution, and of its influence.[1]

For the intellectual aristocracy of Europe, translations were now to a large extent superfluous, and French looked like becoming the universal language. Such, at any rate, was the view of Guy Miège, a Genevan who had settled in London. He brought out a French-English and English-French dictionary, because, he said, "French, in some respects, bids fair to become the universal language". Gregorio Leti, who, when in Amsterdam, published a French version of his Life of Cromwell, was of the same opinion. He did so because "French has become in this present century of ours, the most widely spoken language in Europe. That is either because the political power of France has brought about the spread of the French tongue, just as in ancient days the might of Rome carried the Latin speech into all the countries of the known world; or else it is that the French language, highly refined as it is, possesses a charm peculiar to itself in the precision, the delicacy and naturalness for which it is so widely celebrated". Such tributes were common, and it would be easy to multiply them; however, the most significant of them all is, without doubt, this utterance of Bayle's: "The French language", he said, "is the rallying point for all the countries of Europe. It is a language which we might truly call transcendental, for the same reason that philosophers bestow that epithet on natures which spread far and wide, and freely manifest themselves in every clime and country."[2]

Books, language, manners, to say nothing of the material apparatus of life! Here is a country mansion, designed to look like Versailles, and here is the French tutor, whose business it is

---

[1] We shall see later on, in Part IV, chapter II, what reservations should be made, according to the different countries, regarding the effects of this influence.
[2] *Nouvelles de la République des lettres,* Nov. 1685, Art. 5.

to direct the studies of the young nobleman, its future lord. Clothes, gowns, wigs—all are à la française. To whom should we go for dancing lessons, if not to one of those past-masters of the airs and graces, the French maître à danser, who has managed to beat the Italians at their own game. Now go down to the culinary regions. What do we find there? French chefs and master-cooks, butlers uncorking and decanting French wines. "It looks as if you couldn't give a dinner or a supper-party of any consequence unless you produced imported wines served from thick glass flagons, which we have to call bouteilles, forsooth, since even the containers must have a French name." "And we Italians", says Muratori, "stupid ninnies that we are, hurry, as if there wasn't a moment to lose, to do whatever the French do, slavishly to copy their fashions, as if they had been imposed upon us by order of great Jove himself."[1]

"If some of our ancestors were to come back to earth", said the German Thomasius in his Discourse on imitating the French (1687), "they simply wouldn't know us, degenerate hybrids that we are. Nowadays, everything about us has got to be French— clothes, cookery, language, all French. French are our manners, and French our vices".[2]

Not only Italian and Spanish, but also Latin, Latin which had been one of the corner-stones of European solidarity, had to surrender to French. Everybody had to speak French; it was looked upon as a mark of good breeding: "People wonder why everyone is so mad on French; but mad they are, and what is more they don't look like getting over it. There are some towns where, for one school that teaches Latin, there are ten or a dozen that teach French. Translations of the classics are coming out all over the place, and classical scholars are beginning to fear that Latin will be dispossessed of its ancient sovereignty."[3]

To the various reasons adduced to account for this phenomenon, all of them sound enough, such as the intrinsic merits of the language itself, the high standard of its literature, the care bestowed on it by a nation to whom such things as grammar and the choice of words are matters of first-rate importance, and who are the only people in the world to boast of a Department of

[1] Cf Giulio Natali, Il Settecento, Milan, 1929, p. 68 et seq.
[2] Christian Thomasius, Von Nachahmung der Franzosen, Nach den Ausgaben von 1687 und 1701. Stuttgart, 1894.
[3] Nouvelles de la République des lettres, Août 1684, Article 7.

State specially appointed to safeguard its purity, namely, the *Académie*,—to all these reasons, profound, subtle, and opposite as they are, one other may be added, the needs of a Europe that was about to enter upon a *Vita Nuova*. Latin smacked of the schools; of theology: it had a savour of the past. Little by little, it had lost touch with the present. Excellent as it was as an instrument of mental training, a man wanted something more than Latin when the days of his schooling were over. French, on the other hand, made it seem as if civilization had renewed its youth. The virtue that was in Latin was present in French, too; but it was a virtue brought up to date, as it were. It was clear, it was definite, it was firm, and, above all, it was alive. Science, which was seeking to explain the world otherwise than by direct causation, needed a different medium of expression from that which had done duty in the Middle Ages. So, too, in 1714, when the Peace of Rastadt came to be signed, the diplomats required a medium more roomy, more flexible, less rigid, than that which had satisfied the needs of the Chancellery of the Holy Roman Empire. Even that engaging, happy-go-lucky way of theirs, for which many were wont to blame them, told in their favour: they were like people who had been relieved from the burden of a tyrannical past. They came in for some strictures from the moralists of other countries, who blamed them for being effeminate and worldly-minded. The moralists might have saved their breath. France and things French were all the rage. The same francophil spirit made its way into Italy towards the close of the seventeenth century; about this time, dolls dressed in the latest Paris fashions began to make their appearance in shop windows and showcases. The English did not lag behind. Ladies wore their hair *à la mode*; booksellers recommended "the *à la mode* secretary"; Thomas Brown in the *Stage Beaux tossed in a Blanket* makes fun of Hypocrisy *à la mode*; Farquhar in the *Constant Couple* compares *à la mode* London with *à la mode* France; Steele puts on *The Funeral*, or Grief *à la mode*; and Addison, in his prologue to that comedy, lets us into the secret of the infatuation:

> Our author . . . .
> Two ladies errant has exposed to view:
> The first a damsel, travelled in romance;
> The other more refined: she comes from France . . .

A particular instance of a general tendency; a matter of supply and demand. This explains how it was that France established her dominion, not by coercion, for force would have been powerless to found an enduring sovereignty in the domain of the spirit, but by the gentle and unforced accord of all parties, everywhere. Yes, everywhere: in Spain, and in the Spanish colonies, even in Lima where, in the year 1710, an adaptation of *Rodogune* was performed in the theatre, as well as a play founded on *les Femmes Savantes*; in Holland, too, where the national genius tried, through Antonides van der Goes, and tried in vain, to keep French influence at bay; likewise in Poland, where the star of France grew brighter as the star of Italy declined. Everywhere you hear the sound of the French tongue, everywhere French plays are acted, French books are read; everywhere the genius of France leaves its imprint on the mind of man.

Nevertheless, not long after France had thus established her pre-eminence, a rival appears on the scene; and this rival, strange to relate, hails from the North.

England it was that first ran counter to the political ambitions of France. Neither on the high-seas, nor on the Continent was she disposed to let France have everything her own way. She not only contested her hegemony, but impugned the very principle of authority on which the power of the French king was conceived to be founded.

And so a duel begins between Louis XIV on the one side and William of Orange on the other. The two champions stand forth and confront each other, each symbolizing a principle, an idea. When, in the year 1688, William drove James II from the English throne, and undertook to rule in his stead as a constitutional monarch under parliamentary control, Louis took the royal fugitive under his own personal protection, installed him in palatial quarters at Saint-Germain-en-Laye, and, in thus protecting the person of the fallen monarch, flattered himself that he was upholding the divine right of kings. But when, after a protracted struggle, France was at last compelled to yield to the forces of the Coalition, and when the treaty of peace was signed at Ryswick, how the pride of the *Grand Monarque* must have been humbled! He was forced to admit that his adversary was too strong for him, he also had to recognize in that same adversary a lawful ruler; and that meant the betrayal of the cause of his cousin, and most Christian brother, James II of England.

What manner of people were these English who thus imposed their will on Europe, and, at a single stroke, inflicted on France a more crushing blow to her pride than she had suffered these fifty years or more? A wave of indignation swept through the length and breadth of the country, from court to commonalty; so at least it would appear, if there is any truth in the allegation that *Athalie* was really nothing more nor less than the English Revolution tricked out in an elaborate stage-disguise. Moreover, we come across this sort of thing, a song that was sung at Dijon in the year 1709:

> Le grand-père est un fanfaron,
> Le fils un imbécile,
> Le petit-fils un grand poltron
> Ah! la belle famille!
> Que je vous plains, peuples français,
> Soumis à cet empire,
> Faites ce qu'ont fait les Anglais,
> C'est assez vous le dire . . . .[1]

In the earlier stages of their revival, the English, though energetic and tenacious, did not exhibit any very definite aptitude for letters. When Louis XIV asked his ambassador in London to give him some particulars about the artists and literary folk in England, the ambassador replied that literature and science have a way of forsaking one country in order to go and honour another with their presence, and that, for the time being at any rate, they had taken up their abode in France. He added that if any traces of such things survived in England, they lingered on in the traditions that men like Bacon and Buchanan had left behind them. He made mention also of one Miltonius, and declared that he had covered himself with deeper infamy by his dangerous writings than the regicides had incurred by murdering their king.

But before long, one strong point at least had to be conceded

[1]The grand-dad is a braggart, the son an imbecile, the grandson is a mighty coward, oh! what a lovely family. How I pity you, you French, to be under such a rule. Take my tip and do as the English have done.

to the English; it had to be admitted that they were profound and original thinkers. Thus, here again, a contrast was beginning to develop: to France belonged the art of social life, of good conversation, elegant manners, intellectual adornments. To England, a sturdy individualism, an earnest and courageous spirit of enquiry, complete independence in the realm of philosophical speculation. Had England been able to boast only writers of the trivial, popular order, devisers of amusing but dissolute comedies, which still kept alive on the stage the profligacy that had characterized the Restoration, men such as Wycherley, Congreve, Vanbrugh or Farquhar, then England would have had to be content with playing second-fiddle, since in these things she was merely imitating the French, and openly borrowing from French authors. But that was not the limit of her output. . . . She was engaged in debating loftier questions than, say, how to carry on a secret love-affair, or how to portray the character of a rake. So far from shelving religious questions, on the ground that they had been settled long ago, English writers were ceaselessly discussing the various ways in which different individuals explained the nature of their relationship with God; there was the puritanical mysticism of Bunyan; the enlightened conformity of a Clarke or a Tillotson, and there was the uncompromising deism of a Toland. One of her sons, Locke, was busy building a new philosophy; another, Newton, was bringing about a revolution in scientific thought: the *Principia mathematica philosophiae naturalis* dates from 1687. These were some of the outward manifestations of the living force which England stood for, a force from which France herself could not withhold an admiring tribute:

> Les Anglais pensent profondément;
> Leur esprit, en celà, suit leur tempérament;
> Creusant dans les sujets, et forts d'expériences,
> Ils étendent partout l'empire des sciences . . . .[1]

But at length the time arrived when the English made a bid for fame in the sphere of letters, and from that day forth, the empire

---

[1] The English think deeply; in that their mind is one with their character; delving deeply into things, and rich in experience they extend far and wide the empire of the sciences. La Fontaine, *Fables*, Book 12 (1694), *The Fox and the Grapes*.

of the intellectual world was definitely divided. When Dryden died, in 1700, England considered that she had lost her one great poet. But now, behold! a marvellous revival takes place. If the English were asked what philosophers they could muster, they replied with Cudworth and Berkeley; what moralists? with Addison, Steele, Arbuthnot; what scholars? with Bentley; what poets? with Pope and Gay. And if they were asked whether they had anyone capable of excelling in all these different spheres together, they said they had; his name was Swift. So quickly and so keenly did they come to realize the value of this asset, that they overwhelmed their writers and men of learning with honours and rewards. It was now the turn of the French writers and scholars to show envy of the English. The actors had changed rôles. The hour of triumph had arrived; the hour when the sturdy plant in which the sap had so long been rising was to burst into blossom at last.

One cannot but be struck by the sort of nostalgic emotion which the historians of English literature are wont to display when they set themselves to treat of this memorable period in its evolution. "In 1702", wrote Edmund Gosse, "Queen Anne ascended the throne, and her brief reign is identified with a brilliant revival in English letters, in the hands of a group of men of the highest accomplishment and originality. . . . Between 1711 and 1714, a perfect galaxy of important works in prose and verse burst almost simultaneously from the London Presses. It was as though a cloud which had long obscured the heavens had been swept away by a wind, which, in so doing, had revealed a splendid constellation. In 1702, no country in civilized Europe was in a more melancholy condition of intellectual emptiness than England; in 1712, not France itself could compare with us for copious and vivid production." Ah, 1713! what a prodigious year! "The little volume of dialogues which Berkeley issued under the title of *Hylas and Philonous* belongs to the *annus mirabilis* 1713, when Pope, Swift, Arbuthnot, Addison, Steele, were all at the brilliant apex of their genius, and when England had suddenly combined to present such a galaxy of literary talent as was to be matched, or even approached, nowhere on the continent of Europe."

It had come to pass; the light had shone forth—and it had come from the North! The North could now stand erect, and proudly confront the South. To the fruits of the mind, could now be applied these words of a contemporary rhymster:

> What fine things else you in South can have,
> Our North can show as good, if not the same . . .[1]

And now that they had come to the front, these Englishmen, how they plumed themselves on their triumph! They turned and took a backward glance along the way they had travelled. But a little while since, they said, and their case had been all but hopeless. Their liberty, their religion, the very integrity of their soil, had been threatened by the most puissant of monarchs. Then, in the twinkling of an eye, the whole face of things in Europe had changed, and changed so thoroughly that, thanks be to God, the wicked were cast down and the righteous exalted; the righteous, needless to say, being themselves. They belauded their philosophy, their literature, indeed, everything connected with them. During these years a movement began whose consequences survive to this very day. Who, as a matter of fact, would dream that, as far back as 1713, English was being spoken of as a substitute for French? "The English language, a rival of the Greek and the Latin, is as fertile as it is forceful; a foe to all constraint (like the people who speak it), it readily admits whatever is calculated to lend beauty and nobility to verbal expression; whereas French, weakened and impoverished by over-refinement, is always afraid to launch out, always labouring under the relentless necessity of conforming to rule and precedent, and never permits itself the smallest deviation. Risking nothing, it never reaps the reward of daring."[2]

In order that this force, this energy might have enough elbow-room to play its destined part, a number of prerequisites had to be fulfilled. To start with, the old stereotyped ideas about England had to be got rid of, and a new picture, at once more accurate and more engaging, put in their place. Up to now the "Quality" had always been more than delighted to betake themselves to Paris, but who in the world had ever thought of going

---

[1] John Rawlet, *An account of my life in the North* in *Poetick Miscellanies*, London, 1687.
[2] Abel Boyer, Preface to the translation of Addison's *Cato*, 1713.

to London? Yet, from about 1660, the expedition to England became a sort of recognized thing. The drawbacks were many, no doubt. English manners and customs were generally supposed to be barbarous. Then there was their incomprehensible language; but by far the most redoubtable obstacle of all was the inhospitable sea that had to be crossed before you could get there; a terrifying prospect indeed. Most people know the story of the good Normandy *abbé* who set forth for Cherbourg, fully resolved to risk the crossing. Arriving at the coast, he gave one glance at the white horses in the offing, faced about, and promptly made for home. But the actual coast-dwellers were not so easily daunted. It was they who set the example. Among those who did the crossing were the important personages proceeding to the Court of St. James's, eminent scholars, men of letters, not to mention mere sightseers. The packet, the preventive men, the mail-coach, the inns (anything but "The Traveller's Rest", these!), the London road, the fields, the meadows, the lawns— the finest in the world—the metropolis and its motley sights, the Thames thronged with shipping, Westminster, the Tower, the strange customs of the English, their odd table-manners, the solemn gravity with which they took their pleasures. When these doughty travellers got home again and told of their adventures, painful and pleasurable, their stories took on a quasi-heroic tone. Finally, in 1715, the notion of England took definite shape; men saw her as she really was. The picture was complete. Henceforth, all that had to be done to it was to touch it up here and there, adding fresh details, as required, to a piece of portraiture that was henceforth to hold its rightful and permanent place in the gallery of nations.

Before long we shall find English ideas pullulating in Germany. When the Hanoverian dynasty succeeded to the English throne, the two countries were knit more closely together by political bonds. They were further united, at least in a certain measure, by their Protestantism, by their common dislike of the Papacy, their common hostility to Rome. In 1697, a Tübingen professor, Andrew Adam Hochstetter, delivered himself of a Latin oration in which he dwelt on the advantages of visiting England. He entitled it, *Oratio de utilitate peregrinationis anglicanae*. "It is not", said the speaker, "on the fertility of the English soil that I wish now to dilate; nor will I dwell on the sights which London, that great city, has to offer. I shall address myself rather to the consideration of scientific thought in England, and still more to her religion. Who", he went on, "who of us here is not aware of the magnificent courage with which, in the reign of James II, a band of elect spirits stood boldly forth against the emissaries of the Roman Synagogue, and championed a cause which is dear to us both?" Then came philosophy and Locke. Then literature in general. One effect English ideas were bound to have on German thought; they were bound to draw it away from the influence of France, an influence which was entirely alien to its real spirit, and to offer it instead something more akin to itself, more familiar, to help it to slough off extraneous accretions, and regain its pristine form. As the eighteenth century wore on, Germany was to give evidence, and that in no uncertain fashion, of the effect the emergence of England had had on her, notably by her revolt against French hegemony, and by the formation of a northern league to counteract it.

But those southern countries—how was England to reach them? What means of approach was open to her? Books published in London were likely to hang fire a prodigiously long time, English being a dead letter on the Continent. Few were those of the Latin family who could read English; fewer still could speak it. Something little short of a miracle would have to happen if the *tempo* of diffusion was to be appreciably accelerated. If only the English would use French as an instrument for the propagation of their ideas, the language that was universally familiar; then the French would undertake that the treasure hidden away in the island of its origin should be made accessible to all. "It would be lamentable indeed if so many excellent works were to remain imprisoned, as it were, within the narrow confines of the British Isles. However excellent a language English may be, French has one great advantage over it, the advantage, namely, of being the normal means of communication between almost all the different European countries. Indeed, as touching the range of its influence, we may say of English, as compared with French, what Cicero in his *Pro Archia* said of Greek, as compared with Latin: *Graeca leguntur in omnibus gentibus*: *Latina suis finibus, exiguis sane, continentur.*[1] Precisely; but sup-

[1] From Ricotier's Foreword to his translation of S. Clarke's *The Being and Attributes of God*, Amsterdam, 1717.

posing a team of translators could be enlisted; supposing a sufficient number of Frenchmen could be induced to come and take up their quarters in London; diligent, scholarly men. Then, when they had settled down, let them make themselves acquainted with English literature; let them get interested in it, and choose and publish French versions of the books that appealed to them. In this way they would be earning their daily bread and showing their gratitude to the country that had made them welcome". No better plan to meet the case could possibly have been devised—but it was all in the air, a dream.

Nevertheless, the dream came true. And this is how it happened. When the religious persecution drove pastors, teachers, authors and the like out of France, and compelled them to take refuge in London, they there became the interpreters of English thought. To be absolutely correct, things did not happen in quite such a cut-and-dried fashion. As a matter of fact, there had been some preliminaries, some preparatory feelers. Nothing happened *ex abrupto*. Moreover, these exiles were at least as eager to disseminate a knowledge of French literature in England as they were to export English literature to the Continent. All the same, one of the effects least foreseen of the Revocation of the Edict of Nantes was to furnish England with a whole swarm of intermediaries, interpreters, who did in fact notably stimulate the propagation of her literary output and promote the extension of her influence. On the very eve of her revival, she found herself with heralds at her disposal ready to trumpet her glories far and wide among the civilized nations of the world.

What manner of men were they, these heralds? Not exactly geniuses, perhaps; but, at any rate, men of eager and enquiring minds, of lively intelligence, of tough moral fibre, prepared to face, with stout heart and steady eye, whatever that great adventure, exile, might have in store for them. Not the sort of men, these, to think only of their material well-being, to live by bread alone. What manner of men were they, these seekers after pastures new? Well; there was Abel Boyer, who began his studies at the Protestant Academy, Puylaurens. He was nineteen when Louis XIV revoked the Edict of Nantes. Making his way into Holland, he arrived in England in the year 1689, and, as a means of keeping body and soul together, took up teaching. He brought out a number of translations from the French, as well as some school-books. Then, in 1702, came the *Dictionnaire Royal* to which whole generations of students were to be indebted and which, useful in England, in France became a classic. Later, he translated Addison's *Cato* which, on the Continent, was regarded as the crowning example of English tragedy. He came to be looked upon as a semi-official chronicler of English national affairs. He took part in the literary controversies of the day, and at last, after innumerable balks and set-backs, died peacefully in a house which, like a good, sound Londoner, he had built for himself at Chelsea. Then there was Pierre des Maizeaux, a pastor's son. When the persecution of the Protestants began, he crossed the border into Switzerland and applied himself to the study of theology at Berne and Geneva. His father hoped he would become "his faithful successor in the task of rebuilding the shattered walls of Jerusalem". However, he went to try his fortune in Holland and there fell in with Pierre Bayle, whose strong point was anything rather than religious orthodoxy. Consequently des Maizeaux did not become a pastor. Instead, he embraced the calling of a man of letters and was something of a free-lance. His next home was England. Switzerland, Holland, England—what an endless procession of refugees wound their way along that well-worn route! Owing to the fact that, among other things, he brought out editions of Saint-Évremond and Bayle, that he was a friend of Shaftesbury, Toland and Collins, that he published selections from Locke and Toland, that he was a student of Chillingworth, that he got together the records of a controversy of first-rate importance between Leibniz, Clarke and Newton on philosophy, religion and science, and, finally, because, frequenting various cafés, contributing to gazettes and writing endless letters, finding jobs for the workless and help for the needy, he was stationed so to speak, at the spot where all roads met, a vantage-point whence he could see the long procession of ideas, and of men, go streaming by—for all these reasons combined, he represents, as it were, the intellectual clearing-house of the times, as well as all the restlessness, all the enterprise and daring, and, be it added, all the usefulness, all the infinite promise, that are implicit in the life intellectual.

But it is when we come to Pierre Coste that we reach the summit in this hierarchy of sound workmen. Pierre Coste, who was born at Uzès in 1688, and was intended for an ecclesiastical

THE LIGHT FROM THE NORTH

career, was sent to the Academy at Geneva. On the completion of his studies, he would, in the ordinary course, have become a schoolmaster or a pastor somewhere in the Cévennes. In that capacity, he would have duly conducted his religious services and taught his flock the way they should go, conscientiously performing his duties in that little world, until death came for him at last. But it was not to be. The Revocation of the Edict of Nantes prevented his returning to France, and he took to a wandering existence. We see him successively at the Universities of Lausanne, Zurich and Leyden: he was accepted as a student for the ministry by the Synod of the Walloon Church at Amsterdam; a little later, he obtained employment in a firm of printers as a proof-corrector; in 1697 he crossed over to England, and thenceforth his place in the history of ideas was definitely determined. He became in due course a tutor in illustrious houses, and travelled about Europe with the young hopefuls, his charges, doing the *Grand Tour*. He was elected a Fellow of the Royal Society. He brought out a number of philosophical lectures and historical treatises; he edited La Bruyère, Montaigne, La Fontaine. He translated Xenophon from the Greek and Gregorio Leti and Redi from the Italian; but, most important of all, he translated Shaftesbury's *Essay on the Freedom of Wit and Humour* and Newton's *Optics* into French. To have been the means of introducing these great men —Newton and Shaftesbury—into France, and, through France, into all the countries of the Latin family of nations, would have been no small achievement. But his was greater still, for he became the interpreter of John Locke. Intellectually alert and passionately absorbed in his work, he translated the *Essay concerning Human Understanding* into French and so laid the way open for a European appreciation of English philosophy. "The French are as deeply indebted to M. Coste as the English are to Locke."[1]

If, in considering the general trend of ideas, we are sometimes led to marvel at the unexpected lines they followed, there is no less cause for astonishment in the readiness, the willing alacrity, with which France accepted the rôle which circumstances allotted her. The rise of that new power in the North, though it threatened her own hegemony, she not only regarded with equanimity, she even aided and abetted it. To her own creative activities she added yet a further one, she undertook to secure the quotation,

[1]D'Argens, *Lettres morales*, l. XXIII.

so to put it, of those Nordic stocks on the markets of the South. With notable assiduity, she assumed the rôle of a broker introducing British ideas to an Italian, Spanish and Portuguese clientèle. Sometimes she even acted the part of a connecting-link between one northern country and another, as happened when a work, produced in London, passed by way of Paris in its passage across the Rhine. But far more often she despatched, not only her own, but British and, later on, German, products to Rome, Madrid and Lisbon. Moreover, she treated them, not like the ordinary carrier, who is stolidly indifferent to the nature of the goods he conveys. On the contrary, she titivated them up, trimmed them to suit the prevailing European taste, that is, of course, the taste for which she herself was responsible, the French taste. These English writers were obscure, and they needed careful filtering; they transgressed the rules of logic, their ideas must be properly co-ordinated; they were diffuse, and needed pruning; they were inelegant, and needed refining. So she set to work with her scissors, altering, cutting up, refashioning the clothes, touching up the features with a modicum of paint and powder. The people she presents to the world, after she has finished with them, are perhaps a trifle foreign-looking, but attractively, not alarmingly so. She knows where she excels; she knows what her public likes; and so she sets to work, with an eye to her own interests as well as to those of England and Europe. The translators she commissions are fully aware of the dignity of their office. They are no unimaginative drudges, no mere hacks inexorably fettered to a slavish verbal fidelity. No; they, too, are creators in their own right, or, at the very lowest, ministers armed with unlimited discretionary powers. "Whenever I have had difficulty in mastering a passage in English, owing to some term or other being insufficiently defined (the English are none too particular on that score) I have tried, as soon as I have thoroughly grasped what the author is driving at, to express the thing so clearly in French that no one could possibly fail to understand it. It is mainly in its clarity, its lucidity that French is superior to all other languages. In that connection, it occurs to me that a translator might be likened to a minister plenipotentiary. The comparison is somewhat on the grand scale, and I fear I may be criticized for making too much of a calling which the general run of people do not esteem very highly. Be that as it may, I think that the translator and the plenipotentiary would both find themselves seriously handicapped if their discretionary powers were too rigidly curtailed"[1]—France, the intermediary between English thought and the Latin races: another stream to which this period gave birth, a stream that was destined to flow right through the eighteenth century, and beyond it.

Vessels come gliding in to discharge their cargoes in the very heart of the city. People speak truly when they describe the city as one vast port. There is no lack of fine buildings—the Bourse, the Bank, the headquarters of the India Company; there are substantial-looking houses along the waterside; the people as busy as bees, and just as methodical; a general air of well-being and comfort; no poverty, no beggars; prosperous business men, well-to-do burgesses. That was how Amsterdam struck a foreigner. Holland, for the foreigner, was a haven of delight.

> Je vois régner sur ces rivages
> L'innocence et la liberté.
> Que d'objets dans ce paysage,
> Malgré leur contrariété
> M'étonnent par leur assemblage
> Abondance et frugalité,
> Autorité sans esclavage,
> Richesses sans libertinage,
> Noblesse, charges, sans fierté:
> Mon choix est fait . . .[2]

Holland was prosperous, and Holland was powerful. If, in the commercial field, she had a rival in England; if, after 1688, she began to look rather like a dinghy alongside a big ship; if she gradually lost that fighting, adventurous spirit that had made her a great maritime and colonial power, it must not be supposed that she was impoverished by her altered circumstances. She

[1]Pierre Coste, Foreword to his translation of the *Essay concerning Human Understanding*, Amsterdam, 1700.
[2]Innocence and liberty I see prevailing along these shores. What a crowded prospect. What a number of various things I see—all different yet harmonised in a way that makes me marvel: Abundance mated with frugality, Discipline but no servility, Wealth, but no undue indulgence, Authority without arrogance. That is the place for me. Attributed to J. B. Rousseau and included in *Œuvres de Œhaulieu*, 1774, vol. II, p. 304.

was wealthy, and she was tasting the sweets of wealth. She had, moreover, another means of filling her coffers with gold and silver; and that was banking. She offers the first example of the capitalist State, and she throve on her financial activities.

In view of this process of taking in and paying out, this give-and-take of wealth, it was of course natural that she should aim at maintaining her neutrality, for she needed a stable and peace-loving Europe. Thus, too, it was that she willingly offered asylum to all manner of different religions. A man who tries his best to convert a Jew is doubtless a good Christian; but he is a poor man of business. Holland stood for freedom of conscience, because long and bitter experience had taught her what it was to be persecuted for one's religious belief. Her whole history, in fact, is the record of an heroic struggle for religious liberty. That was one consideration. Another was that you cannot carry on a banking, or any other business, if you have to start by asking your customer to produce his certificate of baptism. And so, alongside the Protestant conventicle, the Catholic may build his church and the Jew his synagogue. But this toleration of hers has its limits. The pastors quarrel among themselves, and then Authority has to intervene, and nowhere in the world does Authority show a more uncompromising front against principles calculated to undermine her. Nevertheless, relative though it was, the liberty that Holland offered was a rare and gracious thing.

Then, too, Holland exerted an influence for peace through her universities. From North and South, from East and West, students came in crowds, came to profit by the teaching, not of Dutch scholars only, but of French and German, too. In Holland, you could come in contact with the people, the books and the ideas of all sorts of countries and this intellectual give-and-take was, at least in those days, unmatched in any other part of the world. All through the seventeenth century, and through most of the eighteenth, Englishmen, Frenchmen, Scots, Danes, Swedes, Poles, Hungarians, and a still larger number of lieges of the Empire came to pursue their studies at Leyden, Franeker, Gröningen and Utrecht. . . .[1]

The Revocation of the Edict of Nantes found Holland well

[1] J. Huizinga, *The Netherlands as intermediary between Western and Central Europe*. European branch of the Carnegie Trust, Bulletin No. 7, 1933.

prepared. Long since, that tolerant and benevolent land had been accustomed to see exiles from England coming to seek the hospitality of her shores, Royalists in Cromwell's time, Republicans in Charles II's. All through those troublous times, whenever an Englishman of mark deemed that his safety was in jeopardy at home, he made for Holland, were he a Shaftesbury, or a Locke, or a Collins, and there he could dwell in security until the evil days were over. It was round about the year 1685 that the French Huguenots came to beg admittance at the gates of her cities, and she welcomed them, as she always did, with a compassionate heart, regardless of their numbers. She did everything her ingenuity could devise to find them posts of some sort, in her workshops, her army, her schools. She took them to her bosom because she herself was Protestant, because she detested the policy of Louis XIV, and because she had a human heart.

Then it was that she began to play her great part among the nations. Europe, seeking to give utterance to the ideas that were stirring within her, could not do so because she lacked the means, there being available no organs of a truly European character. But now, in exchange for the freedom and the hospitality she had so generously lavished on them, the Huguenots bestowed on Holland a splendid recompense. Many efforts had been made to supply the deficiency, but, for a variety of reasons, they had proved abortive. That venerable publication, the *Journal des Savants*, despite repeated attempts to make contact with foreign ideas, was still too exclusively French in tone to answer the purpose; the *Philosophical Transactions* were occupied much more with science than with philosophy; the *Giornale dei Letterati* had little life in it, and its scope was far too limited. The *Acta Eruditorum*, a Leipzig journal, was ponderous in the extreme. In short, there was a vacuum, and it was clamouring to be filled. Now, then, it was that those long looked for periodicals made their appearance, and they made it in Holland. In March, 1684, came the *Nouvelles de la République des Lettres*, Pierre Bayle's review; this was followed in January, 1686, by Jean Le Clerc's *Bibliothèque universelle et historique*; then, in September, 1687, there appeared Basnage de Beauval's *Histoire des ouvrages des savants*. Here, then, were three periodicals which, though printed in French, were hopefully on the look out for a European clientèle. Nor was it long before they got what they wanted. The writing

fraternity were deeply stirred at the prospect of a journal undertaking to allot, wherever it deemed it due, that fame which
overleaps frontiers, which disdains to distinguish between
nation and nation, and whose writ is current throughout the
civilized world. What writer would not aspire to be judged by
such a tribunal? What writer would not voice his gratitude if he
deemed he had been praised according to his merits? What
writer would not be loud in his resentment, if he deemed he had
been treated with injustice? "I have reason, Sir, to complain of
the unhandsome manner in which you refer to me in the supplement to the *Nouvelles de la République des Lettres* for July". . . . "Do
not transgress the law of human rights". . . . "You should
have some regard for fair play in your *Nouvelles*". . . . "Don't
forget the dictates of Christian charity."[1] Or, in a different tone,
"Everybody is asking for my work since the preliminary reference
to it in your December issue. Our scholars are already highly
prepossessed in its favour, convinced that there was never anyone
better able than you to get at the heart of a book, or to form a
just estimate of its value."[2] "Ever since I have had the advantage of reading your publications I have looked on them as
ranking among the most hallowed shrines of enduring fame,
where only works which are the twofold outcome of conscientious toil and conspicuous talent are worthy to be admitted."[3]
But most moving of all was the appeal which Vico once sent to
Jean Le Clerc from Naples. At Naples he was not getting his
deserts; yet Jean Le Clerc had but to say the word, and the name
of Vico would resound throughout the whole of Europe.[4]

So now it is from the North that we discern the light. But
Eastwards, too, some changes of significance are under way.
Poland, weary after her protracted struggle, after all the heroism
she had so freely displayed, and on the morrow of that gesture of
Sobieski's which had fired the admiration of Europe, was now
wholly engrossed with internal dissensions. For a long time, and
with great thoroughness, she had been imprinting on Russia the
stamp of European civilization, seeking to mould her uncouth

[1]From the Abbé de Ville to Pierre Bayle, Chambéry, 31 August, 1686. Selections
from Bayle's unpublished correspondence, published by Émile Gigas, Copenhagen,
1890.
[2]François Bernier to Pierre Bayle, Paris, 28 February, 1686.
[3]Denis Papin to Pierre Bayle, 26 June, 1685.
[4]E. Nicolini, *Due lettre inedite di G. B. Vico à Giovanni Le Clerc.* (*Rev. de litt.
comparée*, Vol. IX, 1929, p. 737.

neighbour by her literature, her fine arts, her science and her
political philosophy. Now Russia was on the look-out for other
models. Meanwhile, the power of Sweden was crumbling, and
the star of Charles XII was soon to be extinguished for ever at
Pultowa. Thus, while some of the great actors in the political
drama were withdrawing from the footlights, others were moving
forward to take their place. The news reached Paris (without,
however, causing any great sensation, at all events at first) that,
on the 18th January, 1701, the Elector of Brandenburg,
Frederick III, had assumed the royal crown, under the style and
title of Frederick I, King of Prussia. Meanwhile, what was afoot
in the land of the Muscovites? One of those grand-dukes whom
in their language they call czars designed to transform this great
Asiatic mass into a civilized power, and he looked to Germany, to
Hungary, to Holland, to England and to France to tell him how
to set about it. The result was that year by year, the transformation continued and on an ever-increasing scale. Manners and
customs of all sorts, from hairdressing to the cut of their clothes,
all began to change. A Dutch traveller, Cornelis Van Bruyn, was
so struck by these innovations, and the rapidity of them, that he
made haste to sketch the costumes of the people about him so as
to preserve a record of them: "As these changes will sooner or
later do away with these distinctive national costumes, so that
none will remember what they looked like, I have recorded on
canvas the sort of dresses the young women wore. . . ." The
older nations were amazed, and looked with wonder at the
colossal stature which Peter the Great, the Emperor of all the
Russias, was beginning to assume.

But the emergence of these two great powers was not a matter
of present concern. It was not until later on that we shall find
Prussia and Russia playing their full parts in the intellectual
arena. In the meantime, what we have to emphasize, the point
we have to bear in mind, is this: intellectual hegemony is no
longer the exclusive prerogative of the Latin races. England
insists on her share of power. She knows her worth, and freely
proclaims her own greatness. For those Portuguese, Spaniards,
Italians, and French, for the whole Latin horde, she entertains a
contempt which she is at no pains to dissemble. They are slaves,
all of them. "As for us Britons, thank Heaven, we have a better
sense of government delivered to us from our ancestors. We

have the notion of a public, and a constitution: how a legislative, and how an executive is modelled. The maxims we draw from hence are as evident as those in mathematics. Our increasing knowledge shows us every day, more and more, what common sense is in politics; and this must of necessity lead us to understand a like sense in morals; which is the foundation."[1]   And Addison, comparing England with Italy, extols her sense of the value of Freedom. O, Italy, how beautiful thou art. . . .

> How has kind Heaven adorned the happy land,
> And scattered blessings with a wasteful hand!
> But what avails her unexhausted stores,
> Her blooming mountains and her sunny shores,
> With all the gifts that heaven and earth impart,
> The smiles of nature and the charms of art,
> While proud oppression in her valleys reigns,
> And tyranny usurps her happy plains?
> The poor inhabitant beholds in vain
> The reddening orange and the swelling grain;
> Joyless he sees the growing oils and wines,
> And in the myrtle's fragrant shade repines:
> Starves, in the midst of nature's bounty curst,
> And in the loaden vineyard dies for thirst.
>
> O Liberty, thou goddess heavenly bright,
> Profuse of bliss, and pregnant with delight!
> Eternal pleasures in thy presence reign,
> And smiling plenty leads thy wanton train;
> Eased of her load, subjection grows more light,
> And poverty looks cheerful in thy sight;
> Thou mak'st the gloomy face of nature gay,
> Giv'st beauty to the sun, and pleasure to the day.
> Thee, goddess, thee, Britannia's isle adores;
> How has she oft exhausted all her stores,
> How oft in fields of death thy presence sought,
> Nor thinks the mighty prize too dearly bought!
> 'Tis liberty that crowns Britannia's isle,
> And makes her barren rocks and her bleak mountains
>   smile.

[1]Shaftesbury, *Freedom of wit and humour* (1707), I, 3.

Others with towering piles may please the sight,
And in their proud aspiring domes delight;
A nicer touch to the stretched canvas give,
Or teach their animated rocks to live:
'Tis Britain's care to watch o'er Europe's fate,
And hold in balance each contending State,
To threaten bold, presumptuous kings with war,
And answer her afflicted neighbours' prayer . . .[1]

"The more I see of the English, the more I admire them; generally speaking, they surpass us in everything."[2] Well; at any rate they were a force to reckon with; they represented a new spirit, a new outlook. But what was it? What did it portend?

---

[1]Addison, *A letter from Italy, to the Right Honourable Charles Lord Halifax, in the year* 1701.
[2]Daniel Laroque to Pierre Bayle, 12 July, 1686.

IV

HETERODOXY

IT was the year 1678. Bossuet had agreed to contend in debate with the Pastor Claude. Mme de Duras, still hesitating between Protestantism, which she was about to quit, and Catholicism on which her heart was set, had asked that this debate might be held, and the two apologists now confronting each other were fighting desperately for a woman's soul, for the truth as they saw it, for the faith that was in them. When they came to discuss the rights of the individual conscience, Bossuet pressed his antagonist with some vigour. What, he invited Claude to tell him, what was this liberty to which these gentlemen of the Reformed Church laid claim? How far did it go? Were there no limits to it? No limits at all? Did they mean to say, that anybody, no matter who, any man, or woman, an ignoramus, *anyone*, was free to believe, nay, *ought* to believe that he might have a clearer understanding of the Word of God than a whole Council, though its members were recruited from the four corners of the earth and from the centre thereof, clearer than all the rest of the Church put together? And Claude made answer saying, "Yes, it is even so."[1]

The age-long conflict between Freedom and Authority, transferred on this occasion to the religious field, that day became

---

[1] Bossuet, *Conférence avec M. Claude touchant l'infaillibilité de l'Eglise*, 1682. In the *Réponse au livre de Monsieur l'Evêque de Meaux intitulé Conférence avec M. Claude*, Quévilly et Rouen 1683 (p. 485 et seq.), Pastor Claude explains his position as follows: "I will begin with the proposition advanced by this Prelate namely, that according to us (Protestants) anybody, however ignorant, is bound to believe that he may more truly interpret God's word than the most universal of Synods and the whole of the Church put together. This proposition may be taken in two ways, one, that every individual, no matter how ignorant, is obliged to hold that he may understand the word of God better than the most universal of true

acute. That day, the principles which men are called upon to choose as their guides through life, were brought into violent opposition. Claude and Bossuet, champions of the two conflicting causes, mighty men of valour, both of them, entered into combat, what time a woman, searching the inner recesses of her soul, and France, and the whole of Europe watched the progress of the duel. One upholds a man's right to believe what he chooses, without let or hindrance; the right of the individual conscience to hold what it believes to be true, no matter what the rest of the world may say. The other puts forward the desire to share in a common belief, the austere joy of conforming to a rule of life once for all accepted, and, that life might continue its course, the need for recognizing a supreme authority.

Claude was defending a cause which at that time seemed to be nearing defeat, Bossuet a cause that was on the up-grade. The tide of heterodoxy was on the ebb; Lutheranism was degenerating, losing vigour, waxing worldly; the most enlightened of its pastors confessed as much. In England, Protestantism was confronted by a twofold menace: on the one hand were the Catholics, who were loyal to the Stuarts; on the other the innumerable sects, the divisions and subdivisions, of the Protestants themselves. The offensive launched by the forces of the counter-reformation had won back a large part of central Europe to the Catholic cause, and never had the Jesuits, those peerless champions of law and order, wielded greater power than now.

France, the most logical and, where ideas are in question, the most uncompromising of all nations, was bound to be carried away by this ideal of perfect unity. An all-powerful monarch who had settled the political problem by the simplest of formulas, was sure to feel a certain amount of dissatisfaction, a sense of frustration, so long as there lingered in the hearts of a section of his people any feeling of discord, so long as any form of sectarianism continued to claim the allegiance of the minority. To

---

synods made up of good, devout, wise and learned people together in the name of Jesus Christ and than all the rest of the Church. The other is that every believer, whom God attends with his Holy Spirit, is bound to hold that he will understand the word of God better than the most universal of false synods made up of worldly self-seekers and hypocrites, that is to say of people to whom God does not communicate his Spirit, and better than all worldly folk together, albeit they falsely call themselves "The Church!" The first meaning, says Claude, is an unwarranted assertion which Protestants repudiate; the second expresses an obvious truth from which Bossuet can hardly derive much comfort.

extend his control so as to bring within its orbit the religious beliefs of his subjects, to establish uniformity in the religious, as well as in the political, sphere, to have but one faith, one form of religion in what would then be a perfectly organized State, such was the dream of Louis XIV. His aim was to extinguish the so-called reformed religion, by argument, by voluntary conversions to begin with, but later on, where these failed, by the increasing application of force. He was told, and he was only too willing to believe it, that the Reformation, which in the past had ravaged the country with fire and sword, was now not only defenceless, abased, humiliated, but well-nigh crushed out of existence, virtually in its death throes. One more honest effort, wrote Père Maimbourg in his *Histoire du Calvinisme*, and "the disastrous conflagration which has wrought such ruin in France and of which to-day little more than the smoke remains, will soon be utterly extinguished. And as we are all united in this most Christian monarchy in the bond of a single law which constrains us to render fealty to the King whom God has appointed to rule over us, so I trust that we shall all be united by a single bond in one and the same faith". France thus pointing the way, and France being the example which Europe followed, why should we not hope that England, too, would find her way back to the One True Fold? Père Maimbourg already seemed to catch a glimpse of such a conversion: "There are grounds for hoping that the day will come when God, dispelling by the light of His grace the darkness which heresy, born of a disastrous schism, has spread like a pall over England, will once again cause the sun of truth to shine upon the English people and so bring them back into the unity of that faith which St. Gregory the Great caused to be proclaimed to them". Thus, by the good offices of the Most Glorious and Most Christian King, the erstwhile fair and seamless robe of Christ would be made whole once more; and thus would the triumph of orthodoxy be assured.

When, in the month of October, 1685, Louis XIV revoked the Edict of Nantes, he was perfectly loyal to the logic of his principles. Where he fell short was in loyalty to the Christian spirit and in his understanding of the human conscience. That conscience will not brook coercion; wherein lies its glory and its pride. Oppression carried to extremes only drives it to revolt. And so, few measures were ever more decisive in their results, or exerted a weightier influence on the shape of things to come, than that fatal revocation. In so far as it is possible to assign dates to great trends of human thought, we may surely say that the year 1685 denotes the high-water mark of the counter-reformation. After that, the tide turned.

And abroad what a clamour, what cries of alarm, arose! The English revolution of 1688 was not wholly political in character, it had a religious side as well. The triumph of William of Orange was not only a victory for Parliament, it was a victory for the Reformers. In William, it was not only the defender of the people's rights who was exalted, but the saviour of religion, the champion of the Protestant cause. To all the countries of the North, Louis XIV stood forth as the arch-enemy, the foe *par excellence*, of freedom of conscience. Over and over again it was insisted that this enactment of his was the convincing proof, the manifest symbol, of his tyranny, his injustice, his ruthlessness, his violence, his contempt for the most elementary human rights. This tyrant, this Machiavelli, this Beast of the Apocalypse, this Antichrist, not content with imposing his will upon the world by force of arms, not satisfied with his conquests and his so-called "protectorates", now claimed dominion over the souls of men, and put his own decrees above the voice of God. So violent was the denunciation that its effect was felt even in the New World. Benjamin Franklin relates that, as a child, in the Old South Church in Philadelphia, he heard words of withering rage and scorn poured forth on that accursed old man, the persecutor of God's people, Louis XIV.[1]

And then all those Frenchmen who had been driven forth as exiles from their native land, what a ferment they must have caused in Protestant Europe! They called on the world to bear witness to the ills they were compelled to suffer. Year by year they had been frustrated, baulked, spied upon, and now, because they refused to forswear themselves, they were treated like common criminals. Leaving Geneva, Berlin, Budapest out of the count, Holland and England, both of which counted churches by the dozen and followers by the thousand, constituted veritable strongholds for defence and offence. These rugged, inflexible Frenchmen, who had so long been inured to resistance and

[1] *Writings of B. Franklin*, Smith's edition, vol. VI, pp. 86-7.

conflict, bore the prestige of men who had suffered for their faith, and were the living evidence of the wrongs they had endured. They brought with them a bitter, rankling sense of grievance which would end only with their lives, and, even then, would still live on after they were dead, in the hearts of their descendants.

What a change in the voice of Pastor Claude after Louis revoked the Edict of Nantes! The time was passed, said Claude, for meeting argument with argument, reason with reason, the time when, if a victory was won, it was by fair means, and in good faith. He had been deceived, he cried, he had been dragged from his church, and given twenty-four hours in which to quit his country as an exile. Terrible were the memories of those days; the arrival of the dragoons, who seized the gates and approaches to the towns, set guards upon them, and then, advancing with drawn swords, shouted "Kill, kill them if they won't be Catholics!" "Amid a pandemonium of shouting and blasphemy, they strung up their victims, men or women, by their hair or by their feet, to the rafters in the roof, or the hooks in the chimney, and then set fire to bundles of mouldy hay heaped up beneath them. They plucked out their beards, and tore at their heads till not a hair was left. They flung them into huge fires which they lit for the purpose, and left them there till they were half-roasted. They fastened ropes underneath their arms, and lowered them into wells, pulling them up and down till they promised to change their religion." Was the King of France then unaware that Faith is a gift that comes from on high, and that nothing that man can do can make or destroy it; that violence and coercion can only create unbelievers, or hypocrites, or else engender in the hearts of the sincere a staunchness, a longanimity that no suffering which man can inflict will ever avail to overcome? Does he not know that by perpetrating such atrocities he has put himself beyond the pale, in the eyes of every European country: and that having scandalously violated both the solemn covenant of his predecessors, and the law of nations, his promises and his treaties will henceforth be credited by none?[1]

Many another pastor, weeping by the waters of Babylon, voiced his abhorrence of such enormities, calling down curses on

[1] *Les plaintes des protestants cruellement exilés du royaume de France*, Cologne, 1686.

the head of the evil-doer: Jacques Basnage, Jacques Saurin the gifted orator, Élie Benoist, Isaac Jaquelot. But to form a notion of the lengths to which ungovernable fury could carry a man, we must listen for a moment to Pierre Jurieu. Nature had made him a fighter, but so long as he remained on his native soil he kept himself within bounds. No sooner, however, did he find himself an exile, than he fell to raving like a man possessed. What others said with dignity and restraint, he flung out in wild and whirling words, harming rather than helping his cause by the outrageous extravagance and reckless irrelevancies of his words, though the feelings which inspired his ravings he shared with many another. From his look-out on the ramparts, he kept ceaseless watch and ward, thundering anathema at the Council of Trent, belauding the Reformation, stirring up his co-religionists to revolt; exhorting them never to yield to force, and circulating pastoral letters among them like those which the Bishops of the early church had been wont to distribute among their persecuted flock. He spoke with the voice of the prophets: the day is nigh when the reign of Antichrist shall come to an end; the fall of Satan is at hand, and his kingdom shall go down in headlong ruin, and God's true Church shall regain its crown of glory. By 1710 or, at the latest, by 1715, all that was to come about, and the Protestants would return to France in triumph. There were people who believed him, who hung upon his words and solemnly exchanged views as to the exact date when the auspicious home-coming would come to pass: in 1720, or 1730, the exiles would regain possession of Jerusalem.

But these tirades, these frenzied outbursts, these delirious ravings were not enough for him. He must needs take up arms against France in the service of the Elector of Brandenburg and the King of England; he incited the Protestants in various parts of the country to revolt; he organized a spy-ring that was to operate in his own country; his agents were constantly coming and going, and it was he who found the money for these activities. Such were the depths to which the bitterness of hatred had brought him, such was the rôle he played, and continued to play, till the day of his death in 1713.

Now the true spirit of these French pamphleteers in Holland, the spirit we have been endeavouring to capture, is really this: they are organs of nonconformity, they are the mouthpieces of heterodoxy.

In the *Nouvelles de la République des Lettres* there is nothing about tragedies, or comedies, or romances, or odes, or epistles. Nor is there in the *Bibliothèque universelle* any mention of such things. The *Histoire des ouvrages des savants* begins by giving a little space to *belles-lettres*, but not much, and without any fixed plan. To be sure, we shall observe progress in one direction. As the years pass by and England becomes richer in authors of talent and genius, the field will widen; but, prior to 1715, the essential interest for them was not so much literature as a fine art, but literature as a vehicle of ideas. These journalists were all brought up in Protestant seminaries. No sooner did they hear people talking about morals, or some matter concerning religious doctrine, than they began to quiver with excitement; such things were what they had had to learn about in their academies, and remembering their studies and their meditations, they recognized once again the sort of thing they were born for. They seized the pen, and on those old familiar themes, began to improvise at large. Don't for a moment mistake them for dilettantes eagerly on the look-out for works of beauty to appraise as artists, rolling them, so to speak, on the critical palate, like literary epicures. For beauty they do not care two straws. The great works of M. Arnauld, M. Nicole; the exegetics of M. Richard Simon; and, if we must bring England into the picture, the treatises of Isaac Barrow, Thomas Brown, Gilbert Burnet and Henry Dodwell, put them on their mettle. Those are the sort of writers with whom they have something in common. They know what such people are driving at; those controversies are the breath of life to them, their daily bread. Jansenism or Molinism, Free-will or Pre-destination, Providence or Blind Fate, those are the sort of things that are in their line. The law of the three unities offers a very pale interest indeed compared with the philosophical exploration of the universe. Nor have they by nature any cosmopolitan leanings. They belong to a different category from that of the travellers and globe-trotters; an ardent tribe, they include commentators on the Bible, the Fathers of the Church, heresiarchs, the Renaissance philosophers, the instigators of the Reformation, the judges of the Inquisition, the doctrines of the Council of Trent; while, among those of their living adversaries whom they encounter in the flesh, are Père Maimbourg, François Lamy, Bossuet: in a word, they are of the tribe of the theologians.

To keep alive, and in the plenitude of its vigour, the animating spirit of the Reformation, such was the primary aim of the gazeteers of Holland. They carried on the work of their Huguenot ancestors, while broadening its scope, and lending a new tone to its message. Neither France nor Rome is under any illusion regarding them. Despite Bayle's efforts to soft-soap the authorities and the King, his journal was banned in Paris and condemned in Rome. Let us glance a little closely at Jean Le Clerc, the author of the three *Bibliothèques*, a man of inexhaustible fertility. His volumes pile up and up, and the sight of them warms his heart. He gives out that he is weary, but in reality he is mightily content. In addition to his journalistic activities, he turns out a prodigious number of books. He represents a type of which there were many examples in these days, learned men who, after writing all day, must have gone on writing all night, otherwise how could they have contrived to leave such stacks of printed matter behind them? His output included criticism, exegesis, philosophy, history; he edited Erasmus and Grotius; he translated portions of the Scriptures, and all this takes no account of his miscellanea; all formidable tasks which even included a revision of Moreri's Dictionary. . . .

The way was long and varied, but the man himself never changed. Jean Le Clerc is scarcely to be called a man of letters; his prose style is completely devoid of grace and charm, and he is apparently quite insensitive to the music of words. Bulk and weight are his main *desiderata*. Jean Le Clerc was a preacher; but he was also a man of action. He studied at Geneva, his birth-place, and in due time became a minister of religion. He also went through a course at the Saumur Academy, did duty in the Walloon church and subsequently at the chapel of the Savoy in London. At last he came to anchor in Amsterdam, and for twenty-seven years he was professor of philosophy, humane letters and Hebrew at the Armenian College in that city. "He specialised in three subjects: *belles-lettres*, philosophy, and theology . . ." As he was in life, so he was in his books and in his articles. He seized every possible opportunity of discussing religion and expounding his views thereon. "He was devoid alike of personal magnetism and of the teacher's art,

things far above mere knowledge."[1]   The truth is, he was
indifferent to these things, and never troubled about them, his
great object being, as he explained in the preface to his *Bibliothèque ancienne et moderne*, not to amuse people, but to teach them
virtue and truth.

It was the same with book-production. Holland turned out
books as fast as she could. "In the whole world there are not
more than ten or a dozen cities where books are printed on any
considerable scale. In England there are London and Oxford; in
France, Paris and Lyons; in Holland, Amsterdam, Leyden,
Rotterdam, The Hague, and Utrecht; in Germany, Leipzig; and
that is about the sum of it."[2]   Five great centres of publishing,
whereas England and France can barely muster two apiece!   A
pretty fine contrast if you like!   There were, we are told, some
four hundred printers or booksellers in Amsterdam. They were
not exclusively Dutch, but included German, French, English
and Jews. Among them, too, were men of notable intelligence,
men by no means wholly absorbed in the commercial side of their
business; there were also book-pirates.   The *Journal des Savants*
for the 29th June, 1682, calls attention to a barefaced piece of
piracy, and not of piracy only, but of gross misrepresentation, on
the part of a publisher in Amsterdam.   It is especially indignant
because the work has not only been stolen, but shamelessly
travestied in Holland.   "That is just the sort of thing they do",
complained Bayle in 1693.   "They pay the author practically
nothing at all, particularly when the copy lends itself to being
printed in Paris.   They just await their opportunity and then
pirate it over here, making no payment whatever to the
author."

The consequence was that books came out in swarms; some
you could get elsewhere, some you could not.   A very daring
manuscript had no great chance of getting published in France,
unless, indeed, the authorities turned a blind eye to the proceedings, a thing that was not altogether out of key with the
popular temperament.   It was harder still in Italy; while in Spain
and Portugal it was practically hopeless to make the attempt.
On the other hand a book that had been rejected by the censors

[1] Voltaire, *Siècle de Louis XIV, Catalogue des Écrivains Français*.
[2] A report dated 1699 and quoted by H. J. Reesink, *L'Angleterre et la littérature
anglaise dans les trois plus anciens périodiques français de Hollande*, 1931, p. 93.

and banned by the public authorities would have no difficulty in finding a printer in Holland and a bookseller to push it. Fénelon, when he was sent into Poitou to catechize the new converts, hinted that it might be no bad thing if some books of Catholic apologetic were issued with the imprint, fictitious of course, of some town or other in Holland; such a label would inspire confidence in readers who still had something of the Protestant left in them. That a Catholic like Arnauld should get his books published in Holland was, in Jurieu's eyes, a scandalous, an abominable thing. Holland was the Land of Saints, the Citadel of God, and ought, in his view, to be closed to the Papists: Catholic books in France; Protestant books in Holland. Occasionally, some French free-thinker would have a current account at The Hague. Out there you could speak your mind freely; a writer was not obliged to trim his sails to the breath of political prejudice, or theological dogma. That, then, was the place for a man of independent ideas to make his supply base.

Thus, despite the most vigilant frontier precautions, banned books, books that had been formally condemned, books that were regarded as anathema, were, in fact, smuggled into France, and in the reign of Louis XIV himself. Travellers brought them hidden away in their baggage; they came in hugger-mugger, *via* some of the northern towns, or by way of the Channel ports, and so managed to get through to Paris. The guardians of orthodoxy raised an outcry, as may be imagined. The *Mémoires* of Trévoux, whose authors kept strict guard, make it clear that their vigilance was often eluded. "Excellent paper and print, first-rate illustrations, altogether a gem; almost always a Dutch marvel. A good exterior, but the goods inside are not always to be relied on. We get a lot of contraband from that country."[1] And Bossuet: "Not long since, we received a book from Holland entitled, *Critical History of the Principal Commentators on the New Testament*. Its author was M. Simon, a priest. It is one of those books which have been refused the Church's *imprimatur* and therefore cannot be printed here. It can only be circulated in a country where there are no restrictions, and among the enemies of the faith. However, despite all the precautions and vigilance of the authorities, such books do manage to worm their way in. They go the round, and pass from one reader to another. They are the more

[1]February, 1719; article XV.

eagerly devoured because they are not easy to come by, because they are a rarity, because they excite curiosity, in a word, because they are forbidden."[1]

Holland was not the only country to bring out books hostile to Louis XIV and to Rome. Switzerland was another. In Germany and in England they abounded for, in the words of Richard Simon, the English are keen enquirers where religion is concerned. The position, then, was that France was beleaguered from Geneva to London by the forces of heresy. The part played by Holland, and particularly by the French Huguenots who had taken refuge there, was directed to ensuring to the utmost of their power that these revolutionary sentiments and ideas should get through to the very heart of France.

The rift grew ever wider and wider. "How terrible was that voice divine which in the past century had echoed through the world crying, Hew away the rotten branches! England, breaking the sacred bond of unity, the only bond by which man's wayward spirit is restrained from plunging to perdition, has yielded to the misleading promptings of her heart; part of the Netherlands, the whole of Germany, Denmark and Sweden are just so many branches which the avenging sword has sheared away and which cling no longer to the parent trunk."[2] The Revocation of the Edict of Nantes did but add force and emphasis to that terrible injunction. It marked the renewal of an intellectual and moral alliance that was destined to endure even when the contending armies had laid aside their weapons and bound themselves to keep the peace in Europe. "To-day, it is, virtually, the North that is ranged against the South, the Teuton races challenging the Latin."[3] Indeed, the forces of the Reformation, though seemingly routed in France, were stronger and more united than ever outside her borders. "Your so-called Reformation, so far as its foreign supporters are concerned, was never stronger or more united. All the Protestant peoples are now united in a single *bloc.* . . . Abroad, the Reformers are more powerful, more united, more arrogant and more menacing, than ever."[4]   The Reformers, or,

[1]*Défense de la tradition et des Saints Pères*, Preface (Ed. Lachat, p. 8).
[2]Fénelon, Sermon for the Feast of the Epiphany, 6 January, 1685.
[3]Leibniz to Bossuet, 18 April, 1692.
[4]Bossuet, *Premier avertissement aux Protestante*, 1689.   See also the Abbé Prévost in *Le Pour et Contre*, vol. I, No. 10.

to be more precise, the Calvinists, for Lutheranism was being pushed back "more and more into the farther north."[1] It recoiled upon itself, content for its action to be circumscribed and local. It was not led on to conquest by a great expanding power; and, lacking in ambition, it was likewise lacking in adaptability. Calvinism, on the other hand, triumphed side by side with triumphant England. The two treatises that John Locke brought out in 1690 to sanction the advent to power of the leading representative of Calvinism in Europe, namely, William of Orange, were designed to serve as the up-to-date political code. Resplendent in the shining armour of recent victory, they are obviously inspired by the spirit of Geneva. The masters and the friends of John Locke in England, France and Holland were Calvinists; his ideas, his arguments are all the products of his Calvinistic studies, and, of course, he supports them with frequent quotations from the Bible. His refusal to promise unconditional obedience to authority is on a par with the resistance which the Calvinists of the sixteenth century offered to the bishops and princes, their oppressors. Calvinism, in this case, represents the right to freedom of conscience, transplanted from the religious into the political sphere. Even the fact that he was now taking service under the English Government does not compromise this right in his eyes, so lively is his recollection of the struggles that government went through to maintain it, so glaring the abuse of power which, in the name of the divine right of kings, Louis XIV had just committed.

It was now, too, that the understanding entered into sometime since between capitalism and religion attained its formal status, its crowning glorification. England, as Holland's successor, was now slowly but steadily capturing the world's markets, and as England's influence grew, so also did that of a religion which, so far from discouraging interest in the affairs of this world, in business, actively favoured it. For, as a contemporary pamphleteer points out, "There is a kind of natural unaptness in the Popish religion to business, whereas on the contrary among the Reformed, the greater their zeal, the greater their inclination to trade and industry, as holding idleness unlawful".[2] Called upon to attend to his business, or rather to his duty, by an ineluctable decree

[1]Le P. Maimbourg, *Histoire du Luthéranisme*, 1680, p. 268.
[2]R. H. Tawney, *Religion and the Rise of Capitalism*, London, 1926. Preface.

from above, ordained to buy and sell, as others are to write and preach, practising those virtues which God and his business alike demanded of him, such as energy, conscientiousness, prudence, thrift, the merchant, whose position in European society was to become more and more considerable, hurries off, without the least sign of compunction, from his counting-house to his chapel, his head high, fully persuaded that he is doing his twofold duty, proudly convinced that he is making sure of a place both in this world and in the world to come. Calvinism comes into its own. That, at least in one respect, shows how the transference of power from South to North finally came about.

However, it may readily be conceived that religious dissent, growing more orderly and disciplined as time went on, would sooner or later aspire to a unity of its own, to a code of belief which, while utterly opposed to Catholicism, would admit of no departure from itself, in other words, to the setting up of a Protestant orthodoxy.

Such a desire, such an aim, is frequently discernible amid the turmoil and confusion of those years of strife. The danger of the whittling down process, the danger of crumbling bit by bit, was sufficiently obvious. There was no mistaking where this dividing and sub-dividing, this multiplication of sects within sects, would ultimately lead to if it went on. The final result would be a multitude of separate individuals all haggling and bickering among themselves. The great thing then was to close the ranks, to form a compact, united body, to share as one community in one common *Credo*. And why not? If they had been able to unite against the common foe, the Papists, why should they not unite again? Therefore, a confession of faith was drawn up outside which, it was declared, there could be no salvation. Work towards this end went on in England, but, perhaps, still more actively in Holland, where the arrival of Protestant divines from France gave rise to further preoccupations. An orthodox confession, that, and nothing less, was what was drawn up at Dordrecht and presented to the pastors for signature in April, 1686. To refuse to sign was to be expelled from the reformed church. The synods held in the succeeding years kept a vigilant eye on the maintenance of doctrine, summoned alleged schismatics to answer for themselves, passed sentence, excluded members from the Holy Table, suspended ministers from their functions. Their verdicts were hardly less drastic than those of the Roman Church. "The association, whose sovereign aim it is to safeguard the unity of belief among those of us who are called upon to preach the doctrine of Truth and the Gospel of Peace, having earnestly and devoutly considered the precautions it behoved them to take to secure the exclusion of all dangerous doctrine, have, after many prayers to God, and in conformity with our long established regulations, decided to declare no pastor eligible for admission to our body unless he shall have satisfied us that his views are in accordance with our confession of faith in general and with the decisions of the Synod of Dordrecht in particular, and declared his willingness to submit to all the requirements of our disciplinary code."[1] Jurieu played the part of Grand Inquisitor. He denounced people, he haled them before the Court, he thundered anathema at them. Against those who defaulted in matters of conscience, he did not hesitate to invoke the secular arm, and to demand the imprisonment or dismissal of all who did not think as he did. "God preserve us", wrote Bayle, whom Jurieu was arraigning before the magistrates at Amsterdam and whom he was trying to get dismissed from his post. "God preserve us from the Protestant Inquisition; another five or six years or so and it will have become so terrible that people will be longing to have the Roman one back again, as something to be thankful for."[2]

But it was not there that the danger lay. The best that the England of William of Orange could do for the dissenters was, not to unite them, but simply to tolerate them. All she demanded of them was their political adherence; the conduct of their religious affairs she left to them. She outlawed Catholicism because it was answerable to Rome; she tolerated Nonconformity because it was answerable only to itself. As for Holland, well, Holland was now nothing more nor less than a swarming ant-heap of differing sects—those that had arisen in the earliest days of the Reformation, and those that had come into being as time went on, the first comers and the last, all were forgathered there within her borders, and all were engaged in an endless succession of

[1]*Extrait des articles résolus dans le Synode des Églises wallonnes des Pays-Bas, assemblé à Rotterdam* (1686), *Article VI*, quoted by Frank Puaux, *Les précurseurs de la Tolérance en France au XVIIe siècle* (1881). See also in the same work, the *Délibérations du Synode d'Amsterdam* (1690).
[2]Letter of 17 December, 1691.

pitched battles, Arminians and Gomarians, Cocceians, Voetians, Trinitarians, anti-Trinitarians . . . , each and every doctrinal view and shade of opinion about Grace, about the Scriptures, about the Rights of Conscience, about Toleration, and even about the Civil Power, were ranged one against another in angry dispute. The battle was unceasing, not only because the opposing parties were utterly sincere in their championship of what they believed to be the truth; not only because of the satisfaction they derived from carrying on a battle so well worth fighting, a battle which engendered light, even as the impact of two stones conjures a dazzling spark from a dull and lifeless mass; no, there was another reason, which lay in something, in a principle, that is inherent in the very soul of Protestantism.

If Protestantism does in truth include among its various manifestations a revolt of the individual conscience against the intrusion of authority in matters of faith, then what right has such authority to claim jurisdiction over the conscience and its workings? Who shall presume to decide where orthodoxy ends and heterodoxy begins? To declare, in the name of Protestantism, that such and such an opinion about Free-will and Predestination is to be elevated to the status of a dogma; and, more than that, to hold that a civil magistrate is perfectly within his rights in exerting his authority to put down idolatry and to stem the spread of heresy: to say that one man is perfectly justified in forbidding another man, not only to teach, but even to believe, what his conscience tells him, is simply to fling logic to the winds.

Hence the powerlessness of the synods to bring the various pastors and their respective flocks together and to unite them in one obedient and contented whole; to check the multiplication of sects; to pronounce the magic word which should cause the ever-enquiring mind to cease its quest. One term crops up with notable frequency in the theological discussions of the day, and that term is Socinianism. Socinianism, which in its original phase was a heresy inaugurated by Faustus Socinus, came into prominence in Poland about the end of the sixteenth and the early part of the seventeenth century. Expelled from Poland, the disciples and successors of Socinus poured into Prussia and France, but it was in Holland that they found their home of homes. In that country it was that the Congregation of the *Frères Polonais* was founded; there, in 1665, Wiszowaty, a grandson of Socinus, published his *Religio rationalis*, a book which the Socinians regarded as a sort of second bible. Four years later, Pastor Isaac d'Huisseau of Saumur brought out his book on the Reunion of Christendom; he proposed that the principles whereby Descartes had revolutionized philosophy should also be applied to religion; henceforth, nothing was to be believed that was not clearly set forth in the Scriptures; only the primary, universal truths inscribed therein, truths that squared with the dictates of reason, were to be retained. So Tradition went by the board, and so, to tell the truth, did the idea of a Church; God, the Bible, the individual conscience; that was the sum of it; no more and no less. The whole French reformed church began to argue about these matters. Penal measures, banishment itself, far from healing these divisions, did but the more exacerbate them. Papon, Isaac d'Huisseau's son-in-law, having become infected with heresy, there followed a battle royal between Paponists and Anti-Paponists. Nowhere could a single synod succeed in stemming the tide of Socinianism.

If there was any truth in what was alleged about the diminution of the sect, *qua* sect; if to the outward view it seemed to have contracted, that was only in its superficial aspect. Inwardly, its influence had greatly increased. Its ideas were seeping insensibly into men's minds, leading them to substitute a rationalistic for a religious view of things. But what precisely do we mean by a Socinian?

According to Bossuet, the main plank in the Socinian platform is the assertion that we cannot be compelled to accept what is not clear to our understanding. *Socinianismus*, wrote Poiret, *fidem et scripturam subjicit rationi*. According to Pufendorf, the Socinians regard Christianity as nothing more than a system of moral philosophy. Jurieu got it into his head—it was sort of monomania with him—that he saw Socinianism everywhere; and perhaps after all he was not far wrong, so widespread and so unmistakable was the general lapse into rationalism. The Socinians, he cried, declare that it is a matter of indifference what religion a man holds. They reject the element of mystery. Yet a sense of mystery is the very essence of the religious spirit. But the most trenchant comment came from Richard Simon. Referring to d'Huisseau's condemnation, he said, "The little herd, by treating the minister d'Huisseau with such conspicuous severity, hoped to intimidate the many other ministers who hold similar ideas. They confided their intentions to a number of ministers in the provinces, who signified their approval; and we may take it that, if they had not thus shown a firm hand, it would have been all over with Calvinism in France. The leading men of that sect would have openly proclaimed themselves Arminians, if not downright Socinians. As it is, they have contented themselves with being so inwardly, letting only their most intimate friends into their secret. It was because they were afraid of losing their posts that they acted as they did. They subscribe the Confession of Faith purely and simply for reasons of policy, *holding, as they do, that Calvin and the other early Reformers left their work but half-done*".[1] A malicious and calumnious declaration that may be, but it shows, at any rate, that Richard Simon saw one thing clearly enough, and that was that the Reformation continued to reform itself.

The Dutch pastors were at loggerheads with their brethren in Germany. The pastors who had made their way to London were at war with Socinianism. Efforts had been made to unite Calvinism and Lutheranism in a closer bond than that of their original kinship, so that both might subscribe to a common confession of faith; but these efforts proved abortive.

It was, therefore, clearly open to the Catholics to argue that since they had quitted the Roman fold the Protestants had wandered into a trackless maze. And Bossuet scored heavily when, in 1688, he brought out his *Histoire des Variations des Églises Protestantes*, which purported to show that these churches had differed all along, that they differed still, and that to differ was the very essence of their being. Little by little, they fell in sunder until at last they came to dust. It was impossible to bring them together in the bond of unity, since each and every one of them had as good a claim to exist as any of the others. They proceeded, one and all, from that same principle of independent judgment which, criticizing now this, now that, was always demanding that something should be changed. Hence the number of different confessions, so numerous, so multifarious, that the historian can do no more than barely enumerate them. That is why it is vain to attempt to reconcile groups whose very nature is one of perpetual and progressive disintegration.

[1] Richard Simon, *Lettres choisies*, vol. III, l. 3.

In reply to Bossuet it might be retorted that the Catholic Church, too, has varied. And that was precisely the line taken by Jacques Basnage, one of his many opponents. Or, again, it might be urged that the Protestant Church has never varied in regard to essentials. That was Gilbert Burnet's argument. On some such lines as these you might argue, unless, of course, you preferred to regard his remarks, not as a reproach, but as something to be proud of, and unless you looked on private judgment as the privilege of a race not possessed of the truth by virtue of a supernatural revelation, but laboriously striving to disengage it, to construct it, piece by piece, by its own efforts;[1] and unless, while weighing the dangers of too much authority on the one hand, or too much liberty on the other, you decided, since dangers there must be, deliberately to choose the latter. Thus it is, and almost in those very words, that Jean Le Clerc in his *Bibliothèque Choisie* for the year 1705, presents the alternatives. How he is hemmed in on every side by atheists! Many books of which he makes mention in his paper are directed against them, proof positive that atheism is becoming an ever-increasing menace. In days gone by, men did not question, did not doubt, the truth of what their teachers imparted to them. They took it all on faith. But now, it is quite different; authority is respected no longer. Is the former state of things to be preferred, or is it not? Jean Le Clerc does not beat about the bush: unbelief is an evil, no doubt; but the disposition which encourages us to believe everything without examination is still more of an evil. It arises from mental stupidity and an indifference to truth. Better a country where there is much enlightenment and a certain number of unbelievers, than a nation of ignoramuses who believe everything that has hitherto passed for truth. Light is productive of virtue, even if there be some who use that light amiss; whereas the sole brood of ignorance are barbarism and vice.

The ideas to which Jean Le Clerc, the Arminian, the Socinian, thus gives expression are those which were destined to prevail throughout the whole of the first half of the eighteenth century. Past and gone are the days when Descartes, conscious that his views were calculated to bear him away into vague, uncharted regions, voluntarily imposed on himself some prudent restraints. "The first was to render obedience to the laws and customs of my

[1]See A. Rébelliau, *Bossuet historien du Protestantisme*, 3rd edn., 1909, p. 571.

country, always keeping firm hold on the religion in which God's grace had suffered me to be instructed from my childhood upwards, and regulating my conduct in all other matters in accordance with such moderate ideas as were approved and adopted by the most level-headed of those with whom I had to live." The day of heterodoxy has dawned, of every kind of heterodoxy, the day of the malcontents, the rebels who during the reign of Louis XIV had multiplied out of sight and had been awaiting the hour of their emancipation; of learned men, who declined to accept tradition at its face value, and insisted on enquiring into its credentials; of the Jansenists, who were to kindle new fire from their dim but never wholly extinguished embers; of the Biblical exegetists; of the philosophers; the day of Pierre Bayle!

V

PIERRE BAYLE

PIERRE BAYLE came from the county of Foix, and was one of the host of Southerners who were driven by fate to the North and who brought with them their quick-wittedness, their passion for ideas, their sturdy character, and their astounding vitality. He was a Protestant, his father being a minister. He had learnt Latin and Greek at school, and then went on to continue his studies at the Academy of Puylaurens. But just as he was entering on the path he had chosen, the path which was to lead him far afield, so far that he was fated to leave all his companions behind, and to journey on in almost utter loneliness; the path along which we shall fare beside him, so that we may note the stages of a pilgrimage which began with religion and ended on the very borders of scepticism—just as he was setting foot on that path, he came to a sudden halt. He had been delving into works of theological controversy, and the result was that he became a convert to Catholicism, and went to read his philosophy with the Jesuits at their College at Toulouse. But, anon, "recollections of his early schooldays resuming their sway,"[1] he went back again to the Reformed Church, "happy as one who, after a long sojourn at the Pole, beholds the sun before him once again." In 1670, he set out for Geneva. "At that time, I was a pretty good hand at argument. I had been tutored in the Schoolmen's art of verbal jugglery, and I am not exaggerating when I say I was not at all a bad performer."[2]

One step more; it brought him from Aristotle to Descartes. A course of philosophy lectures which he prepared on being

[1] Bayle to Pinson de Riolles, Rotterdam, 25 June, 1693.
[2] Bayle to Basnage, 5 May, 1675.

appointed to a professorship at the Sedan Academy reveals him to us as a disciple of the clear-thinking, evidential school. Ideas of that kind always engender a zeal for converts. Would he have been content with his teaching work? Would he have gone on, year in, year out, drumming in the same old lessons, over and over again? We doubt it. While he was at Sedan, he sent the *Journal des Savants* a letter dealing with the subject of comets and omens. The editor flatly declined to print it. A revised and greatly augmented version of this same letter was published in 1682, and it loudly proclaimed that he had cut the painter.

He felt within him that a voice was calling. His nature insisted that he should ever be seeking, enquiring, probing into things. He must needs be always weighing the for and against, taking nothing for gospel until it had satisfied the tribunal of his own reason. When the Sedan Academy was closed down on religious grounds, when, *incertum quo fata ferrent*, he was looking round for a means of earning his daily bread, the worthies of Rotterdam offered him a post in their own illustrious seat of learning. This must have looked like the handiwork of a beneficent Providence, if, indeed, he still retained any belief in Providence and its watchful care. He would go on with his teaching, then, because he had to do so, in order to live; but his real work, his real calling, should be journalism, because, by that means, he could direct people's minds towards those relentless truths which had already laid their spell upon him.

There, then, in his study at Rotterdam, let us picture him, frail in body but ardent in spirit; a solitary, far removed from all material preoccupations. Certainly, he nourished strong family affections, but a lover he was not. Books, books, piles of books! Of books he could never get enough. And news—he implored his friends in the various capitals of Europe, if they had any love for him at all, to send him news. "I recognize quite plainly that my insatiable craving for news is one of those inveterate diseases that set all treatment at defiance. It's dropsy; that's what it is. The more you give it, the more it wants."[1] But books are another matter. They present a definite idea, something tangible, something you can get hold of, something that won't slip through your fingers. Books stimulate the mind, they provoke ideas. You've got your adversary right in front of you, with all his

[1] Bayle to Minutoli, 27 February 1673.

arguments drawn up in order of battle. Oh, the joy of encountering him with some of your nimblest troops—replies, rejoinders,
reasoned arguments. Through a man's book you can get at the
man himself, tell him where he stands, show him the poverty of
his land. But the author is only the corollary, as it were, of the
actual book, and it is books that Bayle attacks in force. Henceforth, the only things that counted in life for Bayle were things
intellectual. Reading, writing, discussing, that was what life
meant to him. He found in study as much of pleasure and delight
as the common run find in gambling and the tavern. The *libido
sciendi* had got its grip upon him. Learn first, all you can; and
then form your judgment, and criticize.

When he started journalism, he did not at first fully show how
formidable he could be in argument. "We think you are like a
good Italian wine, *dolce piccante*; but we are rascally fellows, and
would much rather you put the accent on the *piccante*." That is
what Bernier wrote him on the 11th April, 1686. But even when
he goes out of his way to impose some restraint on himself, the
tone and substance of the *Nouvelles de la République des Lettres* are
evident enough. He invites the reader to bring his mind to bear
on questions of the gravest import; could there be anything
more important than knowing what you believe, what you do
not believe, and your reasons for doing the one and the other?
Therefore, let all ideas, wherever they come from, be allowed a
hearing; a fair field and no favour! And let those ideas which
have been of set purpose kept in the background, let the infidels,
the revolutionaries come out into the open, and take an honoured
place among us. Heterodoxy, smothered and hushed up elsewhere, shall here come into its own. Let everyone have his say,
and let the boldest of them bear themselves like heroes. Those
who gird and complain about the toleration of heresy and
heretical publications must understand that what is sauce for the
Inquisition is not sauce for everyone. The orthodox in particular
should look heresy fearlessly in the face, unless of course they
would rather put the gag on their opponent, and then brag that
they have reduced him to silence.[1]

There was a touch of the febrile in his nature; else how could
he have managed to get through such an enormous amount of

[1] *Nouvelles de la République des Lettres*, Juillet, 1685, Art. 9. *Réflexions sur la tolérance
des livres hérétiques.*

work? He wrote the "copy", he corrected the proofs, but he did not mind that; printer's ink smelt sweet in his nostrils. No; but those captious readers with their finicking objections, each believing that he had the whole truth on his side, gave one a pretty good idea of the depths to which human stupidity could sink; the endless correspondence he had to enter into—that was what wore him down. When you are writing a book you can leave it for a while, if you want to, and then take it up again; you can do a little reading, for example, for there is no recreation like a change of occupation. But letter-writing! When you've got that to do, you have to keep hard at it, all the time. That is what takes it out of you. He carried on at this feverish rate for three years, from March, 1684, to February, 1687; then he put on the brake.

But before that happened, he had already got on his own proper road again, and it had brought him to a notable stage. He held a foremost place among the champions of Protestantism. With a prodigious flow of words, with the force of a torrent that sweeps all before it, with a spate of argument and invective, he had dealt faithfully by le Père Maimbourg. When the persecution had become more ruthless than ever, it happened that he lighted on a book which had come from France, a book in which the author sang the praises of Louis XIV for having used his power to render the country wholly Catholic again.[1] Thereupon Bayle took up his pen. He, Bayle, would give that monarch to understand what he thought of him. "If people only knew the force and present significance of the expression, no one would ever envy France the distinction of being 'wholly Catholic', under Louis the Great. It is now a long time since those who arrogate to themselves the name of Catholic *par excellence*, have been perpetrating deeds that excite such horror in every human heart that any decent person must regard it as an insult to be called a Catholic. After the evils you have wrought in that most Christian kingdom of yours, it is evident that to speak of the Catholic religion and the religion of the unrighteous is one and the same thing."[2]

In the fourteenth chapter of the Gospel according to St. Luke we may read the parable of how a certain man made a great supper,

[1] *La France toute catholique sous le règne de Louis le Grand, ou Entretiens de quelques protestants français*, Lyon, 1684.
[2] *Lettre écrite de Londres à M. l'abbé de . . . ,chanoine de N. D. de . . . Ce que c'est que la France toute catholique sous le règne de Louis le Grand*, Saint-Omer, chez Jean Pierre Lami, 1686.

and how the guests who had been bidden to it with one consent began to make excuse. Then the master of the house being angry said to his servant, "Go out quickly into the streets and lanes of the city and bring in hither the poor, and the maimed, and the halt, and the blind." And the servant said, "Lord, it is done as Thou hast commanded, and yet there is room". And the Lord said unto the servant, "Go out into the highways and hedges and compel them to come, those whom thou shalt find there".

Compel them to come in; *compelle intrare*. Those are the words which St. Augustine employed when exhorting the Donatists to return to the African Church. And since then, Catholic apologists have quoted them time and again to show how right it had been to use force against the Protestants.[1] This roused Bayle to an unexampled pitch of fury; it was an outrage on the deepest and the dearest of his convictions.[2] To use force in a matter of conscience—the thing was monstrous, horrible. And from his armoury Bayle discharged volley after volley of denunciation, vituperation and invective. The Roman Church, which claims to speak with infallible authority; which would govern the souls of men by the law of the strong right-arm; which is not ashamed to employ "converters"—dragoons shall we call them, or fiends?—is nothing but a fury and a whore. There can be no dealings with the Catholics. Have done with them! They are always harping on the same old string: "We are the Church and you are rebels; therefore, while we may chastise you, you have no right to do the like unto us." What intolerable effrontery! Ah, let divided Europe remain divided, and may the nations who have shaken themselves free from the tyranny of Rome never fall again beneath her yoke. Doughty, heart-stirring words, these, for his co-religionists, and they owed him some gratitude. But now the whole business is once more in the melting-pot. The right to coerce, which you deny to the Catholics, you can scarcely concede to the Protestants: from the point of view of pure reason, a mystery is never anything more than a temporary obstruction, no matter how many priests or pastors may accept it. Sooner or

[1] *Conformité de la conduite de l'Église de France pour ramener les protestants avec celle de l'Église d'Afrique pour ramener les Donatistes*, 1685.
[2] *Commentaire philosophique sur ces paroles de Jésus-Christ: "Contrains-les d'entrer"; où l'on prouve par plusieurs raisons démonstratives qu'il y a rien de plus abominable que de faire des conversions par la contrainte, et où l'on réfute tous les sophismes des convertisseurs à contrainte, et l'apologie que saint Augustin a faite des persécutions*. Traduit de l'anglais du sieur Jean Fox de Bruges, par M. J. F. (1686).

later, the broad light of day will replace the dim religious lamp
that glimmers tremulously before the tabernacle, be it in a
Catholic church or a Protestant bethel. Thus, with the very
weapons which he used to rout his foes, did Bayle procure the
undoing of his friends. He said that the conscience is answerable
only to itself; that if, in good faith, you believed what your conscience told you was the truth, no one had a right to interfere
with you. If, with the best intentions in the world, one's conscience misleads one, sin must not be imputed to it, nor must
force be applied to correct it. An atheist who believes it his duty
to be an atheist is in no wise to be accounted less worthy than the
most orthodox of Protestants.   And that word *orthodox*—it
really ought to be suppressed, seeing that it implies the interference of authority with freedom of thought and belief. When
he heard these words, Jurieu veiled his face. "Bayle", he cried,
"Bayle is a Socinian." A Socinian he was, and something more as
well, if we are to take him at his word in this apology of his:
"God forbid that I should extend the jurisdiction of human intelligence and the domain of metaphysical speculation as far as
do the Socinians, who lay down that any interpretation of Scripture which does not square with the said human intelligence and
metaphysical ideas is to be set aside, and go on to declare that, in
the light of this rule of theirs, they reject the doctrines of the
Trinity and the Incarnation. No, no; I do not commit myself to
any such sweeping and unqualified statements. I am fully aware
that there are axioms which the clearest and most categorical
denials in Scripture itself would be powerless to discredit. I mean
such things as, 'If equals be taken from equals, the remainders
are equal.' or 'Of two contradictory statements both cannot be
true' or that 'the essence of a thing can survive the destruction
of the thing itself'. Even if Scripture proclaimed a hundred times
over that those propositions were not true; even if more miracles
than Moses or the Apostles ever wrought were performed to
support a doctrine opposed to these universal conclusions of our
natural intelligence, man, being what he is, would refuse to believe it. Rather would he say, either that Scripture was expressing
itself by way of metaphor and paradox, or that the said miracles
were the work of the Devil. He would, I say, rather take that line
than believe that man's natural intelligence had erred in regard to
the matters in question.

"I repeat: God forbid that I should wish, in such matters, to go as far as the Socinians. But if limits are to be assigned to speculative truths, I think there ought to be none in respect of the ordinary practical principles which have to do with morals. What I mean is that we ought always and without exception to refer moral laws to that natural conception of equity which, no less than the metaphysical light, illumines every man that comes into the world.

"That is the conclusion we are bound to come to, the conclusion, I mean, that any particular dogma, whatever it may be, whether it is advanced on the authority of the Scriptures, or whatever else may be its origin, is to be regarded as false if it clashes with the clear and definite conclusions of the natural understanding, and that more particularly in the domain of Ethics."[1]

A dictionary, the compilation of a dictionary! A queer sort of undertaking truly for a man of his tastes and talents! Well; this is what he himself has to say on the matter: "Somewhere about the month of December, 1690, I conceived the idea of compiling a critical dictionary, i.e., a dictionary which should comprise a complete inventory, as it were, of the various errors perpetrated, not only by lexicogaphers, but by writers in general; the details of each such error to be set out under the name of the individual, town or city associated with it."[2] Such was his plan, but he did not fulfil it to the letter. The names are set down in alphabetical order, and under each name he has furnished a certain amount of factual information. But his most daring ideas, his most provocative utterances are to be found *passim*, or tucked away in the notes. The result is that the things he was really anxious to convey are, except in a few instances, to be met with anywhere, rather than in the places one would naturally expect to find them. He rather liked this game of hide and seek, it appealed to him, and he excelled at it. But, despite all the modifications he had to introduce into his original plan in order to avoid scaring publishers, booksellers and public alike, this Historical and Critical Dictionary stands out as the most damning indictment that was ever drawn up by man to the shame and confusion of his fellows. Well-nigh every name calls up the recollection

[1] *Commentaire philosophique*, Première partie, I, 1.
[2] Bayle to his cousin Naudé, 22 May, 1692.

of some delusion, error, misdemeanour or crime. All those
Kings whose misrule brought misery to their people; all those
Popes who debased the Catholic religion to the level of their own
ambitions, their own passions, philosophers with their futile,
foolish systems, all those cities, towns and countries whose names
call back the memory of wars and plunder and massacres. Next
came offences against decency, against all that is good and seemly,
moral perversions. If Bayle tells of these with obvious zest, the
reason may be, as he says, that the book-trade had asked for them
as a bait to attract readers, or it may have been that he himself
wanted a little diversion, reminding us, as he does, that it is
one thing to give an account of man's delinquencies, another
deliberately to brighten up a narrative with a sprinkling of broad
and spicy anecdotes. But is not the real reason to be sought in
the fact that, in addition to our errors, we must also take stock
of our wilful transgressions, and that in addition to our errors
in the realm of the intellect, we must not lose sight of offences
committed by us in the moral sphere. Thirdly, and finally, we
have to consider the fables and stories invented by those who have
related the deeds of others, fables and stories so many of which
are born of the levity, stupidity, greed or corruption of the
narrators. What an edifying spectacle!

All that had to cleared away, and that is precisely the task to
which, with a sort of melancholy satisfaction, Bayle first addresses
himself. Away with the myth-mongers! Mankind, one and all,
have gone astray: the Ancients, who lied as glibly and freely as
we speak; the Moderns, because they were dazzled and carried
away by the prestige of the Ancients. The most competent, the
most respectable of authors have made mistakes; La Mothe Le
Vayer, and Gassendi included. There are professional liars like
Moreri, who compiled a dictionary which was everything a
dictionary ought not to be, a dictionary bulging with falsehoods.
He was a public poisoner. He must be refuted point by point;
we must make a list of his lies: a dozen here, fifteen there; we
must take him by the throat; no quarter for him! Toil on, make
sure of every step, and Truth will be established on her throne
once more. Stern yet seemly are the laws that govern the Republic of Ideas. "This republic is a state in which wide latitude is
allowed. The only powers whose writ is acknowledged there are
Truth and Reason, and under their auspices men take the field

impartially, wherever they are called upon to fight. Friends may be called to account by friends; sires by their own children."[1]

Courage such as this, such an ardour for battle, such determination to free men's minds from error, presupposes the conviction that truth prevails, and may be attained, no matter what obstacles stand in the way: objective, factual truth, which criticism and positive knowledge combine to set free from all encumbrances. But that positive knowledge, that objective truth, how hard it is to grasp it! How potent is error and how deep-rooted, so deep that, do what you will to destroy it, it will always contrive to spring up again somewhere or other. "There is no perversion of the truth, however absurd it be, that is not passed on from book to book, from generation to generation. Lie with a bold face, we may say to the sorriest mountebank in Europe, print what outrageous extravagance you will, you will find plenty of people to copy your tales, and, if you are extinguished now, the day will come, circumstances will arise, when it will be in someone's interest to bring you back to life again."[2] We shall never convert any but the converted, so impervious is the mind to truth, even when it is as plain as daylight.

Are what we call facts really what we take them to be? The new school of philosophy would have us believe, would it not, that they are merely modifications of our own consciousness?[3]

The name of Sextus Empiricus was hardly known in our schools. The allurements of the epoch which he described so subtly were as unknown there as was the southern continent, when Gassendi gave us a brief account of it and opened our eyes. Cartesianism put the finishing touches on the work, and now no sound philosopher has any doubt that the sceptics were in the right when they said that the qualities of the objects which we apprehend with our senses are merely appearances. Anyone may say "I feel the heat when I am close to the fire", but not "I know that heat is in itself, what I think it is". That is the way these early Pyrrhonists looked at the matter. To-day, the new school adopts a more positive tone. They say that heat, smell, colour and so on are not objects of our senses but modifications of our mind. We know that external objects are not what they appear to us to be. There was an idea that extent and motion might be excluded from this rule, but that was found to be impossible; for if the

[1]*Dictionnaire*, art. *Calius*, note D.
[2]*Dictionnaire*, art. *Capet*, lettre Y.
[3]*Ibid.*, art. *Pyrrhon*.

objects of our senses appear to us to be coloured, hot, cold, odorous, when, as a matter of fact, they are not so, what is to prevent their appearing to be of such and such an extent, of such and such a shape and design, at rest or in motion, when in reality they are none of these things? Those are the kind of ideas with which the new school of philosophy would strengthen the Pyrrhonist position, and which I decline to admit.

But Bayle did not decline for ever. That he was uneasy in his mind is quite evident. Despite himself, perhaps, or, it may be, because he had a natural inclination that way, he slips insensibly into Pyrrhonism as he goes on confronting truth and error. Can you ever be quite sure where a principle is going to lead you? "The same theory which serves as a weapon against error, may sometimes do a disservice to the cause of truth.[1] One thing you will always find if you look long enough, and that is antinomy, contradiction."[2] In a word, man is in an unhappy posture, because the light which enables him to avoid one evil leads him into another. Banish ignorance and barbarism and childish credulity, so profitable to the powers that be, and the only use the people make of the advantage they have gained is to wallow in sloth and debauchery; but then, when you point out to them the evils of such a mode of life, and inspire them with the desire to find out all they can about things, they become so hair-splitting, so logic-chopping that nothing is good enough to satisfy the demands of their miserable reason.

There *is* a method, and, with a little trouble, you can see what it is, and even reduce it to a formula: In every system, if it is to be made to work, two things are essential; the first is that its terms should be plain and unequivocal; the second, that it should square with practical experience.[2] By this method you get at abstract truth, and at the concrete proof of it. But when it comes to putting this method into practice, how is it to be done? As for getting at the concrete truth, people are for ever distorting and misrepresenting facts. In the *Dictionnaire historique et critique*, the critical part demolishes the historical. As for abstract truth, men can never get an adequate grasp of ideas, and if they did, if they saw those ideas as they really were, they would find that they were all equally cogent, all equally probable and all mutually destructive.

[1] *Dictionnaire,* art. *Takiddin.*
[2] *Dictionnaire,* art. *Manichéens,* note D.

But Bayle does not stop there. If we would take stock of his philosophy as a whole, and see how constantly, as though by a sort of logical obsession, it kept harking back to questions which he could never persuade himself he had satisfactorily settled, we must go further and study his *Réponse aux questions d'un Provincial*, the publication of which, begun in 1704, was cut short by his death. In it, he discarded neither his style, with its characteristic outbursts and coruscations, nor his habit of turning from the actual chapter and verse of what he was dealing with—historical narrative, philosophical treatise, dissertation, or whatever it might be—to launch out into a flood of criticism and counter-argument; nor was his pitiless irony any the less in evidence. His propensity to go off at a tangent was, if possible, more marked than ever, his reactions more vehement, his analysis more relentlessly logical. The man of the provinces is supposed to be making enquiries about the contents of a book, or about the exact determination of the date at which something happened, about some event in history, or about some matter of ordinary, everyday interest. In a few sentences Bayle defines the bearings of the question with a clarity that is always admirable; no shirking the point at issue, no equivocation, no hidden corners where any vestiges of error could linger on unnoticed, no leniency, no indulgence, no pardon. Around him the same problems are for ever recurring. Does God mean that universal consent should be taken as proof of His existence? Has God endowed man with free-will, or is he the bondslave of ineluctable destiny? If there be a God, why does He permit injustice and every imaginable evil to exist in the world? With unflagging persistence, Bayle advances his ultimate solution, a solution which leads to the conclusion that certainty can be affirmed of nothing, that nothing can be known beyond all doubt.

And back again goes the labourer to resume his task, but more boldly now, and with an added consciousness of his responsibility. And that task is to show convincingly, beyond all doubt, that there is no common ground between religion and philosophy. So long as you continue to mix up the one with the other you will be but a voice crying in the wilderness. Bayle protests that he is not attacking religious belief as such; he even goes the length of averring that he respects it; he does, he declares, but follow and restate the arguments of its apologists. Do they not admit that in every form of religion there is at the outset an element of mystery? That is the crucial point of the whole matter, for mystery is incompatible with reason, and implies an attitude of mind irreconcilable with the mental processes, nay, with the very nature, of a reasoning being. It is now truer than ever to say he is inside the fort in order to betray it, that he mingles with its defenders in order to sow alarm and despondency among them. He tells them that if Revelation is true, religion is true, and that its dogmas follow logically, one upon another. But then, he goes on, Revelation cannot be proved to be true. To believe is one thing, to employ one's reason is another. There can be no middle course, no picking and choosing. To reject a dogma here, to retain a dogma there, is a flagrant anomaly, a manifest absurdity. "I fancy I gathered from some of you that, as regards the Trinity and some other articles of the Christian faith, reason must bow to the word of God, but that, as regards the Fall of Adam and its consequences, the Scriptures must defer to the judgment of the philosophers. I should be sorry for you if you really took this view and believed you could differentiate to that extent."[1] You say you believe in the element of mystery. Believe in it then, whether philosophy tells you to do so, or not. Believe in it, even if the arguments against it are irrefragable. But if you do take that line, don't go and pretend that you are acting according to reason. It is not the Catholics or the Calvinists only that Bayle would tax with stupidity or folly, but the Jews and Mohammedans into the bargain; nor these alone, but the deists as well, the deists who maintain that the existence of God may be demonstrated by human reason. All these he lumped together as "religionnaires",[2] as he called them. In the opposing camp are the Rationalists.

But the two forces once well in sunder, it behoves the Rationalists, if there is any logic in them, to see about setting their own house in order, to examine their own basic principles, and this is where the trouble begins.

Unhappily, philosophy does not make good the breaches it creates, in spite of all its efforts so to do. The philosophers are very good at knocking down received beliefs, but having done so, all they can supply to fill up the gaps are notes of interrogation.

---

[1] *Réponse aux questions d'un provincial*, vol. III, 1706, ch. CXXVIII.
[2] *Ibid.*, ch. CXXXIV. "*Les Religionnaires (permettez-moi de me servir de ce mot pour désigner en commun les Juifs, les Payens, les Chrétiens, les Mahométans, etc.)*"

Is man the captain, or the captive, of his fate? Argument about this question of freedom is never-ending. The resources of either side are inexhaustible.

"So intricate is this question of free-will, so rich in ambiguities, that the deeper into it you go, the more you get involved in contradictions. As often as not, you find yourself echoing the words of your antagonist and forging weapons for your own discomfiture."[1] Is the soul immortal? It is; unless, of course, the contrary is the case. If that is so, it is merely a property of matter. Is there an all-wise and all-beneficent deity? There may be, but, if there is, how are you going to explain, by what possible argument *can* you explain, that this wise and beneficent deity permits his creatures to suffer as they do in body and soul, and freely allows them to compass their own perdition? When he contemplates, even for a moment, such a picture of things, a picture which appals the feelings as much as it outrages the reason, Bayle is filled with horror. He is also filled with indignation. "Those who permit an evil which they are perfectly able to prevent are to be condemned; those who permit someone to go to his doom when they could readily save him are guilty of his death. Put this question to any simple peasant woman: A mother, though her breast is full of milk, lets her little one die of hunger. Is she not as much its murderess as if she had flung it into the water to drown? A father who, seeing his son about to put something poisonous into his mouth, lets him do so, when a word or a glance would have stopped him, is he not as great a criminal as if he had given him the poison himself?"[2]

Can we imagine that God could be as cruel as that inhuman mother, as criminal as that father? Some worthy souls there were who did their utmost to find a way out of the dilemma. One William King, an Anglican theologian, was guileless enough to think that he had disposed of the problem of evil once and for all. He published a voluminous treatise in Latin in which he fondly believed he had solved the insoluble. He had solved nothing. He might as well have tried to square the circle.

What a tangle of contradictions is man! Man is the toughest morsel to digest that any system could have to tackle. He is the

[1] *Réponse aux questions d'un provincial*, ch. CXLII.
[2] *Ibid.*, Ch. LXXIV et seq. Refutation of W. King's treatise, *De origine Mali*, London, 1702.

reef on which, like waves, the false and the true are shattered. He is a trial to orthodox and unorthodox alike. He is a harder knot to untie than any the poets ever dreamt of. Men try to do battle with error, but when the fight is over they have the uncomfortable feeling that the human soul is more at home with illusion than with truth[1] and that they ought to admit it. A man stakes his all on reason, only to find that he has been leaning on a broken reed. Reason cannot hold out against the feelings. Time after time she has to follow the chariot wheels of the passions, sometimes like a docile captive, sometimes like a fawning sycophant. For a time she strives against the passions, then she holds her peace and chafes in secret, finally she gives in and lets them work their will.[2] It is clear that she is never quite certain of what she lays down and that propositions which seem on the face of them self-evident, have, nevertheless, a shade of the problematic about them. Once again scepticism renews the attack, and the truth that seemed so crystal clear begins to grow thought-sick and cloudy.

Did he reach the point of absolute scepticism? He would have done so had he suffered his mind to follow its natural bent. Nothing ever pleased him better than that interplay of *pro* and *con*. He would have floated away into that far-off void, where actions lose their significance and life its purpose, had he followed logic to its final term, and taken cognizance only of his human experiences, which day by day impressed him more and more. He might, nay, he must, have arrived at last at what Le Clerc calls metaphysical and historical scepticism, at universal doubt.

But this he resisted. His intrepid spirit, the feeling that he had a mission to fulfil, an abhorrence of error, more potent than any doubts he might have entertained about truth, a reasoning mind that would not willingly accept defeat, and above all his strength of will enabled him to stop short of the final step. He never would, and he never did, divest himself of the belief that he had a definite moral task to accomplish, a definite line of progress to recommend. In this connexion, the *Dictionnaire* furnishes a moving passage; it occurs under *Mâcon, note D: Why I touch on*

[1]Ibid., ch. CIII.
[2]Ibid., vol. I, ch. XIII, 1704.

these appalling disorders. These appalling disorders are the wars
of religion, which have served as a pretext for the most shocking
barbarities. Were it not better to pluck them from the memory,
to raze them from the tablets of the mind? If we recount them
afresh, shall we not be feeding the fires of irreconcilable hatred
among men? "Shall I not be told that I seem to have a special
desire to revive old passions, to rekindle the fires of hatred, when
I go out of my way, in various parts of my work, to describe the
most atrocious deeds in the history of the bygone century?"
The answer is, No! "As everything has two faces, we may, for
sound reasons, be permitted to hope that the memory of all those
frightful disorders will be kept studiously alive." Rulers,
churchmen, theologians must be constantly reminded of former
evils, so that in the future they may be avoided. Thus, of the two
faces which everything presents, Bayle chooses the one in which
he is able to discern a modicum of hope. He may have doubted
whether absolute truth would ever be attainable, but he was at all
events convinced that the liability to err was a contagious disease
and that it behoved him to limit its ravages. A physician to the
blind, it was at least his duty to give sight to the sightless where-
ever he could.

He did not, however, imitate those weaklings of whom he
had mockingly declared, "They make a mighty brave show of
their hostility to God when health and prosperity are on their side,
but when sickness comes upon them, and misfortune, or old age,
they mostly change their tune, and become the veriest slaves of
superstition; and when they think they are drawing near to death,
they make the most elaborate preparations for their journey
hence." He remained a fighter to the end of his days. With whom
had he not crossed swords? Sherlock, Tillotson, Cudworth,
W. King, Le Clerc, Jurieu, Arnauld, Nicole, Bernard and, finally,
M. Jaquelot. M. Jaquelot, who had attacked the *Dictionnaire*
and claimed to have established a synthesis between Faith and
Reason, was something more than an antagonist. He was a
living symbol of ideas which shrink from being definitely
brought out into the daylight, of difficulties which shrink from
being resolved by reason, a symbol, in short, of human frailty.
Utterly weary, tortured by a persistent cough, with attacks of
haemorrhage of the lungs, worn out with fever, Bayle devoted his
dying hours to formulating yet another answer. If he had

anything to regret, it was being compelled to depart this life before refuting the errors of M. Jaquelot.[1]

Bayle's brand of criticism is much too potent to be taken neat. It needed to be diluted, to have something added to it, and that was what happened. Being decanted into the *Dictionnaire* it was removed from the province of purely theological controversy and came within reach of people in general: there were the arguments, plain as plain could be, and so it became the inspirer of heterodoxy in every land, the sceptic's bible. "It is notorious that the works of M. Bayle have unsettled a large number of readers, and cast doubt on some of the most widely accepted principles of morality and religion."[2]

The ideological battles of the XVIth century had been followed by proposals for peace. All those problems which had so long tormented the minds of men, why not regard them as settled? If that were done, men could live in peace, without being a prey to everlasting doubts and fears, without reopening old sores again and again. It should be a time for doing things, a time for achievement. Man's zeal for creating should be directed towards things of the spirit; people would enjoy the amenities of social life, and, having learned to live amicably together, they would be, if not completely and absolutely happy, at all events content. There should be a touch of the grandiose, the heroic in this mutual arrangement, and even their patched up peace would have a hint of the sublime about it, just as in the organization, the hierarchical disposition of a hive of bees, in its productive activities, there is a rule, an order, which presupposes sacrifices without number.

But how was such a peace to be made lasting, if the psychological foundations on which it was based began to change even before it had been properly established? Travellers, wanderers, seekers after new things, the hungry-hearted, those who turn

[1]Isaac Jaquelot, *Conformité de la foi avec la raison; ou Défense de la religion contre les principales difficultés répandues dans le Dictionnaire historique et critique de M. Bayle*, Amsterdam, 1705. These were the brave old days when no one would willingly suffer an adversary to have the last word, when stubborn warriors pursued the foe to the death, ay, and beyond it. See Le Clerc, *Bibliothèque choisie*, vol. XII, 1707; art. V; art. VII, *Remarques sur les Entretiens posthumes de M. Bayle*; and Foreword: "I knew everything M. Bayle could say against me and I made up my mind that I would put up with all his fury, all his insults rather than give him the satisfaction of having the last word, which was what he was so eagerly longing for."

[2]*Bibliothèque germanique*, vol. XVIII, 1729.

with disdain from the ordered, regulated life; and those moder-
nizers, those who see in history, and historians, nought but
childishness and make-belief; and those newcomers to the scene,
who have not so much as an inkling of the classical tone of mind;
and all those doubters and fault-finders who regard the political
question as anything but settled, still less the religious—how
should all this heterogeneous and multitudinous agglomeration
of human beings keep themselves within any settled or enduring
bounds? To that question the answer was war, and, to begin
with, war on traditional beliefs.

PART TWO

The War on Tradition

I

THE RATIONALISTS

WHEREAS for some years past an obscure person, who goes by the name of Reason, has been attempting to make forcible entry into the schools of our University; and whereas the said person, aided and abetted by certain comical quidnuncs calling themselves Gassendists, Cartesians, Malebranchistes, vagabonds all of them, designs to arraign, and then to expel, Aristotle . . .[1]

It was even so. Reason, all primed for battle, was coming on to the field. It was not only Aristotle she insisted on putting through the mill, but anybody who had philosophized, anybody who had done any writing at all. She gave out that she was going to make a clean sweep of all the old lumber and then start life again on a fresh lease. She was not unknown; not by any means; every age had called her in; but now she came in a new guise. The cause, and in particular the *causa causans*, the *final* cause? No; she had given up claiming to be that. Well then, was she a "faculty" whereby man is supposed to be distinguished from the lower animals, and wherein it is evident he greatly surpasses them? Yes; that would be acceptable enough, provided no limits were set to the operations of this faculty, provided it could go to any lengths, even the most daring. Its province was to lay down certain definite, incontrovertible principles, and then, in the light of those same principles, to deduce conclusions equally definite and incontrovertible. Its essential function was to examine, to enquire into things, and its initial task, the first item on its agenda, was to go into the question of the mysterious, the unexplained, the hidden, in order to dispel the shadows, to give a little light to

[1]François Bernier et N. Boileau Despréaux, *Requête des maîtres es arts* . . . 1671.

the world. The world was full of errors, errors born of human self-illusion and encouraged by irresponsible authority, disseminated by the favouring winds of credulity and indolence, intrenched and fortified by Time. The first thing then she had to do was to effect an enormous clearance, to get rid of that gigantic mass of error. That was what she had to do, and she was impatient to get through with it. It was a mission she took on herself, a mission which the consciousness of her own worth justified her, she considered, in undertaking.

Active, zealous, full of daring, the rationalists hastened to obey her call. From France they came, from England, from Germany and Holland, too. A Jew, but a Jew detested by the Ghetto, Spinoza put his genius at the disposal of the cause. What a motley crowd they were, hailing from the most divergent starting points, and all uniting in a single aim. It was a concentration of force that stirred the imagination.

To start with, there were the Freethinkers, English members of that brotherhood, like William Temple, who, emancipated now from the ties and the cares of office, sought solace and repose in a life of quiet, mildly Epicurean seclusion. Next, and more especially, there were the Freethinkers of France. They were not a recent growth, these Freethinkers. They had disseminated, and, in the process, diluted, at least two philosophies; the Paduan school, with Pomponazzi and Cardan, to begin with; then came Gassendi and his system, at least the non-Christian part of it. Gassendi's ideas derived from Epicurus, with his atoms and his materialistic conception of the soul, but it was an Epicurus refined upon and made more complicated. However, they attained the dignity of a philosophy, these ideas, but a philosophy not at all easy to understand, a philosophy which united the glamour of novelty with the prestige of ancient tradition. Those who professed it formed a distinct group, and gained in dignity and importance.

Gassendi having challenged Descartes, the result was a duel, with some lively exchanges. The adversaries joined battle before an audience who were keenly interested in the issue of the combat. "O *mens*! O spirit pure and immaterial!" cried Gassendi to Descartes. "Say rather, I beg of you, O flesh!" said Descartes to Gassendi.[1]

---

[1] *Petri Gassendi Disquisitio metaphysica, seu dubitationes et instantiae adversus Renati Cartesii metaphysicam, et responsa.* Amstelodami, 1644.

Gassendi got the worst of the encounter. True, he still counted some disciples; there were some in England, some in Germany, some in Switzerland, and some in Italy, but they were a scanty remnant, overshadowed, eclipsed, by the glory of Descartes, who had the whole of Europe at his feet, and soon after by Locke, a new planet in the intellectual firmament. In Paris, in the year 1674, François Bernier brought out an *Abrégé de la Philosophie de M. Gassendi*. It was very well received by the public and ran into several editions. It kept alive the influence of a doctrine which its author had received from the lips of the master himself. He praised it, but not quite with the same ardour, the same conviction as of old. He praised it, but with a qualifying "After all" which rather limited the range of his panegyric. "Gassendi's philosophy", he says, "which, after all, seems to me the most reasonable, the simplest, the most sensitive, the most understandable of them all. . . ." The dominant element in his intellectual make-up was doubt. "For more than thirty years now I've been philosophizing; about *some* things very confidently. But now I confess I am beginning to have my doubts about them." He was like Simonides, who was asked by Hiero to tell him what God was. Simonides asked for one day's grace to think it over. Next day, when Hiero repeated his question, he asked for two days more, the day after that, for four days, and so on. On Hiero expressing his astonishment thereat, Simonides confessed that the more he pondered on the matter, the more involved he found it.

These Freethinkers had no very hard and fast doctrine of their own. They were not very profound—we may as well confess it—these *dilettanti*, dinner-party philosophers. The Odes of Horace were their customary breviary. Their metaphysics did not go very far. How came they, then, to cause so much commotion among the guardians of orthodoxy? Precisely because their metaphysical sense was lacking. They are, by nature, rebels, malcontents, obstinate; their aristocratic culture did but reinforce their scepticism. They are like those little sparkling rivulets so often encountered in the intellectual field, little tributaries that go to swell the broad river of incredulity. Claiming to think for themselves, refusing to be dictated to by anyone, profound philosophers they are not, but "philosophers" all the same, for whom a mystery is merely a riddle so far unsolved, just that and nothing more. And if they can't solve it, they just ignore it.

What does it matter? They live on the margin of religion, not within it. Since shadows there are, and we cannot dispel them, let us make the most of our allotted span; let us enjoy, with taste and elegance, the pleasures it has to offer, and when the time to take our leave arrives, submit with a good grace to the will of destiny. A moral surrender, if you will, a making the best of a sorry business, but, nevertheless, a *modus vivendi* which in those days commended itself to many, and those by no means of the common herd.

Take the French freethinkers, for example. Over-refined, too delicate by half, they must needs invigorate their stock by bringing in a rougher and a tougher breed, or perish. Such a one was Jean Dehénault, who followed in the steps of Guy Patin and La Mothe Le Vayer. Like many another, he translated Lucretius, more skilfully than most, and gave melodious utterance to his mournful but monotonous negations:

> Tout meurt en nous quand nous mourons;
> La mort ne laisse rien et n'est rien elle-même;
> Du peu de temps que nous vivons
> Ce n'est que le moment extrême.
> Cesse de craindre ou d'espérer
> Cet avenir qui la doit suivre.
> Que la peur d'être éteint, que l'espoir de revivre
> Dans ce sombre avenir cessent de t'égarer.
> L'état dont la mort est suivie
> Est semblable à l'état qui précède la vie.
> Nous sommes dévorés du temps.
> La nature au chaos sans cesse nous rappelle.
> Elle entretient à nos dépens
> Sa vicissitude éternelle.
> Comme elle nous a tout donné,
> Elle aussi reprend tout notre être.
> Le malheur de mourir égale l'heur de naître,
> Et l'homme meurt entier, comme entier il est né.[1]

[1] All dies in us when we come to die; death leaves nothing behind and is nothing itself; of the short time we have to live, it is but the final moment. Fear no more, and hope no more about what follows after. Let the fear of annihilation, or the hope of living again in that sombre future mislead you no more. Your state when life is ended will be even as it was before your life began. We are the prey of all-devouring time. Nature is for ever calling us back to chaos, satisfying, at our expense, her never-ending love of change. As she gave us all, even so she takes

Such, too, was Mme. Deshoulières, and such was Ninon de Lenclos, who was convinced that she had no soul, and never abandoned that conviction, not even in advanced old age, not even at the hour of death.

However the choicest flower of them all was messire Charles de Saint-Denis, Brigadier-General in the armies of His Most Christian Majesty. In 1661, he fled to England to avoid the consequences of ministerial and royal disfavour, and thenceforth, until the day of his death in 1703, Saint-Évremond had little else to do but to live the life of the cultured sceptic. Thus he became the type and exemplar of his set, the sceptic *par excellence*. As such, he appeared to the French, who lamented his departure from their midst, and to the English who loved him, and also to the Dutch with whom he abode for some considerable time. He may have been a little old-fashioned, in his appearance as well as in some of his ideas; a man suddenly called upon, in his riper years, to change his habits and his mode of life, naturally finds it a little difficult to divest himself of the associations in which he had been brought up. That is why he never ceased to be a "gentleman" when examples of the breed were growing scarcer and scarcer about him, and when that fine type of humanity, ceasing to be a reality, was fast becoming but a memory, a tradition of a vanished age. Being a gentleman, he did not blow his own trumpet, and if he frequently took up the pen he was careful to make it clear that he did so, not as one having a lesson to impart, or presuming to lay down the law, but as a man of the world who, having an abundance of time on his hands, wanted to pass it as agreeably as possible. Those mathematics, those physics, in which the people about him were so deeply immersed, were very little to his taste. In his view, the only branches of intellectual activity which it became a gentleman to concern himself with were ethics, politics and polite letters; an attitude of mind decidedly out of date at a time when Science would soon be aiding and supplementing the work of the philosophers, and when, to hold oneself aloof from Science was to run the risk of finishing up in a backwater. Saint-Évremond took a scholar's pleasure in studying the writers of

---

all away. The doom of death balances the happy hour of birth, and man dies wholly, even as he was born.

·   Adapted from the chorus of the second act of Seneca's *Phoenissae*, Miscellaneous Works, 1670; quoted by Frédéric Lachèvre, *Les œuvres de Jean Dehénault*, 1922, p. 27.

classical antiquity, in the nice comparisons by which the discerning critic brings out the special qualities whereby the orator or
the historian lends distinction to his work, the parallels, the
portraits, all the divers directions in which a mind, naturally
acute, finds occasion for the exercise of his psychological powers.
Needless to say, he cultivated the art of conversation. When
Hortense Mancini, Duchesse de Mazarin, settled in London and
opened a salon there, a salon to which he could daily resort, he
found therein the focal point in which life for him had hitherto
been lacking. He was definitely an Epicurean, believing that of all
the views laid down by the various philosophers regarding the
summum bonum, there was none which made a more powerful
appeal to reason than the system of Epicurus. His aim was to live
according to nature, and if we are forced to admit that he had no
very clear idea as to what he meant by nature, there is no denying
that he was wonderfully successful in ensuring for himself a most
comfortably cushioned existence. Protected by the powers that
be, even when the sceptre passed from James II to William III,
parcelling out his days into a number of little regular occupations;
fond, perhaps a little too fond, of the pleasures of the table; taking
his diversions in scrupulously measured doses, the better to
appreciate their savour, he was no doubt an egoist, but a very
engaging one. The very notion of going without, of self-denial,
of mortifying the flesh, of asceticism gave him the horrors.
Moderation, restraint, a temperament naturally proof against the
fury of the passions, a delicate and discerning selfishness—all
these he looked on as necessary virtues, these, and a due attention
to bodily health, which, when we regularly enjoy it, we may be
sometimes tempted to take too much as a matter of course. On
attaining the age of seventy or thereabouts, he became troubled
with a distressing infirmity. "M. de Saint-Évremond had blue
eyes, keen and sparkling, a broad forehead, bushy eyebrows, a
shapely mouth, a quizzical smile, a lively and engaging expression, an erect and well-proportioned figure and a general air
of distinction and good-breeding. Twenty years before his
death he was troubled with a wen which made its appearance
between his eyes and increased considerably as time went on."
So we are told by des Maizeaux, his earliest biographer and
his publisher. But he took the wen philosophically. Suppose
you do get a great wen between the eyes, what matter, if you

go on living? "Better a week of life, than a week of fame after you are dead."

He was very much in love with life, which, in his own case, he managed to prolong to an advanced old age; the trying experiences of his earlier days were things of the past and life was propitious and kindly to him. That was all he asked for and, among the various epitaphs composed in his honour, this one would assuredly have pleased him:

Aimé de plus d'un roi, cher à plus d'une dame,
Il connut peu l'orgueil, peu l'amoureuse flamme:
Écrire, et bien manger, fut son double talent.
Il nourrit pour la vie un amour violent,
Connut à peine Dieu, mais point du tout son âme.[1]

A passionate love of life he certainly had, and of that which makes life worth living, namely, freedom, and of all freedoms more especially that of a mind which is a law unto itself.

But ought we to see in him a spirit of greater complexity than the foregoing implies? Are we to take it that he deliberately invented and propagated his own legend? Are we to believe that, while he wanted to appear in the eyes of the world as the typical sceptic, the real Saint-Évremond, his heart filled with longing, was far less of a doubter than he would have us believe, and that he never ceased to hope. We cannot say for certain, though that view of him has been stoutly maintained. For when deploring the miseries of this our mortal state, he asks either that we should be raised as high as the angels, or depressed as low as the beasts, it is not the God who died for him upon the Cross that he implores, and whom such an appeal would have offended, it is Nature:

Un mélange incertain d'esprit et de matière
Nous fait vivre avec trop ou trop peu de lumière,
Pour savoir justement et nos biens et nos maux.

[1] Loved by more than one king, dear to more than one lady, he felt but little pride and little of love's flame. To do some writing, to eat well, for these he had a twofold talent. He was passionately fond of life, knew little of God, and nothing of his soul.

Change l'état douteux dans lequel tu nous ranges,
Nature, élève nous à la clarté des anges,
Ou nous abaisse au sens des simples animaux . . .[1]

In any case, even if the portrait elaborately counterfeited differs
from the real man, a man with far more doubts and contradictions
in his nature, then the real man was careful to keep in the background. It was the sceptic who did the acting, who figured on
the stage. If you start on the study of his life and work expecting
to acquaint yourself with a man of grave and sober disposition
living the life of a sage, you will not get very far before you realize
that you have made a vast mistake; you will perceive, in fact, that
if you were to model your life on his, no one would ever take you
for a serious-minded philosopher indifferent to the gratification
of the senses. As touching his writings, if you expect to meet
with any profound knowledge of philosophy, or antiquity; if you
expect to find yourself in the austere company of a stoic or an
anchorite, it will soon dawn on you that you have come to the
wrong address. It may perhaps annoy you to realize that you
might read him from beginning to end without coming across a
trace of the sort of thing you expected to meet with. "A shallow
Epicurean"; such is the judgment passed on him by Jean Le Clerc
in his *Bibliothèque choisie*, when reviewing a collected edition of
his works published in Amsterdam.[2]

What, then, is to be learnt from this equivocal freethinker and
from others of his school? What has this forerunner of the New
Age got to tell us? What is there new about him? To begin with
there is some sort of suggestion of a cosmopolitan outlook on
things, and that, not merely because he took an interest in the
literature of his adopted country, not merely because he translated *Volpone*, and wrote a comedy of his own in the English
manner which he entitled *Sir Politick Would-be*, but also because
he conceived some sort of inkling of relativity, just as he conceived the idea of evolution in history. He recognized the fact
that any nation which has a way of life, a number of customs, a

---

[1] An uncertain mixture of mind and matter causes us to live with too much or too
little light to have any true notion of our good and ill. Change the dubious state
in which you keep us, Nature, and either raise us to the brightness of the angels, or
lower us to the level of mere animals. ,
  Quoted by A. M. Schmidt, *Saint-Évremond ou l'humaniste impur*, 1932, p. 141.
[2] In 1706, vol. IX.

spirit, a genius peculiarly its own represents a set of values which no other nation can possibly judge by its own yardstick. He declined to regard every foreigner as a barbarian; and the same tolerant spirit which he displayed in the sphere of ideas he extended to international relationships. Just as there is some truth in every philosophy, so also there are some valuable qualities in every nation: "To tell the truth, I have never come across people better calculated to get on together than the French, who give careful attention to the theory of what they are considering, and the English who avoid getting lost in the abstract by giving concrete expression to their ideas with an independence of mind that we should do well to imitate. The salt of the earth are the French, who do the thinking, and the English, who put the thoughts into words."

It is this comprehensive attitude that linked him up with the coming age; so, also, and still more, did the atmosphere of peace and easy tranquillity which pervaded his non-religious mind. He has not the slightest consciousness of being a rebel. With a few concessions to custom, to appearances, he settles down in his scepticism with as much peace of mind as other men find in their religion. If there were freethinkers who suffered persecution for their ideas, he was not one of them. Honour, renown were his reward. Saint-Évremond is not the freethinker militant; he is the freethinker triumphant. Do not his bones lie honourably entombed in Poets' Corner in Westminster Abbey? Above all, he personifies the trend towards a more forward, a more aggressive school of thought, a school better fitted to produce a pabulum suitable to minds athirst for novelty. During his stay in Holland, which lasted from 1666 to 1672, he became acquainted with a certain Jew whose name was Spinoza. It gave him pleasure, des Maizeaux tells us, to see "some of the famous philosophers and men of learning who were then at The Hague, particularly, Heinsius, Vossius and Spinoza". We do not know precisely what passed between them; what we do know is that, long after the interview took place, Saint-Évremond was still haunted by the memory of Spinoza. "In the humble and pensive solitary of Ryneburg and Stilla Veerkade, French libertinism, which, till now has been no more than a vague desire to be free, an impatience of rule, and a revolt against dogma, a spiritual Fronde in other words, is on the look-out for, and now thinks it has found, the required apologist for its unbelief, the right man to give a logical basis and formal expression to the aims it has most at heart."[1]

First and foremost, then, the freethinkers want to be quoted, in spite of their lack of any definite philosophical basis. They had refused point-blank to have anything to do with the *concordat* proposed by the French classical school. They flatly declined to regard any doctrine whatever as finally established. All along, their stock-in-trade had consisted of doubts and denials. Their intransigence paved the way for rebellions to come. It is an un-doubted characteristic of the controversies of the period, when people were in too much of a hurry to draw any fine distinctions between the various shades of opinion, that whenever they wanted to give an idea of the sort of people who were dangerous to religion, such as those who were given to criticizing the Gospel texts too closely, people who rejected Revelation and miracles, the deists, the atheists or those who were merely indifferent, they lumped them all together under a single label and called them "libertins".

But it is also no less true that the "libertins" could not stand on their own feet, and that they were obliged to seek the support of a philosophical system more coherent and more stable than their own. If one of the meanings of the word "libertin" signified a person who had no religious belief, another denoted one who was living a life of gross self-indulgence; if the word con-noted two such different sorts of freedom, freedom of thought and freedom to wallow in the sensual sty, the time was coming when these two types of freedom would be put in their respective places. The sceptics were on the look-out for a new philosophy to replace their pinchbeck and threadbare Gassendi-ism. In Voltaire they were to discover something at once different from, and more than, a "libertin". The hedonists clamoured for

[1]Gustave Cohen, *Le Séjour de Saint-Évremond en Hollande et l'entrée de Spinoza dans le Champ de la pensée française*, 1926. Dehénault undertook the journey to Holland for the express purpose of meeting Spinoza. He was a man of brains and learning, taking his pleasures with taste and refinement and his grosser indulgencies with a certain amount of delicacy and art. But he suffered under the greatest handicap a man could possibly have: he plumed himself on his atheism, he bragged about it, and flaunted it abroad with detestable flamboyance and affectation. He had elaborated three separate theories about the immortality of the soul and went to Holland on purpose to propound them to Spinoza who, however, formed no great opinion of his learning. (Dubos to Bayle, 27 April, 1696; in *Choix de la Correspondance de Pierre Bayle*, by E. Gigas, 1890.)

grosser, more unbridled sensuality; they wallowed more openly in debauchery, grew more blatantly cynical. Under the Regency there was no attempt to strike a balance between the mind and the senses, but much rather a deliberate determination to flaunt every kind of excess. The *roués* were more conspicuous for the indecency of their behaviour than for the independence of their minds. La Fare and Chaulieu mark the transition, especially Chaulieu, who held that wine and women were the principal boons which we owe to a wise and beneficent Nature, and who, in reply to some verses of his friend Malézieux, delivered himself of the following profession of faith:

> Pour répondre à tes chansons,
> Il faudrait de la Nature
> De Lucrèce ou d'Épicure
> Emprunter quelques raisons;
> Mais sur l'essence divine
> Je haïs leur témérité,
> Et je n'aime leur doctrine
> Que touchant la Volupté.
>
> Je suis cet attrait vainqueur,
> Ce doux penchant de mon âme
> Que grava d'un trait de flamme
> Nature au fond de mon cœur;
> Dans une sainte mollesse
> J'écoute tous mes désirs;
> Et je crois que la sagesse
> Est le chemin des plaisirs . . .[1]

The word itself was in process of changing its connotation and we must now draw a distinction. We must talk of "*libertins d'esprit*,"[2] if we are to avoid confounding the free-thinkers with

[1]To reply to your songs it would be necessary to borrow a few arguments from Nature as described by Lucretius or Epicurus; but as touching the divine essence I hate their temerity, I only like their teaching when they treat of Pleasure. I follow that triumphant attraction, that sweet inclination of my soul which Nature with a stroke of fire engraved in the depths of my heart. In a state of blessed acquiescence I give ear to all my desires; I believe that wisdom tells us to follow the path of pleasure.

[2]Pierre Bayle, *Dictionnaire*, article *Arcesilas*: "The real principles which regulate our moral conduct have so little to do with the speculative conclusions we form regarding the nature of things, that nothing is more common than to see orthodox Christians living evil lives and freethinkers living good ones."

the free-livers; while those who declare for Deism and other similar brands of unbelief refer to themselves as *"esprits forts"*, or intellectuals *par excellence*.[1]

Nulla nunc celebrior, clamorosiorque secta quam Cartesianorum, loudly asserts a contemporary writer in a work bearing the significant title *Historia rationis*.[2] And it is a fact that, by the end of the century, Descartes had become King. But his sway was not unlimited, for there is not, and never has been, such a thing as an absolute monarchy in the realms of the intellect. There is a certain national or racial element that persists in clinging to every philosophy no matter how impersonal and abstract, an abiding and inalienable note, or characteristic. Descartes never succeeded in ousting that stubborn *residuum* which gives to the Englishman or to the Italian his unmistakable national character. It was only when, and in so far as, speculation was raised to the universal plane, that Descartes established his ascendancy. There was not a Frenchman who, if he thought about such things at all, was not to some extent affected by him; and that is true even of his opponents; nor was there a single foreigner of note who was not indebted to him, if only for stimulating him to think, to philosophize on his own account. Locke made no secret of the debt he owed him; Spinoza began his writing career with an account of the Cartesian system, and probably no one had a profounder understanding of the Master's philosophy than he. When, a little later on, Vico sought to endow his country with a philosophy that should be essentially Italian, the adversary with whom he had to measure swords was not Aristotle, now dethroned, but Descartes, who reigned in his stead. Descartes' philosophy was officially taught in Dutch schools, and from Holland it was imported into Hungary by students returning thither after finishing their course at the Universities of Leyden, The Hague, Amsterdam, Utrecht and Franeker. It was his teaching which Germany took up, with the idea of freeing herself from the trammels of Scholasticism. Here again, if the intensity of the impact is to be measured by the vehemence of the reaction it provokes, it is significant that no less a person than the great Leibniz himself made it his business to refute the philosophy of Descartes. At

[1]Pierre Bayle, *Pensées sur la Comète*, § CXXXIX.
[2]*Historia Rationis*, author D.P.D.J.U.D. (P. Collet), 1685, Art. XIII, p. 107.

first denounced, put on the index, persecuted, condemned, the disciples of Descartes, when fifty years are passed, are appointed to learned professorships, deliver lectures, bring out books. Theirs are the honours now; *they* wield the sceptre.

When a system of philosophy has attained such wide currency as to be familiar to people who have never put it into practice, when people who have never read the books in which it is expounded are influenced by it all the same, it may be safely assumed that it has shed a good many of its riches on the way, and that the only operative part remaining is that essential core which has been permanently incorporated into the human heritage. The pineal gland, in which he deemed the soul was lodged; those robots or mechanical animals insensible alike to pain and pleasure, the "plein"; the whirlpools; the physics, and even the metaphysics, of Descartes had fallen by the wayside. What, then, of essential significance survived? His spirit; his method—a lasting acquisition, that—his rules for guiding the operations of the mind, so simple, yet withal so powerful, that even if they did not illuminate the whole domain of truth, they at all events caused some of the shadows to recede.

Reliance on reason as a sure means of arriving at certitude, "the movement which proceeds from within to without, from subjective to objective, from psychological to ontological, from affirmation of the consciousness to affirmation of the substance",[1] such were the inalienable values which Descartes bequeathed to his successors of the second and third generation. Hear what Fontenelle has to say on the matter: "He, in my opinion, it is to whom we are indebted for this new method of reasoning, a method far more valuable than his actual philosophy, a good deal of which, judged by his own rules, is either doubtful, or definitely unsound".

And now Reason breaks loose and there's no holding her any longer. Tradition, authority are nothing to her; "What harm," she says, "in wiping the slate clean and beginning things all over again?" Of the concrete she intends to make a clean sweep. The talisman, the magic word which was to pull up forces when they looked like getting out of hand and running into danger; the word of warning which the wise master had so promptly and so prudently pronounced, his apprentices knew nothing of, and if

[1] Menéndez y Pelayo, *Historia de las ideas esteticas, Siglo* XVIII. *Introducción.*

they had, they would have declined to heed it. Heaven was theirs, and earth was theirs; theirs was the whole domain of the knowable. There was nothing, they thought, nothing in the whole universe which the geometrical mind could not grasp. Theology, too, was their business. A certain professor of mathematics, one Jean Jacob Scheuchzer, belauding the geometrical mind in its dealings with theology,[1] quotes with proud and grateful satisfaction from Fontenelle's Preface to his *Histoire de l'Académie royale des sciences depuis le règlement fait en* 1699. "The geometrical method is not so rigidly confined to geometry itself that it cannot be applied to other branches of knowledge as well. A work on politics, on morals, a piece of criticism, even a manual on the art of public speaking would, other things being equal, be all the better for having been written by a geometrician. The order, the clarity, the precision and the accuracy which have distinguished the worthier kind of books for some time past now, may well have been due to the geometrical method which has been continuously gaining ground, and which somehow or other has an effect on people who are quite innocent of geometry. It sometimes happens that a great thinker gives the keynote to the whole of his century. He to whom the distinction of endowing us with a new method of reasoning may most justly be awarded was himself an accomplished geometrician." No more was needed. The wheel had come full circle; Descartes the geometrician had called the tune for the new era. But what if the geometrical mind collides head on with religion? What will happen if it is applied wholesale to matters of faith? It would mean putting the sponge over the religious slate; every religion would be wiped out.[2]

Was there ever a more singular example of the way in which after a while a doctrine may develop ideas completely at variance with those with which it started? The truth of that has been demonstrated with an insight so unerring that we need do no more here than offer it the tribute of our admiring recognition.[3] To the cause of religion, the Cartesian philosophy came bringing what seemed a most valuable support, to begin with. But that same philosophy bore within it a germ of irreligion which time was to bring to light, and which acts and works and is made

[1]*Praelectio de Matheseos usu in theologia habita a Jh. Jacobo Scheuchzero. Med. D. Math. P.*, Tiguri, 1711.
[2]*Nouvelles de la République des Lettres*, Nov. 1684, Art. I.
[3]G. Lanson, *Etudes d'histoire littéraire*, 1930.

deliberate use of to sap and undermine the foundations of belief. One thing the Cartesian philosophy established as a certitude; to the sceptic's "No" it replied with a resounding "Yes"; it demonstrated the existence of God, the immateriality of the soul; it distinguished thought from extension, the noble idea from mere sensation; it registered the triumph of will over instinct; in short, it was a bulwark against the freethinkers. But now, lo and behold! it is actually comforting and aiding them; for examination, enquiry, criticism are the very things it insists upon. It must have evidence even in matters which authority had aforetime ruled to be outside the laws of evidence; it laid rude hands on the temporary structure it had erected to give shelter to religion. Whether you would or no, and provided you did not wilfully blink the truth, you could not fail to see what it would ultimately lead to; it would lead to the calling in question not only of dogmas but of the very basis on which the dogmatic principle reposes. Thus Aristotle had been driven from the field: "The poor Peripatetics and the disciples of Aristotle must be feeling themselves in a very disagreeable quandary when they perceive that the Eternal Word has turned Cartesian in its later years . . ."[1] But wait a while and you will see to what a pass the Cartesian line of thought will bring you: "You would be not a little astonished if Descartes were to come back to earth to-day. I fancy you would see in him the most redoubtable enemy of Christianity."[2]

Against this antagonism, which became more and more acute as time went on, one man fought with all the strength at his command, and that was Malebranche, who, throughout his life, never wavered in the belief that "religion is the true philosophy."

Malebranche bears a striking resemblance to the philosopher of popular imagination: he is never really at home save in the regions of the Infinite; ideas are his staple food; his material needs are almost negligible. If there had been no such thing as metaphysics before his time, he would assuredly have invented them. A queer yet engaging physiognomy was his, simple and ordinary enough at a first glance, but on closer inspection not a little intriguing. His constitution was delicate and his health

[1] Jurieu, *L'esprit de M. Arnauld*, 1684, p. 78.
[2] L. A. Caraccioli, *Dialogue entre le siècle de Louis XIV et le siècle de Louis XV*, 1751, p. 39.

uncertain. Fontenelle, who looked on him as a quaint and amusing specimen of humanity, pawkily remarked that, with Malebranche, the feelings prompted what the will enjoined, so that, for once in a way, desire and duty, the flesh and the spirit, found themselves pulling in the same direction. Fearful of the world and its ways, bewildered at life, he sought peace and seclusion in the Congregation of the Oratory. There, he shrank from the responsibilities of office and the burden of honours, and it was with genuine humility of spirit that he chose the lowliest of duties. He was rich, but he divested himself of his riches by bestowing them on others. He had at least some of the virtues that go to the making of a saint. Open-hearted and utterly guileless as he was, he was subtle, too, and stubbornly determined. Nothing in the world would have induced him to abandon his ideas; when they provoked difficulties, he had a way, peculiarly his own, of plunging into still more difficulties, till at length the tangle became inextricable; then he was elated.

One day he fell in with the Cartesian philosophy. It was as though the scales had suddenly fallen from his eyes. Till then, he had had no clear idea of where he was going; the path had been uncertain before him. But from that day forth, he hesitated no longer. He would be a Cartesian and a Christian, at one and the same time. If there were discrepancies, he would adjust them. That day, the road he was to take was decided on, once and for all.

Much time he spent in prolonged and concentrated meditation, and then, at last, when he deemed that he could add no more to his ideas, he incorporated them in two big volumes on metaphysics which, on their publication, caused nothing less than a sensation. Fame now came to him as it were unbidden, and a very dazzling fame it was; so dazzling that at this distance of time it is not easy to realize its brilliance. Its rays penetrated far beyond the frontiers of his own country, and it lasted longer than his life. He had his army of readers, his devoted disciples, his fanatical admirers. A Neapolitan seminarist, one Bernardo Lama, shook the dust of Italy from his feet, and hastened with what speed he might to Paris, that he might have speech of the famous Malebranche. Essentially a man of peace, and in no wise given to quarrelling, his ideas elicited rejoinders so numerous and refutations so passionate, and he answered them with such zest and thoroughness, with such fierce conviction, that he seemed to be living in the thick of an everlasting battle. From that bare and austere cell in which he immured himself to think his thoughts, cut off from social intercourse, heedless of the charms of nature, there issued forth, with a resounding flourish, what he referred to as "This last essay towards a liberal Christian philosophy," and this final effort, characterized as it was by all the vigour of a mind that loved to play for the highest stakes, moved the hearts of men, and became an outstanding landmark in the history of ideas.

Rational evidence: such is the perfect light whereunto Malebranche aspires, with all the fervour of a mystic, for in him mysticism went hand in hand with the cult of reason. In all piety of spirit he endeavours to fulfil his aim, namely, that individual life and cosmic life, life as one indivisible whole, should be seen as the realization of an order in which religious faith is at once included and explained.

Now, when we look out upon the world, we see there, side by side with a generally prevailing order, some disconcerting breaches of the same. There are distorted and monstrous shapes presented to the view which betoken the existence of physical evil; while the existence of sin proclaims evil in the moral order. These anomalies it is the business of the philosopher to explain.

If we suppose a world in which nothing contrary to the general order is ever to occur, in which every soul on the brink of sinning is either to resist the temptation, or, having yielded to it, is to obtain the grace necessary for its redemption, we shall have to postulate a God prepared to intervene at any given moment, prepared at any time to go out of his way to work a miracle, in other words to interfere with the very laws which he himself has declared inviolable. The countless breaches of the general order would need to be met by special divine interventions no less multitudinous than themselves.

Here it is that Malebranche, who refused to believe that the Almighty would put himself to such endless trouble as these constant interventions would involve, comes on the scene to inform us that God acts by way of general laws, and not by special *ad hoc* enactments to suit each individual case. God must needs follow the path of wisdom, because He is Himself Supreme Wisdom. God loves wisdom with invincible love; because it is

at once natural and necessary that He should so love it. He cannot
fail to adopt the course of action which exhibits the visible signs
of His own attributes, a course of action which is at once rational
and consistent.

The rain falls on the field which needs water in order that it
may bring forth fruit; but it falls likewise on the highway, and
on the river, and on the sea: whereat we marvel. But which of the
two lines of action is the more closely consonant with reason; to
interfere every time it rains in order to restrict the area affected
by the downpour, or to suffer the general law of motion to
operate without let or hindrance. If this latter mode is the more
logical and the more befitting, then God cannot do other than
adopt it.

True, God desires not the damnation of this unbeliever, or of
that transgressor; but He cannot be perpetually intervening to
instil the faith into each and every unbeliever, or righteousness
into the heart of each and every sinner, for this would be a mode
of action incompatible with the idea of an All-wise and Infinitely
Perfect Being; whence it would follow that salvation of the
world could never be accomplished.

The utmost that God can do is to establish occasional causes:
ministers, that is to say, who act as His deputies, and whose
functions are unalterably defined. Jesus Christ is established by
His Father as the sole occasional cause of all grace of every kind,
which He causes to be outpoured on all for whom He makes
special supplication, all of whom will attain salvation without the
Father having been called upon to intervene in each or in any
particular case. And Jesus Christ must needs pray as the rule of
order requires Him, according, that is to say, as the spiritual
edifice which God designs to raise, has need of further living
stones. God obeys this same principle of simplification, of
economy of means, because it is logical, because it is the truth and
the life.

Such was Malebranche's line of argument. Wherever a divergence threatens between philosophy and religion, whether it has
to do with transubstantiation or with some disputed passage in the
Scriptures, he hastens away to set things right, to explain: allow,
he would say, an ampler scope to reason; cultivate a better appreciation of the value and power of order, and all will become as
clear as daylight; harmony will be restored. His dexterity is

boundless; his *tours de force* partake of the miraculous; one upon another, he poises his airy castles of ideas, and, since by a miracle, they do not topple down, he takes that unstable equilibrium as proof that they are founded on a rock. The only thing is, he does not see that, by making God subservient to that all-powerful Order of his, that all-conquering Reason, that remorselessly logical Wisdom, he despoils Him at a stroke of His prerogatives and of His *raison d'être*; either God is merely an agent, or He is the universe taking shape in accordance with ineluctable law. Therefore involuntarily, and despite his declared intention, despite his miracles of dialectical acrobatics, the most Christian Malebranche lays himself open to the charge of preaching an anti-Christian doctrine. "You did not see", said Fénelon in his *Réfutation*, "that what you were really doing was subordinating religion to philosophy, and aiding and abetting the Socinians in their attacks on our mysteries". Nay, one of his admirers even, Pierre Bayle himself, who calls Père Malebranche and M. Arnauld the two greatest philosophers in the world (a somewhat ominous compliment) and who sees in the *Traité de la Nature et de la Grâce* "a work of soaring genius and one of the noblest examples of human intellectual endeavour", even Bayle is under no illusion as to where these metaphysical theories will ultimately lead. "What it really amounts to is this; Malebranche takes it that God's goodness and power are confined within more or less restricted limits, that God has no freedom of action, that His own wisdom compels Him, first, to create, then to create this and not that, and finally to create it in this particular way, and in no other. Here, then, we have three inescapable conditions which together make up a *fatum*, a Fate, more relentless than any the Stoics ever conceived. . . ." Whereupon Bayle enunciates two syllogisms, telling us that the minor premises of the first, and the major of the second give an accurate definition of the doctrine of Père Malebranche:

Here, then, is syllogism No. 1.

God cannot will anything repugnant to the love He must necessarily have for His own wisdom;

Now, the salvation of all mankind is repugnant to the love which God must have for His own wisdom;

Therefore God cannot will the salvation of all mankind.

And here is syllogism No. 2.

The worthiest work of God's wisdom includes among other things the sinful nature of mankind and the eternal damnation of the greater number of them;

Now, God must necessarily will what is most worthy of His wisdom;

Therefore, He must necessarily will that which includes among other things the sinful nature of mankind and the eternal damnation of the greater number of them.[1]

What an ironic turn of fortune! Here is a man, not only pious and devout but profoundly Catholic, Catholic in all the multi-farious manifestations of his active life, Catholic to the inmost core of his being, yet here is this same man assigning to Reason such a transcendent rôle that she would appear to draw everything, even God Himself, into her bosom.

We had our contemporaries as far back as Louis XIV's time, remarked Diderot, referring to himself and his brother philo-sophers. And he was quite right; he had contemporaries under Louis XIV, not only in the later years of the *Grand Monarque* when, as we know, the social and political fabric was beginning to totter, but long before that, when we are commonly wont to see Orthodoxy enthroned in solitary state, and the splendours, as yet undimmed, of regal majesty. The truth is, however, that it was just when the power of Church and State appeared unshakable that their foundations were showing signs of giving way. If we only look at the literature, and particularly the French literature, that appeared between 1670 and 1677, we shall come away with an unclouded impression of sovereign might, and peace, and grandeur. *Les Femmes savantes* goes back to 1672, and *Le Malade Imaginaire* to 1673. Racine gave us *Bajazet* in 1672, *Mithridate* in 1673, *Iphigénie* in 1674, *Phèdre* in 1677. It was in 1670 that Bossuet pronounced his funeral oration over Henrietta Maria, and was appointed tutor to the Dauphin, for whose edifi-cation he was in due time to compose his *Traité de la connaissance de Dieu et de soi-même*, his *Politique tirée de l'Ecriture sainte*, his *Discours sur l'Histoire universelle*. Boileau's *Art poétique* belongs to the year 1674. This array of literary works was not merely dazzling,

[1] *Réponse aux questions d'un provincial*, vol. III, ch. CLI.

it was compact, it was firm, and it was evenly balanced. But let us turn from literature for a moment, from a literature which is so fascinating that, often much to our loss, it prevents us from perceiving influences at work even more potent than itself, influences to which it will itself become subservient later on. Let us now take a glance at the main currents of philosophical speculation. There we shall discern movements, already fully under way, which are tending to disintegrate the established order even before it has reached the stage of final development. One is reminded of a tree that still goes on blooming and bearing fruit, after its roots have begun to wither.

We must not lose sight of the fact that the *Tractatus theologico-politicus* appeared as far back as 1670, and that, of new and startling ideas, it contained quite enough to cause a terrible commotion in the social order on which it descended. Spinoza, in his Latin, blandly declared that a clean sweep would have to be effected of all traditional beliefs, and a fresh start made from the very beginning. Things, he said, had come to such a pass now that you couldn't tell a Christian from a Jew, or a Turk or a Heathen. Religious belief, he declared, no longer had the slightest effect on conduct; the soul had begun to fester. The trouble, according to him, was all attributable to the fact that religion was no longer an inward thing, something deeply pondered on and then spontaneously embraced, but purely and simply a matter of external observance, of mechanical practices and of blind obedience to the priesthood. Ambitious men had wormed their way into the sacerdotal office and substituted sordid greed for brotherly love, and the result was envy, hatred, malice, and all uncharitableness. Of the Christian religion, all that remained was a soulless formalism and a blind credulity which turned men into brute beasts by denying them the exercise of their own judgment, and extinguishing the light of human reason. Reason must be the starting-point of the new quest. In the name of Reason, a clearance would have to be made of two cities, one the City Celestial, the other the City Royal, both illogical, both fraught with disaster.

The Scriptures: the Scriptures were constantly being quoted by those who wanted to exact obedience. From the Scriptures were derived all dogmas, all superstitious beliefs and practices. And what precisely were the Scriptures? Prophets! Never had they existed, those mouthpieces of God, writing the words which He dictated to them. What were they, these so-called prophets, but a few fallible mortals who, beneath a vivid imagination and a gift for glowing metaphor, concealed the poverty of their own ideas? There was never any chosen race specially set apart to be the perpetual trustees of God's law; only a people which, like all other peoples, had its day and perished. Miracles there had never been. Inasmuch as Nature followed uninterruptedly an immutable order, any violation of that order would prove, not that God was mighty, but that He did not exist. If we divest the Scriptures of all the glosses which have been superimposed upon them so as to make them appear something different from what they really are, if we interpret them by the rules of criticism which we apply to all other writings, their real nature will be apparent; we shall see them as the work of human hands, full of doubts, contradictions and errors. Moses could not have been the author of the Pentateuch, nor can the books of Joshua, Judges, Ruth, Samuel and Kings be regarded as authentic; and so on. Thus Spinoza, making sure of every step he took, pausing whenever it seemed necessary to see whether his followers were duly coming along behind, arrived at length at his initial conclusion, which was, that the Christian religion was nothing but an historical phenomenon, whose striking character was to be accounted for by the peculiar nature of the times which witnessed its birth, and by the circumstances which prolonged its influence. Nevertheless, it was essentially transitory, not eternal; relative, not absolute.

So much for Christianity. Spinoza next trained his guns upon the kings, and proceeded to show that they had always made a great fuss about religion because it was in their own interest to do so. The monarchical form of government made an art of deceit by investing with the glamour of religion the awe on which the powerful rely to keep the masses in permanent subjection. What the people call loyalty to the throne means, in plain language, playing into the hands of the king. They imagine they are fighting for themselves, when the truth of the matter is, they are merely forging fetters for themselves. They shed their life's blood in order to buttress the power and exalt the pride of a single individual, who uses them as tools to secure his own ends, and, by robbing them of their freedom, robs them of all that makes life worth living. If they wish to escape from these servile conditions, they have but one course open to them, and that is to apply to the nature and aim of political institutions the same spirit of free and independent enquiry which enabled them to give the death-blow to superstition; and to achieve that end, let them begin by thinking freely for themselves. If they do, they will see that the State is not made for the despot, that political power rightly understood is the delegation of authority carried out with the free consent of the people, that democracy is the form of govern-ment which is most closely consonant with natural law, and that, whatever may be said about the matter, the primary object of political institutions is to guarantee to the individual freedom of conscience, freedom of speech and freedom of action.

If we bear in mind what must have been the explosive poten-tialities of this sort of doctrine in the year 1670, it will not be surprising to learn that Spinoza was regarded by his contem-poraries as the Arch-iconoclast, the Destroyer *par excellence*, the Accursed One. This Jew, this spawn of a hated race by whom he himself was reviled and spat upon, this abnormal creature who lived like a hermit, caring not a jot for pleasure, or money, or public esteem, who did nothing all day but polish his lenses and think, think, think, was an object of mingled curiosity, amazement and repulsion. His name was Benedictus, but Maledictus would have been nearer the mark. He was the Thorn, even one of those thorns which spring up in the field that has fallen under the curse of God. It was the Italian Renaissance which had given birth to Atheism, the Italian Renaissance which had called back Paganism from the grave. Machiavelli had helped to spread it abroad; so, likewise, had Aretino, and Vanini. Lord Herbert of Cherbury and Hobbes had been its champions, and now here, to join them, was the most unholy of them all—Spinoza![1]

Nowadays, it is among the builders, far rather than among the destroyers, that he would be assigned a place, and among the very busiest of those builders. Against the allegation that he pulled down without building up, he himself most vehemently protested; and it is a fact that the *Tractatus* cannot be properly understood unless we realize the positive vein that runs right

[1] *De tribus impostoribus magnis liber, cura editus Christiani Kortholti, S. Theo. D. et Professoris Primarii*, Kilonii, 1680.

through it. More striking still, the *Ethic*, which appeared post-humously in 1677, introduces us to a sort of palace, a palace wrought of concepts so aspiring they seem like a vaulted roof soaring up as though to mingle with the heavens. Geometrical, no doubt, but tremulous throughout with the breath of life itself, the *Ethic* is woven of tissues both human and divine, making of the two a single category, and over its portals are engraven the words, God is All and All is God. The supreme daring of the author lay in the structural design of the building which those who are lacking in the metaphysical sense will always find some difficulty in following. Spinoza displays his plans, his theorems, his deductions; he explains them as follows: I understand by the cause of a thing, something whose essence envelops its existence, or something whose nature cannot be conceived as non-existent. By substance I mean something that exists in itself and is conceived through itself, that is to say something of which the concept can be formed without there being any need of the concept of anything else. By attribute I mean that which reason conceives in the substance as constituting its essence. There exists a unique substance constituted by an infinite number of attributes of which each expresses an eternal and infinite essence: God. All that is, is in God, and nothing can be, or be conceived, apart from God. God is thought; God is extension, and man, body and soul, is a mode of Being. As such, he tends to persevere in his being by an effort which, when it applies to the soul is called will; when it applies to the body, appetite; and when the soul takes cognizance of the effort, desire, so that desire becomes the fundamental element in the moral life.

Thenceforward all established values are upset. Men had always taken themselves as their starting point, their transitory appearance, their habits, their failings, their faults, their vices, and by a ridiculous twist of their complacent imagination had made themselves a god in their own image—greedy, selfish, open to flattery, vindictive, cruel. But he, Spinoza, took quite a different line; he started with God, and into that rational God he re-integrated man. Man was no longer an *imperium in imperio*; he was merged henceforth in the universal order. By the same token the problem of evil no longer presented itself. "All that is, is for the same reason, a necessary expression of the divine essence; every force that acts is, in the measure in which it acts, a manifestation of the divine power; wherefore, God being absolute good, each creature has as much right as power, every deed, being attached by the same bond of necessity to the being of God, is fulfilled with the like lawfulness."[1]

The problem of freedom presented itself otherwise; of the liberty of indifference there could no longer be any question, but only of the progressive assimilation of the thought to a substance which understands that it is no longer pre-ordained to act save through itself. A man is a slave when he is powerless to govern and restrain his passions; but, an inclination ceasing to be passive as soon as we form a clear and distinct idea of it, man becomes free when he is capable of directing and controlling his bodily appetites as his understanding directs, and of subordinating them to the love of God.

The pursuit of happiness also took on another significance, and, changing its road, at length reached its goal. Happiness does not consist in the gratification of the passions, as some grosser natures, who do not aspire to the loftier heights of knowledge, believe to be the case. Neither is it the renunciation of all the pleasures of this world in expectation of a paradise to come as, under one form or another, the various religions suppose. Happiness consists in understanding truth; in adherence to the laws of the universal order, and in the consciousness, in one's own particular instance, of having done so. In his own case Spinoza believes that he has attained that happy state, which is the bringer of peace; he looks with compassion on poor, erring humanity, and he points out the practical effect which his philosophy is bound to have on the conduct of life:

"I. According to this theory, we act only through the will of God, we share in the divine nature, and this participation increases as our actions approach perfection, and our knowledge of God grows more complete. Such a doctrine, in addition to bringing perfect tranquillity to the mind, has this further advantage, in that it shows us wherein our sovereign felicity consists, that is to say, in the knowledge of God, which knowledge leads us to act only as love and our duty towards God may direct. II. Our system . . . teaches us to await, and to bear with equanimity, whatever of good or of ill fortune may have in store for us. The truth is that all things are brought to pass by God's eternal law

[1]Léon Brunschvicg, *Spinoza et ses contemporains*, 3rd edn., 1923, p. 105.

with the same absolute necessity as that which ordains that the
sum of the three angles of a triangle are together equal to two
right angles. III. Another respect in which our system is beneficial to social life is that it teaches us to refrain from hatred or
contempt, and to make no man a target for mockery, envy, or
wrath. Furthermore, it teaches every man to be content with
what he has, and to render aid to others, not from a womanish
sense of pity, nor from partiality, nor from superstition, but
solely because his reason bids him."[1]

He who ensures for himself a place in heaven is no longer the
god-fearing man who cleanses himself from the stain of original
sin and wins his way aloft by his good works—not he, but the
Sage, the philosopher:

"The principles I have laid down bring out clearly the lofty
character of the Philosopher. . . . It is hardly possible that his
spirit should be troubled. Possessing by virtue of a kind of
eternal necessity knowledge of himself, of God and of things in
general he never ceases to be, and true peace of the spirit is his for
all eternity."[2]

But the wisdom he has in mind is no cheap, commonplace
brand, easily acquired, but something that surpasses the stoicism
of the Stoics themselves. Harmonious, and not to be won
without a struggle, it is worthy to rival Christianity. And so we
might have looked for a grand intellectual trial of strength
between the two opposing champions, the Christian and the Sage.
If, as has been truly pointed out, Pascal's *Pensées* and Spinoza's
Ethics furnish "the most perfect description of the goals towards
which the two ideals, religion on the one hand, philosophy on the
other, respectively direct their efforts,"[3] what a noble contest we
might have witnessed between these two conceptions of life,
these two attitudes of mind, these rival sovereignties.

But Pascal, as we have already remarked, had no disciples, and
Baruch Spinoza, as an architect of ideas, was not, for the time
being at any rate, sufficiently understood. He will have his
revenge later on. The time will come when the German metaphysicians will take their cue from him, and when the appearance
of the *Ethics* will be looked back upon as one of the great

[1] *Ethics*, part II, *Of the soul.*
[2] *Ethics*, part V, *Of the Soul's Freedom.*
[3] Léon Brunschvicg, *loc. cit.*, chap XIV, p. 150.

landmarks in the history of the West.[1] But we had not arrived at that point in 1677. The time was not ripe. The nutriment was too strong. If the *Tractatus* was better understood than the *Ethics*, it would have been on its negative side, as an instrument of destruction.

These ideas of Spinoza—what crowds of people attacked them without knowing what they were about, without studying them, without so much as troubling to glance at them! Even among those who did make some sort of an effort, how many had a sufficient grasp of them to discuss them intelligently, to do anything more than utter vain words of protestation! The Cartesians at any rate, his intellectual kinsfolk, would, one might have thought, have given him a hospitable reception. But no, it was precisely those ideas which made them so uncomfortable and caused them to shut the door in his face. They found this cousin of theirs too embarrassing by half, and blushed for him. More vigorously than Bekker, the author of *le Monde enchanté*, who repudiated him, more trenchantly than Jean Le Clerc who dubbed him "the most notorious atheist of our day", Malebranche refused to have anything whatever to do with him, vehemently denying a charge which his adversaries took a malicious delight in laying at his door, and from which his friends thought it incumbent on them to defend him. On at least two occasions, in 1683, in his *Méditations chrétiennes*, and again in 1685, in his *Entretiens sur la métaphysique et sur la religion*, he speaks of the injustice done, not only to his religion but to his philosophy, by people who likened his ideas to those professed by "the wretched Spinoza".

Bayle was obsessed by Spinoza. He frequently refers to him by name. Time and time again, when disinterring some bygone heresy, he remarked on the resemblance it bore to the views of Spinoza. He could not help admiring the man, the man who did not willingly brook interference in matters of conscience, who had had the courage to express freely and openly what he thought and believed, and who, having lived a worthy life, had departed from it without recanting. To have been the first to reduce atheism to a system, to have given it definite doctrinal form, to have integrated and inter-related its several parts, after the

[1]Léon Brunschvicg, *Le progrès de la conscience dans la philosophie occidentale*, 1927, p. 188.

manner of the geometricians, all this was by no means calculated
to evoke Pierre Bayle's disapproval. Far from it. Still there was
one point in Spinoza's metaphysic which did repel him. If he
describes his teaching as the most monstrous hypothesis anyone
could possibly imagine, the most irrational, the most diametri-
cally opposed to the clearest deductions of human reason, it was
not that he was trying to give that teaching a wider currency
while pretending to denounce it. His antagonism was sincere; it
crops up too often to be regarded as a ruse, as a move in the game.
Not so; his wrath, his indignation were thoroughly genuine. He
himself was profoundly preoccupied with the problem of evil.
Nothing had ever been more present to his mind, but, of all the
solutions ever dreamt of, Spinoza's struck him as the worst.
What! Are we to regard the Infinite as producing within himself
all the follies, all the aberrations, all the crimes of the human race?
He is to be not only the cause efficient, but the passive subject
thereof. He is to mingle with them in the most intimate union
the mind can conceive. For it is a penetrative union, or rather
it is an actual identity, since the mode is not really distinct from
the substance modified. "That men should hate one another,
that they should spring out of a thicket and murder one another,
that they should range themselves in armies to butcher one
another, that the victors should sometimes make a meal off the
vanquished—all that one can understand because men are, we
suppose, different from one another, and because 'What is yours'
and 'What is mine' excite warring passions among them. But if
men are but modes of one and the same being, if the God that
changes himself into a Turk is one and the same as the God that
changes himself into an Hungarian, then, that there should be
wars and battles between them, is the most outrageous idea ever
thought of, surpassing the wildest ravings of the craziest brain
that ever found a home in a madhouse."[1]

If we look about for a philosopher capable of standing up to
Spinoza on equal terms, capable of understanding his *Ethics* and
of countering his ideas with a reasoned refutation based on a
philosophy of his own, we shall find but one, and he was Leibniz.
The *Tractatus*, however, was another matter; no need to be terribly learned to understand that, at least the gist of it, and to quarry
it for stones to throw at the Bible, and at the royal power. Hence,

[1]Bayle, *Dictionnaire*, article *Spinoza*.

in defiance of the censorship, masquerading under borrowed names, the wide circulation it attained; hence, the bitter criticisms it provoked; hence, too, and in freedom-loving Holland, its denunciation to the authorities, and its formal condemnation.

This explains the widely divergent estimates that have come down to us regarding the nature and scope of his influence. Arnauld has it that the freethinking school got all their ideas from Spinoza. Jurieu retorted that not ten unbelievers in a million ever so much as heard of him. Dubos declares that to read Spinoza, and to get at his meaning, one must have a vast deal of stamina; that is why your freethinker makes the most of this world, without troubling himself about the next, or about Spinoza. Fénelon is of the same opinion; whoever may have been the freethinkers' favourite author in his day, he gives us plainly to understand that it was not Spinoza. On the other hand we find Père Lamy declaring that the number of Spinoza's followers increases every day: many are the members of the younger generation that have had their heads turned by his erroneous teaching; someone who ought to know what is going on in the world has told him so for a fact. Contradictory witnesses, and all of them telling the truth. Of disciples, in the strict sense of the word, Spinoza had scarcely any, outside Holland and Germany. "Very few people are suspected of sharing his doctrines and of those, few have seriously studied them, and of those who have, fewer still have grasped his meaning and not been put off by the obscurities and incomprehensible abstractions which they are called upon to encounter. But the truth of the matter is this: by and large, everyone who has little religion in him, or none at all, and doesn't much care who knows it, is dubbed a Spinozist."[1]

He betook himself to the freethinkers to fire their audacity and urge them to revolt. And he betook himself to the Italian unbelievers; for such there were; you get a hint of him in the pages of a rebel like Count Alberto di Passerano who attacked religion and the political power of Rome. He provided weapons for the German school of unbelief, Mathias Knutsen and his band of *Conscienciari*, F. W. Stosch and the rest of them, as well as for the English Deists, Shaftesbury, Collins, Tindal, and, most blatant and conspicuous of them all, John Toland.

[1]Bayle, *Dictionnaire*, article *Spinoza*.

A queer personage indeed, this John Toland! He had got drunk on "reason"; it had gone to his head. *Christianity not mysterious* was his war-cry, in the book that made him famous in 1696. "No mystery about Christianity", he gave out, and that for the plain and sufficient reason that there *are* no mysteries, they simply don't exist. Mystery—the very word is pagan, like so many others we have clung to. It either means a superstition of some sort, and should be stamped out, or it denotes some problem by which we are temporarily baffled, but must sooner or later resolve. Either Christianity is reason, and is part and parcel of the universal order, sloughing off all that is extraneous thereto—tradition, dogmas, rites, creed, faith; or else it could not exist, since nothing in the world can be above reason, or contrary to it.

John Toland was not an unlettered individual. He had taken his M.A. at Glasgow; he had studied at Edinburgh, Leyden and Oxford. He had delved into ancient history, only to discover that it was one colossal imposture and that its chroniclers were, one and all, a pack of deceivers. The Scriptures he had gone into, only to inform us that they were apocryphal, and that the so-called miracles they recorded were susceptible of a perfectly natural explanation, laying about him right and left, slashing, dashing, foaming at the mouth, trumping up all manner of things and, altogether, making confusion worse confounded. He acquainted himself with polite letters, poetry, great oratory, only to report that the utterances of the sanctified humbugs of every religion were merely their way of deceiving people, and leading them by the nose. He was a born mischief-maker and scandal-monger, puffed up with vanity, fond of creating an uproar, very cock-a-hoop when fortune favoured, yet not averse to being pelted at because the brick-bats at least made a clatter about him as they fell.

But in this John Toland, whose iconoclastic energy lent vigour to the activities we have just enumerated, we must not expect to find originality. Time and again, as we read him, we catch echoes of Fontenelle and Bayle, of Bekker and Van Dale, of Hobbes and Spinoza. Moreover, if we were in any doubt about the matter, the overt quotations he makes from these authors would satisfy us that the similarity of ideas was not fortuitous, but the result of conscious plagiarism. His head was crammed with things he had read, and the ideas of his predecessors keep cropping up in little shreds and patches in everything he wrote. No; for originality in the man we shall look in vain, but what we shall find in him is a sort of morbid mental excitement, uncontrollable rage: the explosion of feelings long dammed up by Irish Catholicism and English Puritanism, to say nothing of respect for common decency—all these shackles one day burst asunder and the report sounded like a mighty shout of defiance.

John Toland was born in Ireland, a Catholic. Subsequently, he turned Protestant. He declared, with a self-satisfied toss of the head, that, from his cradle upwards, he had been nourished in an atmosphere of superstition and idolatry, but that his own reasoning, certain friends abetting, had been the auspicious means that had led to his conversion. When he was but a lad of sixteen, he had been as full of zeal against the Papists as ever he had been since. And that zeal of his was not only anti-Papal, but anti-Anglican, in fact "anti" any religious body which might have made an effort, however slight, to curb that exasperated spirit of his, or raised a finger against his ideas of freedom, ideas that refused to brook so much as the shadow of a yoke. After the successful appearance of his *Christianity not mysterious*, he went across to Ireland, there to bask in the sunshine of his scandalous reputation, to show off his eloquence in the various cafés and, generally, to cut a dash. But his luck was out. No one would look at him. Everywhere he was snubbed, cold-shouldered, shown the door. He was regarded as a sort of lower animal; beyond the pale. Molyneux, the mathematician, to whom Locke had recommended him when he first began to attract attention, wrote to the philosopher telling him about his downfall. "Mr. Toland has at last been driven to quit the country. Poor fellow, his own untactful behaviour made him so universally disliked that it was risky to be known to have exchanged a single word with him. And so everybody who valued his reputation gave him a wide berth. At last, according to what I heard, he was actually going hungry; and no one would have him at his table. When the modest sum he brought over with him was all spent, I am told he was reduced to going round borrowing half-crowns from all and sundry. They say he had not the wherewithal to pay his barber, his tailor or his landlady. To complete his discomfiture, Parliament condemned his book and gave orders for it to be burned by the public hangman. After that, he disappeared from these parts, and no one knows where he has made for."

This state of outlawry explains to some extent his mental attitude. The touch of the aristocrat, of good breeding you find in the French "libertin"; the purely intellectual make-up of a Bayle; the dignified bearing of a Spinoza are all very foreign to the character of Toland. His dream was to become the founder of a religion, a sort of Mahomet; but he lacked the power and prestige. Yet what a hater he was, using all the resources of a ready tongue and a nimble wit to envenom his vituperations. And how he loathed priests, every single one of them, from the tribe of Levi onwards; for the Levites, too, were tricksters, nothing more nor less. On the priesthood he poured forth all the vials of his wrath. He denounced them for liars and malefactors; he was anti-clerical to the marrow of his bones.

In England, a political discussion was going on: who was to succeed to the throne when Queen Anne departed this life? Toland in his *Anglia libera* (1701) definitely plumped for the House of Hanover. England must never risk falling under the Papal yoke again; she must safeguard her political freedom, immeasurably the most precious of all her national assets. Such sentiments, we may well imagine, were by no means disagreeable to Hanoverian ears. John Toland became a political agent in the pay of the government. He was continually starting off on confidential missions to somewhere or other abroad. He was to be seen in Berlin, Hanover, Düsseldorf, Vienna, Prague, The Hague. Sophia Charlotte, Queen of Prussia, the same lady that had asked Leibniz to explain the fundamental cause of things, questioned this queer looking gentleman about his philosophy, involving him in arguments with the learned men and Biblical scholars in her entourage. It was thus that he came to address to her his *Letters to Serena* (1704) which contain, perhaps, the pith and marrow of his ideas.

He assured her that belief in the immortality of the soul was not an exclusively Christian doctrine. According to him, it was of pagan origin, and the Egyptians had been the first to profess it. Belief in a personal God, he further explained, was the fruit of idolatry; mankind had decreed divine honours to beings of their own species, built temples to them, raised altars, erected statues, and instituted a priestly and sacrificial order. At a very early date, the people were encouraged to look on God as a being closely resembling their own rulers and that is how it was that God came to be regarded as capricious, changeful, jealous, revengeful and despotic. There is nothing new about these ideas; we have heard them all before, and we need not dilate upon them here. As far as his ideas went, Toland, whose writings were designed with the express purpose of refuting Spinoza, was none the less influenced by him; indeed, it was he and none other who first gave currency to the word *pantheist*. He did not look very closely into things, and a few contradictions caused him no very serious embarrassment.

Yet how thoroughly is our second impression of him borne out. What vehemence! What a tempest of anti-religious fury! No sooner does he come to touch on the subject of "superstition", than he flares up and flies into an ungovernable rage. What he calls our "prejudice" is, he tells us, in our very flesh and blood. He sees it everywhere; indeed he sees nothing else; the thing is an obsession with him. From the moment of our birth, "le prèjugé" lies in wait for us:

The very midwife hands us into the world with superstitious ceremonys, and the good women assisting at the labor have a thousand spells to avert the misfortune, or to procure the happiness of the infant; making several ridiculous observations, to discover the omen of his future state of life. Nor is the priest in some places behind-hand with these gossips, to initiate him betimes into his service, by pronouncing certain forms of words as so many powerful charms, and using the gentle symbols of salt or oil, or the severer applications of iron or fire, or by marking him after some other manner, as his own right and property for the future.[1]

As the child grows up, the effect of these superstitions grows with it. His nurses tell him stories about werewolves: the servants tell him fairy-tales; his schoolmasters talk to him of Genii, of Nymphs, of Satyrs, Metamorphoses and all manner of other strange or miraculous things. They make him read the poets, fabulists and orators, all of them adepts in the art of lying. When they go up to the university they get no better, no wiser. Their teachers, who have to do what the law tells them, are neither free nor sincere. "The Universities are positive hot-beds of superstition . . ."

All our life long, superstitions are on the watch to lead us

[1]First letter to Serena.

astray, and when death draws near, it is still from superstition that we gain our hopes, from superstition that we draw our fears. But he, Toland, has none of these superstitious ideas. His business in life is to combat them in others; that is what he was born for; in him is the truth. He never had the faintest doubt about that. His vanity, his intrepidity, his ferocious energy find expression even in the words he composed for his epitaph: Here lies John Toland who was born in Ireland, near Londonderry, and in his youth studied in Scotland, in Ireland and at Oxford. Having visited Germany more than once, he passed his adult years in the neighbourhood of London. He cultivated the various literatures, and was acquainted with more than ten languages. The Champion of Truth, the Defender of Liberty, he bound himself to no man, on no man did he fawn. Neither threats nor misfortunes deterred him from his appointed course, which he pursued to the very end, always subordinating his own interest to the pursuit of the Good. His soul is united with the Heavenly Father, from whom he first proceeded. Beyond all doubt he will live again unto all eternity, yet never will there be another Toland. He was born on the 30th November: for the rest consult his writings.

Such were the Rationalists.

Dragging along behind them companions as different from the main body as Malebranche, who followed them reluctantly, protesting all the while, they set forth on the long trail, to regions where evidence, and logic, and order were to reign supreme. Any obstacles that got in their way, well, they just had to be removed. They began to play the critic: *Siamo nel secolo dei censuristi*; we live it seems in a fault-finding age.[1] They were always attacking something or other. They condemned all slavish submission, apathetic acquiescence, any sort of sham or absurdity. Once more they set themselves the task, the ever needful task, of freeing us not only from error, but also from cowardice. When they argued that they were doing a good turn to the believers themselves by forcing them to give reasons for their beliefs instead of passively accepting them, they were, in a way, not so very wide of the mark. They deserved respect for their sincerity,

[1]Gregorio Leti, *Il Teatro britannico*, 1684, Preface; Aaron Hill, *The Ottoman Empire*, 1709, Preface.

their courage and their daring. It was no primrose path that they had chosen, but a very thorny one on which they well knew the difficulties they would have to encounter from the start. They had not got the big battalions to back them, nor the influence of the powers that be; they were, on the contrary, but an inconsiderable minority, and knew they had no one to rely on but themselves. "The trouble one has to take in looking for the truth with one's own eyes is mighty indeed when one reflects how easy it is to be one of the blind following the blind."[1] "The longer error has held sway, the more pluck it takes to attack it." "I must say that it causes much less fuss to combat errors before they have had a chance to take root in the minds of men in general, than it does when time has conferred on them a sort of sacro-sanctity. But there is no statute of limitations where truth is concerned, and it would be wrong to let it remain perpetually buried in oblivion on the grounds that no one had ever recognized it."[2] The trouble they went to, the scandal they provoked, they regarded as a measure alike of the need, and of the greatness of their mission. "I think far more highly of a man who swims against a rushing tide than of one who lets himself be carried unresistingly along with the current. Similarly, my opinion of a man who thinks things out for himself and who, on occasion, makes a stand against some general view, however long established, is infinitely higher than it is of people who take their ideas from their ancestors, and who cling to them for no other reason than their antiquity or their lofty lineage."[3] The thing to note, however, is that these champions of reason were displaying just as much of the dictatorial spirit as the most imperious of their religious antagonists, whom they held in such detestation. They never thought of asking themselves how it was that countless generations of Jews, Mohammedans and Christians had had recourse to prayer; never paused to enquire whether these people had nourished in their hearts a religious fire that nothing could extinguish. They had simplified the problem, as they thought, and deemed that they had said the last word when they brought in such terms as "Prejudice" and "Superstition". They never stopped to enquire whether, in those very terms prejudice and

[1]Claude Gilbert, *Histoire de Caléjava*, 1700, p. 35.
[2]Pierre Bayle, *Pensées diverses . . . à l'occasion de la comète*, 1683.
[3]Tyssot de Patot, *Voyages et aventures de Jacques Massé*, pp. 28-29.

superstition justly so called, they were not including beliefs that were at once lawful and necessary. Hasty, presumptuous, they likened history to a huge sheet of paper covered all over with creases. Those creases had to be ironed out, and the sheet restored to its pristine smoothness; that was all; as if it were an easy thing to do; as if it could be done at all; as if, in the long course of our immemorial pilgrimage, man had done nothing but pile error upon error. They had eyes for the crimes and aberrations of mankind, they had none for their deeds of heroism and devotion; they forgot all about the saints and the martyrs. They assumed in their pride that they had laid bare the whole truth; that they had kindled the light that should make the shadows flee away and dispel the darkness, so that in the last resort they made a god of man himself. "By obeying reason we depend on no one but ourselves and so, in a sense, we, too, become as gods."[1]

[1]Claude Gilbert, *Histoire de Caléjava,* p. 57.

II

MIRACLES DENIED: COMETS, ORACLES AND SORCERERS

MIRACLES, rudely violating the laws of Nature; miracles with their grandiose pretensions—they were the enemy *par excellence*. Miracles bedazzled the multitude, and it was the multitude, people in general, religious folk who went to church to say their prayers, the women, these it was that the rationalists sought to convince, to win over.

Miracles—yes; but they had to tread warily. Impossible to risk a frontal attack. Nevertheless, it was open to them to single out some particular form of superstition; and there were plenty to choose from. They therefore proceeded to assail some more or less obvious popular delusion, showing how absurd it was, and how harmful. They dug down to the bed-rock origin of such errors—authority, general consent, custom; and as it was authority, general consent and custom that bolstered up belief in miracles, they contrived to return to their main objective by this circuitous route. The attack falls into three separate stages.

Journal des Savants, Monday, 1st January, 1681:
"Everybody is talking about the comet, and there is no doubt that the comet is the outstanding event of the early part of the year. The astronomers are busy charting its course, and everyone says it portends all manner of disasters. . . ."
This was a reference to a comet that made its appearance in December, 1680. It was followed by others in the ensuing years. All this was the signal for a recrudescence of an old controversy, which this time, however, took on quite a different tone.

Comets are a danger in themselves, said some. They consist of a mass of gaseous exhalations given off by the earth. When these exhalations catch fire, it betokens some major disturbance of the elements, and some notable upheaval invariably follows. That is precisely what the old-fashioned philosophers used to say, said the other side, but nowadays we know better; we know that these comets are just ordinary celestial bodies, and that our earth has nothing whatever to fear from them.

Comets are portents, said the credulous, warnings from above of the coming of some great retribution which mankind have brought upon themselves. When comets appear, woe unto them who repent not of their sins. Remember that throughout the ages their appearance has ever been the precursor of dire events to follow; kings foully done to death, earthquakes, wars, pestilence, and famine. Weep, then, and pray. Crime has reached its peak, God is declaring His wrath, and sends forth these messengers from heaven.

"Are we such important folk as all that?" ask the others. "So important as to imagine that the heavenly powers should go out of their way on purpose to send us a comet?" Look where we will, we can discover nothing to support the popular belief, nothing in what learned men have to say about the matter, nothing in Holy Writ to warrant us in adopting such a conclusion. What are comets but unusually beautiful stars, jewels of the sky? Suppose, if you like, that a comet is a collection of nebulous vapours, why should we regard it as an omen? Could a wholly material body, devoid alike of thought and feeling, give us any inkling of the shape of things to come? Comets obey the laws of nature as laid down by God, laws whose harmonious working no taint of original sin has ever marred. Comets obey those laws; they do not change them. *O vis superstitionis, quantos motus, quantas tempestates in illorum animis excitas, quos oppresisti!* O mighty superstition, what troubles, what tempests thou stirrest up in the minds of those whom thou hast enslaved!

Here Bayle intervenes,[1] analysing the difficulties one by one, in due order. On what, I ask you, does the belief that comets are the sign, nay, more than the sign, the *cause*, of disaster repose?

[1]"Letter to M.L.A.D.C., Doctor of the Sorbonne. Wherein it is proved in the light of various arguments derived from Philosophy and Theology that comets are in no sense portents of disaster . . .," 1682. "Divers reflections recorded in writing for a Doctor of the Sorbonne in connexion with the comet which appeared in December, 1680. . .," 1683; 3rd edition, 1699. "Additional matter appended to Divers reflections on the comets . . .," 1694. "Continuation of Divers reflections . . . ," 1705.

On what the poets, those professional purveyors of falsehood, have to tell us? On the authority of the chroniclers of strange events? On astrology, the world's supreme absurdity? The fact is, the belief has no logical foundation at all. Even if it were established that comets have always been followed by a series of disasters, that would be no ground for saying that they were either the sign or the cause thereof: "Unless, of course, you are prepared to allow that, because a woman cannot look out of a window in the rue Saint-Honoré without seeing a lot of carriages go by, she has a right to assume that she is the cause of the phenomenon; or at any rate that her appearance at the window ought to warn her neighbours that carriages would soon be going by . . ." In point of fact—and facts duly authenticated are, or should be, the sole *criteria* in these matters—it is not true that the years immediately following the appearance of a comet have been specially fruitful of disaster. There have been comets without disasters, and disasters without comets. To discern a sequence of cause and effect in what is merely a fortuitous coincidence, is an abuse of common sense; to affirm that such a sequence occurred when it did no such thing, is downright lying. Leave the comets to mind their own business. They have no concern with men. Only conceit, stupidity, or mental inertia, all potent allies of error, could ever lead us to imagine that we are of any interest to them.

With this line of argument no enlightened Christian would have any fault to find. But Bayle does not stop there. Stop? He never does stop. When you think he has arrived at his Q.E.D., he has other chapters to tack on, long and solid ones at that. And when at last the book is finished—he starts on another one. And, even then, we are only just beginning.

You are not to believe in the power of comets, even if whole nations have borne witness to it, even if millions have sworn to it; nay, even if it is proclaimed by universal consent. Universal consent, the argument used to convince the unbelieving of God's existence, Bayle energetically repudiates. He also rejects tradition, on which the faithful put their trust as the means by which religious truth is preserved and handed down from age to age. "I have said it before, and I say it again; it is the purest delusion to suppose that because an idea has been handed down from time immemorial to succeeding generations, it may not be entirely false."

And so the battle begins anew. Bayle produces the argument which is dearest to his heart, which he deems the most original and most novel of them all, the argument, namely, that if comets were a presage of evil, God would have wrought miracles to confirm idolatry in the world. He warms to his task, he waxes eloquent, almost dithyrambic: Ah, he says, let us not, every time we encounter something difficult to explain, let us not jump to the conclusion that it is a miracle. Miracles are against all reason. There is nothing more consonant with God's infinite greatness than His maintenance of the laws which He Himself established; there could be nothing more unworthy than to imagine Him intervening to interrupt their regular operation. And intervening for what, pray? Intervening about something as paltry and insignificant, compared with the march of the Universe, as the birth or death of a prince!

"*The more we study the ways of man, the more we are forced to recognize that pride is his ruling passion, and that he will give himself grandiose airs even when his affairs are at their sorriest. Frail and infirm as he is, he quite persuades himself that when he comes to die, the whole of nature is stirred to its very depths and that Heaven itself must needs go out of its way to lend a touch of splendour to his obsequies. Foolish, ludicrous vanity! If we looked at the universe aright, we should soon realize that the birth or death of a prince was a very small matter indeed against the background of the universal order, far too small for Heaven to make a pother about. We should say, with the wisest and loftiest of all old Rome's philosophers (Seneca), that it is true indeed that the solicitude of Providence includes even ourselves, but that, though we have our allotted place in the general scheme of things, the Heavenly purpose is directed to something far greater than our particular preservation, and that, while we derive great benefits from the movements of the heavenly bodies, it is not merely for the sake of this earth that they set themselves in motion.*[1]

Universal consent, tradition, miracles: Bayle goes on. The idea that comets are to be regarded as portents of public calamities is an ancient superstition which contrived to establish itself among Christians in pagan times, and has lingered on ever since. For it is a fact that many of the errors of paganism have survived throughout the ages and are discernible in the customs, ceremonies and in the actual beliefs of Christians. Nay, more; God, when He delivered the pagans out of darkness, did not take it

[1]Pierre Bayle, *Pensées diverses . . . à l'occasion de la comète*, 1683, § 83.

upon Himself to reveal to them the secrets of Nature, or so to arm them against popular errors and superstitions that they should never succumb to them again. Revelation or no revelation, human nature, liable as it is to all manner of illusions, prejudices, passions and vices, is fundamentally what it always was. Christians fall into the same sins as do the general run of men. Indeed, it may be that religion, so far from dispelling the darkness, has actually intensified it: to revert to the superstitious tendencies which the Evil One has observed in the human mind, I say that that Arch-enemy of God and of man's salvation has put his shoulder so strenuously to the wheel, and exploited his opportunities so profitably that he has transformed what was best and most valuable in the world, namely, religion, into a conglomeration of quaint, foolish or extravagant customs and, what is worse, of staggering crimes. Worst of all, it has sent mankind down the slippery slope that has landed them at last in the most degrading form of idolatry imaginable.[1]

It may be that idolatry is a characteristic of all the religions that are. It is very evidently a characteristic of religion today. Now there can be no greater evil than idolatry, not excepting atheism itself. We may say, speaking in the abstract, that imperfection is as inimical to the nature of God as complete nonexistence. One way of illustrating the detestable nature of idolatry would be to collect all the solemn denunciations which the Church herself has uttered against it; but instead of doing that, let us examine the facts of the case, for we should always come back to the facts. Is it not a fact, then, that Christians offer examples of every vice that is? Is not the most flagrant immorality found in practice to be perfectly compatible with a belief in God? Conversely, are there not many atheists who live the most exemplary lives, who are keenly sensitive to the dictates of honour, and who, though they do not believe that the soul is immortal, nevertheless strive their utmost to invest their name with the halo of imperishable renown? One might readily imagine an atheistical society, not only as good as, but better than a Christian one. Finally, if the worth of an idea is to be gauged by the heroes it inspires, by the martyrs who lay down their lives for its sake, are we not aware that atheism, too, has had its heroes and its martyrs?

[1]*Ibid.*, § 68.

And so Bayle, taking a few inoffensive comets for his text, winds up at last with a panegyric on atheism. People there were in plenty, who, like Bayle, wanted to push out beyond the purely philosophical specialists, and to bring their ideas to bear on the world of ordinary men and women; but none of them, not even Toland, though he took a leaf out of his book now and again, can emulate the ferocity of Bayle. Numerous as were his supporters and fellow-travellers, his contradictors and opponents were more numerous still, but they only picked out isolated details for their attack, finding fault, now with this point, now with that. Many years were to elapse before a thinker came along, who, rising above the consideration of mere *minutiae*, opposed him with general principles as weighty and as cogent as his own. It was not until 1712 that Élie Benoist, a pastor of the Walloon Church, Delft, challenged him in a composition which, though somewhat limited in scope, adumbrated some very material arguments. If, says Élie Benoist, we were to adopt the method employed by Bayle in his discussion of comets, if that is to say we insisted on first-hand evidence and regarded every other testimony as inadmissible, we might quite well prove that he was not the author of his Dictionary. He assures us that he is, but what proof of his *bona fides* can he offer? He swears on oath that he is telling the truth, but what I want is direct evidence. Many a man has perjured himself ere now. He brings along friends to vouch for his good character; but who's going to vouch for his friends? He will cite me his publisher, the printer, the proof-reader, but I shall question the trustworthiness of all these witnesses; and so, having found something to challenge in one witness after another, I shall show that, before I have grounds for believing M. Bayle, I shall have to summon a general synod of the whole human race. . . .

What he meant was that there are cases in which one must content oneself with a moral proof, and where Bayle errs is in trying to confine the spirit in a strait-jacket and in insisting on applying his method to every conceivable circumstance that life can offer. Moral proof, though it may not dispose of every difficulty, or dispel every shadow of obscurity, does enable one to make a choice, to have a mind of one's own, to say "yes" or "no", to come to a decision and to act on it. "Absolute proofs are so rare, so difficult to come by, that they can play no part in matters in which circumstances call for immediate action, and if it be asserted that to decide on a line of conduct one must have grounds that would be proof against every conceivable objection that some ingenious philosopher, some subtle casuist, might allege against them, we should have to abstain from almost all the functions of life. The Arts, the Sciences, Societies, Laws, Commerce, all depend on such practical demonstrations." And, he might have added, Religion also.[1]

From the day that was said, forgetting all about comets, the members of the Walloon Church of Delft, and, like them, all the men and women in the world, were free to choose between abstract rationalism, on the one hand, and pragmatism on the other.

Those beauteous Sibyls that Michelangelo depicted in the Sistine Chapel were women inspired of God who, albeit pagans, foretold the coming of Christ, his life, his miracles, his death and resurrection. The Fathers of the Church made great and fruitful use of the oracles of these prophetesses when converting unbelievers. When, in the books wherein the oracular utterances of the Sibyls are recorded, the Gentiles beheld the mysteries of the Christian faith set down in advance, they were constrained to avow that that faith was divine and true. Ten famous Sibyls; eight books, Greek and Latin; the testimony of great writers, such as Virgil, Tacitus, Suetonius; the authoritative pronouncements of the Fathers—St. Justin Martyr, St. Augustine, St. Jerome—what an imposing array! What a rampart against unbelief! Nor will you fail to remark that oracles continued up to the birth of Christ, and not beyond. After that they were silent; they were no longer needed. That miraculous aposiopesis is yet another mark of their heavenly character.

Howbeit, some learned men there were, who were bent on putting their spoke into the wheel. These so-called Sibylline Books, were they genuine? Weren't they in all probability the fabrication of a group of Messianic Jews? Or, perhaps of the Christians themselves? They had all the appearance of an artificial concoction, and a pretty unskilful one at that. As for

[1] *Mélange de remarques critiques, historiques philosophiques, théologiques sur deux dissertations de M. Toland, intitulées l'une, L'Homme sans superstition, et l'autre, Les Origines judaïques, par Élie Benoist, pasteur de l'Église wallonne de Delft,* Delft, 1712.

the Fathers of the Church, all their learning, all their sincerity was no guarantee against error. They lacked the critical sense; they were prejudiced, *ex parte* witnesses, and accepted as true certain statements that were palpably false; they had been misled themselves and, with the best intentions in the world, they had misled others in their turn.

Showing scant respect for the Sibyl of Delphi, or for her sisters of Cumae, of the Hellespont, of Phrygia or of Tibur, the learned Vossius, Canon of Windsor, inclined to the theory that the books were of Jewish origin; whereas Johannes Marckius, Doctor in Theology at Groningen, was disposed to ascribe them to the early Christians. Then came a Dutch physician, one Antony Van Dale, heavy-handed but powerful, who, without entering into any learned details, dealt a couple of sledge-hammer blows: in the first place, all these oracles were just a lot of impostures; in the second, they did not cease with the coming of Christ.

Next, a Frenchman arrived on the scene, very much at his ease and very subtle-minded. Moreover, he was the very sort of man who, amid the noise and tumult of the fray, lets fall the telling and decisive word, the word that no one can better, however long the debate goes on. Fontenelle furnishes us with a typical example of the manner in which an idea may evolve. He was a nephew of the great Corneille, but the heroic did not long detain him; the Sublime, to him, was merely so much meaningless bombast. For a time, he toyed with the "precious" school; he had a taste for elegant versification, for writing pretty compliments to ladies, for turning out madrigals, and the discovery of a single silver thread among some fair one's raven tresses inspired him with a wealth of wonderful conceits. He contributed to the *Mercure*; he wrote comedies, tragedies, operas; his conception of the art of letters was that it meant producing work in faithful conformity to rigid formulas, and in this occupation, such as it was, he took an infinite delight. Of all these tastes and pursuits he retained a good deal more than the mere recollection, and all his life long there was about him something of the Cydias whom La Bruyère so pitilessly delineated for us.

But he was by nature of an enquiring mind; enquiring, and something more besides, eager to arrive at clear and sound conclusions, mathematically exact if possible. No pastime, sport or other recreation could rival the pleasure he derived from analysis and deduction, the pleasure of drawing ever closer and closer to the shadows he is trying to overtake. Fontenelle's intellect offers an almost ideal example of a gift that was peculiarly his own, the power, that is, to grasp a thing in all its parts and grasp it quickly, allowing no external influence or inward prompting to mar or distort it. To see his mind at work, you would be reminded of a surgeon's scalpel, so keen it was, so glittering. Add to all this the enthusiasm natural to the convert, enthusiasm from which no one in those days was exempt, no one as yet being wholly disillusioned. However, it must be admitted that he was a terrible egoist, that he was equally immune from the passions of anger and love, that his attitude to the fair sex was dictated by pure selfishness; he disliked the extremes of heat and cold and did his best to avoid them; he detested draughts, and fought shy of people who might ask him a favour, fought shy even of friends, of everyone and everything, in fact, that could possibly curtail his freedom or tax his strength. Finally, the very delicacy of his constitution, by the care which it forced him to take of his health, enabled him to see many of his robuster contemporaries precede him to the grave, and to prolong his own life to a hundred. There is no justification for the reproach that, having his own hand full of truths, he never offered to share them with others. Proselytes are not, all of them, loquacious and ill-bred. Some are delicate and refined, as was Fontenelle himself. So great was his abhorrence of error, that it sometimes led him to forget the caution which held him back from falling into scepticism: "Error is to be found everywhere", he sadly remarked.

Such, then, was this Fontenelle who came to inspect the Sibyls, and looked at them with a mistrustful eye. It was in 1686 that he brought out his *Histoire des Oracles*. He had examined no very recondite sources of information. Van Dale furnished him with all he needed. Van Dale indeed was so vigorous and so sound that he almost thought it would suffice merely to translate him, and leave it at that. But then Van Dale was ponderous, bristly, overloaded with quotations, turgid, and, at first sight, anything but inviting. Better titivate him up a bit and put some attractive French trimmings on him, so that people should not be put off by his appearance for "the women, and, there's no denying it, the vast majority of the men, of this country at any rate, are more taken by the choice of words, by elegance and

grace of diction and turns of thought, than they are by the more
solid virtues of accurate research and learned arguments. Then
again, most people, being averse to mental exertion, like a well-
planned book, straightforward and easy to follow, so that they
don't have to keep their brains on the stretch more than is absolutely necessary." The upshot was that the task was divided,
Van Dale supplying the matter, Fontenelle the wit, the grace, the
charm, and the trenchant style.

In the first place, there was no truth in the statement that oracles
were pronounced by demons. How, then, could such an idea
have got abroad? Because a whole literature, devoted to recording strange and startling events, gave it currency; because
Christians, having once accepted the idea of oracles, naturally
worked them as hard as they could. Besides that, this demon
theory seemed to fit in with the Platonic philosophy, and finally,
most cogent reason of all, there was the power of the supernatural over the minds of men.

But the whole structure was unsound, unsound from the
foundations upward. The tales on which these fabulous ideas
were based were apocryphal, or contradictory, or so manifestly
untrue that they fell to pieces the moment the light of reason was
brought to bear on them. Thus Fontenelle—laying about him
right and left. The current idea about oracles does not square so
well with religion as people think; the existence of spirits is not
satisfactorily established by Platonism; whole schools of pagan
philosophy have declared that there is nothing supernatural
about oracles; while numbers of people, not philosophers, have
also, often enough, shown scant respect for oracles; the early
Christians themselves were far from being convinced that
oracles were the utterances of spirits. Wherever he came up
against something that was affirmed as a certainty, he questioned
it, or flatly denied it; and he always gave the reason why.

Having amply demonstrated that oracles were a fraud, that
they were invariably worded to suit the wishes of the great; that
the pagan priests employed every trick they could think of to
impose them on the credulity of the public; that they were am-
biguous and therefore useless; that they proceeded from human
knavery and not from divine intervention, he next went on to
deny the assertion that they had ceased with the coming of
Christ. There had been many oracles subsequent to that date,

and, if in the end they had ceased to make themselves heard, it was because they bore within them the cause of their own decay, one which was logically sufficient in itself, apart from any divine interposition, and that was the evidence, the clear evidence, that they were deliberately designed to deceive: "The crimes of the priests, their overweening insolence, the various events that had exposed their knavery, the ambiguity or downright falsity of their answers would have discredited these oracles and made an end of them sooner or later, even if the Pagan system itself had not ceased to exist." In short, there was nothing supernatural about the matter at all. It is sufficiently accounted for by ignorance on the one side, and fraud on the other. The supernatural—that is the ordinary recourse of human kind; it is also the most misleading, the most deceptive. We rush away to search for the cause without stopping to find out whether the supposed fact is a fact in reality. That is where we make the great mistake. The remedy lies in a rule which we should always bear in mind: *Make sure of the fact before worrying your head about its cause.*

Everybody knows about the story of the Gold Tooth, a diverting tale, well conceived and full of significance. Let us read it once more, for its lesson never grows stale, and as we read let us recall the sensation it made when it first came out. Fontenelle, while seemingly indulging in a little harmless amusement, touches in reality on three matters of profound human concern: Science, History, and Religion.

In the year 1593, the report got about that, somewhere in Silesia, a child of seven had lost all its teeth, but that one of the missing molars had been replaced by another, all of gold. In 1595, one, Horstius, Professor of Medicine at the University of Helmstad, wrote an account of this tooth, giving it as his opinion that it was partly natural, partly miraculous, declaring that God had bestowed it on the child in order to console the Christians for the sufferings they had undergone at the hands of the Turks. Truly, a strange sort of consolation! And of what possible concern could this tooth have been to the Christians, or the Turks? That same year, so that the Golden Tooth should not be lacking in historians, Rullandus wrote another account of it. Two years later, Ingolsteterus, another man of learning, wrote a work in which he contested Rullandus' views on the Golden Tooth, whereupon Rullandus came out with an elaborate and erudite rejoinder. Yet another eminent person, named Libavius, collected and collated all the statements that had been put forward in regard to the tooth, to which he appended a theory of his own. These works were all very impressive; only one thing was lacking and that was any clear evidence that the tooth was a gold one at all. On its being handed to a goldsmith for examination, he discovered that a piece of gold leaf had with amazing dexterity been superimposed on the tooth. First came the books about it; afterwards, the expert examination by the goldsmith.

That is what happens in all manner of cases. It is just human nature. What in my view brings home the extent of our ignorance is not so much the facts which really are facts, but which we cannot explain, as the explanations we produce of the facts which are not facts at all; which is as much as to say that while we have no principles that should lead us to the truth, we have plenty of others well calculated to lead us away from it.

Learned men of science clearly demonstrated how it was that underground places were warm in winter and cool in summer; then other scientists still more learned, came along with the discovery that the whole thing was a mistake and that the original statement was entirely incorrect; underground places were not warm in winter and cool in summer.

Historical questions are still more liable to this sort of error. We discuss and argue about what the historians have told us. But these historians—what manner of men were they? Had they not their own passionate predilections? Were they not credulous, or ill-informed, or inaccurate? Find me a single one who examined his subject, whatever it may have been, with a completely unprejudiced and attentive eye.

All this is especially pertinent when your particular subject-matter happens to be concerned with religion. In such cases, according to the side you are on, it is no easy matter to avoid ascribing to a false religion virtues which it cannot claim, or to a true one, virtues which it does not need. However, we ought clearly to understand that, just as we can never add truth to what is true already, so we can never impart truth to what is intrinsically false.

At first, he seems to be indulging in a little playful banter; but gradually, as he proceeds, his tone becomes graver and graver. Through all these airs and graces, the underlying idea, profound though it be, is clear enough and it obviously tallies with what Bayle had said in the matter of comets; the likeness is unmistakable. There is the same appeal to a wider audience than that of the professional philosophers and theologians, the same pitiless denunciation, first, of human frailty, the primary cause of all error, next of tradition, which blindly takes error to its bosom, fortifies it and renders it all but invincible. Some absurd

idea or other crops up; the Ancients take it seriously and give it
their *imprimatur*; then we, the later generations, accept it with
our eyes shut, on the authority of the Ancients. The process
never varies. Get half a dozen people to believe that the sun is
not the source of daylight, and the thing is done. In time, whole
nations will come to believe it. Like Bayle, Fontenelle is a fierce
opponent of authority; the doctrine of universal consent he
considers absurd as affording proof that such and such a proposition is true. Whether a fairy-tale is believed by a hundred people,
or a hundred million, for a single year, or for generations, it still
remains a fairy-tale. Like Bayle, too, he would not hear of
miracles, and lastly, like Bayle, he declined to recognize any
specific distinction between Pagan and Christian. Christian
truths were not prefigured in Pagan rites; the Pagans bequeathed
their errors to the Christians.

A lover of the good things of this world, almost uncannily
"wise", he was too fondly addicted to his little comforts to risk
calling down the wrath of the gods about his ears. Therefore he
fought without making any great noise about it; but he fought all
the same. He knew that at Bologna there was a scientific academy
that went by the name of the Academy of Restless Souls. Restless! That was the word. The name was admirably suited to
those "modern philosophers who, being independent of control
by any authority, are seekers now and for ever".[1] He is one of
the Restless Ones. Like the rest of the band he feels that he has a
mission to fulfil, and he feels that it is not going to be an easy
one. To reject some new idea out of hand, or to concur with
some old and commonly accepted one, does not require any
exercise of the reason; but to abandon a long-standing opinion
or belief, to take sides with the innovators, that is not so easy,
that deserves some credit: "It takes some effort to strive against
the stream, but none to drift along with it." Believers are nothing
in his estimation; unbelievers everything, as this dictum makes
clear: "What people who believe in a thing have to say in its
praise, is nothing to its credit; but what people who disbelieve in
it may have to say to its detriment may serve to destroy it. The
believers may know of no reason why they should not believe;
non-believers can hardly be ignorant of the reasons for believing."

[1] *Éloge de M. Marsigli.*

Of still more ancient date, still more deeply rooted in the popular mind, still more general was belief in witches; abominable creatures who hied them to their Sabbath, bestriding weird mounts, who held high festival with the Evil One. Dreadful tales were told of them. By their spells, they could stop a husband from fondling his spouse; they led well-conducted, virtuous young women astray by dropping a charm of some sort into their food or drink. They poisoned the beasts of the field, they made the fruits of the earth to wither, and man to languish and die, maimed women big with child, and wrought scores of other iniquities. Still more wicked are magicians; they hold familiar intercourse with the Spirit of Evil, whom, to such as are curious to behold him, they can present under whatsoever guise they please. They have a secret trick for winning at card-play and of enriching those to whom they reveal it. They can foretell the future. They can take the shape of any animal they please, and assume the most terrifying forms; they enter houses where they utter shouts and yells and appalling groans; they take on fiery shapes loftier than trees, dragging chains behind them with their feet and brandishing serpents in their hands. After a while, they fill people with such terror that there is nothing for it but to send for the clergy to come and exorcise them. . . .

They were very numerous: they were found among the American savages; among the Laplanders. These Lapland wizards, having made a compact with the Devil, have power to stay a vessel in its course, and to change the aspect of the sky. They beat for a long time on a kind of magic drum, after which they go off into a trance and lie motionless, face to the ground, what time their soul leaves the body and ranges far and wide. In Lapland, you might almost say, you come across a sorcerer every step you take.

However, there is no need to go all the way to Lapland for your sorcerers. For example, at Tedworth, in old England, there is a house from which a drum-beater had to be expelled by the occupier. However, by some unearthly means, the creature got in again, and began making a horrible rumbling sound, intermingled with divers other diabolical noises. The truth of the story is established beyond all possible doubt. A clergyman, the Reverend Joseph Glanvil, went to the house and examined every nook and corner from cellar to attic; he heard noises, but he saw

no one. People who refuse to accept such a clear proof of the
Devil's existence and power are impious, unbelieving Sadducees.
The Sadducees are making some headway in England, paving the
way for atheism by casting doubts on the existence of an Infinite
Being; but all good folk, mindful of the sinister activities of the
Tedworth ghost, will give them the trouncing they deserve.

So we see how this question, no new one, but one that time
after time recurred afresh, still had power to disturb men's
minds. Witchcraft, charms, spells and so on—what exactly *were*
they? The spiteful deeds of infernal spirits, of ubiquitous demons
who take pleasure in tormenting human beings and in luring them
on to commit evil? Or do we mean the multifarious manifestations
of the power of the Devil, of Satan who, leading Jesus Christ to
the top of a high mountain and showing him all the Kingdoms
of the Earth, and the glory thereof, essayed to tempt him? Or
are they but evil dreams, mere illusions, figments of the mind, to
which we mortals are always prone, cheating fantasies of an over-
heated imagination, imagination, mother of lies?

And so, for yet a third time, there was nothing for it but to
renew the contest, or, more properly, to intervene in a contest
which seemed endless, but which, if it were humanly possible,
should now at last be brought to a conclusion. And it was high
time to intervene, and to intervene energetically, since it was now
no longer a mere abstract question of truth or error that was at
issue; it was a matter of flesh and blood, of accusers and accused,
of courts of law, of judges and of victims. If some European
countries were inclined to leniency in these matters, forbidding
proceedings to be taken against a lot of poor unfortunate wretches
suspected of having commerce with the Devil but in point of fact
quite innocent of that or any other crime; if, in 1672, an edict of
the King of France had forbidden the courts to take cognizance
of bare, unsupported charges of sorcery, other countries went on
pursuing alleged magicians, necromancers and demoniacs with
the utmost rigour of the law, sending them to prison, the torture-
chamber, the gallows or the stake.

A Dutchman, then a German, Balthasar Bekker, and next
Christian Thomasius, with more vigour than any of the others,
are typical of the triumphant rationalism of the time. A queer
figure of a man was this Balthasar Bekker. From a pair of broad
white bands emerged a massive square jaw, a huge mouth, an

enormous nose and two great staring eyes surmounted by a pair
of bushy eyebrows. And the man himself was as queer as his
appearance. Though a pastor, he was—he couldn't help it—a
disciple of Descartes from whom he acquired the art of clear
and logical thinking. An incident that had happened to him
earlier in his life had imbued him with an enduring contempt for
the judgment of his fellows. It appears that, while carrying on
his pastoral work in Frisia, he had compiled a catechism which
was condemned by more than two hundred pastors in solemn
synod assembled, not a single one of whom, according to him, was
able to give any reason for the condemnation. On two subsequent occasions, the book was formally approved, although he
had not made the smallest change in its doctrinal content. How,
after a thing like that, could one help concluding that a sound
Christian, and particularly a teacher, would do well to pay no
attention to what others thought and said, but to rely, for his
rule of faith, on himself alone? Henceforward, he would pursue
one object in life, apart that is to say from the care of his flock,
and that should be to denounce error and unmask shams wherever
he found them. He was not going to follow in the footsteps of
anyone, not even of the learned, who were always ready to play
the sedulous ape to those who had made a name for themselves
in the world, and were simply hide-bound with prejudice. He
would do his best to make people wiser, though it was to be
confessed that few betrayed any very enthusiastic desire to submit
to the process. It is always so convenient to concur, in thought
and action, with the general run of people; to repeat what you
hear others repeating day after day; so easy to shout with the
crowd; such an effort to think for yourself! Like Toland, he was
intoxicated with reason, this Balthasar Bekker. But, at all events,
he was valiant, sincere and full of energy. He was fired with that
revolutionary ardour which is an indispensable part of the
armoury of an intellectual crusader.

Setting out to do battle with prejudices, he had no difficulty in
finding them; there were plenty of them ready to his hand. He,
too, began by exculpating the comets; but the subject that
engrossed him beyond all others was the Devil. The Devil was
his major obsession; the Devil puts in an appearance in all his
sermons, and went on doing so till at last in a weighty volume
which he brought out in 1691: *De betooverte Wereld*, the World

Enchanted, he cast him out. It was his mission to disenchant the world.

He starts off at a lively pace. Belief in the Devil and all his works, in his supposed agents and their evil deeds won't bear examination in the light of day. We have only to trace the idea to its source, to note its development throughout the ages and in various countries, to recognize that it was of Pagan origin and that Christianity had been tainted with it. And although Protestants, since their rupture with the Pope, had to some extent shaken it off, it still exercised a baneful effect on them. Don't tell me that it is founded on the Scriptures. On the Scriptures as interpreted by the Fathers of the Church, perhaps; but not on the Scriptures interpreted in the light of reason; that is to say, interpreted by him, Balthasar Bekker. For example, the Scriptures speak of angels; since, however, they tell us nothing of their nature, of their essence, we may assume that they are ordinary mortals entrusted by God with a special mission and therefore endowed by Him with extraordinary powers. The Scriptures make mention of evil spirits, but here again they simply mean men, but men depraved and given to sin. They describe the temptation of Adam, but here again there is not a word in the whole narrative to warrant the idea that the Devil can exert any direct influence on the soul or the body of man. They give an account of the temptation of Jesus Christ, but they say nothing to lead us to believe that the Devil was other than a wicked man. They tell us that Jesus Christ healed folk who were possessed of the Devil, but it was customary in those days to attribute serious diseases to devils, and indeed to apply the word to the diseases themselves. Christ was merely availing himself of the metaphorical mode of expression current in his day; consequently, when we speak of the healing of persons possessed of the devil, what we mean is, not the literal driving out of devils, but the healing of maladies only too real. In brief, "if we consider the Scriptures with a perfectly open and unbiased mind, we shall certainly not attribute to the Devil those powers and activities which their preconceived ideas led the commentators and translators to ascribe to him". In our own day, we have had experience of magicians, enchanters or sorcerers, who have been very wicked people, spiritually and morally corrupt; but without having had any private or exclusive communication with the Devil.

Balthasar Bekker's opinions brought upon him the censure of his Church, but he died still clinging to them. He had made a point of having his book translated into French, himself keeping an eye on the rendering, lest it should be disfigured by any of those distortions and misrepresentations which seem to be the inevitable portion of the most successful works. The precaution was a wise one, for the book, in its French guise, had a very extensive circulation. It was also translated into English and German, and was read all over Europe.

However, the country in which sorcerers were hunted down with the grimmest determination was, at that time, Germany. No great while since, the death had occurred of a celebrated jurist, one of those terrifying people who are quite sure that they are the repositories of all truth and all justice, and remorselessly condemn their brothers for their own good. Benedict Carpzow is said to have boasted that he had read the Bible right through from cover to cover fifty-three times and that he had received Holy Communion at least once a month while devoting his life to tightening up the regulations directed against, and increasing the penalties exacted from, the practitioners of the black art. He had convicted, or been the means of convicting, some thousands of them. However, it so happened that it was Germany that was destined to produce, a generation later, the man who, of all others, was most effective in opposing these barbarous cruelties. His name was Christian Thomasius and his mere emergence on the scene is sufficient to show how the times had changed.

At Leipzig, where he was born in 1655, Christian Thomasius had been reared on sound principles, as befitted a respectable professor's son. He had been taught to think on Aristotelian lines and to believe precisely what those austere guardians of orthodoxy, the pastors, taught him to believe. At the age of twenty, having completed his training, he went to Frankfort, there to become a teacher in his turn. He knew exactly what it behoved him to do in order to uphold authority, and to safe-guard traditions which left no scope for independent thinking in matters intellectual, or for any sort of latitude in the conduct of everyday life.

But it so happened that, in the year 1675, he made acquaintance with the works of Pufendorf who, by drawing a distinction be-tween Natural Law and Divine Law, had completely laicized the character of juridical studies. For Thomasius, this was nothing short of a revelation. The doctrine of Natural Law, which he had opposed without having had any close acquaintance with it, was henceforth his *Credo*; he traced it back to its basic principles, and now behold the one-time Champion of Dogma transformed into a firebrand of revolution! No more passive acceptance of doctrines, no more blind following of the blind, for him! In future when I examine a doctrine I shall not enquire as to the position and reputation of its upholders, I shall simply ask what degree of evidence there is to support it. I shall study the arguments for and against, and in making my decision I shall be guided solely by the light of my own intelligence. Instead of behaving like the submissive vassal of an intellectual oligarchy, I shall model myself on one of those heroes of ancient times who took up arms against the tyrant they had served, so that liberty might triumph.

He was by nature a tough customer. He dearly loved a good set-to, with plenty of fire and fury, and he revelled in the commotion, which, starting in the university, spread throughout the city. He was especially fond of practising those subtle ruses whereby an overweening, blustering adversary is baffled and befooled, or officious pomp deflated by a pointed sally or a shaft of satire. Nor was he unduly troubled by the scandalous reputation he bore, which caused people to nudge each other as they saw him in the street and whisper, "There goes Christian Thomasius, a fellow that stands in awe of nothing and nobody."

In 1680, he returned to Leipzig as a *privat docent* and gave full rein to his ideas. His teaching soon became widely known as something both novel and provocative. Metaphysics, he said, was simply beating the air; as for theology, let the theologians keep it to themselves. There were only two branches of knowledge that really mattered: logic and history; the former because it taught you to think clearly; the latter because it afforded you a number of useful examples, some to be imitated; some, not. Knowledge, he said, should have some tangible object in view, should lead to some immediate practical advantage; justice should be social justice. Of prejudice of every kind, of prejudice, the parent of every ill, he was the determined and relentless foe. Prejudices came of giving children and young people the most pitiable rubbish to swallow, and never encouraging them to reason things out for themselves. Another cause lay in the haphazard way people take in whatever they are told to believe. And he would wind up by repeating his favourite *dicta*: the light of Nature is one thing; the light of Revelation, another. Theology belongs to the Biblical world; philosophy to the world of Reason. Theology sees to man's welfare in the next world, philosophy to his welfare in this one; and that is by far the more pressing.

That sort of thing was more than the University authorities could stomach. Thomasius was poisoning the minds of the young; he was leading them straight to atheism. They attacked him; he hit back. Swathed in the ample folds of his academic gown, behatted with a monumental wig whose ringlets foamed in profusion about his shoulders, tall and massive, he stood his ground, firm as a rock. They pelted him with arguments, with pamphlets, with threats; they dragged him before the beaks and big-wigs, they ordered him to stop his lectures—they only added to his zest for the fray. Sometimes, he had positive flashes of genius, as on the day, still a red-letter one in the annals of German Universities, when he posted up the syllabus of his forthcoming course of lectures written, not in Latin, but in the vernacular. And what a subject he had chosen! As he wished to talk to his students as man to men; as it was his object to make them, not so much barristers, or judges, as thoughtful human beings, it was his purpose, he told them, to study the sort of human type which Baltasar Gracian presented to the world, the type, that is to say, of the hero. This led him to consider another type of humanity, the "honnête homme", the "gentleman", the "man of breeding"; and this brought him to "la civilisation française", to those arts of social life of which France is *par excellence* the mistress, the exemplar. In his inaugural lecture he dealt with the question how far Germans ought to imitate the French. Well, they ought to study them, of course, and to acquaint themselves with their leading writers, with their famous books, the *Logique* of Port Royal, for example; they should familiarize themselves with their language and with all the delicate, psychological subtleties which it reflects. But they should not imitate them slavishly, with ape-like fidelity, or play the common plagiarist. The French, he said, are ahead of us in Science, in Taste, in Manners. Instead of trotting along submissively behind them, let us get up-sides with them and not allow these highly superior gentlemen to put us on a par with a lot of Muscovy savages. We've got to show them what we Germans can do. Our future will be what we ourselves make it.

In the thick of the fight, he would laugh aloud; for, says Gracian, it is an advantage, not a drawback to have a merry spirit, provided we keep our merriment within bounds. There's no better seasoning than a pinch of humour. He spiced his rationalism with a very generous pinch indeed when, in 1688, he brought out a journal on the lines of what he thought a journal ought to be. Again there was a mighty fluttering in the dove-cots of the doctrinaires. It turned out, this journal, not to be in Latin, like the *Acta eruditorum* of which Leipzig was so immensely proud, but in German. Thomasius thought the world of it. A journal at once flippant and serious, frivolous yet sober, a journal which talked about books, some grave, some gay, a journal inspired by the spirit of a man who was himself the very personi-fication of Irony and Reason: Erasmus!

The tension went on getting worse and worse till at last, in 1693, things reached breaking point, and Thomasius had to say goodbye to Leipzig. Those who refuse to go with the swim must expect things like that; they are all in the day's work. So he betook himself to Berlin. He happened to arrive just when Frederick III of Brandenburg was in the middle of turning the Academy of Nobles at Halle into a University, and one which was destined to become a great centre of intellectual activity. There Christian Thomasius found himself in clover; he was in fact the life and soul of the whole place, its real creator, its in-spiration. It was there that he began to busy himself with the Devil.

And what energy he put into it, piling argument upon argu-ment, some of them a re-hash of Bekker, some his own particular brew. Neither the evidence, nor the Scriptures if read aright, nor common sense, nor logic furnished any grounds for maintaining such a superstition: This sort of thing, for example—Satan presents himself to a man in animal or human shape; they strike a bargain; Satan gets the man's soul; the man gets the power to put the evil eye on men and things. Sometimes Thomasius re-fines upon his theme, as thus: This absurd idea about the Devil is taken from books and pious books at that. That is where—in books—Catholics, from their childhood upward, have seen the Devil in the guise of some horrible monster; that is where Lutherans, from their childhood upward, have seen the Devil wearing a monk's habit, complete with cloven heel and horns poking through his cowl. Sometimes, he waxes indignant: You would think, he says, that after Luther, after all the fables, Roman and papistical, had been exploded, the Reformers would have shed this absurd delusion. Not so; it still holds its ground in popular belief; indeed, it seems to be actually gaining ground among the Protestants, among Lutherans in particular. The shame of the thing!

But it is not only the philosopher that speaks; the professor of law, the barrister who has had some experience in defending people charged with witchcraft in the criminal courts takes up the tale. In Saxony, there were laws, and quite recent ones, which laid down that anyone who should so far forget himself as a Christian, as to make a compact with the Devil, should, whether he had harmed anyone or not, be tied to the stake and burned until he was dead. Ah! by the ever-spreading light of the Cartesian philosophy, by the march of reason, let the German jurists and theologians cease to fall into an error that leads to crime! Nothing, perhaps, is more characteristic of Thomasius than this practical intervention of his; it is a sort of outward and visible sign of his zeal for justice and humanity.

In 1709, he had the intense satisfaction of refusing a professorship of which, in repentant mood, the University of Leipzig made him the offer. At Halle he had come to stay, at Halle he passed the remaining years of his long life; at Halle, in 1728, he breathed his last, the glorious inaugurator of the German *Aufklärung*, a hero in the great struggle for enlightenment.

We do not have to delve very far into the depths of the human consciousness before encountering a seam of superstition; there are always plenty of outcrops. The Marquise de Brinvilliers and her female accomplice Voisin were not only poisoners; they were also held to be witches. In 1680, one of the most exalted personages in France, the maréchal de Luxembourg, was arrested and flung into prison on a charge of having made a pact with the Devil. The discussions about the Loudun women, said to be possessed, ancient history though it was, still went on; and plenty of other cases of the same kind. In 1692, the skill of a certain wizard with his magic wand—his name was Jacques Aymar—had led to the arrest of the murderers. He became famous. Whenever he got near a thief, or a dicer, his hazel-twig would begin to turn and twitch violently. He threw himself into the spirit of the part; he swooned, he went off into trances, he was everywhere in demand, the sensation of the age! And he was not the only one. At Toulouse, in the Dauphiné, in Picardy, in Flanders, similar marvels were all the talk. Curés, monks, women, children could detect the hidden presence of water or of gold. We must not run away with the idea that this sort of thing was confined to France. Germany, too, came into the picture. The magic wand was used in reducing dislocations, healing wounds, staunching haemorrhages. Similar practices were rife in Bohemia, Sweden, Hungary, Italy and Spain. "Zahuris is the name given in Spain to certain men possessed of such extraordinarily penetrating vision that they can detect springs of water under the soil, as well as metals, hidden treasure and dead bodies. They have very red eyes."[1] In Egypt, the hazel-twig is used to relieve animals swollen with excess of urine. In all these stories there were plenty of impostures, but as in some instances the twig did undoubtedly move of its own accord in the hands of people of unquestionable probity, its mysterious motions were inevitably ascribed to the Devil. And besides this kind of practitioners, there were wonder-workers of every conceivable description, adepts in black magic, fortune-tellers, interpreters of cards and I know not what.

But all this time, opposing forces were at work; the forces of common sense. The number of books that were written about Jacques Aymar—for and against! In fact, it was the affair of the Gold Tooth over again. "Following up two short books that had already appeared on the subject, Vallement came out with a third, consisting of six hundred duodecimo pages, purporting to explain on ordinary mechanical principles why it was that the divining rod twisted about as it did. M.P. of the Oratory would have none of it and clearly demonstrated that the rod could not possibly move without the Devil's having a hand in it. The upshot was that, after all these excellent books had been written, Jacques Aymar was discovered to be a swindling knave, and M. le Prince had him bundled out of the country. What from the

[1]Pierre Bayle, *Dictionnaire*, art. Zahuris.

philosopher's point of view is particularly amusing about this story is that Vallement began his book by telling his readers that M. Van Dale's story of the Gold Tooth had put him on his guard, and that before attempting any explanation of the marvel, he had taken particular care to establish its authenticity." Dubos told this story with a chuckle in a letter he wrote Bayle on the 27th April, 1696. Brossette, who had seen, yes *seen*, the wonderful man with his own eyes, and had not quite recovered from the experience when he unburdened himself at some length about the matter in a letter to his friend Boileau, was inclined to think there was something in it all. The letter is dated Lyons, 25th September, 1706, and it reads as follows: "I saw a man here yesterday whose powers, or natural gifts if you prefer it so, are by no means easy to explain. I refer to the celebrated Jacques Aymar, or the Man with the Magic Wand, who, as a matter of fact, is a peasant belonging to Saint-Marcellin in Dauphiné some forty miles or so from Lyons. They get him to come here when there is anything particular they want to investigate or discover. He told me some really extraordinary things about this water-divining skill, how he can locate hidden springs, trace displaced landmarks, hidden coin, stolen goods and how he can expose murder and foul play. He described the violent pains and paroxysms that come upon him when he is on the scene of a crime or in the neighbourhood of its perpetrators. First of all, he gets an acute burning sensation about the heart, this is followed by nausea and the vomiting of blood and then he goes off into a dead faint. All this happens to him without his being in the least aware that there is anything for him to find out, and these manifestations seem to have more to do with his body as a whole than with his divining-rod. If you would like any further particulars, I can supply them." No; Boileau doesn't want any further particulars. He is not at all impressed by his friend's account and his reply is distinctly gruff: "Auteuil, 30th September, 1706. My dear Sir, I really am bound to confess that it utterly passes my comprehension how a man like you could have been so foolish as to let yourself be taken in by a knave whose rascalities have been thoroughly exposed, and who wouldn't find anyone in Paris, not even among the nursemaids and little children, to listen to his balderdash. In the days of Dagobert or Charles Martel, people might have been deceived by such mountebanks, but are we, in the enlightened age of Louis the Great, to give ear to such rubbish? And doesn't it look as if our common sense had deserted us not long since, together with out victories and conquests?" Not at all; common sense was very much on the alert. "I am told that there used to be a number of people in Paris who made out that they were diviners and that they got a lot of money by that means. I am not in the least surprised. There are so many fools of all sorts and conditions in that vast city that it is no wonder the diviners do a brisk trade there."[1]

These were the ideas and protestations of a few independent thinkers; but, apart from them, there was a concerted movement on foot which, while aiming a blow at superstition, aimed an equally shrewd one at religion. There was never the slightest attempt to differentiate between the two; they were invariably treated as one.

Comets are not portents of ill. Oracles are hoaxes, pure and simple. God never wrote His decrees on the entrails of animals; nor did He confide them to moonstruck madmen. If by sorcerers you mean knaves or lunatics, then sorcerers there are; otherwise, there are none. There are no such things as devils, nor is there *the* Devil. There is no ultimate authority from whose verdict there is no appeal. There are no traditions free from the taint of error or misrepresentation. There are no miracles, for Nature does not take its cue from man's delirium.[2] Nothing is supernatural. No mystery is insoluble by human reason: "Would you like me to tell you, as one old friend to another, how it is you follow what the crowd hold in your ideas about things, instead of consulting the oracle of Reason? It is because you believe that there is something divinely inspired about it . . . because you imagine that the common consent of so many peoples down the ages, can only be the outcome of some manner of inspiration —*vox populi, vox dei*; it is because, being a theologian, you are accustomed to give up reasoning when you think you are in the presence of a 'mystery'."[3]

---

[1] Richard Simon, *Lettres*, t. III, p. 51.
[2] *Tractatus theologico-politicus*, Preface.
[3] Pierre Bayle, *Pensées diverses . . . à l'occasion de la comète*, § 8.

III

RICHARD SIMON AND BIBLICAL
EXEGESIS

IT WAS not to be expected that the Bible would escape
the critical onslaught. The symbol, as it was, of Authority,
it was only natural to submit it to the searching eye of
criticism.

When the critics could manage to make out that it was self-
contradictory in this passage or in that, how they exulted! For
example: We are told in the Book of Genesis that Adam was the
first man, and Eve the first woman, and that they had two sons,
Cain and Abel; that Cain killed Abel; that Cain said unto God,
"My sin is too great to be forgiven me . . . therefore whoso
shall find me shall slay me". *Whoso shall find me*; so there were
men in the world already, before Adam. Isaac de la Peyrère had
landed that fish a long time since, and the Pre-adamites were hand
in glove with the "intellectuals".

Take the essay which, purporting to be a letter addressed to a
London nobleman, was written in the year 1695 by an Oxford
M.A. who did not reveal his name. This attack takes a different
line. All the Eastern races, and the Hebrews are no exception,
have a wonderful gift for inventing myths. Just as the history of
the Persians, the Medes and the Assyrians is a farrago of imaginary
tales, so too the Bible, so too the Talmud, are a mass of fables.
The Arabs outshone the Hebrews with their metaphors, their
similes, their gift for fiction, as witness their Alcoran, their many
poets who, in the fulness of time, inspired the writers of Spain
and Provence with their tales of Knights Errant, Giants, Dragons,
Enchanted Castles and all the paraphernalia of Chivalry. Holy
Writ, he concludes, "is altogether mysterious, allegorical, and

enigmatical". It betrays a kinship with those fables of the Orient which are no more than "romantick hypotheses".[1]

The Protestants, setting to work to study the text of the Divine Word, and to disengage it from the accretions which had gathered round it in the course of time, found their task by no means easy. They reproached the Catholics for their passive attitude to the Bible; the Catholics reproached them for their audacity. In point of fact, an appreciable body of exegetical work had been accomplished by the Protestants as the works of Samuel Bochart, a minister of the Gospel and teacher at Caen, and of Louis Cappelle, minister and professor at Saumur, sufficiently testify.

On the Jewish side, there was Spinoza, who held that the methods we employ in studying Nature, should also be applied to the study of the Bible; that was how he put it and we know what came of that. To achieve the object in view it was necessary to have an accurate account of the phenomena and then, starting from that solid ground, to proceed to an accurate definition, but for all this the primary requisite was to know Hebrew, an exceptionally difficult matter, seeing that the ancient Hebrew grammarians have left us no information regarding the foundations or theory of the language; no dictionary, no grammar, no rhetoric. Next, said Spinoza, we should enter into the atmosphere and spirit of the Bible and adapt ourselves to it rather than attempt to force the Bible to fit in with our own presuppositions.

"The third requirement that the history of the Scriptures should fulfil is that it should teach us to understand the various vicissitudes that may have befallen the books of the Prophets whose tradition has been handed down to us; the life, character and aim of the author of each book; the part which he played; at what period, on what occasion, for whom, and in what language he composed his writings. Nor is that enough; we must know the fortunes of each book in particular, the circumstances in which it was originally composed, into what hands it subsequently fell, the various lessons it has been held to convey, by whom it was included in the sacred canon, and, finally, how all these books came to be embodied in a single collection. . . ."[2]

[1] Two essays sent from Oxford to a Nobleman in London. The first concerning some errors about the Creation, General Flood, and the Peopling of the World, in two parts. The second concerning the Rise, Progress, and Destruction of Fables and Romances. By L. P., Master of Arts. London, 1695.
[2] *Tractatus theologico-politicus*, VII.

And the Catholics themselves, on their side, did they not number in their ranks Jean de Launoy, the dethroner of Saints? The learned Mabillon, deeply versed in textual criticism? Nay, the Abbé Fleury himself, the highly orthodox author of the *Histoire ecclésiastique*, divested the life stories of the Virgin Mary and the Apostles of the legends with which the popular imagination had so plentifully embellished them. The thing was in the air.

However, these various tendencies were not effectively polarized until a certain person came upon the scene who had the courage to deliver himself of some very simple, but very decisive words. They ran like this:

Those who profess and call themselves critics should be content to devote themselves exclusively to explaining the literal meaning of their authors and should disregard everything that is irrelevant to that purpose.[1]

With Richard Simon and his *Histoire critique du Vieux Testament*, which was published in 1678, criticism comes into its own.

The term is a technical one, as Richard Simon pointed out in his preface: "As nothing has so far appeared in French on this subject, my readers must not be surprised if I have sometimes availed myself of expressions that may sound a little strangely in their ears. Every art has its own peculiar terminology, which is regarded more or less as its inviolable property. It is in this specialized sense that I have employed the words *critic* and *criticism* in the work which follows, together with some others of the same nature, to which I was obliged to have recourse in order to express myself in the terms proper to the art of which I was treating. These terms will come as no novelty to scholars, who have for some time been accustomed to their use in our language. When we refer, for example, to the book to which its author, Louis Cappelle, has given the title *Critica Sacra*, or to the Commentaries on the Scriptures which have appeared in England under the title *Critici Sacri*, we should, if we were speaking French, refer to *la Critique de Cappelle*, *les Critiques d'Angleterre*."

This particular art, which now proposes to overstep the boundaries of purely learned coteries, to display its power far and wide, is an end in itself. Its purpose is to establish the degree of genuineness, of authenticity, to be ascribed to the texts with which

[1] *Histoire critique du Vieux Testament*, Vol. III, chap. XV.

it is called upon to deal, and it disregards anything and everything that is extraneous to that end. It is not concerned, for example, with maintaining the beauty of this passage, or the moral soundness of that. If it addresses itself to the examination of some sacred work, it does so quite independently of any theological considerations, theology being wholly outside its province. It must neither attack nor defend it. The critic, as such, may not put any gloss or interpretation of his own upon the text, and no authority can make that text other than what it is. If a certain passage runs counter to a given dogma, and if the passage in question is shown to be authentic, then it is the dogma, not the text that has to suffer. If a passage is essential to support a dogma, and that passage proves to be apocryphal, that passage must be expunged. Whether it be the *Iliad*, the *Aeneid*, or the *Pentateuch* that is in question, the principles of criticism are the same. Criticism will have nothing to do with the *a priori*. The moment it comes to busy itself with characters graven on stone, engrossed on parchment, or written on paper, criticism is its own sovereign mistress.

The basis of criticism is philology; philology, once a modest handmaiden, now a queen. What Renan wrote about the lofty status of philology, Richard Simon, from the realm of the shades, must surely have applauded, for such had been his own opinion. To be a critic and a philologist, such was his heart's desire. Critics, the chronologists, too, had essayed to be before him. They, too, had proclaimed that they were concerned with nothing but their own art, that is to say, with the computation of time; but they had been scared at their own discoveries. What they chiefly lacked was any real understanding of the nature of the revolution they claimed to be bringing about, and in no wise had they attempted to sound the inner meaning of the sacred text. Grotius, too, had been a critic in his commentaries on the Old and New Testaments. But he had not been strict enough. Twice he had infringed the very rule which he himself had laid down; in the first place he had invoked the testimony of pagan antiquity, which was entirely irrelevant to the matter in hand; in the second place, he had permitted himself to be biased by his own personal opinions. He was an Arminian, a Socinian, yet, as a general rule, his judgments were impartial, and his readings were chosen on their intrinsic merits; *as a general rule*, but not always; occasionally they were selected because they happened to favour the Arminians, the Socinians. And Spinoza! A critic he certainly was, and one can hardly fail to see in him the direct forerunner of Richard Simon, who, though he very decidedly contests and repudiates his conclusions, does so with that shade, that hint of deference, which a really great mind never fails to inspire. "Do not accuse me of using the same language as does the impious Spinoza, who states his complete disbelief in the miracles recorded in the Scriptures. This idea, which is widely entertained, does me wrong, and I beg you to dismiss it from your minds. It is right and proper to condemn the impious conclusions which Spinoza draws from some of the axioms he lays down; but those axioms are not always false in themselves, not always to be cast aside."[1] Spinoza was endowed with the insight of genius, but he is not always perfectly sound in his philology, and this defect detracts somewhat from the constructive portion of his exegesis; Spinoza allowed his metaphysics to get the better of his science. It was not until Richard Simon came on the scene that criticism attained its purity, prescribing its own laws and rigorously observing them. On the conclusions to which it led, neither philosophy nor dogma had any influence whatever. The manuscript, the ink, the writing, the letters, the way they were formed, commas, full-stops, accents—these were the things, and the only things, that mattered. This mundane science brooked no interference from religious authority.

He was a little man, with a high-pitched voice, plain of feature, and not particularly intelligent-looking. "You couldn't say of him, as you might of some people, that 'his face was his fortune'." Nor had Nature shown him any more indulgence in regard to his birth and worldly circumstances generally. He was the son of a humble Dieppe blacksmith. What, however, Nature *had* bestowed on him was a passionate love of study, a clear-sighted and powerful intelligence, and an indomitable will, and, over and above these things, with a character that was at once stubborn and supple. He got through his humanities and philosophy with the Oratorians at Dieppe, and, following his natural bent, determined to enter the Order, proceeding, in due course, with a bursary, to serve his noviciate in Paris. There, however, he came within an ace of quitting the Congregation altogether "by reason of certain

[1] *Lettres choisies*, éd. de 1730, tome IV, Lettre 12.

aversions which he could not overcome". Thus he would have come to grief at the very start, almost, if a wealthy patron, the Abbé de La Roque, had not put him on his feet again, and provided the money for his return to Paris, so that he might go through with his theological course. It was now that his vocation in life was definitely decided. He was an indifferent humanist, still less of a scholastic. No; what he really hankered after was a subject very much out of the common, and one that was bristling with difficulties. It was Hebrew, and at Hebrew he set to work.

In 1662, he returned to the Oratory, and was allowed to go on with his studies. Here is a story about him, one of those anecdotes that throw a revealing light on characters like his, and symbolize, as it were, their significance. His brethren were shocked to discover a number of heretical books in his room, amongst others, a polyglot Bible from London, and a number of critical commentaries on the sacred text. They went and reported what they had found. But it so happened that M. Simon had an accomplice, and that accomplice was none other than the Father Superior himself, Père Bertad. The pair of them used to get through a portion of the Scriptures in the original Hebrew every day. So it happened that the venerable sexagenarian sat at the feet of this very youthful master, and so it was that M. Simon got the best of the encounter.

Perhaps the happiest days of his life were those which he spent in the library of the Oratory House in the Rue Saint-Honoré, cataloguing the Oriental books which belonged to the Congregation. To broaden and deepen his knowledge of philology; to go back to the sources of things; to have all around him, within reach of his hand, the very best of teachers and, truth to tell, the only ones, all this made every moment a joy. Nor was he content with this daily browsing on books and manuscripts; he made the personal acquaintance of some Rabbinical Jews, in particular of one Jona Salvador, with whom he read the Bible. In 1670, the year he was ordained priest, he drew up, at Salvador's earnest request, a document in defence of the Jews of Metz, who had been charged with committing a ritual murder.

Would you sail the wide Rabbinical Sea? Then choose, said Simon, a pilot thoroughly accustomed to making that long and difficult voyage. For him, it was to last for years, the voyage over those mighty waters. He neglected nothing that might be calculated to make it direct and sure. He consulted all the charts, and studied all the constellations. He braced himself for the effort, called up all his powers—his clarity, for clarity he could bring even into the thorniest of grammatical questions; his sagacity, his discernment, his candour, his perspicacity, his accuracy.[1] He drew on his accumulated stores of erudition, especially on his Hebrew; and at last the day came when he felt that he could give his *Histoire critique du Vieux Testament* with confidence to the world.

"To begin with, we cannot arrive at a thorough understanding of the sacred books unless we know in the first place the various states in which the texts were found, and in what times and places, and unless we have accurate knowledge of all the changes they have undergone . . ." Thus the guiding principle and essential rule of his method are at the outset made clear. He repeated them on every possible occasion. "I am convinced", he said, "that we cannot read the Bible intelligently if we have no preliminary acquaintance with textual criticism". As regards philology, here is a case in point that will give you a vivid idea of its importance: Omit a word, a single word, some seemingly quite insignificant thing, such as a conjunction, and you may find yourself lending countenance to a heresy. The third chapter of the Gospel according to St. Luke begins, "Now, in the fifteenth year of the reign of Tiberius", which implies that something has preceded it, since the particle *now*, which the grammarians call an adversative, necessarily denotes a reference to something already said. On the other hand, begin straightway with "In the fifteenth year of the reign of Tiberius", and you will be playing into the hands of those early Marcionite heretics who maintained that the first two chapters of St. Luke were not part of the original gospel but were a later accretion. Still more true is it that the Old Testament, bristling as it is with difficulties, difficulties of which the uninstructed do not so much as suspect the existence, cannot be profitably studied unless we respect the rules and are actuated by the spirit to which I have referred.

Take up your Bible, look at it with a perfectly open mind. How does it strike you? Can it possibly be regarded as the word

---

[1] All these expressions are used by F. Spanheim in his *Lettre à un ami, où l'on rend compte d'un livre qui a pour titre, Histoire critique du Vieux Testament, publiée à Paris en 1678* (1679).

of God, directly inspired, committed to writing and handed down in its original state to us of the present day?

When looked into, replies Richard Simon, it is abundantly clear that the text has been modified, altered, and that it presents certain chronological problems which call for solution; that in some of the narratives there have been some strange transpositions, sometimes involving whole chapters. Let us, then, put ourselves back into the days when they were written, let us endeavour to discover and to understand the nature of Hebrew civilization. Who and what were the prophets? They were scribes, public writers, men whose duty it was faithfully to record the history of the State and to store these annals in the archives set apart for the purpose. "If there were public writers in the Hebrew State as far back as the time of Moses, as there most probably were, it will be easy to settle the various arguments adduced to prove that Moses was not the author of the Pentateuch, the proof being founded as a rule on the manner in which it is written, the object apparently being to suggest that someone other than Moses collected the facts and recorded them in writing. Granting that these public writers did exist, to them would be allotted all the annalistic part of these books, while the laws and ordinances would be assigned to Moses, and these it is that Scripture calls the Law of Moses." And inasmuch as these prophets or public writers not only performed the task of collecting contemporary information and consigning it to the archives, but sometimes gave a new turn to matter recorded by their predecessors, this explains the alterations and additions that are found in the other sacred books. Furthermore, as these books are but epitomes of much longer records, it is not surprising that it is impossible to elicit a strict and definite chronology from the Scriptures. It would be absurd, for example, to ignore the existence of other Persian kings besides those named in the Bible, and to base our computation of time on the duration of their successive reigns, seeing that the Scribes confined their records to matters exclusively concerning the Jews, while the profane writers make mention of several other kings, and thus greatly extend the chronological period involved. Lastly, we must bear in mind the ravages of time, and the carelessness of copyists; let us also picture to ourselves the physical conditions in which these latter did their work. "As the Hebrew originals

were written on little rolls or sheets, which were put one on top
of another and of which each made up a volume, it followed that
if these rolls were accidentally put in the wrong order, the
sequence of the events recorded would be correspondingly
disarranged."

Briefly, what happened was that Richard Simon explained his
ideas with such seeming simplicity and with such cogent force
that ordinary folk, though to begin with they had followed him
but falteringly into regions so hallowed and mysterious, now
began to listen with ever growing attention to what their guide
had to tell them. He possessed the secret of imparting to his
demonstrations of concrete matters an air of luminous and convincing logic. Furthermore, he purposely avoided expressing
himself in the language of the theologians and resolved that his
Histoire critique should be given to the world in good, honest
French. Latin was appropriate enough for professed exegetists
arguing some knotty and recondite question, but the evolution
of the Biblical texts, in its general aspect, should be set forth in
such a manner as to be understood by the world in general.

The characters of the great actors we have been studying
hitherto were comparatively simple. Born rebels, they were never
really happy unless they were breathing the atmosphere of opposition. The psychology of Richard Simon is somewhat more
complex. A Catholic priest, he would have it that he was strictly
faithful not only to the letter of Catholic doctrine, but also to
the spirit of the Church. The Church may condemn him, but
he sets to work with all his might to prove that she is mistaken,
that she is acting in error.

He *would* insist that he was orthodox. And it is a fact that, so
far from denying the inspiration of the Scriptures, he extended it
so as to include even the people that re-moulded them. He declared that God, who had made known His will to Moses, made
it known also to the scribes and annalists who, at various times
in history, recast the Mosaic text. The persons who were responsible for the alterations we find in the Bible "having the
power to write the Sacred Books had likewise the power to revise
them." The prophets, the scribes still continue to be the spokes-
men of God. Though patently human in the way they were carried
out, those successive changes were none the less inspired by God.

Those who edited and re-edited the Biblical text were appointed by God to fulfil that sacred mission. The revisions began in the days of Moses and went on throughout the ages. The Jews were the chosen people, not in any figurative sense, but in fact and reality: "The Hebrew Republic differs from the other countries of the world in that it has ever acknowledged one sole head, namely God, who continued to guide it even when it was subjected to the rule of kings. That is why it has been given the name of the Holy and Divine Republic; its people likewise assumed the title of Saints in order that by that glorious appellation they might be distinguished from the other nations of the world. Therefore also it was that God, through Moses and the prophets that came after him, Himself gave the law to the race he had chosen to be exclusively his own."[1]

Others may decry tradition, he, for his part, defends it. It is not true that the Scriptures are always easy to understand, nor that, by the mere reading of them, you may easily learn God's will. Tradition is the indispensable complement to the Scriptures; it is its office to explain and interpret. The *Histoire critique du Vieux Testament* lays great stress upon it: "It will be shown in the pages which follow, that, if the rule of law is divorced from the rule of fact, in other words, if the Scriptures are unaccompanied by Tradition, one can be sure of scarcely anything in religion. It is in no way to derogate from the Word of God to associate with it the Tradition of the Church, since he who bids us search the Scriptures has bidden us also to betake ourselves to the Church, to whom he confided the sacred treasure."[2] And Richard Simon goes on to explain that, before the law was committed to writing by Moses, the early patriarchs preserved the purity of the faith wholly and solely by tradition; that after the time of Moses, the Jews, in cases of difficulty, always consulted the interpreters of the law. Look also at what happened in the case of the New Testament, where we find that the Gospel was regularly taught in several churches before any of it had been committed to writing; the same unwritten word was preserved and perpetuated in the principal churches, which had been founded by the Apostles. So true is this that an Irenaeus or a Tertullian would rely on it in his disputes with heretics in

[1]Book 1, chap. II.
[2]Ibid., Preface.

preference even to the Word of God as contained in the Sacred Books. In the Councils, the Bishops quoted the tradition of their respective churches in order to elucidate obscure passages in the Bible. "That is why the Fathers of the Council of Trent laid it down in their wisdom that no interpretation of the Scriptures should ever conflict with the unanimous decisions of the Fathers. Furthermore, that same Council ascribed as much authority to duly authenticated oral tradition as to the Word of God in the Sacred Books, it being held that those unwritten traditions originated with our Lord, who communicated them to the Apostles, whence they have come down to us of the present day. We may regard these traditions as forming, in their entirety, a compendium of the Christian Faith as it was propounded in the earliest days of Christianity in the first churches, independently of Holy Writ. . . ."

Fully sure of his position as defined by these forthright declarations, Richard Simon let loose his thunders against the Protestants, who, by taking their stand on the Bible, the whole Bible, and nothing but the Bible, were really relying on writings that had been altered and mutilated, so that, rejecting tradition, they rejected, *ipso facto*, the guidance of the Spirit, which preceded, accompanied and illuminated whatsoever was doubtful or obscure in the said writings. He carried on a fierce and prolonged controversy with Isaac Vossius, Canon of Windsor, and with Jacques Basnage, a pastor, first at Rouen, afterwards at Rotterdam. His most violent fulminations were reserved for the Socinians who not only looked on tradition as possessing no authority whatever, but ignored certain portions of the Bible itself so that they might believe just what it suited them to believe, that is to say what was generally held to be acceptable to reason, and nothing else. In this sense, he represented himself as a defender of Catholicism.

In this sense; but who could fail to perceive the flaw in his argument, how he passes from an idea in one category to another in a category wholly different. He begins by stating that the text of the Mosaic law is overlaid by a number of subsequent alluvial deposits. That is a fact; or at least he regards it as such. But then he goes on to say that the writers who altered the wording of the law, so far back as we can trace them, were also inspired by God. Now that is not a fact; it is simply a personal belief, a theory of his own devising. On the one hand we have an historical circumstance which may be scientifically proved; on the other, something to be believed, to be taken on faith. A non-Christian might very well assent to the former proposition; but not the latter. Arguing from a non-religious standpoint we might very well agree to the first part of his thesis, namely, that the Scriptures betray countless traces of man's handiwork, without going on to admit that the Jews who rehandled the original text were divinely inspired, which was what he held himself, not in the light of any evidence he could produce to support it, but solely from his own personal conviction. So here Richard Simon stepped out of the sphere of criticism and philology, the sphere whose laws and limits he himself had so rigidly defined.

He quits those confines when he gives an account of his aims and intentions in his prefaces. But, if we follow him through the details of his *Histoire critique*, we see quite clearly to which side his natural bent inclines him. Note him as he sets to work on the Pentateuch. His object is to show that Moses could not have been its sole author. It contains quotations, proverbial sayings, poetical verses which belong to a period subsequent to that of Moses. It recounts things that happened after Moses' day. "Could anyone, for instance, maintain that Moses wrote the last chapter of Deuteronomy, the chapter that gives an account of his death and burial?"[1] The Pentateuch contains innumerable repetitions. "Take for example the account of the Flood in the seventh chapter of Genesis"; in verse 17 we read, "The waters increased, and bare up the ark, and it was lift up above the earth". In verse 18, "And the waters prevailed and were increased greatly upon the earth: and the ark went upon the face of the waters." In verse 19 we have, "And the waters prevailed exceedingly upon the earth, and all the high hills that were under the whole heaven were covered", which is again repeated in verse 20, which reads, "Fifteen cubits upward did the waters prevail, and the mountains were covered". "Is it not reasonable to suppose that if one and the same writer had been describing that event, he would have done so in far fewer words, especially in a history?" Richard Simon pursues his labours, and when he has finished them, what is the reader's impression? That the

[1]Book, I, ch. 5.

Biblical account of the creation lacks coherence, that it was put together at widely separated dates by hands little fitted for the task; that, to put it mildly, it was retouched so often and so clumsily that it is impossible to get at the original wording. In such a chaotic state of affairs, what assistance could tradition afford?

And so Richard Simon sets to work to enquire into tradition, doing so in the strictest critical spirit and not at all in the spirit of a believer. Here, too, let us contemplate him at his task, and see at close range how he approaches St. Augustine. That great Saint occupies a place apart in Biblical criticism by reason of his spiritual and intellectual power and the soundness of his judgment. "He has pointed out, in his books on Christian doctrine, and elsewhere in his writings, the qualities requisite for the due interpretation of the Scriptures". Only, "being of a modest nature, he frankly confessed that most of those qualifications were lacking in him", and he displayed but a small degree of accuracy in his commentaries. Being ignorant of Hebrew, he recognized that the work he had undertaken on the book of Genesis with the object of refuting the Manichaeans was beyond him, "nor was he ashamed to condemn work that he had done over-hastily and without the equipment necessary for a proper explanation of the Scriptures". Instead of aiming at the literal meaning "he busies himself almost entirely with allegorical interpretations as remote from history as from the letter of the text". "His subtle and penetrating intelligence readily enabled him to recognize the difficulties presented by the Scriptures, indeed, he sometimes discovered difficulties where none appeared to exist; but he was not sufficiently experienced in this kind of work to offer solutions satisfactory to the reader." "Moreover, he was full of certain theological and philosophical prejudices which he introduced into everything he wrote. . . ."[1] And so on. We will only add that Richard Simon took a mischievous delight in pitting St. Augustine against St. Jerome, and that it would be interesting to know what sort of an idea of St. Augustine's authority a non-Christian reader would be likely to form.

He soon gets back to criticism and philology, the things which really excite his interest. He is firmly convinced that nothing can stand up against "sound reasoning", least of all the intuitions of

[1]Book III, ch. 9.

"the *illuminati* and their brother fanatics". All that talk about an "inward voice", an "inward spirit", "which reveals to us the innermost truths of the Scriptures" was well enough for legendary times. "Today, the 'inward spirit' is little heard of except among the Quakers and other similar enthusiasts, who, for lack of brains and common sense, are glad to have recourse to it to fill the gap."

Battling against wind and tide, he held on his course. On the 21st May, 1678, he received notice of his expulsion from the Oratory. The same year, the *Histoire critique du Vieux Testament* was banned by an order of the Royal Council, in pursuance whereof the Lieutenant of Police impounded the printed copies and consigned them to the pulping machine. In 1683, the Congregation of the Index formally condemned the book. But Simon, seeing that he would never be able to satisfy the censors, actuated also by the fact that a spurious edition printed by "M. Elzevir" from a manuscript copy was in circulation outside France, obtained an authentic text and had it published in Amsterdam in 1685. He continued his labours; his abundant energy must needs find an outlet, and having dealt with the Old Testament, it was only logical that his next objective should be the New. By way of clearing a path for himself, he produced a number of introductory studies: in 1689, *l'Histoire critique du Texte du Nouveau Testament*, in 1690, *l'Histoire critique des Versions du Nouveau Testament*, in 1693, *l'Histoire critique des Commentaires du Nouveau Testament*. Each title contains the word "critique" and in case anyone should misconceive its meaning, he explains it again; he has never done with explaining it: From the earliest Christian times, there have been learned men in the Church who have devoted themselves to the task of carefully correcting such errors as had from time to time crept into the Sacred Text. The present work, which demands an accurate knowledge of the books together with diligent searching of the manuscript copies, is called "critique" because it forms a judgment as to the readings which should be adopted. The word "critique" is a technical one, mainly employed in works whose aim it is to examine the various readings in order to decide which are authentic and to be retained. That this art should have been unrecognized during the Dark Ages is understandable, that it should continue to be neglected in these days is inexcusable. Nowadays, criticism

should play the part that was formerly assigned to Theology . . .
One can picture the theologians holding up their hands in
horror when they heard those words. "And so, according to this
critic, if we want to understand the New Testament properly,
what we have to do is to confine our attention to the rules of
grammar and let theology and tradition go by the board! I can
think of nothing that would suit the Socinians better than that."[1]

At last the great work, the *Nouveau Testament de N.-S. Jésus-*
Christ, traduit sur l'Ancienne édition latine avec des remarques, made its
appearance. It was published at Trévoux in 1702. It was a translation based wholly and solely on the text, having no other aim
than to give an exact literal rendering of that text, and disregarding all those traditional interpretations which, according to
Simon, were paraphrases, glosses, often inaccurate and sometimes completely misleading, but which had come to be looked
on as sacred. Its margins filled with comparative notes, which
Simon's knowledge of Greek and Hebrew suggested to him, it
was, if one may so call it, a "critical" translation. "In conclusion,
I would add that as I had no other object in my notes than to
bring out the literal meaning of the Gospels and the Apostles, it
will be useless to look for any of that mystery-mongering which
only the ignorant and the thoughtless find to their taste." The
meaning, the literal meaning, that and nothing else: Otherwise
one often gets involved in that sort of unintelligible verbiage
which some people call *spiritual.* This Trévoux version was
condemned.

We must not class Richard Simon among the romantics; still
less must we sugar-coat him. He was grim and harsh in nature.
His intellectual force was intense; his emotional, very much less
so. He delighted in the major contests, the great clashes of ideas,
but he also had a taste for the subtler devices of warfare: "Know,
my dear Sir, that a certain anonymous theologian of the Paris
Faculty, and René de l'Ile, priest of the Gallican Church, and
Jérôme le Camus, and Jérôme de Sainte-Foi, and Pierre Ambrun,
Minister of the Gospel, and Origenes Adamantius, Ambrosius
and Jérôme Acosta and the Sieur de Moni, and the Sieur de
Simonville—know, I say, that all these writers, and a good many
others besides, are just one and the same person"; to whit,

[1] Arnauld to Bossuet, July, 1693.

Richard Simon. In his controversies with the Catholics he was not always quite fair and above board. In the copy of his *Histoire critique* which he sent to the Doctors of the Sorbonne for examination, the dangerous chapters were omitted; it is also to be observed that in his clashes with the Protestants, Christian charity was the last, and the least, of his concerns. Overbearing and harsh, he could utter words of scathing irony; his arrows, which he discharged with gleeful satisfaction, were cruelly barbed. Even in his principal works, despite his pretended self-effacement, the satisfaction with which he evidently regards himself is more than equalled by the disdain he evinces for his opponents. But it is when we come to his letters—which more resemble pamphlets or lampoons than letters—that a certain strain of ill-nature— or should we say of gall?—becomes especially evident in his moral make-up. It is not merely a man at war with the powers that be, a man oppressed, frustrated, embittered, ready to stick at nothing to defend himself, that we behold, but a man for whom heresy has a positive lure, a man who delights in expatiating on doctrines of doubtful orthodoxy, to dwell on theologians who have cut themselves adrift from the Church, to harp on books that circulate under the rose, forbidden books that foster the seeds of schism, books charged with dynamite. How is such an attitude of mind to be reconciled with the devoutly religious character which he claimed to maintain?

> For some, who have his secret meaning guess'd,
> Have found our author not too much a priest . . .[1]

But of his inward struggles, if such he had, he never lets us into the secret. To know what kind of faith was really his, we should need to know something of those voluminous notes which, in a cautious moment, he himself committed to the flames. He had sought refuge in his own parish of Bolleville in Normandy. One day he was sent for and put through an interrogation by the intendant of the province, and he was afraid the next thing would be that they would come and seize his papers. So what did he do but stuff them into some big casks. These he trundled off by night to a field hard by and there set fire to them. What Simon believed in his innermost soul He from whom no secrets are hid

[1]Dryden, *Religio laici*, 1682.

alone can tell. Though expelled from the Oratory, he always considered himself a member of the Order, and no one ever clung more stubbornly than he to the *Tu es sacerdos in aeternum*, the ineffaceable sign of the priesthood. To the very end, he went on with his learned studies as one to whom knowledge was all in all, always obstinately regarding himself as a son of the Church, despite the Church's censure. "He received the Sacraments in an edifying and Christian frame of mind and fell asleep in the Lord in the month of August, 1712, in the seventy-fourth year of his age."[1]

In protesting against those stereotyped forms of expression, "It has always been held", "It has been constantly taught", "It is a tradition as old as the world", and the like, Richard Simon lent a hand in that re-assessment of values which we have already so often observed to be taking place in men's minds. Yet again his influence made itself felt because it was he who inspired criticism with a consciousness of its power and its duties. *Critici studii utilitas et necessitas.* His adversary, Jean Le Clerc who, judging by certain elements in his character, differed from him much less than either of them suspected, published, in 1697, a sort of official code of this triumphant *Art critique*. Lastly, he was responsible for starting a widespread movement of Biblical exegesis, if not among the Catholics—he rather alarmed *them*— at all events among the Protestants. More than forty works refuting his *Histoire critique du Vieux Testament* are sufficient indication of the sensation he caused. He had few direct disciples, though a pupil of his, Raphael Levi, otherwise known as Louis de Byzance, translated the Koran on lines he had learnt from Simon. But there were many whom he stirred on to new and daring flights. For example, in 1707 a Neapolitan, one Biagio Garofalo, showed that there are many metrical passages in the Bible, a number of them in rhyme. Would he have dared to draw attention to these traces of human handiwork in the sacred text, if the author of the *Histoire critique* had not paved the way for people to say what they liked, however bold it might be?

And then the sceptics, what an ally he was for them! They were not capable of examining the sacred texts themselves, but

[1]Bruzen de Lamartinière, *Éloge de Richard Simon.*

they were only too ready to believe anything that tended to diminish the authority, and derogate from the power, of the Scriptures. On the whole, what they said amounted practically to this: "How can you expect me to believe what I am told in these Bibles, things written ages ago, translated from all sorts of different languages by ignorant people who mistook their meaning, or by dishonest ones who changed it, heightening it up, or toning it down, into the words we read today."[1]

[1]Baron de Lahontan, *Dialogues curieux*, 1703, p. 163. Ed. G. Chinard.

IV

BOSSUET AT BAY

WHENEVER we think of Bossuet, we always behold
him in his sovereign majesty, as Rigaud depicted him
in his famous portrait. It may be a commonplace to
bring in a reference to that magnificent work of art; if so, it is an
excusable commonplace, for the simple reason that it is un-
avoidable. The manner of the thing, its pomp and splendour,
once seen, never fade from the recollection. Or again, we may
behold the great orator delivering one of his famous funeral
panegyrics. From the very opening sentences, we feel as though
borne aloft into the realms of the ineffable; the swelling flood of
eloquence, thrilling with the sound of tears and passionate
entreaty, awakens in our hearts emotions so deep and so poignant
as to be almost beyond endurance. And when, at last, that
religious music culminates in a paean to the world beyond the
grave, it is as though we had been listening to some prophet of
God, some dweller in a region more than human.

Such an idea of Bossuet is a perfectly true one; but it implies
that we are viewing him in one particular aspect. The river of
time has borne everything away save the noble, the majestic, the
triumphant. But there was another Bossuet, a Bossuet humbled
and plunged deep in sorrow. In saying this, we are urging
nothing against his convictions, at once so admirable, so simple,
so profound. Once, and for all, he had dedicated himself to the
Eternal, the Universal: *quod ubique, quod semper* . . . "The truth
that came from God was perfect from the beginning." In that
statement is mirrored his unshakable belief; there exists a truth
which God revealed to man; that truth is contained in the
Gospel, it is attested by miracles, and, being divine and therefore

perfect, it is unchangeable; if it admitted of variation it would not be the truth. The office of the Church is to be the guardian thereof: "The Church of Jesus Christ, watchful guardian of the dogmas committed to her charge, makes no change in them; she adds not, neither does she take away, robbing them of nought that is essential, adding to them nought that is superfluous. Her sole task is to keep burnished the things entrusted to her from of old, to confirm what has been sufficiently explained, to guard and protect whatever has been confirmed and defined."[1] To this sole and immutable truth it is the duty of everyone to conform, for if everyone took it into his head to embrace what he individually looked on as the truth, chaos and confusion would result, it being clear that in regard to any given question there cannot be a million truths, nor a thousand, nor a hundred, nor ten, nor two, but one and only one. "And so we get a clear idea of the real fundamental meaning of the words Catholic and Heretic. A heretic is one who has his own opinion. What does having an opinion mean? It means following one's own ideas, one's own particular notions. Whereas the Catholic, on the other hand, is what the name signifies, that is to say one who, not relying on his own private judgment, puts his trust in the Church, and defers to her teaching."[2]

O Bible, beloved Bible, how beautiful, how rich in colour, how moving is the manner in which thou makest known to man the history of his race and settest forth the rules of conduct he should follow. In the Bible are the principles on which the Catholic faith is based, interpreted in the light of tradition; the Bible is the authority which prevents those principles from being incessantly called in question. Bossuet never gave up his Bible; from his early childhood he had loved it dearly, and dearly he continued to love it, till the end of his days; he could not do without it; it was his sustenance, his daily bread. Just as some humble country *curé* will con over and over again his book of prayers, albeit he knows those prayers by heart, so did Bossuet, who knew his Bible by heart, continue to read it again and again. Since it was the Fathers of the Church who had expounded, confirmed and developed the original deposit of truth, what wonder

[1] *Premier avertissement aux Protestants*, 1689. Ed. Lachat, vol. XV, p. 184 (Citation de Vincent de Lérins).
[2] *Première instruction pastorale sur les promesses de l'Église*, 1700. Ed. Lachat. vol. XVII, p. 112.

that he should betake himself so frequently to them? He had a passion for the printed word. No sooner did a controversy spring up than he collected all the documents he could that bore upon the matter. His faith, indeed, was firmly based, but that was no reason for his not seeking all the information he could gather; to do so was at once his duty and his pleasure. But of all the books that were, those which he consulted most freely, most eagerly, were the Fathers, the servants of the Church; and of these, most especially, most particularly, St. Augustine; a fact that Le Dieu, his secretary who narrowly scanned his ways and habits, does not fail to record. "He was so steeped in St. Augustine's teaching, so deeply attached to his principles, that he never explained a dogma, never gave an instruction, never replied to an argument without first having recourse to St. Augustine. In him he found all. When he had to preach a sermon to his flock he would ask me for his Bible and for St. Augustine."

Sure in his belief, enlightened by recourse to books, Bossuet integrates himself into an order which justifies his own existence, and the significance of what he was and what he did lies in his adherence to this conception of the world, and in the way in which he established it and rendered it visible to the minds of others. He did not chafe at the limits imposed, he accepted them. In the inwardness of his own consciousness, he felt perfectly free to devise a scheme of life for himself: our effort in life should not be perpetually directed to criticizing a rule freely and deliberately accepted, but to profiting by the certitude created by it that we may live a life of charity and good deeds. There was an admirable saying of his which he borrowed from the Book of Kings: "Obedience is better than sacrifice". We obey; we obey God; we obey the King, God's representative on earth; and we have the comfort of consciously acting in accordance with the will of Him who established the order by which we live, and which is indeed the Truth and the Life. We are done now with guesses at truth, with anxious searchings of the heart. He was even as a writer of the classical school who, having subscribed once for all to the law of the Three Unities because it seemed to him to be sound and based on reason, takes his stand inside the limits it prescribes and, within their protecting shelter, constructs a masterpiece.

Temperamentally, he was no ascetic. He regarded Rancé with

esteem and affection. When he went to visit him at la Trappe the
monks saw their Prior and the Bishop walking and talking for
long periods together, devoting to friendly intercourse the time
which they did not spend in prayer. But he did not prolong his
stay at the monastery. Like the classic again, he shunned excess
of every kind; there was danger, he thought, even in an excess
of piety. Implacable towards the obstinate, the self-opinionated,
he was gentle towards the weak, and charitable to the poor. His
table, to which the wines of Volnay and Saint-Laurent were no
strangers, was liberal, but not luxurious. He was susceptible to
the charm of nature, he admired the comeliness of the gardens of
Germigny, the finest in the world; he dearly loved a tree-shaded
alley, where he could read and meditate at his ease upon his
breviary, and with the emotions that a piece of landscape may
sometimes awaken in a sensitive heart he was far from being
unfamiliar. There were times when he could be very stern, yet
he was capable also of extraordinary tenderness. And he had the
gift of friendship. In his bosom, St. Augustine was on the best
of terms with St. Vincent de Paul, his master. If his attitude
towards life was sturdy and robust, it was also evenly balanced.

Doubt gained no entry into a mind and soul thus constituted, a
mind which yielded allegiance to nothing which had not satisfied
the tribunal of its own judgment, a mind which possessed the
clearest possible consciousness of its own ideas, its own aims; for
Bossuet, quite as much as the most exacting sceptic, took accurate
note of the trend of his ideas and of the goal to which they were
tending. Chatting one day with his nephew, the Abbé, he told
him about a question that had once been put to him by a dying
man, and the answer he had given.

*An unbeliever, being on his death bed, sent for me and asked me to
come to him. "Sir", he said, "I have always regarded you as an upright
man. Now that I am near to death, speak frankly to me, for I trust you,
and tell me truly what you hold about religion."*

*"I tell you that it is sure and certain, and that I have never had any
doubts about it."*[1]

About that ineradicable faith there is no more to be said. But
instead of viewing him in his solitary splendour, let us put him
back into the throng and press of his contemporaries, let us try
to visualize him amid that restless welter of disputes, trials,

[1]Le Dieu, *Journal*, 15 May, 1700.

frustrations that were his portion; let us contemplate him, not in his younger days, or in the period that witnessed his glorious rise to the plenitude of his power and influence, but in his later years, when the burden of old age lay heavy upon him; let us try to see him, not as he is within the gilded frame of that famous portrait, but in actual life, as the champion of a tradition that was now attacked on every side, as one forsaken and, as it were, left derelict by his time.

The *Tractatus Theologico-politicus*, which Antoine Arnauld sent him, and of which he had a copy in his own library, was not merely an impious book, it was an exasperating one. What! This Spinoza fellow! This wretched Dutch Jew, giving himself these high and mighty airs simply because he knew Hebrew! According to his ideas, Latin was not enough; no, nor Greek either. Don't talk about the Bible at all, or else learn Hebrew!

Bossuet had been quite satisfied with the Vulgate. Of Hebrew he knew not a word. This was a serious matter, and he realized that it was so. If he was to reply on equal terms, as one who was well up in his subject; if he was not to seem old-fashioned, behind the times, and, maybe, ridiculous; if, moreover, he was to obey the still small voice which spoke within telling him where his duty lay, he would have to put himself to school again. That was easier said than done. But he worked with a will. It is pleasant to conjure up the picture of those little gatherings; a few serious-minded laymen and some priests meet at regular intervals; each one brings his Bible. One of the party reads the Hebrew version, another the Greek. Then they look up St. Jerome and the doctors of the Church; comments are offered, the passage is discussed, Bossuet sums up and pronounces judgment, the Abbé Fleury writes the minutes of the meeting. They form a definite group. They are anxious to increase their knowledge; they brace themselves for the struggle, for something tells them there is trouble ahead. But Hebrew—will Bossuet ever master it? On Maundy Thursday, 1678, the Abbé Eusèbe Renaudot, a member of the group, acquaints the Bishop with the contents of a work which is just about to be published. It is the *Histoire critique du Vieux Testament*, by Richard Simon. The book had been granted the royal licence, it had been passed by the ecclesiastical censors, it had been approved by the Superior General of the Congregation of the Oratory; the King was on the point of accepting the dedication of the book, for Père La Chaise had undertaken to use his good offices to that end. Bossuet was filled with indignation. This so-called "critical" history was nothing more nor less than a mass of impiety, a fortress for sceptics. It must not appear. Despite the sacred character of the day, despite the ceremonies and penitential observances connected with it, Bossuet hurries away to the Chancellor, Michel Le Tellier; he puts the case before him; he uses all his powers of persuasion; he brings to bear all the pressure he has at his command, and at last he gains his point: the book shall be banned.

But the pity of it all! That a priest, of all people in the world, a priest of the Oratory, should treat the Bible in such a manner! All his life long Richard Simon was fated to be a grief and a trial to Bossuet. He might show him the most attentive deference, might do his utmost to prove that he was not a rebel, Simon could not conceal from those keen and watchful eyes the real nature of the impulse that was bearing him irresistibly along. He would fain dethrone theology, and set up grammar in its place: the man was a criminal!

If, when reading the second part of the *Discours sur l'Histoire Universelle*, we recall how Spinoza and Richard Simon haunted and obsessed the mind of Bossuet, we shall the better understand, not only the passionate language of the champion of Catholic orthodoxy, but the real nature of the book itself. His purpose is not so much to expound as to refute. He has to reply to arguments which are, in their nature and essence, completely foreign to his own. No easy task to apply to a profession of faith, to an *a priori* principle, the sort of historical method of proof which his adversaries demand of him and which he must inevitably adopt if he is really to come to grips with them. His position is clearly laid down. The Scriptures, being of divine origin, must not be treated as if they were mere mundane compositions. This said, he has now, in order to reply to these new exegetists, to look at matters from their level, to examine them from a purely human standpoint. That was where Bossuet's difficulty came in. He has to explain how Moses got together the material for his history; he has to dispose of the hypothesis which would ascribe to Esdras the authorship of the Pentateuch. He must examine the text *qua* text, dispel the obscurities, explain the difficulties, account for the alterations to be found in it. Impatient to get clear of these profitless disputes, he drives straight ahead. Never mind details; let us come to essentials. In all the versions of the Bible, we find the same laws, the same miracles, the same prophecies, the same historical sequence; in all, the doctrinal content, in a word, the substance, is the same. What signify a few trifling differences of detail, when we contemplate the massive and immutable whole? Perfectly frank and above-board as he always is, he makes no attempt to evade the case against him; he faces it fairly and squarely, and then essays to demolish it by the sheer sweep and impetus of his attack.

"Finally, and this is the *gravamen* of the charge, have not things been added to what Moses wrote? And how is it that we find an account of his death at the end of the very book he himself is supposed to have written? Well, what is there to marvel at if the writers who continued his narrative added an account of his edifying end, by way of rounding off the story? As for the other additions, what do they amount to? Are we told about some new law, some new rite, or dogma, or miracle, or prophecy? No one dreams of such a thing, nor is there the faintest trace of it. That would have been tantamount to adding something to God's own work. The law forbade such a thing, and the outcry would have been tremendous. Well then, what are they, these additions? Perhaps someone continued an uncompleted genealogy, or supplied information about some town that had changed its original name, or, in regard to the manna wherewith the people were fed for forty years, had stated the time when this celestial food had ceased to descend, and this piece of information, taken from some other book, was recorded in the book of Moses in the form of a note or memorandum regarding something of common interest and common knowledge. Four or five such notes added by Joshua or Samuel, or some other prophet of like antiquity, inasmuch as they related only to matters within everybody's cognizance, matters of plain fact, may easily have been incorporated into the text, and tradition, which brought us the rest, would have brought them along with it. Is there anything so very terrible about that?"

Thereupon, Richard Simon chuckled to himself and indulged in a little mocking laughter. The concession was vastly important. So His Lordship of Meaux *does* admit that additions were made to

Moses' writings, he *does* admit that the Pentateuch was tampered with. That being so, His Lordship the Bishop of Meaux (as well as M. Huet, the Bishop of Avranches) is, in the eyes of the theologians, a Spinozist, and deals a death blow to the Bible.

Irony is not at all to Bossuet's taste. "Right-minded people have little liking for jests of that kind." The thing would not have mattered so much if he had not felt that it was not going to stop there, that there was more to come, that Richard Simon was getting more and more daring with every successive attack, and that "the whole affair was becoming one of extreme importance for the Church". In his already overtaxed existence there was no room for any other task; there was the Dauphin's education, all the work of his diocese, the guidance of the Church of France, whose moral leader he had now become, heresies springing up all round him that had to be coped with, the sermons he was called upon to preach, his official attendances at Court—ah! what a life of toil it was, toil that took up, not only his days, but his nights as well. When all the palace is wrapt in slumber, he rises, lights his lamp, turns to his notes, and begins to write. Something must be done to curtail his multifarious responsibilities, so that he may strike a blow for Tradition and the Fathers, against the onslaughts of Richard Simon; nothing could be more urgent than that.

When the translation of the New Testament appeared, his indignation burst forth anew: Quick! there's not a moment to lose. The book must be stopped, even as the *Histoire critique du Vieux Testament* had been stopped. He must see to it immediately. But four and twenty years have hurried by since then, and we are now in the year 1702. He himself had pronounced the funeral oration over Michel Le Tellier, who had always been so willing, so obedient to his wishes—in the days gone by. But now Pontchartrain was Chancellor in his stead, and Pontchartrain was not compliant, nay, he was hostile, and actually wanted to make him submit to the censors the *Instructions* he was writing with the object of confuting Monsieur Simon. Had it not been for the King, who still stood by him, he must have lost the game. What! Was he, Bossuet, to knuckle under to the Censor? Was he to be bearded by a civil magistrate? Was he to be looked on as a mere drag on the wheel, a hindrance, something out of date and done with? His authority was slipping away from him. Times had changed; the Freethinkers were getting the upper hand; and nothing pained him so cruelly as that.

Often he called for his *magnum opus*, his *Défense de la tradition et des Saints Pères*. He conned it over, he set to work on it again. But he was never to finish it. He must needs go on adding chapter upon chapter, the trouble being that he was combating, not so much some definite person, as something impalpable, an influence, a spirit which permeated everywhere, on every possible occasion. The Richard Simon affair was no sooner disposed of than the case of Ellies Du Pin had to be dealt with. He, too, was a priest, less recalcitrant than the other, it is true, but evincing an air of bland and tranquil innocence that was highly significant. In a voluminous compilation of extracts from various ecclesiastical writers which he brought out, he went the length of saying that sometimes heretics had had deeper insight, and come nearer the truth in their enquiries into the sacred texts than had the Catholics. And he went on to say—a monstrous thing, this!— that some points of capital importance regarding the sacraments, even some of the Church's fundamental dogmas, were still not settled, still undecided in the minds of the Fathers, as late as the third century A.D. The first to commit himself to a definite statement about Original Sin was St. Cyprian, who was also the first to treat fully of penance, and the power of the priesthood to bind and loose; and more in like vein. Bossuet was keeping a wary eye. He did not want to come down too heavily on Ellies Du Pin, who was a relation of M. Racine's, and who, moreover, was always quite willing to confess himself in the wrong. But there were some things he could not tolerate: this soft-soaping of the heretics, to begin with: and this belittling of what Tradition had taught about Original Sin; these, and a good many other things besides. He could not bear to hear the Fathers spoken of with an off-handedness which Catholics in bygone days had never permitted themselves. The most glaring licence was becoming the fashion of this age of ours, "so critical is its temper".

On the 23rd March, 1692, Fénelon wrote him saying: "I rejoiced to see the vigour of the old teacher, the old bishop still unimpaired. I seemed to see you in your big skull-cap, grasping M. Dupin, as an eagle grips a frail sparrowhawk in its talons." It was all very well for Fénelon to treat the matter lightly; the

Lord's sheepfold would be grievously infested if the eagle of Meaux were not on the look-out. But times there were when a sense of mortal weariness descended upon him.[1]

He was fated never to complete the *Défense de la tradition et des Saints Pères*, or the *Politique tirée des propres paroles de l'Écriture Sainte*—ah! how many were the works he was destined never to complete!—all of them of essential and urgent importance. He longed ardently to go to England, to discuss matters with the theologians there, to open their eyes; but to England he never went. England was deep in schism; England had driven out her King and taken in his stead the bitterest foe of France and the Catholic faith. "I can but mourn for England!"[2] Time was when he had dreamed of raising a crusade against the Turks: Ah! for the days when he pronounced the panegyric of Saint Pierre de Nolasque in the Church of the Fathers of Mercy, when he gave such passionate utterance to his indignation at the great and terrifying inroads of Islamism! Or when he lamented that the most redoubtable empire beneath the sun was being abandoned to that arch-enemy the Turk. "O Jesus, Lord of Lords, Ruler of all Empires, King of all earthly Kings, how long wilt thou suffer thine arch-enemy, seated on the throne of Constantine the Great, to uphold with his many armies the blasphemies of his Mahomet, to cast down thy Cross beneath his Crescent, and day after day, with fortune-favoured arms, to encroach farther and farther upon the realms of Christendom?" In those days, Louis XIV—he was a young man then—looked with approving eye on this and such-like high adventures. But no one now thought of setting out for that far-off East. Farewell, now, to all such dreams! Whenever the word "crusade" was mentioned, the sceptics smiled, and even devout ecclesiastics deemed it best to leave the Turks alone: "Crusades! We are past all that sort of thing", said the Abbé Fleury, "only a few flowery and romantic poets clamour for crusades these days".

He was still the same; still as staunch and unshakable as ever; yet somehow it seemed as if things were eluding him, presenting themselves in such novel and unwonted colours that

---

[1]Le Dieu's *Journal*, 1 December, 1703. "In the midst of it all, he said to me, 'I feel that I cannot bear this burden any longer. God's will be done. I am ready for death. He will provide other defenders for His Church. If He gives me back my strength, I will use it to that end'."

[2]22 December, 1688, to the Abbé Perroudot.

he failed to recognize them for what they really were. He had always been treated with consideration; even in the cut and thrust of the liveliest debates, his zeal, his charity, his good faith had always commanded respect. To him Bishops in other lands, and foreign rulers, had paid their tributes of veneration, showering marks of distinction upon him. But since the Reformers had taken root in Holland, this deference had disappeared. Even the marks of ordinary civility were lacking. Insults were now the order of the day. Jurieu, who hit at everyone all round, fell upon Bossuet with peculiar ferocity. He charged him with deceit, with downright lying; he hinted that his morals were not everything they should be, and muttered dark things about concubinage. He was coarse and ill-bred in his mode of attack, as here for example:—Bossuet liked people to address him as "Monseigneur"; Ah, ha! Those episcopal gentry have gone up a peg or two since the days of the founders of Christianity whose only title was Servants of Jesus Christ. Bossuet is a ranting cushion-thumper devoid alike of honour and sincerity; Bossuet has neither common sense nor common decency; his ignorance is vast, his impudence prodigious. To deny the things that Bossuet denies you must either have a face of brass, or be abysmally ignorant.

There are some people who are quite insensitive to insults, who even feel a certain satisfaction at provoking them, and at being a target for obloquy. But Bossuet was not one of these. He had outbreaks of impatience, of wrath which showed how deeply he could suffer. He was terribly hurt when anyone whom he had greatly loved turned against him; Fénelon for example; or when vituperation seemed calculated to diminish his authority, to make him appear unworthy to be the interpreter of God's word.

As he trod his *via dolorosa*, Jurieu was there to fling mud at him, to call him a man devoid of faith and honour, a liar and a hypocrite. Then at last a cry escaped him, a moving appeal to One to whom all things are known, and who orders all things for the best.

"*O Lord, hear my prayer. O Lord, I have been called to Thy dread judgment seat as a slanderer, as one who charges the reformers with impiety, with blasphemy, with intolerable errors, and as one who not only imputes these crimes to them but has further accused one of their ministers of making open confession of them. Lord, it is before Thee that I have been accused. . . . If I have spoken the truth, if I have convicted of*

*blasphemy and of calumny those same persons who have called Thy
judgment upon me as a slanderer, a deceiver, dishonourable, conscienceless,
vindicate me before them. Let them be covered with shame and confusion,
but O God, I implore Thee, let their confusion be such that from it may
spring repentance and salvation.*"[1]

Every passing breath of unbelief caused him a pang; what the
Freethinkers were putting into print he knew well enough. He
was not satisfied merely to study Grotius the Socinian; he took
the trouble to read up what Crellius had written in the *Bibliotheca
Fratrum Polonorum*, and Socinius the originator of the doctrine.
This was the very source whence the poison had spread far and
wide and infected so many minds. Do not let us imagine that he
was unaware of all the talk that was going on about those Austral
Lands; and how people were using them as an argument against
Catholicism: How could Catholicism be universal when there
was a whole continent which had never so much as heard of the
name of Christ? He knew all about that. Go and take your
wrangles to St. Paul and Jesus Christ Himself and tell them about
these Austral Lands, and argue with them about the tidings heard
throughout all the earth.

Nor is he unaware of those embarrassing Chinese: on the
contrary he himself is in the plot which the Reverend Fathers of
the Foreign Missions are hatching against the Jesuits to make
them confess that the ceremonies practised by the Chinese are
nothing more nor less than downright idolatry. It was under his
roof that a decision was arrived at to print the *Lettre au Pape sur
les idolâtries et les superstitions chinoises* before it was shown to the
King, since he might have vetoed it out of regard for the Reverend Fathers. Missionaries came in numbers to the Palace to tell
him about all that was happening in Peking: "M. de Lionne,
Bishop of Rosalia, came this morning and again this afternoon,
and told M. de Meaux all about the country, the manners and
customs of the people, their national characteristics, and so on".
All this talk about a Chinese Church was sheer blasphemy. "A
queer sort of church!" he indignantly exclaimed; "No creed, no
promise to hold out, isolated, no sacraments, no trace of divine
sanction, knowing not what it worships, to whom it offers
sacrifice, whether to heaven or earth, or to the spirits of rivers

[1]*Deuxième avert. aux Protestants*, 1689, Ed. Lachat, XV, 275.

and mountains, an inextricable tangle of atheism, politics, god-
lessness, idolatry, magic, soothsaying and sorcery!"

He knows about the chronologists and their recondite investigations. Who that knew the man would have been surprised
to find on his shelves Marsham's *Chronicus Canon Aegyptiacus*?
Jean Le Clerc accuses M. de Meaux of borrowing from Marsham
without acknowledgment. The fact is that in his *Discours sur
l'Histoire Universelle*, which was published in 1681, he recorded
his own reactions to the discrepancies which were becoming
glaringly apparent between sacred and profane history, and
causing so much agitation among his contemporaries. He took
his stand on the side of Tradition, and thought that it was his
duty to give the Dauphin some of his reasons for so doing.
"What a quandary these chronologists are in, to be sure! Holy
Writ, on the one hand, tells us how Nabuchodonosor made
beautiful the city of Babylon, which had grown rich on the spoils
of Jerusalem and the East; how, after him, the Babylonian
Empire, unable to brook the might of the Medes, made war
upon them; how the Medes chose for their general, Cyrus, son
of Cambyses, King of Persia; how Cyrus overthrew the Babylonians, and united the Kingdom of Persia, hitherto unknown to
fame, with the Kingdom of the Medes, the extent of which had
been so largely increased by conquest. Thus he became the peace-
loving ruler of all the East, and founded the greatest empire that
the world had yet seen. Not so the writers of profane history,
Justinian and Diodorus, and the majority of the Greek and Latin
authors whose works have come down to us. They tell a different
tale. They know nothing of these Babylonian kings; they assign
them no place among the dynasties of whose successive repre-
sentatives they make mention. We find little or nothing in their
works concerning those famous kings Teglathphalasar, Salman-
asar, Sennacherib, Nabuchodonosor, and all those many others
renowned in Scripture and the histories of the East."

Now trust them not, Monseigneur, those profane historians.
There are Greek histories that have been lost to us, and it may
well be that they contained just what we find in the Scriptures. The
Greeks, whom the Romans copied, wrote at a later date. Putting
style above accuracy, they aimed not so much at instructing, as at
diverting, the people of Hellas with their tales of far-off days,
based on vague and floating hearsay. Believe them not, I say.

Put your trust, rather, in the Holy Scriptures, which are more especially concerned with the things of the East, and therefore more likely to be true—and that, apart from the fact that we know them to have been divinely inspired.[1]

But it was in 1700, when he brought out the third edition of his aforesaid *Discours*, that his deep anxiety of mind became more apparent still. Père Pezron's *Antiquité des temps* had come out in 1687, Père Martianay's and Père Lequien's replies followed in 1689 and 1690. The mass of facts and theories which they contain, Bossuet had duly mastered. As with the chronologists, his trouble was the Egyptians, the Assyrians and, in particular, the Chinese, who claimed such an immense period of time for the unfolding of their history that they altogether exceeded the limits of ecclesiastical chronology. Like Père Pezron, he favoured, as a way out of the difficulty, the adoption of the Septuagint version, as that allows an additional five centuries for the accommodation of these importunate gentry; like him, he felt that a date was the ruling factor in settling his choice between two versions of Scripture that were chronologically at variance. Never had he found himself on the horns of such a cruel dilemma.

Gradually the lineaments of the real man come into focus, grow more and more distinct. No imperturbable, untroubled builder, he, of some splendid cathedral in the sumptuous Louis XIV style; no, not that, but much rather a harassed workman, hurrying away, without a moment to lose, to patch up cracks in the edifice that every day grow more and more alarming. He sees deep down into the underlying principles of things. He was not deceived about the extent, the power, the diversity of what the sceptics had done, and were doing, to undermine and destroy the very foundations of the Church of God.

Spinoza, by rejecting miracles, would make God subservient to the laws of Nature. Ah! let not men suffer themselves to be led astray by this God-Being idea, a God that is no more than a shadow. Mightier by far is the God of Moses, "He can make and unmake at will; He dictates laws to Nature and revokes them at His pleasure. If, in times when His name had been forgotten of men, He wrought miracles and compelled Nature to break even the most constant of her laws, in order that He might make His

[1] *Discours sur l'Histoire Universelle*, 1681, p. 41 et seq.

presence known to them, He did not cease to show in like manner
that He was the absolute ruler of all things and that His sovereign
will, His sovereign will alone, prescribes and maintains the
Natural Order." Take the Creation: "By calling the world into
being by His mere word, God shows that nothing is an effort to
Him; and in doing so repeatedly, He proves that He has sovereign
power over His material, over His own actions, over all that He
undertakes, obeying no law but His own infallible will". Concerning the Deluge: "Let it not be thought that the world goes
on of its own accord, and that what has been hitherto, will be so
for ever, by virtue of its own momentum. God who made all
things and to whom all things owe their continued existence, will,
if it so please Him, drown all the animals on earth, and, with them,
all men, that is to say the fairest portion of His handiwork."[1]
Bossuet is thinking of the dangerous notions that the God of the
Ethic may engender in Christian consciences, and it is on their
account that this God fills him with apprehension.

Malebranche also adds to his misgivings; at the root of his
philosophy he discerns the same idea. "How I despise"—he
exclaims in the funeral oration he delivered over Maria Theresa
of Austria on the 1st September, 1693—"how I despise those
philosophers who, making their own intelligence the measure of
God's purposes, would regard Him merely as the creator of a
certain general order which He then left to develop as best it
might. As if, like ours, God's aims were vague and confused
generalities, as if His sovereign intelligence were powerless to
include in its scheme those individual existences which alone,
strictly speaking, can be said to live." That Père Malebranche
was a modest man, that his intentions were excellent, he did not
deny; nevertheless, he, Bossuet, knew perfectly well that his
disciples were heading straight for heresy. When you manage
to find your way through the fearsome jargon in which he
envelops himself, you discover that his philosophy is based on a
theory of life which wholly excludes the supernatural, and that
same theory is itself dependent on a method which involves some
"terrible drawbacks". Nowhere does Bossuet show himself
more clear-sighted or more admirably himself than here:

Arising out of these principles imperfectly understood, another idea, in-
volving the gravest difficulties, insensibly gains possession of men's minds.

[1]*Discours sur l'Histoire universelle*, Part II.

For, on the ground that we ought not to assent to anything which we do not perfectly understand—which, within limits, is a perfectly sound contention—everyone considers himself entitled to say: "I understand this; I do not understand that"; and with that as a starting point, he accepts or rejects just whatever he likes, forgetting that, above and beyond our own clear and definite ideas, there are other ideas of a vague and general character which, though not clearly definable to our intelligence, nevertheless contain truths so fundamental that to deny them would be to reduce everything to chaos. In this way he invests himself with a right to accept or reject which ends in his discarding Tradition and boldly adopting whatever conclusions he, as an individual, may happen to come to.[1]

But from whom does Malebranche derive? From Descartes. Living in an age that was intoxicated with Cartesianism, and, up to a point, a Cartesian himself, Bossuet meditates, draws distinctions, and defends his own position. In Descartes we find at least three things: in the first place, sound arguments against the atheists and the freethinkers; then, physical theories which we are free to accept or reject, but which, having no bearing on religion, are of no great intrinsic importance; and lastly, a principle which threatens the very foundations of religion:

I see . . . preparations for a great onslaught on the Church in the name of Cartesian philosophy. From the womb of that philosophy, from its principles, to my mind imperfectly understood, I foresee the birth of more than one heresy. I foresee also that conclusions deduced from it hostile to the dogmas our fathers taught us will bring down hatred upon the Church and rob her of the fruit she was entitled to expect from them by enabling her to implant in the philosophic mind a firm belief in the divinity and immortality of the soul.[2]

Might there not be an attitude of mind of which the philosophy of Descartes was, to begin with, merely the exponent, but which, later on, it reinforced? Might we not discover, more widely diffused, more deeply interwoven in men's lives, a fixed resolve all-embracing in its objects, a resolve to renounce allegiance to authority, an invincible urge to criticize, which was at once "the disease and the temptation of our time?"[3] Time was when men humbled themselves before God, when they rendered obedience to their King. That day was past. It was now the day of

[1]To a disciple of Malebranche, 21 May, 1687.
[2]*Ibid.*, and *Lettre à Huet*, 18 May, 1689.
[3]Bossuet to Rancé, 17 March, 1692. *"La fausse critique qui est la maladie et la tentation de nos jours'".*

"intellectual intemperance". In this passage, eloquence adorns the truth which Bossuet discloses, and in these solemn words it is the preacher who sets forth the attitude of mind which is constantly gaining ground, which bids fair to achieve a universal victory, and which fills him with nothing short of terror:

"Reason is the guide of their choice, but reason only brings them face to face with vague conjectures and baffling perplexities. The impossible positions into which they are forced by their rejection of religion are found in time to be more untenable than those truths whose loftiness astounds them, and, because they refuse to put their faith in mysteries beyond their understanding, they go on from error to error, all of them as far beyond their comprehension as the mysteries. What, then, Gentlemen, when all is said and done, is this lamentable unbelief of theirs but one interminable error, temerity that exposes everything to hazard, bewilderment deliberately sought, pride which can suffer no curb, a pride, that is to say, which cannot brook the restraint of legitimate authority. Do not imagine that it is only by their sensual desires that men are swept off their feet; intellectual desires are no less alluring. They, too, have their clandestine pleasures, they, too, are made the keener by opposition. Look at this man, puffed up with pride, who deems that he rises superior to everyone, superior to himself, when he rises superior, as he imagines, to the religion he had so long held sacred. He regards himself as one of the enlightened. He flatters himself that he is not one of those weak-minded people who blindly follow in the footsteps of others, never making the slightest effort to strike out a line on their own account. And so, becoming the sole object of his own admiration, he ends by becoming a god unto himself."[1]

Simplicity has departed; balance and moderation are alike no more, now that men have withdrawn their allegiance from authority. However devout, however learned, a man may be, there is no knowing what strange fancies he may not take into his head. We can be sure of nothing, and knowledge is no more. Is there not some talk now of publishing and crying up the book of some Spanish nun, whom they call a mystic but who is in fact

[1]*Oraison funèbre d'Anne de Gonzague*, Ed. Lachat, vol. XII, p. 552.

a madwoman, Maria de Jesus, Abbess of Agreda? And then Fénelon, his beloved Fénelon, see how grievously he has gone astray! People try to defend the theatre; they cudgel their brains to show that the Church countenances the licence of the Stage; the Fathers are ransacked for quotations to show that they approved of these things; they even quote the Bible to prove that it, too, contains passages about the passions, and that, if things are to be banned because of the undesirable after-effects they might conceivably have on some people, you would have to stop them reading the Latin Bible, since that is the innocent source of all the heresies. And who, pray, is it that gives utterance to these absurdities? Who is it that can lay his tongue to such a string of blasphemies? A monk, of all people in the world, who goes by the name of Père Caffaro! People plunge from one excess to another: on the grounds that they owe obedience to the King, some people, for two pins, would withhold it from the Pope, and the Gallican Church would fall into schism if he were not at hand to see that unto Caesar were rendered the things that are Caesar's, unto God the things that are God's. Unceasing were the excursions and alarms. No sooner is an attack driven off in one place, than another develops somewhere else, and he must rush off to repel it. The fact of the matter is, he has got to be everywhere at once. How glad his foes would be to see him depart. From time to time a rumour gets about that he has had a stroke. M. Simon is even reported as saying, "There's no help for it, we must just let him die; he hasn't far to go." But M. de Meaux still holds on.

It may be because he lives in a constant state of angry vigilance, with never a moment to call his own, that he so furiously condemns this world and all its vain deluding ways; including in one single denunciation the allurements of the flesh, the eyes and the mind. Nothing now finds favour in his stern regard, neither the urge to experiment and discover, nor the love of history, nor the pursuit of knowledge, if it be but pride in another guise, nor the thirst for renown, nor heroic deeds: sick of the countless failings of humankind, he himself puts óff his own humanity, and, having done so, turns his gaze to the divine, to Heaven, with a heart that is hungry for consolation. So he returns to the Gospel, not to argue or dispute, but to dwell in pious meditation upon its fairest pages, to taste the joy of calm, unquestioning belief, of tenderness and love. "Read yet again, O my soul, and rejoice in this sweet command to love." Mounting upward from height to height towards the celestial abodes of joy and love, he reached at last those realms sublime where, Prayer and Poetry merging into one, his words give utterance solely to his spirit's yearning for Truth and Beauty that will never die.

V

AN ATTEMPT AT REUNION AND WHAT CAME OF IT

"HE was a pale-faced wisp of a man; long, tapering fingers extended from hands that were criss-crossed with innumerable lines. His eyes, never very keen-sighted, had left him with no very clear-cut visual impressions; he walked along with his head well forward and he disliked sudden, jerky movements. He delighted in sweet scents and derived much comfort from them. Talking had no great attractions for him; he would much rather be alone, so that he could read and meditate in peace; all the same, if a conversation did happen to start up in his neighbourhood, he would play his part with zest. He liked to work at night. In things that were past and done with he took but little interest; but anything that had a bearing on the present, however slight, held his attention far more closely than the most outstanding events of bygone days. So it came about that he was always starting to write on something new, and always leaving it unfinished; if next day he had not forgotten all about it, he, at all events, made no effort to take it up again."[1]

Such was Leibniz. What an appetite for knowledge his many-mansioned mind displayed! Knowledge was his ruling passion. He longed to know everything there was to know, and, reaching the confines of the real, to invade the realms of the imaginary. He declared that the man who had studied the largest number of pictures of plants and animals, of drawings of machines, of descriptions or plans of houses or fortresses, who had read the greatest number of ingenious romances, listened to the greatest number of strange narratives—that man would possess more knowledge than his fellows, even though there were not a grain

[1] Jean Baruzi, *Leibniz* (*La pensée chrétienne*), pp. 10-12.

of truth in all that he had heard, read, or seen depicted. He had mastered every branch of study; Latin and Greek to begin with, rhetoric, poetry. . . . His tutors, amazed at his insatiable zeal, began to fear lest he should remain for ever fettered to these pre-liminary studies, whereas the truth was he was even then begin-ning to slip away from them. From scholastic philosophy and theology, he passed on to mathematics, in which department he was destined to make discoveries that marked him down a genius. From mathematics, he turned to jurisprudence. He took up alchemy, attracted as he was, by all that was rare, secret, out of the way, by things which, by ways inaccessible to the common run, might peradventure furnish a key to the world of phenomena. Every book he took up, every person he fell in with, he regarded as a means of learning something new. "To fix, to nail himself down", to one particular spot, to one unvarying routine, to one solitary subject—that was a thing he could not endure at any price. To choose some particular calling, lawyer or schoolmaster, to do the same things day after day, at the same fixed times—not he! He travelled about, he visited various towns in Germany, he went abroad, to France, England, Holland, Italy; visited museums, attended the meetings of learned societies, enriched his mind through innumerable different contacts. Life for him, was always a bringer of new things. He consented to become a librarian, with an ear open to the ceaseless appeals of every branch of human thought; an historiographer, so that he might embrace as much as he could of past and present; a world-correspondent; a counsellor of princes; an encyclopaedia always open for con-sultation. But his real mission was to give the world an example of a dynamic force that seemed to be inexhaustible, because it never ceased to replenish its stock of facts, ideas, sentiments and human interests.

From a mind that gave itself no rest, mingling together and brewing all manner of fresh additions to its stock, there issued, as time went by, practical inventions, philosophical systems, noble dreams. In the end, he came to possess all the sciences, all the arts, to say nothing of the inexhaustible materials whereof his dreams were woven. He was, as someone described him, "mathematician, physicist, psychologist, logician, metaphysician, historian, jurist, philologist, diplomat, theologian, moralist". And, in all this prodigious intellectual activity, which perhaps no other mortal ever rivalled, what most delighted him was the variety of it all: *utique enim delectat nos varietas.*

Utique delectat nos varietas, sed reducta in unitatem. To reduce to unity; such was, indeed, Leibniz's second love, more prone to see where things agreed than where they differed, eager to detect the imperceptible gradations which link light with darkness, zero with infinity. He would have liked to persuade the scientists of every kind to pool their knowledge and ideas; for what is it that accounts for the slow progress that is made by science, if not the lack of contact between those who pursue its several branches? Academies should be created in every country in order to facilitate the exchange of knowledge and ideas among the various nations. Before very long, those intellectual conduits, carrying the streams of new discoveries, would fertilize the world. But more than that, Leibniz would institute a universal language. Truly the world presents a dismal spectacle of strife and misunderstanding; barriers everywhere; questions left unanswered; soaring guesses at truth, fated to fall, like birds on broken wing, into the void again; a welter of confusion that has prevailed for centuries. Would it not be possible to do away with some, at least, of the stumbling-blocks, the very sight of which is an outrage on good sense? And, as a beginning, could not some agreement be arrived at regarding the meaning of words? It might be possible to invent a language which everyone could use, and which would not only facilitate international intercourse, but carry with it such intrinsic merits of clearness, precision, adaptability, richness, that it would be a truly rational and unequivocal medium of expression. It could be used in all departments of intellectual activity, just in the same way as mathematicians make use of algebra, only this would be algebra in a concrete form, every term offering at a glance the vision of its possible relations with the terms next to it. Thus we should have a universal medium of expression, the most telling instrument ever placed at the service of mankind.

He is pained by the disunity of Germany, by the disunity of Europe, to which he would bring peace, even if that meant letting loose against the East the overflow of its warlike energies. And if we penetrate into the inmost recesses of his mind, there too we shall find a kindred longing. His great mathematical discovery, the infinitesimal calculus, is the transition from the non-continuous to the continuous; his great psychological law is the

law of continuity: a clear perception is linked to obscure perceptions by a series of insensible degrees which lead us ever closer and
closer to the initial vibration of the vital principle. Harmony is
ever the supreme metaphysical verity. Diversities which seemed
irreconcilable end by merging together at last in one harmonious
whole, where each component has the place designed for it by a
divinely constituted order. The universe is one vast choir. Each
individual has the illusion that he is singing independently of all
the others, whereas, in reality, he is singing the part allotted to
him in one mighty score, wherein every note is so placed that all
the voices have their answering counterparts, the whole creating
a concord more perfect than that music of the spheres dreamed
of by Plato.[1]

Let us here read over again that noble passage in which Émiel
Boutroux put on record the difficulties which such a thinker
would have had to encounter at the time of his entry into the
world: "The problem does not present itself to him under the
same conditions as it did to the Ancients. He finds confronting
him, developed by Christianity and the influence of modern
thought, sharply opposed ideas and contrarieties, if not downright contradictions, such as the Ancients never knew. The
general and the particular, the possible and the real, the logical
and the metaphysical, the mathematical and the physical, mechanism and finality, mind and matter, experience and instinct,
universal co-ordination and individual spontaneity, concatenation
of causes and human liberty, providence and evil, philosophy
and religion—all these contraries more and more divested of their
common elements by the process of analysis, have now reached
such a degree of divergence that their reconciliation seems no
longer possible, so that to choose one to the complete exclusion
of the other seems the only course open to a mind that has any
regard at all for clarity and consistency. To resume, in such
conditions, the task of Aristotle, to try to arrive at that underlying unity and harmony in things which man seems to despair
of ever finding, which, perhaps, he even regards as non-existent,
such was the task that Leibniz set himself."[2]

And so this admirable intelligence, daring but serene, at a

---

[1] We shall have occasion to revert to this philosophy in Part IV of the present
work, chap. V.
[2] *Préface à la Monadologie*, 1881.

time when ideas were warring with one another with unprecedented vehemence and wrath, resolutely posted himself on a height so lofty that any choice which excluded a contrary seemed to him a sign, not of strength, but of weakness and surrender. Would he succeed in his high emprise? When Leibniz comes down to earth, exchanging the airy heights of speculation for the ground of solid fact, when he essays to heal the religious consciences of his contemporaries, so lacerated and so bruised, by offering them the balm of peace and reconciliation, will he succeed, or will he but deepen the existing rift between them and prove it beyond repair? Would it be possible for anyone, no matter how great a genius, among such a diversity of religious traditions, to rescue and preserve the true spirit of Christianity?

No sooner do we come to contemplate Europe as a whole than it is its divided state that forces itself upon our attention. Ever since the Reformation, its moral unity has been shattered. Its peoples are divided into two hostile camps, each bidding defiance to the other. Wars, persecution, bitter feuds, cruel words, such are the things that fill the daily lives of these contentious brethren. Whoever longs for harmony must first of all essay to cure an evil that every day grows more acute. Since 1660, in fact, the quarrel between Catholics and Protestants had been raging with renewed and ever increasing intensity, and there was no telling to what extremes of violence it might not ultimately lead. If it continued very much longer it would soon be all over with Christianity, indeed with religion of any kind. Deists, and atheists, too, are waging against religion a joint campaign, which grows bolder every day, opposed only by forces fatally weakened by division. How different it might be if Catholics and Protestants could compose their quarrel. Then would all Christians, united once again, and invincible in their union, triumphantly confront the forces of impiety, and save the Church of God.

This task of reconciliation Leibniz was to pursue with all the power he could command. He was thoroughly versed in the claims of the two sides. He had for a long time been conversant with the works bearing on the controversy, and found in them, on the whole, nothing to commend. He knew his men. Nor, on his side, was he an unknown quantity, a mere "man in the street",

so to speak. He had shown, by what he had achieved, that he
was a force to be reckoned with in the intellectual field. In every
country in Europe, scholars, intellectuals of the first rank, could
testify to his worth. He was a Lutheran, but, to quote an admirable remark of his own, in the pursuit of so grand an aim as
that of reunion, he was not going to dwell on fine distinctions,
"he was not out to split hairs". As for choosing a plan of campaign, a *modus operandi*, he had but to follow his natural inclination
and make it clear that the points of difference were not essential,
that the points of resemblance were so numerous as to amount to
something like identity, and then to call for a united rally to
formal professions of faith at once the simplest and the most
profound.

In the course of his stay in Paris, he had paid a visit to Arnauld,
the Jansenist, and recited to him a *Paternoster*, to which, he
claimed, everyone could assent: "O God, who alone art eternal
and almighty, the one true and infinite Lord of all, I, Thine unworthy creature, do put my faith and trust in Thee. Thee do I
love above all, to Thee do I send forth my prayers, to Thee do I
give praise, and into Thy hands I resign my spirit. Pardon me
for all my sins, and be pleased to vouchsafe unto me and unto all
men whatsoever may accord with Thy will and be expedient for
us in this world and in the world to come, and keep us from all
evil. Amen." But Arnauld considered this prayer inadmissible,
because it did not include the name of Jesus Christ. Well; there
would always be people to reject his formulas, and his task was
not going to be an easy one; all the same he was going to shoulder
it. If he succeeded, he would have played his part in restoring
that harmony which is the law of the universe. If he failed, then
others, the stubborn, the blind, must be answerable for the failure.
They it would be who would perpetuate the schism, and render it
irremediable, and bring ruin, final and complete, upon the cause
of religion in Europe.

The preliminary stages were gradual, and extended over some
years. As far back as 1676, when Leibniz was in the early, tentative stages of his studies in alchemy, he fell in, at Nuremberg,
with an adept called the Baron de Boinebourg, a convert from
Protestantism, who devoted the best part of his life to what in
those days were known as "irenical negotiations". Boinebourg
took him to Frankfort, and from there on to the Court at Mainz,

where religious controversies were in full swing. On his return from Paris, he accepted, in 1676, an appointment as librarian at Hanover and there met, in the person of Duke John Frederick, a Catholic prince ruling over Protestant subjects, the man through whom Rome hoped to bring Northern Germany into the Catholic fold. The movement gathered impetus; the actors on the Hanoverian stage got busy. There was Ernest Augustus, John Frederick's successor; Bishop Spinola, a protégé of the Emperor's, who kept going to and fro between Vienna, the German principalities and Rome, spinning the threads of union. In 1683, Spinola produced a formula designed to serve as a basis for discussion, *Regulae circa christianorum omnium ecclesiasticam reunionem*. Theologians from both sides assemble, confer together, and, under the inspiration of Molanus, abbé of Lockum, a broad-minded, large-hearted man, elaborate a plan which is to lead at last to the long desired reconciliation: *Methodus reducendae unionis ecclesiasticae inter Romanenses et Protestantes*.

Leibniz goes farther than any of the others. About the time when the Revocation of the Edict of Nantes was being planned and put into effect in France, he, paying no heed to what he believed to be temporary outbreaks of violence, holding fast to the conviction that the spirit of concord is the truth and the life, drew up, after long and careful meditation, the profession of faith, so grave in tone, so beautiful in diction, which goes by the name of *Systema theologicum*. "After invoking the divine aid by long and earnest prayer, putting aside, so far as is humanly possible, all party spirit, looking at the religious controversies as though I had come from another planet, a humble learner, unacquainted with any of the various communions, bound by no obligations, I have, after due consideration, arrived at the conclusions hereinafter set forth. I have deemed it incumbent upon me to embrace them because Holy Writ, immemorial religious tradition, the dictates of reason, and the sure testimony of the facts, seem to me to concur in establishing them in the mind of any unprejudiced human being."

What, then, is the conclusion, the conviction, to which he thus alludes? Having examined and considered not only dogmas, the existence of God, the creation of mankind, and of the world, original sin, the mysteries, but also the most hotly debated points in regard to religious practices, monastic vows, works, ritual, statues, invocation of the saints, he was convinced that there was nothing to prevent Catholics and Protestants from coming together in unity and, by making mutual concessions in regard to a few apparent difficulties, from restoring the unity of the faith. This is how he speaks of the Roman system, and of the things which aroused the wrath or contempt of his co-religionists, the Lutherans:

I confess that the religious orders, pious brotherhoods, sacred con-fraternities, and all other institutions of the kind, have, in me, always excited a particular admiration. They are like an army from Heaven fighting on earth, so long as they are free from abuse and corruption, and provided that they are carried on in accordance with the spirit and rules of their founders, and that the Sovereign Pontiff employs them to serve the needs of the Church Universal.

And more striking still:

Thus the strains of music, the sweet concord of voices, the poetry of the hymns, the beauty of the liturgy, the blaze of lights, the fragrant perfumes, the rich vestments, the sacred vessels adorned with precious stones, the costly offerings, the statues and the pictures that awaken holy thoughts, the glorious creations of architectural genius, with their effects of height and distance, the stately splendour of public processions, the rich draperies adorning the streets, the music of bells, in a word all the gifts and marks of honour which the pious instincts of the people prompt them to pour forth with lavish hand, do not, I trow, excite in God's mind the disdain which the stark simplicity of some of our contemporaries would have us believe they do. That at all events is what reason and experience alike confirm.

After that, need it surprise us that, at Rome, whither his duties as historiographer and his all-seeking curiosity take him in 1689, he is offered the curatorship of the Vatican Library? Were there not ample grounds for assuming that he was a Catholic at heart, and on the very verge of conversion?

But there was Bossuet, and Bossuet would have to be won over if the cause was to prosper. "You are like a second St. Paul, for your works are not confined to any one nation, to any single province. Your words are, at this very moment, making them-selves heard in well-nigh all the languages of Europe, and your converts are blazoning abroad your triumphs in tongues to you unknown."[1]

[1]Lord Perth to Bossuet, 12 November, 1685.

For a long time Bossuet had believed that the Protestants could be brought to heel by argument. When, in 1671, he published his *Exposition de la doctrine catholique,* he seemed to be stretching forth his hands, opening wide his arms. As with Leibniz, it was not his wish to split hairs, to aggravate differences; rather it was his aim to stress the things that might lead to reunion. Disengaging Catholic doctrine from the various accretions with which mistaken or excessive zeal had overloaded it; showing that the fundamentals of belief were the common property of both sides; stating, in the most conciliatory manner, what Catholics really held in regard to the invocation of Saints, statues, relics, indulgences, the sacraments, justification by grace; setting forth the Catholic position in regard to Tradition and the authority of the Church; showing that the doctrine of Transubstantiation constituted the only real difficulty, and that even that was not insurmountable, he displayed such generosity, such a warmth of cordiality, that the whole Protestant world was deeply moved. Some people alleged that his *Exposition* was too liberal to be orthodox, but, backed as it was by the approval of the Bishops and of the Pope himself, it emerged triumphant, and became a force, and an active one, in Europe. "This explanation of our doctrine will have good effects. In the first place, some of the points in dispute will wholly disappear because they will be shown to result from erroneous conceptions of our creed. Secondly, such differences as do remain will when judged by the principles of the so-called Reformers turn out to be far less crucial than at first appeared, involving nothing calculated to impair the foundations of belief."

It is true that he applauded the Revocation of the Edict of Nantes, for that fitted in logically with his line of thought, and that the rift dates from that event. It was Sunday, 21st October, 1685, that he preached his sermon *Compelle intrare* before the whole Court, and that day the Protestants must have seen in him not just an opponent, but a foe. And when the *Histoire des Variations des Églises Protestantes* appeared in 1688, we all know the storm that greeted it. For months, for years, afterwards, refutations and replies came pouring forth; and refutations of refutations, replies to replies; and none of the disputants were exactly mealy-mouthed.

"No need to drink up all the sea to find out that it is salt, any more than there is to repeat everything that is said against us to realize the general hatred with which we are regarded".[1]

It was now that the enterprise took on its aspect of pathetic grandeur. After the Revocation, to seek to unite the Churches— what a hopeless task! Everybody had been longing for it. In Sweden, in England, and even in Russia there were people ready to do their utmost to bring all men of goodwill into a single fold. But now, when the shepherds did nothing but assail one another, how vain to go on hoping for reconciliation. Nevertheless, that was precisely what Leibniz did hope for, and he called on Bossuet to lend him his aid.

And so we behold them in conference, if not in person, if not in the actual flesh, at least in the spirit of the things they longed and hoped for; not sitting face to face, but with the same minute attention as if they were closeted together in some austere chamber with a crucifix above their heads. Aided by a few others who were in the secret, out of the daylight's glare, in the mysterious penumbra befitting long and difficult negotiations, these two mighty spirits begin their long and heartbreaking debate.

If we disregard the opening phase of the negotiations, which consisted in a rapid exchange of letters and polite civilities, it was not until 1691 that the debate began in real earnest. In France, a small group of religious-minded people were gazing hopefully towards Hanover. There was Pellisson, Fouquet's old friend, who had been a prisoner in the Bastille and then set free. Originally a Huguenot, he had become a Catholic and was *directeur de la Caisse des conversions*. He was all on fire to bring about the union of the Church he had quitted, with the Church of Rome. Then there was Louise Hollandine, sister of the Duchess of Hanover, who had abjured the Protestant faith and withdrawn to the Abbaye de Maubuisson, near Pontoise; and Mme de Brinon, her secretary, active and zealous for the glory of God. There was no telling what might happen. Perhaps the Duchess of Hanover might follow her sister's example and come over in her turn; and perhaps her husband might do the same. It might well be that this land of Hanover, where the good seed seemed to be springing up, would yield a glorious harvest. Salutes were

[1] *Seconde instruction pastorale sur les promesses de Jésus-Christ à son Église* (1701). Ed. Lachat, vol. XVII, p. 239.

exchanged. Leibniz and Pellisson exchange letters and arguments, and, across the sundering distance, a mutual esteem and affection springs up between them. Bossuet gets the call to arms, and "enters into the plan".

And so the battle is joined. Leibniz looks about him for a favourable terrain on which to begin his conciliatory campaign, some spot that is weakly held, or slackly defended, so that he may gain a foothold within the fortress; and this is what he chooses: A man may err on a matter of religious belief without being necessarily a heretic or a schismatic, provided only that he be not contumacious. If Protestants agree that General Councils cannot err, and are then led erroneously to deny the oecumenicity of the Council of Trent, which set its seal on the final separation, they at all events err without malice and in good faith. They are neither heretics nor schismatics, and, by agreeing to abide by the decisions of a further oecumenical council, they remain, in spirit, in communion with the Church. What a hopeful line is that, and what a great advance it would be towards religious peace, if Bossuet would but approve!

To turn the positions established by a Council in a way that would be tantamount to regarding it as null and void was hardly a move likely to suit the Bishop of Meaux. "In order to clarify the position in regard to these proposals for reunion, it must be clearly borne in mind that, while it may be permissible, should the circumstances of the time render it expedient, to relax a disciplinary ordinance, or some other non-essential, the Church will never agree to abandon any point concerning doctrine which has been expressly defined, and least of all defined by the Council of Trent". To make concessions to the Lutherans in regard to such matters as Communion in both kinds is one thing; to give way in regard to the principle of authority, which is the Church's very corner-stone, is quite another. Then, in his vigorous, forthright manner—not a very serviceable instrument of diplomacy—he takes the offensive. If M. Leibniz believes in Catholicism; if he proclaims his belief in propositions which are the very essence of Catholicism, the thing is simplicity itself. Let him become a Catholic.

He made a mistake. He did not rightly read his adversary's mind. That vague frontier, that almost imperceptible line which divided him from the Church of Rome, Leibniz was destined never to cross. He would never cross it because it was something individual that held him back, something within the man himself that no pressure from outside could annul or modify; but also, and more especially, because the real point at issue was something of a different nature. The question was not whether the Protestants were going to surrender unconditionally to their opponents, but whether they were going to join them; he, Leibniz, had come to discuss terms, not to crave asylum. Bossuet would have to understand that. He would have to discard those high-handed, imperious ways of his and learn the difference between conciliation and conversion. "We have gone a very long way for the sake of charity and peace. We have pushed on right up to the banks of the Bidassoa, so as to be ready, when the appropriate moment comes, to cross over to Conference Island. We have made a particular point of avoiding anything that might savour of the disputatious and all those superior airs with which one habitually refers to one's own side . . . that offensive arrogance, that confident assurance which every one feels in point of fact but which it is both useless and impolitic to flaunt before people who have no small share of it themselves." Once more, the question put to Bossuet is whether, supposing one honestly holds that the Council of Trent was not oecumenical, it would be allowable to disregard its decisions. The prelate's answer had been too sweeping by half. Let him reconsider the data of the problem. We await his reply.

So Bossuet set to work. Despite the crushing mass of business which weighed upon him, he proceeded to examine in detail the documents so far drawn up, the formulas hitherto put forward, with a view to providing a working basis for a settlement. "At the earliest available opportunity, I will tell you with the utmost frankness what my views are on the matter."—"May this year prove a propitious one for you and for all those who seriously desire to restore the union of Christendom."[1] He worked with a will. "I enter into the scheme and although I cannot enter into all the means, I see plainly that, if we can go by what the Abbé Molanus says, and others as fair-minded as he, most of the difficulties should be cleared away. You shall shortly hear what I think."

Meanwhile Leibniz used the interval to good account. He kept

[1]Letter, 17 January, 1692.

a sharp look-out for any arguments that might support his case. Already, sometime previously, he had pointed out that France herself had not accepted the Council of Trent as oecumenical; and now, to his great joy, he lighted upon a case with a direct bearing upon the question, a precedent which seemed to him to clinch the matter. On one occasion at any rate—there were plenty of other instances in point of fact, but one would suffice as typical of the rest—the Church of Rome *had* annulled the decisions of a Council. The Calixtines of Bohemia failed to comply with the ruling of the Council of Constance in regard to Communion in both kinds. Pope Eugenius and the Council of Basle, over-riding the decree, did not order them to submit, but referred the matter for further consideration and final decision by the Church. What thought Bossuet of the significance of such a precedent as that? Was it not, beyond dispute, on all fours with the question now under discussion? "Consider, Monsieur, whether all these German-speaking peoples do not deserve at least the same measure of indulgence as was meted out to the Bohemians. . . . "

It came at last, the long-awaited answer. It came in the shape of a monograph dealing point by point with Molanus's *Some personal reflections on the manner of bringing about a union between the Protestant and Roman Catholic Churches*, and it set forth the writer's conclusions. Bossuet said the method proposed was unacceptable, in that it aimed at drawing up conditions of peace before any examination of the principles on which that peace was to be founded. The only acceptable method was that which should first declare the principles, and then proceed to an examination of the facts. To begin with a sort of gentleman's agreement, then to meet together for an informal discussion about doctrine, and finally to convene a Council to settle points on which the parties had failed to agree—that was not the way to go to work at all. The first thing needed was to summon a Council to give formal hearing of the Protestant retractation, after which would follow the reconciliation. Anything else would be merely begging the question. If the Protestants expected to re-enter the Roman Communion before making their submission, it would naturally be inferred that they did not acknowledge their error, that they still did not acknowledge the authority of the Church. The whole crux of the matter was there.

The method, in fact, takes for granted the very matter that is under discussion. The Church is infallible: the decisions of the Council of Trent are valid for all time. The notion that France disputed its oecumenicity is a pure delusion, for France's protest had reference solely to questions of precedence, to the prerogatives, privileges and customs of the realm. To quote the incident of the Calixtines of Bohemia is also beside the mark: the enquiry which was agreed to at Basle was to be regarded not as questioning the decision arrived at Constance, but as clarifying and confirming it. And since Leibniz asks point-blank whether people who are willing to submit to the Church's authority, but choose to doubt the oecumenicity of this Council or of that, are rightly to be looked on as heretics, Bossuet replies equally point-blank that they *are*: "Yes, heretics they are, recusants they are." After that, it was useless for Leibniz to try and hit back, retorting that it was a very odd thing to say, "Yesterday we believed such and such a thing, so we've got to go on believing it". It was no good digging up more precedents; they got him no farther. Bossuet had built up a wall, and he could see no flaw in it. The discussion might as well be regarded as closed.

However, it began again. The secondary actors in the play were gradually fading out; death was taking its toll of them; but Leibniz and Bossuet still remained, and hope was not yet entirely extinguished. The 27th August, 1698, found Leibniz in the monastery at Lockum hard at work on a new Plan for facilitating the reunion of Protestants and Roman Catholics, which he concluded with a fervent prayer to God. Then he resumed his correspondence with Bossuet. But the arguments were the same as ever, all save one, that is. Quite determined to show that it was untrue to say that the Church had never changed, he broached the question of the authenticity of the Scriptures. The Church to-day, he remarks, accepts as authentic books which the early Church regarded as apocryphal; consequently tradition *had* changed. The controversy went lumbering heavily on, coming to a stop at every trifling little obstacle. It went on till Bossuet felt that his end was approaching. The letters on either side developed into lengthy treatises; one of them numbered as many as a hundred and twenty-two clauses. There was no getting away from it, Leibniz in questioning the authenticity of the Scriptures had strayed a long way from the paths of conciliation.

These two mighty toilers, whom neither weariness nor work, however heavy, could dishearten, laboured on till the end, each in the light of his own guiding principle. Leibniz made good use of his nimble and penetrating intelligence, of his native gift for diplomacy; he began cautiously, warily treading the path of discretion, for, as he said, it was not a matter of constructing arguments or making books, but rather of getting to read men's hearts, of gauging the opposing powers. Gradually he grew more heated. Chafing at a resistance which neither his goodwill nor his ingenuity availed to overcome, he permitted himself to talk about people "splitting hairs". He accused Bossuet of shuffling, of wilfully obscuring the issue, and of putting on tragic airs. A note of bitterness began to creep in. This Bishop is a die-hard. Better bring a few laymen into the discussion and talk things over with them; these ecclesiastical gentlemen have their own peculiar way of looking at things, their own pre-conceived ideas. He, Leibniz, was all for a friendly compromise, for a little give-and-take on either side. He could always draw on his prodigious memory for something in the past that had a useful application to the present; he had the sort of mind that was constantly urging him to look for points of agreement in seeming opposites, to whittle away differences to vanishing point, to elicit the harmonious elements in things whenever he could. His approach was political rather than religious. The value of the prize to be won seemed to him to warrant a somewhat liberal interpretation of the rules of the game. But on one point, and one point only, he was adamant, though it must be admitted that that point involved all the rest; it was the right of full and free enquiry, the refusal to bow to any dogmatic authority. When, in spite of all his efforts, he failed to achieve his object, his heart was filled with vexation, nay, with grief, and it was a bitter wrench for him to have to abandon a project which had seemed to him to promise so much for Europe and for all the human race. There was bitterness, too, one feels, and a note of reproach to all whom it might concern, in his obstinate harping on the one unvarying theme: He gives notice that "he washes his hands of all responsibility for whatever further ills the existing schism may have in store for the Christian Church"; "We can console ourselves that we have left undone nothing that we ought to have done, and that to reproach us with perpetuating the schism would be the very acme of injustice"; the Church of Rome it is that causes the schism by violating that charity which is the soul of unity.

Bossuet was less demonstrative, and kept his feelings far more to himself. Had he wounded Leibniz, when he charged him with heresy and contumacy? And did Leibniz grieve at such a verdict? If so, he, too, was grieved; but, said he, Leibniz would have been the first to blame me had I shilly-shallied and beaten about the bush when what he demanded was that people should speak their minds and say exactly what they meant. There was a blend of humility and bluntness in the way he replied to his adversary's reproaches: "If you will be good enough to point out just where you consider my answers have fallen short of your requirements, I will undertake to give you full satisfaction, looking neither to the right nor to the left, but going ahead with all the candour you could look for from a man whose joy in collaborating with so able and conscientious a colleague in the task of healing, if it may be, the wounds inflicted on the Church by so lamentable a schism, can never be exceeded".

Leibniz had a new idea. He thought it would be good thing to get Bishop Spinola to draw up a memorandum setting forth the Protestant point of view, while he himself would be responsible for another explaining the Catholic position. The proposal did not commend itself to Bossuet. Truth was not double faced. Truth is one and immutable. Truth is eternal. He holds to the rule which had nourished him, mind and soul, which had been his guide all through his life: cling only to that which abideth.

With less regret, but without rancour, without bitterness, he beheld the disappearance of a mirage which had never wholly captured his imagination. In his case it was the religious sense that triumphed over the political. To abandon the project of reunion was to rob Europe of all hope of that spiritual peace whereof she had never stood more desperately in need. But if reunion was to be attained only at the cost of conceding that the Catholic Church was fallible, that there had been occasions when she had condemned and excommunicated without just cause, that she had sometimes contradicted her own enunciations and varied her teaching—if this was the price to be paid, it was too high, for it meant undermining the Church's very foundations. Suffer but one solitary breach to be made in the breastwork of authority, and all the heresies would enter through it one after another, and the Temple of Truth would be laid in ruins. Between these alternatives Bossuet had to choose, and choose he did: If perforce it must be so then let the schismatics abide in their error, but let the Church continue to flourish even as an immemorial tree that has but shed a withered branch.

It is time, now, to ring down the curtain. He has outlived his destiny and the burden of the years is heavy upon him. The people who should have stood by him in his hour of need, desert him. He suffers agony from the gravel. He groans and cries aloud with the pain of it. No sooner, however, does his malady give him a little respite, than he orders his litter, takes the road again, and repairs once more to the King, from whom in the days of old he had always drawn new strength and courage; but now the King himself is going downhill. Besides, he cannot work miracles. He cannot restore their vanished youth to folk with one foot in the grave.

Bracing himself up against the pain that was racking him, "hardly able to keep on his legs", he was a pathetic figure as he tried to make obeisance to his sovereign. He was continually to be seen at Versailles. The courtiers laughed at the broken-down grand old man, a little ludicrous now, and something of a trial. "Has he made up his mind to die at Court?" said the somewhat heartless Madame de Maintenon, under her breath. In 1703, at the procession of the Assumption, in which he would insist on taking part, he presented a sorry spectacle. His friends were grief-stricken, the general public deplored the sight and the older Court habitués laughed at it. "Bear up, M. de Meaux", Madame de Maintenon kept saying all along the route, "we shall get there." "Poor Monsieur de Meaux!" said some, and others, "He managed very well". But the comment of the majority was, "Why doesn't he go and die in his own house?"[1]

It fared no better with Leibniz. He went on dreaming his dreams. China must be converted, not by showing the Chinese they were wrong, but by bringing out the analogies between their religion and our own, by delving right down to the basic, underlying unity of the human spirit. But he came up against reality, and the experience undeceived him; for reality is not a thing you can mould to suit your own ideas, it is not something

[1] V. Giraud, *Bossuet*, 1930, p. 139.

the mind can shape as it thinks it will. It is proof against all such attempts. There is no characteristic you can declare to be universal; no union possible among the Churches. Vain projects, all of them! Empty, elusive dreams! Fontenelle, describing him to the *Académie des Sciences*, portrays him as a triumphant figure, "something like those dexterous charioteers of old, who could drive as many as eight horses abreast, he can do the like with all the sciences". That was Leibniz the scientist; but there was also Leibniz the man: "At home, he was monarch of all he surveyed; he always took his meals alone. He had no stated times for them, and no domestic staff. He sent out to a cook-shop for something to eat and took whatever was going. Very often he slept the night in his chair, and woke up none the less refreshed at seven or eight in the morning. He worked without intermission, and for months at a stretch he allowed himself no break." The older he got the truer this became of him. He is alone now; the great and the powerful on whose support he had counted have deserted him. When, in June, 1714, the Elector of Hanover became King of England, he had no use for the services of this sick and aged man. As he attended no place of worship and never took the Sacrament, he was looked on as an unbeliever, and the pastors turned their backs on him. He died on the 14th November, 1716. He was buried quietly, no funeral procession, no mourners, no one to pay him the tribute of a tear. "You would have thought it was a felon they were burying, instead of a man who had been an ornament to his country."

The dream: for one brief moment it seemed as if the union of the Churches was at last within reach, a moment such as hardly occurs once in a hundred years. "The arm of the Lord is not shortened", said Leibniz, in a letter he wrote to Madame de Brinon on the 29th September, 1691. "The Emperor is favourably disposed; Pope Innocent XI and a number of Cardinals, Generals of Monastic Orders, the Maître du Sacré Palais, and many grave theologians, having carefully considered the matter, have expressed themselves in the most encouraging terms. I have seen the actual letter that was written by the late Père Noyelles, General of the Jesuits, and nothing could be more explicit. It is no exaggeration to say that if the King of France and the prelates and theologians who have his ear in these matters were to take concerted action the thing would not be merely feasible, it would be as good as done." So the union is imminent. Catholicity is setting its house in order, Teuton and Latin are winning back their spiritual communion, Dutch and English, duly following suit, find their way back to the Church, a Church both Roman and Reformed, and Christians, one and all, present a solid front to the forces that threaten the destruction of their faith.

Such was the dream. Now for the reality. Catholics and Protestants will not come to terms; the psychological moment has gone by; the most able and well-meaning of men has failed in his task, the enemies of the Christian faith rejoice and exult. Ah, what ruin! Ah, what havoc!

Instead of the God of Israel, Isaac and Jacob, we are offered an Abstraction, none other than the Law of the Universe, or, maybe, the Universe itself. This new God can work no miracles; miracles would only show him to be a victim of caprice, or perhaps at war with himself, and, far from confirming his existence, would confirm the contrary. Authority is not, tradition is a delusion, universal consent cannot be guaranteed, and even if it could, what was to prove that it, too, was not contaminated with error? The Law of Moses is not a law dictated on Mount Sinai by God himself and taken down then and there in its entirety. It is a human law which still betrays the handiwork of the various peoples by whom it was handed down to the Hebrews, of the Egyptians in particular. The Bible is a book just like any other book, it is full of alterations and perhaps second thoughts; scrolls joined together by unskilled hands, the careless work of rude, untutored folk, who paid no heed to dates and sometimes mistook the beginning for the end. There was nothing divine about it. Still less was the Monarchy divine. The right of subjects to rise up against their King had been proclaimed far and wide, and when Louis XIV quitted this earthly scene, it looked as if the process were complete.

Never, it is certain, had the beliefs and ideas on which society had so long reposed been laid open to so fierce an attack, Christianity in particular. Swift,[1] in 1717, indulges in one of his characteristic bouts of irony. It is dangerous, he says, it is imprudent, to oppose the abolition of Christianity at a time when

[1] J. Swift, An argument to prove that the abolishing of Christianity in England may, as things now stand, be attended with some inconveniencies, and perhaps not produce those many good effects proposed thereby, written in the year 1708.

all parties are unanimously set on its annihilation, as is clearly
manifested by their speeches, their writings and their deeds. To
defend it, to suggest that its abolition might not be unattended
by inconveniences, and that possibly it might not produce all the
good effects expected of it, would be a line of action that only a
perverted mind would pursue. Swift's sally reflects the misgivings entertained by Christian folk, particularly when they
came to realize the results of the demolition that had been going
on for years, not on a small scale and hugger-mugger, but wholesale and in broad daylight.

However, Europe has no taste for ruins; she only puts up with
them as a passing fancy, making garden-ornaments of them, for
example. And even then, their real purpose is to serve as a sort
of foil or contrast, to set off the living green of the trees, and the
passionate outpouring of bud and blossom. The most advanced
unbelievers among the thinkers with whom we have been
dealing, called a halt when they came face to face with the
Nihilism to which their scepticism seemed about to lead them.
Not theirs "the perfect balance between the Will and the Understanding," which Pyrrho held to be the essence of wisdom and
well-being.[1] If their understanding sometimes presented the
contra in a more favourable light than the *pro*, their will had by
no means resigned its functions. They declared that they were
only pulling down the old edifice to replace it with a new one,
whereof they had drawn the plans, laid the foundations and built
the walls; and that, even while the work of demolition had
actually been going on. Pull down, and at the same time build up,
that was the order of the day. If we would complete our estimate
of the men whose lot was cast in those most critical times, we
must study them at their task of reconstruction, and to that we
shall now address ourselves.

---

[1] Moreri, *Dictionnaire*, art. *Pyrrhon.*

PART THREE

The Task of Reconstruction

I

LOCKE'S EMPIRICISM

SO the great quest had to be started all over again; the human caravan must needs set forth once more, this time along a new road, and heading for a different goal.

To begin with, and most important of all, it must keep clear of Pyrrhonism, a thing which filled even Bayle himself with dread. To be continually arguing about everything under the sun, and then do no more than suspend judgment, means in the end complete inaction, the immobility of death. Pyrrhonism, a useful ally in restoring to the mind its freedom of choice, now looked as if it were going to annihilate the Will, and, with it, the possibility of choosing at all. This was no time for logic-chopping, for weighing the nicely calculated less or more, but for striking out promptly and resolutely for the far-off horizon of Happiness.

Fontenelle explained to his pupil, the marquise, one night when they were contemplating the stars together, that Philosophy was based on two things; one, that we had enquiring minds, the other, that we had very short sight. The result was that philosophers spent their time disbelieving what they did see, and trying to guess at what they didn't; an impossible state of affairs. Far better do the exact opposite; not bother our heads about what we don't see, but trust firmly to what we do. A philosophy that answered both these needs would be an immense boon to the human race. It would preserve them from doubt.

At this point it was that Locke came in.

And he came in the nick of time, like a bringer of good things, because he invested "the fact" with its due status and its sovereign dignity. In speaking of facts, we do not mean the facts of history.

They had been shown up, discredited, done with. There was no going back on that; their fate had been sealed once for all. When one tried to bring to light the facts of history, facts engulfed in the dead, irrevocable past, they came wrenched from their context, misinterpreted, warped, and bestained with lies. No sensible people could put any trust in them. What was needed was a different sort of certitude from that, and it was John Locke who supplied it.

Locke it was who turned the attention of thinkers to psychological truths, truths present in the mind, living, constant and indefectible. In this domain, not only is reason, however doubting it may be, forced to accept some elementary *data* on which criticism has no hold, but, more than that, it delights to discover, what had hitherto been hidden from it, namely, the conditions of its own functioning. And so the rationalists accept an alliance which keeps them on the hither side of scepticism; the eighteenth century, in so far as it has its roots in the seventeenth, is rationalistic in essence and empirical by consent.

Locke seemed expressly designed to play the part of the ideal philosopher. In the first place, he was an Englishman; consequently he thought deeply about things. Secondly, he did not limit himself to metaphysics, but made a study of the empirical sciences, notably medicine. Before turning his attention to the mind, he had made some acquaintance with the body; a salutary precaution which the unpractical were wont to neglect. He had had some experience of public affairs. As secretary and confidential agent to Ashley, Earl of Shaftesbury, sharing his downfall, seeking refuge in Holland, and returning in triumph with William of Orange, he had been one of those who had borne a hand in building the new England, the invincible England. Very wisely, he had contented himself with playing second fiddle, and from his vantage-ground, a trifle to the rear, he studied with observant eye the wiles and manoeuvres of his fellow mortals. Delicate, of uncertain health, he had not flung himself into the *mêlée* of affairs with the zest which takes such complete possession of the more robust; he had kept himself a little in reserve, as one who wanted to ponder on things a little more deeply. His travels had endowed him with ease and flexibility of manner; he had sojourned long in our southern districts, studying at close range those odd, but by no means unlikeable folk, the French; what their national customs were, what they fed on, what line their thinkers took, and what those who were not thinkers did for a living, how they produced those delicious things that England had not, namely, oil and wine, and why there was distress among the peasantry. In Paris he had made friends with medical men, astronomers and learned people of every kind, with all manner of restless and enquiring spirits. But Holland must have profited him still more, if it be true that the best of all schools is the rude school of exile. Driven from his native land, wandering from city to city in the country where he had found asylum, hob-nobbing with pastors, dissenters and the heterodox in general, it was as if he had gone back to school for an intellectual refresher course. Finally, he became a teacher himself, which is but another way of learning, and his pupil was none other than the son of Shaftesbury, his patron, who was soon to conquer a place of his own among the leaders of the new philosophy. Without a trace of pedantry or self-conceit, perfectly natural and, save for an occasional display of temper, as likeable in life as he was in everything he wrote, endowed with a sort of inborn distinction, John Locke was decidedly a gentleman. There was nothing of the learned professor in imposing academicals about Locke; he had not the necessary lung power to hold forth, *ore rotundo*, from the professorial chair; he spoke easily, quietly, and at length, in a style suited to the ordinary men and women of the world. The time had come when the real philosophers were to be found in the ranks of the laity and, with rare exceptions, few were recruited from among the pastors or the *monsignori*, from the pro-fessors of the Sorbonne or the Sapienza. They mingled with the world, the better to direct it.

He started with the peripateticism they had taught him at Oxford, which did not satisfy him. He was a long time feeling his way, with Bacon, Gassendi and Descartes as the guides of his choice, but, in the last resort, he relied on no one but himself. In the course of the winter of 1670–1671, talking over some philosophical questions with a party of friends, it dawned upon him that what was wanted was some sound rule, some trust-worthy guiding principle. The principles of faith and morals could not be securely established until we had examined our own mental capacity and determined what things are, and what are

not, within our intellectual grasp.   It was, therefore, the intellectual faculties which, before we attempted anything else,
had to be measured with accuracy.   It was no use living on charity;
no use calmly relying on the ideas of others, or asking what Plato
or Aristotle has to say about the matter, no use swearing by what
the masters have to tell us.   No; what we had to do was to take
Truth as our one and only aim, and to make our way towards it
along the path of free enquiry.   At the outset of Locke's intellectual career, we notice the same determination to strike out
an independent line, the same desire to begin again *de novo*, the
same anxiety to be intellectually free and self-sufficient, which was
working like leaven in the spirit of the age.

This method is by no means that of a solitary, of one who kept
to himself.   You can almost imagine you hear the voices of those
who have come to their friend Locke to ply him with questions,
hoping he will set their minds at rest.   Typifying the eager per-
sistency of their epoch, they brought their questions to one they
deemed most likely to provide them with a philosophy that
would allay their doubts.   Locke was at the mercy of his times.
All through his apprenticeship, he remained in direct contact
with his contemporaries, listening to the question which they
never ceased to put to him, the eternal question, which, now that
the answer of tradition was no longer held to suffice, again began
to clamour for a solution.   And that question was, *Quid est
Veritas?*   What is Truth?   To him it fell to proclaim the new
truth to the world.   From 1671 onwards, he had been committing
ideas to paper, ideas which soon began to fall into a coherent
whole, and which he might have put forth then and there, had
he been so minded.   However, he spent nearly twenty more years
developing them, putting them to the test, showing his manuscript now to one, now to another of his intimates.   No solitary
he, but a distinctly sociable person.

Journeying along the highways of France, at the various
hostelries where he put up; or in London, amid the preoccupations of his official duties; at Oxford, his haven of peace; at
Rotterdam, Amsterdam, Cleves, he pondered and toiled, bringing
by slow degrees his system to perfection.   When, at length, he
did give it to the world, people recognized that here indeed was a
man endowed with the gift of making his subjects live; for he did
not confine himself wholly and solely to philosophy; he liked to

tell his readers what he himself thought about religion, political matters, education and so forth, and every time he brought out a new book, there was no end to the discussion it provoked. Of a writer who wrote, as he did, only what appeared to be essential, I can recall but one other example, Jean Jacques Rousseau, who, whenever he touched on religion, or politics, or education, inevitably started a conflagration. Locke, burning with a gentler flame, did not, like Rousseau, set fire to everyone who approached him. But, before Rousseau, he sensed the heart-hunger of his fellow-men, and responded to it. His writings are just so many personal talks which grip the reader, and never let him go till they have won him over. Back, again and again, they hark, with countless new and persuasive arguments; patiently, they force him to surrender; his sentences enmesh him like a net.

His means are urbanity, ease, and an indefinably flowing and limpid style. No Sibylline mysteries for him; no excessive esotericism, no vertiginous profundities. He will have nothing that is not readily intelligible; it gives him pain to find himself at grips with a metaphysical thinker like Malebranche: "Wherein, I confess, there are many expressions, which carrying with them, to my mind, no clear idea, are like to remove but little of my ignorance by their sounds".—"Here again I must confess myself in the dark"—"And methinks if a man would have studied obscurity, he could not have writ more unintelligibly than this". Far be it from him to indulge in such obscurity! "My appearing in print being on purpose to be as useful as I may, I think it necessary to make what I have to say as easy and intelligible to all sorts of readers as I can. And I had much rather the speculative and quick-sighted should complain of my being in some parts tedious, than that any one, not accustomed to abstract speculations, or prepossessed with different notions, should mistake or not comprehend my meaning." Such were his feelings and such was his mode of expressing them. Is it not yet another sign of the times that he should thus avow his intention not to address himself exclusively to specialists in philosophy, but to risk incurring the disapproval of speculative and esoteric thinkers, in order to be of service to all who were seeking a sound rule of life?

At last, in the year 1690, the book appeared. Its title was

unpretentious enough: *An Essay concerning Human Understanding.*
Whatever may be said of it by those who care only for the high
flights of philosophy, the date marks a definite change, a new
orientation. Henceforth, man's sphere of exploration was the
mind of man and its unfathomable riches. Let us have done, said
Locke, with these metaphysical conjectures; do we not realize
how fruitless they are? Are we not tired of asking, and always
asking in vain? Was there ever one able to reveal the nature and
essence of the human soul, to show us what must be set in
motion in the animal part of us to give birth, through our bodily
organs, to our sensations and ideas? The body obeys the mind,
the mind acts on the body. No sooner do the metaphysicians
begin to interfere, than this fact, which is borne out by universal
experience, and which is, in itself, self-evident, is transformed
into a mystery whose obscurities even the most learned enquirers have only succeeded in making darker still. Let us, then,
leave it at that, let us cudgel our brains no more about it. If there
are substances external to us (as there certainly are), we have no
means of grasping them in their essence; why then waste our
energies in attempting to apprehend them? Let us abandon that
vain endeavour.

The certitude which we need resides in the mind. Let us look
therein and cease to probe those infinite spaces which do but
breed deceiving visions; thereon let us concentrate our attention.
Clearly recognizing that our understanding is limited, let us
accept its limitations; nevertheless, we should make the most of it
within the limits imposed, studying it and getting to know how
it operates. We should observe how our ideas are formed and
how they combine, one with another, and how the memory
retains them. Of all this amazing activity we have hitherto been
in total ignorance. That, and that alone, is the field of sure and
certain knowledge, and so rich are the prospects it holds out to us,
that the sum-total of our existence is not too long for their
exploration.

"It is of great use to the sailor to know the length of his line,
though he cannot with it fathom all the depths of the ocean. It
is well he knows that it is long enough to reach the bottom at
such places as are necessary to direct his voyage, and caution him
against shoals that may ruin him. Our business here is not to
know all things, but those which concern our conduct. If we can

find out those measures whereby a rational creature, put in that state which man is in this world, may and ought to govern his opinions and actions depending thereon, we need not be troubled that some other things escape our knowledge".[1]

Or to put the matter in other words (for Locke is not shy of repeating himself—far from it!): What is our business here, in this world? To learn about the Creator by learning as much as we can about the creature; to learn what our duties are; to provide for our material needs; no more. Our faculties, rude and imperfect though they be, are adequate to the due performance of those functions. Therefore, putting aside the hope of attaining any perfect and absolute knowledge of the things around us as something beyond the range of finite beings, let us content ourselves with being what we are, with doing what we can do and with knowing what we can know.

The truth of the matter is that, as soon as the mind attempts to reach out beyond its allotted limits, and seeks to learn the causes of things, we realize that the only effect of our exploratory effort is to make us aware how limited is our range of vision; we are confronted by a wall of impenetrable darkness. On the other hand, if only we are content to confine our investigations to the sphere vouchsafed to us, we find ourselves in a world of marvels, and we find wisdom and happiness into the bargain. Should we, then, hesitate to make our choice? Let us give up the impossible. We need have no fear of falling into the abyss, so long as we keep firm hold of the certainties which our hands, weak though they be, are able to grasp.

The real contribution which we owe to Locke's philosophy does not lie in his abandoning metaphysics; that, a number of thinkers had already done, but in his way of circumscribing and protecting a little islet in the illimitable ocean whose horizon recedes for ever as we move.

Still a task remained, the task of ordering the world so as to banish doubt. The *a priori* had to be treated as non-existent. A change indeed! Philosophy would have to be re-made all over again, and on a different plan; all philosophy, from Aristotle down to the latest comers, the Cambridge neo-Platonists, Cudworth and the rest of them, who were for reviving the theory of

[1] Foreword to Pierre Coste's translation.

ideas. There was no such thing as an innate idea; the idea of
infinity is not innate, nor is that of eternity, of identity, of the
whole and the part, of worship, or of God. In the newly born
it is impossible to distinguish any of these alleged realities, borne
from one knows not whence, inventions of the speculative mind,
which had expressed itself in many forms, Greek, scholastic, and
modern, but which had never resulted in anything but words,
words, words. Away with these phantoms. The mind is a piece
of white paper, waiting for things to be written on it, a camera
obscura, awaiting the coming of the sun's rays.

For this wholesale rebuilding work, there is one element
available; one, but it suffices; and that is *sensation*. It comes from
without, it impinges on the mind, arouses it, and, before long,
takes possession of it. By juxtaposition, by combination, it produces those increasingly complex and abstract ideas which result
from the mind's working on its own sense-data. Starting with
sensation, nothing is easier than to construct a theory of knowledge, intuitive, or demonstrative, which will bring with it
indefectible certitude. The relationship now is not between
subject and object, but—something much more simple—between
subject and subject, and henceforth the struggle to eliminate the
possibility of error is no more than a domestic concern, of taking
and maintaining internal precautions. "Since the mind, in all its
thoughts and reasonings, hath no other immediate object but
its own ideas, which it alone does or can contemplate, it is
evident that our knowledge is only conversant about them . . .
knowledge then seems to me to be nothing but the perception
of the connexion and agreement, or disagreement and repugnancy,
of any of our ideas". So that our knowledge, our human knowledge, is at once perfectly possible and infinitely sure.

But now, no sooner do we concede to Locke his principle of
initial sensation, than off he goes to reconstruct a system of
morality. We feel pleasure, and we feel pain: hence we get the
notion of the beneficial and the harmful; hence the notion of
things permitted and things forbidden; hence a moral code based
solely on psychological realities, a system which, for that very
reason, is endowed with a character of certitude which it would
not possess if it depended on some law external to itself. For
inasmuch as certitude is no more than the perception of agreement or disagreement in our ideas, and as proof is merely the

perception of this relationship arrived at through a series of intermediate ideas; as our moral ideas are, like the truths of mathematics, abstractions elaborated by the mind, it follows that there is no difference in kind between the one set of truths and the other, and that both are equally to be relied upon.

Thus, step by step, the dogmatic attitude is replaced by an empiricism which discovers and records all the facts of our psychological existence. What is the origin of language? Did God implant this wonderful intermediary within us by a single act of will? We cannot say. But what we do know perfectly well is that man possesses organs expressly designed for the creation of articulate sounds, that, by means of these sounds, he expresses the changes which his own sensibility experiences, and that words are the signs, first particular and then general, of ideas. All rhetoric and all the art of writing is there. Don't talk to us about works on style, or the art of poetry, unless they are based on those obvious principles. An author who really knows anything about the origin and office of words will scrupulously avoid any that convey no clear idea; the words he uses, he will use with a uniform connotation, otherwise he would create confusion in the ideas of which words should be the unchanging symbols; he will avoid over-refinement, as he will over-emphasis, both of them arch-agents of falsification and distortion. The object of language being to get our ideas into the minds of others, and to do so promptly, he is to be accounted a good writer, or a good speaker, who always keeps these objects in view and adapts his style to their attainment. Grammar was not invented by pettifogging pedants for the purpose of harrying luckless schoolboys; it has its logic, an inward logic, which, beginning with the initial sensation, can be followed in its successive stages.

To see the activities of the human spirit continually growing and expanding, and, with them, the beliefs which enable us to lead a happy life, with the consciousness that there is nothing, no science, no moral idea, no art which is not the outcome of its own activities—what subject for contemplation were better calculated than that to awaken our interest, our pleasure and our pride? Not, indeed, the pride of one who defies the gods, for none can be counted an initiate without sacrifice and humiliation of spirit, without acknowledging his fundamental ignorance, without bowing the head in unquestioning and limitless surrender; not pride in that sense, but the self-congratulation of one who has narrowly escaped drowning at sea and who, having managed to scramble ashore, has contrived to build himself a shelter with his own brave and hard-working hands. Locke's title was a modest one; it was an essay; but it was an essay on that marvel of marvels, the Human Understanding. Two principles, and two only, sufficed him: the impression made by external objects on our senses, and the workings of the mind and spirit consequent upon such impressions. These two principles, contemplated in their active operation, studied and analyzed, suffice to satisfy all our curiosity; such are the miracles which they work, and genuine miracles to boot. Generation on generation of learned men will come and go before we get to know what the Will, for example, or the Memory, really is. The mine is inexhaustible, and the ore it contains indisputably pure. It deceives not, neither does it disappoint. "When men extend their enquiries beyond their capacities and let their thoughts wander into those depths where they can find no sure footing, it is no wonder that they raise questions and multiply disputes, which, never coming to any clear resolution, are proper only to continue and increase their doubts, and to confirm them at last in perfect scepticism." On the other hand:

"When we know our own strength we shall the better know what to undertake with hopes of success and when we have well surveyed the powers *of our own minds we shall not be inclined to sit still and not set our thoughts on work at all in despair of knowing anything."*

Pierre Coste is loud in his praises of the master's work. In the preface he wrote for the second French edition of the *Essay* (1729), he says: "It is the masterpiece of one of the finest geniuses which England produced in the last century. Four English editions appeared under the author's eye within the space of ten or a dozen years; and the French translation which I published in 1700, having made it known in Holland, France, Italy and Germany, it was, and still is, as highly esteemed in those countries as it is in England, and the breadth, the depth, the precision and the clarity which distinguish it from beginning to end are the subject of ceaseless admiration. Finally, as its crowning distinction, the book has been, so to speak, adopted both at Oxford and

Cambridge, where it is read and expounded to the students as being the book best fitted to form their minds and widen their knowledge. So Locke now fills the place which Aristotle and his principal commentators have occupied hitherto in both these famous universities."

It is always a considerable adventure, this bringing of a work of philosophy to the notice of the world in general. In this instance, the process was exceptionally swift and auspicious. Locke benefited by the services of those interpreters whom the changes then taking place in Europe, changes of which he himself had had experience, put at his disposal. The first to herald his importance were the Dutch journalists; and particularly Jean Le Clerc in his *Bibliothèque Universelle*, which published an "Extract from an English work not yet published, to be entitled 'An Essay concerning the Human Understanding' in which is set forth how far the field of certitude in human knowledge extends and the method by which that knowledge is to be arrived at". Two refugees, David Mazel was one, the other the aforesaid Pierre Coste, who is perpetually evoked as his master's very shadow, both interpreted his line of thought, the former in its political, the latter in its philosophical aspect. Locke died in 1704, and as far back as 1710 a translation of his various works afforded French readers a complete grasp of all that was essential in his writings. In Germany, it was about 1700 that Thomasius read the *Essay* and as a result of that perusal became one of the heralds of the age of enlightenment. Locke stands at the turning point whence the roads of Europe start for the New Age.

Admittedly, he underwent some startling metamorphoses. Empirical, "sensationist" as he was, it was he who inspired Berkeley's idealism; nor was that by any means the most illogical of his adventures, since, if we ignore his starting-point and take up our abode inside his system, we find that we are living in a world not of realities but of relativities. Nothing could have been more repugnant to his desire, affirming as he did the existence of an Eternal Being, fountain of all intelligence, of infinite wisdom, than to be taken for a member of the materialistic school. His profession of faith, lengthy and detailed, struck an emphatic, even a solemn note; he proved with admirable cogency that matter could not be co-eternal with an eternal spirit.[1] But in

[1]*Essay*, IV, 10.

passing, and as though carried away by his own conception of God's infinite power, he declared that, after all, God may well have "given to some systems of matter, fitly disposed, a power to perceive and think";[1] a rash statement which was promptly denounced by the theologians, and which, exploited and popularised by Voltaire, resulted in Locke's whole work being for a long time misunderstood: Locke became a materialist despite himself. He wanted to be a Christian, and one of his preoccupations was clearly to define the limits of reason and faith. Reason serves to establish the certainty, or the probability, of those propositions or truths which the mind arrives at by deductions from the ideas it has acquired by making use of its natural faculties, viz., sensation or reflection. "Faith is the assent to any proposition not thus made out by the deductions of reason, but upon the credit of the proposer, as coming from God in some extraordinary way of communication. This way of discovering truths to men we call *Revelation.*" So, then, he believed in Revelation, in the divine mission of Jesus Christ, in the authority of the Gospel, in miracles. He held that the most exacting of thinkers, thinkers most prone to scepticism, could furnish no valid reason for doubting the Gospel Revelation: such was his own statement of the case. On the other hand, he reduced his *credenda* to a minimum: faith in Christ, and in the doctrine of repentance. As he asserted that there was no condition of salvation other than belief in the mission of Jesus, and living a good life; as he refused to believe that all Adam's posterity were doomed to infinite and everlasting torment because of the sin of the first man, of whom millions of mankind had never heard, he was, because of all this, classed among the Deists. He was looked on as a friend of Toland, and his *Reasonable Christianity* was ranged alongside *Christianity not Mysterious.* This was profoundly painful to him, particularly as it was his special aim to bring back to the religious fold all who had been alienated from it by a soulless formalism, by dogmatic hair-splitting, and by the multiplicity of warring sects; and further, because he wanted to show that Natural Religion was intrinsically insufficient; and, finally, because the Deists were the very people he longed above all things to confute; Deists who, in the name of Reason, rejected Revelation.

Such were the consequences, and such the drawbacks, of a line

[1] *Ibid.,* IV, 3.

of thought which was not invariably self-consistent, and which freely exposed itself to attack by its opponents. However, in spite of misinterpretations, and deviations, and cross-currents, his system continued to gain ground, and in a direction that was plainly discernible. Locke was pre-eminently the man who invited every sensible man to cultivate his garden and not go outside it. Cultivating a garden; what better calculated than that to conjure up for a man a picture of the Earthly Paradise? Or at least to bring him comfort and renew his zest for life? Finally, and in particular, Locke it was who aroused a lively interest in that very important and highly fascinating diversion—psychology. Attentively to study and investigate the capacity and workings of the human mind, without any idea of criticizing or finding fault, but solely to observe and understand—this was at once a toil and a pleasure which, refined upon by Condillac, and later on, by Taine, has come down to our own day, losing nothing of its interest and attraction.

II

DEISM AND NATURAL RELIGION

HERE we have yet another of the numerous and powerful links that connect the Renaissance with the period we have selected for our present study. Deism originated in Italy. Early in the XVIth century it migrated to France and settled there, so to say, for it was in France that it acquired its formal titles, in France that repeated attempts were made to fix and define its vague and shifting boundaries. In the earlier half of the XVIIth century, it often showed its head; thereafter, it lived on mainly in penumbra. However, an English offshoot had early detached itself from the parent tree. It was in the year 1624, in Paris, that Edward Herbert of Cherbury composed a Deist's profession of faith, which, far from being a string of negations and impieties, was reverent, religious, indeed, almost mystical in its tone. At the outset, he warns the reader that he proposes to deal, not with religion, but with the understanding. Well, that may be so, but still there are verities of religion which the understanding accepts, and of such were the doctrinal precepts of Lord Herbert of Cherbury: there is a Supreme Power; it is our duty to worship that Power; the practice of virtue is part of the worship which men render to God; impiety and crime are expiated by penitence; reward and punishment await us in the life to come. . . .

And in England; transplanted into this new *milieu*, Deism multiplied and prospered. It had found the climate and the soil that suited it; it felt at home. Openly, in the public *forum*, so to speak, its apologists and its adversaries joined issue in debate. Toland supported it with bitter and fanatical ferocity; Bentley, Berkeley, Clarke, Butler, Warburton confronted him as champions of revealed religion. In short, "there was no other country where Natural Religion was more clearly set forth than it was in England".[1]

Later on, in the ceaseless ebb and flow of ideas, France was again to open her arms to Deism, but this time it was a Deism habited in foreign guise, at least so it appeared to her. Voltaire took his religious philosophy from it, and Rousseau, when he wanted to portray the ideal Deist, that is to say, a materialist and a righteous man, presented him in the person of an Englishman, whom he called Milord Edouard Bomston. But its high blossoming time was yet to come; for the moment it was still endeavouring to take firm root.

The negative elements in its composition are easily discernible. "There must be no sort of constraint, nothing could be more out of keeping with the times".[2] Catholic, Protestant, Jew—there was constraint in all of them. There must be no more of it. No more priests, no more pastors, no more rabbis, all alike claiming to wield authority. No more sacraments, no more rites and ceremonies, no more fasting and mortifying the flesh, no more feeling that you are obliged, willy-nilly, to go to church, chapel, synagogue, or whatever it may be. The Bible is a book just like any other book; there is nothing supernatural about it; no more Tables of the Law; no more Ten Commandments. Deism is a sort of creditor demanding payment of a deferred liability. God is cast in a new mould. The present age will have no more of divine wrath, divine vengeance; nor, for the matter of that, will it tolerate any divine interference with human affairs. Vague, indefinite, remote, God did not look like causing very much embarrassment. The consciousness of sin, the need for grace, the uncertainty of salvation, which for so many centuries had been a weight upon so many hearts, would trouble the sons of men no more.

So much for the negative aspect of Deism. Its positive characteristics, what were they?

If Deism rejected the God of Israel, Abraham and Jacob, it at least believed that there was a God. If it denied Revealed Religion,

---

[1] *Bibliothèque anglaise*, 1717, I, 318.

[2] Le P. Buffier, *Éléments de métaphysique à la portée de tout le monde*, 1725, p. 92. (Metaphysics for everyone.)

at least it would not admit that the Heavens were empty. Nor did it regard man, and man alone, as the measure of the universe. So it happened that among the many denunciatory utterances pronounced by Catholic, Huguenot or Anglican, there crept in from time to time a softer, almost an approving note, as might happen when men share, even with those they are arguing against, the fundamentals, the alpha and the omega, of religion, that is to say a belief in God. Michel Le Vassor, a priest of the Oratory, filled with sorrow and affliction at Richard Simon's attitude, took it upon himself to vindicate the Order, and in 1688 brought out, to this end, a voluminous treatise which he entitled *De la Véritable Religion*, "Concerning True Religion". "More reasonable and more judicious than the Platonists and the Epicureans, some Deists there are today who avow in good faith that certain principles of natural religion and morality do exist, and that man is in duty bound to conform to them. But, they continue, those principles suffice, and we do not need any Revelation, or written law, to remind us of what we owe to God and our neighbour. Reason is guide enough, and God will always approve, so long as we obey the moral and religious instincts which He has implanted in our hearts."[1] And so, for this Catholic apologist, some Deists (some, but not all, for the genus included a diversity of species) stood, not so much for unqualified negation in matters of religion, as for a regrettable deviation from the path.

Now let us see what the Protestants thought about it all. That very learned man, Robert Boyle, taking a dismal view of the encroachments of infidelity, set aside the rent of a house he owned in London to finance a series of annual lectures which bore his name. They were lectures on religion, which were not to concern themselves with sectarian differences, but rather to set forth the general principles on which religious belief could be firmly established, to bring out clearly the proofs of the Christian faith, and to defend them against the assaults of unbelievers, of notorious infidels such as Atheists, Deists, Pagans, Jews and Mohammedans, while disregarding the controversies which the various Christian bodies carried on one with another. The Boyle lectures, which adhered to the lines laid down by their founder, proved a conspicuous success. The most learned theologians in the land, the

[1] *De la Véritable Religion*, Bk. I, chap. 7.

most eloquent preachers, were invited to lecture, among them Samuel Clarke, at that time Chaplain to the Bishop of Norwich. On two occasions he had the honour of speaking, once, in 1704, and again in the year following. Let us hear what he had to say about the Deists. They are of four kinds; those who pretend to believe in the existence of an eternal, infinite, independent and intelligent Being, but who disbelieve in Providence; those who accept God and Providence, but maintain that God does not concern himself as to whether actions are morally good or bad; actions being judged good or bad in the light of arbitrary, man-made laws; those who accept God, Providence and Moral Duty, but decline to believe in the Immortality of the soul, or in a future life.

"*The last sort of Deists are those, who if they did indeed believe what they pretend, have just and right notions of God, and of all the divine attributes in every respect; who declare they believe that there is One, Eternal, Infinite, Intelligent, All-powerful and Wise Being, the Creator, Preserver, and Governour of all Things.*"

The note struck by Samuel Clarke was similar in tone to that of Michel Le Vassor: the most tractable of the Deists retain the elements of a positive religious system; the misfortune is that they deny Revelation.

If we now interrogate a layman—in the person of the sensitive and gifted Dryden—shall we err if we seem to discover in his verse a condemnation indeed, but a condemnation mitigated and almost compassionate, of the Deists, because he is aware of the vague religious sympathies which many of them still retain?

Dryden encounters them on the road when he is dealing with the philosophers who had stated their views about the *Summum Bonum*, and this is how he portrays them:

> The Deist thinks he stands on firmer ground,
> Cries Eurêka, the mighty secret's found:
> God is that spring of good, supreme and best,
> We made to serve, and in that service blest;
> If so, some rules of worship must be given,
> Distributed to all alike by Heaven;
> Else God were partial and to some denied,
> The means His justice should for all provide.
> This general worship is to Praise and Pray:

One part to borrow blessings, one to pay:
And when frail nature slides into offence,
The sacrifice for crime is penitence.
Yet since the effects of Providence, we find,
Are variously dispensed to human kind;
That vice triumphs and virtue suffers here
(A brand that sovereign justice cannot bear):
Our Reason prompts us to a future state,
The last appeal from Fortune and from Fate,
Where God's all-righteous ways will be declared,
The bad meet punishment, the good reward.
Thus Man by his own strength to Heaven would soar,
And would not be obliged to God for more.[1]

The Deists whom Dryden thus depicts are Rationalists, but they are Rationalists with a heart-hunger for Religion. The Deism which we meet with in the writings of the period attenuates the idea of God, but does not annihilate it. It makes God the object of a belief vaguely defined, perhaps, yet positive none the less, and intentionally so. It sufficed at all events to endow its adherents with a sense of superiority over their godless brethren; it enabled them to pray and to worship; it prevented them from feeling that they were alone in the world, lost and fatherless; so that the *Vicaires Savoyards* of the morrow, when they saw the sun gilding their mountain-tops, would be able to pour forth their pent-up emotions and, weeping, return to the ways of faith. It is no easy matter to be an Atheist and brutally to crush out belief in the divine; it is incomparably easier to be a Deist. Those sweeping rebellions, those absolute negations, call for a character not a little out of the ordinary. "The difference", says Bayle, "between an Atheist and a Deist is almost negligible, when you come to look into the matter." But in that *almost* countless *nuances* come home to roost. "A Deist," Bonald will one day be telling us, "is simply a man who hasn't had time to become an Atheist." "A man who doesn't want to be an Atheist", would be much nearer the mark.

It was not for nothing that Deism got its finishing touches among a people who are used to halting their ideas just where they think they will; where a doctrine gets its wings clipped when

[1]*Religio Laïci*, 1682, lines 42-63.

it goes too far and threatens the moral stability of the country. That is so, if we may believe the words of a contemporary: "This was always look'd upon as a good natur'd nation, well dispos'd to religion and receptive of vertuous impressions, and tho' one cannot without astonishment see the wonderful progress that profaneness and immorality have made among us, yet I flatter myself that it is but an acute and temporary distemper, being so much against the native constitution of the people, that I hope is still strong enough to throw off by degrees this malignant ferment, which if it be unable to do so, the event must be deplorable".[1]

The popular mind sees no cause for astonishment or alarm in a deliberate limitation, or even in a contradiction. Such an attitude of mind will do quite well for a religion without mystery. Therefore it discards mystery, but it sticks to religion. However, as an Englishman looks on religion, ideas are not merely a matter of logic; the will, too, has a part to play.

Secondly, what the Deists did next was to preserve the idea of obedience to a law; and that law was the law of Nature. That there is such a law is freely acknowledged by Catholics: *Est in hominibus lex quaedam naturalis, participatio videlicet legis aeternae, secundum quam bonum et malum discernunt.*[2] There is among men a certain natural law, that is to say a part of the law eternal, in the light of which they distinguish good from evil. . . . Protestants, who recognize it the more readily in that they are themselves closer to Rationalism and more disposed to travel some of the way with the philosophers, hold it partly from conviction and partly because they have to harmonize their apologetics with the tone of the times. The reinforcement they thus obtained from the Deists, was by no means to be despised. It would mean a certain amount of territory won from the Atheists, in whose camp would reign consternation and confusion.

The only trouble was that when this concept, Nature, came to be more closely scrutinized, certain divergencies were brought to light, divergencies which could not be glossed over. There were

---

[1] Richard Blackmore, *Essays on Several Subjects*, 1716, Preface, I.
[2] St. Thomas Aquinas, *Summa theologica*, Prima secundae, quaestio 91, art. 2— *Ibid.*, quaestio 94, art. 4 and 6.

at least three of them. In the first place, what neither Catholics nor Protestants could agree to was that this enterprising Nature, not content with figuring as a seven day creation, not content to ascribe all its beauty to Him who called it out of chaos, should little by little be usurping the place of its Creator, that it should pose as His intermediary and even as His substitute, that it should be regarded as the Order, the supreme Order, to which God Himself was obliged to conform; that it was, in fact, the ultimate Essence. We have already seen the repugnance with which Spinoza's ideas were received.

Secondly, what religious folk could not admit was that Nature should be regarded as a kind of moral instinct, capable of becoming a complete religion in itself, a religion which would have been merely a matter of man's adjusting himself to the laws of Nature; that, and nothing more than that.

Thirdly, if we hold that Nature is "a kindly mother", as Lahontan says; or, as Shaftesbury puts it, that "Nature has no malice"; and that, in order to live a good life it is enough to obey the laws of Nature, what becomes of original sin and the corruption that flowed therefrom? What of the need for redemption? Life on earth then is no longer to be regarded as a state of trial during which we are to fight against the seeds of evil that are in us, so that, overcoming them, we may win to Heaven at last.

Now, what *is* Nature? The question sounded peremptorily, as did all questions in those days, in the ears of those doughty men who, to whichever camp they belonged, would tolerate no subterfuges, no evasions. They hungered after truth, and both sides alike were battling for the light. The more involved the problem, the more honour in attempting its solution. What, then, *is* Nature?

It was at once recognized that the word was given all manner of interpretations and that in consequence there was "terrible confusion between what it signified in the mouths of the ignorant, and what it stood for in the mouths of the learned". Nature is very sensible. Nature does nothing in vain. Nature never does more than it sets out to do. Nature invariably does what is best. Nature always takes the shortest cut. Nature is never overburdened by the too much, or cramped by the too little. Nature is self-preserving. Nature is the healer of ills. Nature is ever mindful of the preservation of the Universe. Nature abhors a vacuum. What a host of miscellaneous tags, and what a motley set of meanings to apply to one and the same thing: author of Nature; the essence of anything; the order of things; a kind of semi-divinity, and so on and so forth.[1]

There was no coming to terms, try as they might. But men's minds were sorely troubled. Robert Boyle, who deplored this confusion in the sort of language we have just recalled, and who urges people for heaven's sake to introduce a little order into their various interpretations of the word, was really not so much seeking for a definition of it, as voicing a protest, the protest of the Christian conscience fearful lest men should slip into the habit of putting Nature in the place of God. Against the obviously absurd idea that men are naturally good, Pierre Bayle entered his protest. Nature? To begin with, no one has ever accurately noted precisely how the hearts of men react to its influence. "There is hardly any word more vaguely and loosely used than the word *Nature*. It occurs in all sorts of contexts, meaning now one thing and now another, but it is scarcely ever used with one precise and definite connotation. Be that as it may, every clear-headed person will agree that, if we want to be quite sure that such and such a thing has been implanted in us by Nature, we should satisfy ourselves that the young are conscious of it and influenced by it without any external mention of its existence. I do not know that anyone has ever carried out an experiment in order to discover what takes place in the mind of a man who has never been taught anything at all. If some people had brought up a number of children and had been content to feed them, without teaching them a single thing, we should then see what unassisted Nature was capable of; but as a matter of fact all the people we know have been bamboozled from the cradle upwards and made to believe anything." Later, when their eyes are opened and they come to look around them, men cannot help seeing that Nature and Goodness are anything but synonymous. "We perceive in the human race very many evil things, without having any grounds for supposing that they were not put there by Nature. I see the most god-fearing and affectionate of parents who take the utmost care to have their children instructed in the

[1]Robert Boyle, *De ipsa natura, sive libera in receptam naturae notionem disquisitio*, Londini, 1686.

truths of the Gospel, but who are nevertheless unable to repress in them the desire for revenge, or for praise, or for gambling, or for illicit love."[1]   And further, "I warn you that Mr. Sherlock imagines that the general consent of mankind is the voice of Nature, and that it therefore carries with it the infallible attribute of truth. That proves too much, for, if anything is to be regarded as the voice of Nature, it is the voice that bids us indulge our appetite for revenge and unhallowed love, just as we satisfy the cravings of hunger and thirst".[2]   Something more than all this talk about Nature was required to make us feel that we were the temples of Goodness and Virtue.

All the same, the Deists were satisfied that they were freely acting as indicated by the Unseen Power that ensured the preservation and order of the Universe.   When they worshipped their non-mysterious God, they had the feeling that they were acting in due accordance with a positive law.   Sometimes they went the length of holding that it was the revealed religions which misrepresented the true God, by substituting for the divine idea, images drawn, not from Nature but from art invented by self-interested and deceiving men, and perpetuated by superstition.

Among the Deists a new and advanced group of freethinkers came into being.[3]   This is the line they took.   They defined freedom of thought as "The use of the understanding, in endeavouring to find out the meaning of any proposition whatsoever, in considering the nature of the evidence for or against it, and in judging of it according to the seeming force or weakness of the evidence".

The verdict of this tribunal of the conscience is not invariably unfavourable.   When a testimony seems sufficiently well-founded; when a fact is established in accordance with the rules of evidence, it is accepted.   Your freethinker discards whatever seems to him to be false, but retains whatever seems to him to be true; far from being a sceptic, he believes in the power of reason to furnish the foundations of Truth and Justice.

[1], [2]Pierre Bayle, *Réponse aux questions d'un Provincial*, vol. II, ch. cv. *Ce que c'est proprement qu'une chose qui émane de la nature.   Si pour savoir qu'une chose est bonne il suffit de savoir que la nature nous l'apprend.—Ibid.*, ch. cxl.

[3]Anthony Collins, *A Discourse on Freethinking*, London, 1713.   *Discours sur la liberté de penser, écrit à l'occasion d'une nouvelle secte d'esprits forts, ou de gens qui pensent librement.   Traduit de l'anglais*, à Londres, 1714. *Discours sur la liberté de penser et de raisonner sur les matières les plus importantes.   Ecrit à l'occasion de l'accroissement d'une nouvelle secte d'esprits forts, ou de gens qui pensent librement.   Traduit de l'anglais*, Seconde édition, revue et corrigée. A Londres, 1717.

Thence he derives the inward force which inspires him: the idea that he is possessed of a principle so manifestly true that nothing further could possibly put its truth in a stronger light, lends him confidence and assurance: he has solved the great secret which the weaker brethren will never comprehend. With infinite satisfaction he keeps repeating over and over again the magic formula which assures him of his power over men and things: I am free to think as I will. Not a single person in the whole world but has made mistakes; but so far as he is concerned, he, at any rate, will make no more; at the far end of the strict examination to which he subjects everything that presents itself to his vision or to his understanding, he discovers, as a reward for the courage which led him to cast off the shackles of superstition, the True and the Good. The certitude he derives from the exercise of his reason brings him the same sort of tranquillity and happiness as religious folk once used to derive from their faith: *neque decipitur ratio, neque decipit unquam*; think freely, and all the rest shall be added unto you. Think freely and you shall taste of the fruit of the Tree of Knowledge. Meanwhile, the faint-hearted, the servile will continue to linger in outer darkness, far from the earthly paradise. "Nothing is more foolish than to imagine there is any danger in allowing men freely to examine the bases of received opinions; nothing is more foolish than to suspect the good intentions of those who avail themselves of this freedom. Until men have a better guide than reason it is their duty to follow this light whithersoever it leads them."

To think freely is not only a happiness in itself, but, furthermore, it tells us how to order our lives, with happiness as our goal. It is only by dint of thinking that man can read the secret of human life and tell himself that misery and misfortune are the offspring of vice, whereas pleasure and happy days are always the reward of virtue. Cicero knew that well enough when he expatiated on the blessedness of the man who cheerfully does his duty; who carefully regulates his whole conduct, who obeys the law, not because he is afraid of it, but because he looks on it as a thing excellent in itself. The freethinker gets it into his head that he is merely doing what his enlightened desire, the logical power of his own reason, bids him do: he is the master of his fate, as he is of the universe.

The first to proclaim these definitions of Freethought was

Anthony Collins; first, in his polemical writings and, subsequently, in greater detail, in his famous *Discourse on Freethinking*, 1713. Thenceforth, the words freethinker and *libre-penseur* became current coin in the human vocabulary. There was a gentleman, recognized as such by everyone, an old Etonian and a Cambridge man, possessed, according to Locke, of a house in the country and a library in town, and of friends everywhere; a man of irreproachable character, a perfect example of that *respectability* which his compatriots regarded as the leading social virtue, and this gentleman it was who came in for the mixed inheritance of the freethinkers and the Deists, and produced from it a clear analysis of the aims and principles it involved. It was about this time that the freethinkers came to be regarded as intellectually and socially the *élite*; and that this *élite* began to look with pity or contempt on all who professed any kind of religious belief, although the believers still held the lead in numbers and influence. Anthony Collins refers to Samuel Clarke in terms of the utmost disdain: Samuel Clarke held orthodox views, and that was enough to damn him. "There is one thing which I am very much surprised to find in Mr. Clarke, and of which I did not think him capable, and this is an insinuation that *I believe too little*. For I did imagine that the usage he had had of the like kind, would have given him an opportunity to consider, that such reflections are capable of being made by anybody, and so derive no credit on their author, and that they can please no man of candour and ingenuity. However, I shall not make that return which such an insinuation does suggest and would justify, but instead thereof will give him on this occasion a testimony in his favour, before I finally take my leave of him; that I verily think he neither *believes too little*, nor *too much*; but that he is perfectly, and exactly orthodox, and in all likelihood will continue so."

Such is the line of thought which conduces to the view that orthodox folk are not only incapable of thinking for themselves, like the mentally backward, but that they are positive hindrances to progress; while the freethinkers, on the other hand, are regarded, not merely as sound reasoners, but as people who make a definite contribution to the well-being of society. No more are these latter to be looked on as feather-brained voluptuaries, as pleasure-seeking egoists, or as worthless riff-raff, or as a set of despicable adventurers. Such a freethinker as Collins exhibited an integrity and a dignity that even his opponents were forced to respect.

Without troubling himself about the finer shades of meaning, which never worried him because he never suspected their existence; without entering into his adversary's arguments, Collins, stubbornly driving straight ahead, finds a great deal to deny, but also a great deal to affirm. He reverses the signals; he puts negatives in the place of positives, and *vice versa* he declares that necessity is a doctrine of freedom and that materialism ensures the triumph of the spirit. As early as 1714, Louis XIV being still alive, a French version of his work was made current, and it was apparently a success, seeing that a second edition was called for in 1717. As the translator justly observed, its appeal was universal. Some people had said that the book was only suited to the English, that it would take a deal of explaining to make it intelligible to foreigners, and that no translation would stand a chance. That was obviously incorrect. "Truth, thought, reason belong to every country." "The matter of the discourse concerns people of all kinds." And be it noted—it is not the least interesting thing about it—that Collins adorns his free-thinkers' chapels with his own collection of Saints. The followers of Reason will be able to venerate the great men who, down the aisles of time, helped to establish the new cult; Socrates, Plato, Aristotle, Epicurus, Plutarch, Varro, Cato the Censor, Cicero, Cato of Utica, Seneca, Solomon, the Prophets, Josephus the Historian, Origen, Minutius Felix, Lord Bacon, Hobbes and, besides Synesius Bishop of Africa, Archbishop Tillotson, who is undeniably a Christian apologist, though his sermons tend to enthrone Freethought, with Religion and virtues as assessors, whereof the practice contributes mightily to the peace and happi-ness of society. Besides all these freethinkers on whose merits he enlarges, Collins could add an account of a number of other heroes whom he contents himself with merely naming, lest he should take up too much time and space. Among them he includes Erasmus, Montaigne, Scaliger, Descartes, Gassendi, Grotius, Herbert of Cherbury, Milton, Marsham, Spencer, Cudworth, Sir William Temple and Locke. In short, he concludes, it is difficult, if not impossible, to name a man in any way distinguished for worth and intelligence, any man who has left anything of a name behind him, without having to recognize that he has also given evidence of freedom of thought. On the other hand, it would be equally impossible to pick out an opponent of freethinking, however socially important, however distinguished, who had not some sort of mental twist, was not something of a fanatic; or was not ambitious, cruel, addicted to detestable vices, or who, to put the whole thing in a nutshell, was not always prepared to do anything, no matter what, under the pretext of glorifying God and serving the Church—impossible, I say, to find any opponent of freethought who has not left behind him memorials of his brute ignorance, who has not been the slave of priests, of women, or of chance.

It was all very well, this calendar of lay saints, but what was also needed was a form of initiation whereby the adepts might be officially received and appointed to their appropriate groups. Some sort of ritual was wanted, some new ceremonial. These, it seems, were the needs arising from the ideas whose development we have been contemplating.

Who, asked Swift, would apply the description of "philosopher" to Toland apart from his one and only theme, namely, his aversion to Christianity? It was that, his anti-Christian bias, that eventually led him to found a society which he intended to be a counter-blast to the Church. He wrote a hymn which, although it was addressed to Philosophy and not to God, was none the less a hymn: "Philosophy, thou Guide of Life! thou Searcher out of Virtue! thou Expeller of Vice! What, not only would become of us, but even what would be the life of Man without thee? Thou hast founded Cities, thou hast gathered dispersed Mankind into a Society of Life. Thou hast united them to each other, first by a participation of the same abode, afterwards by wedlock, and finally by a communion of letters and words. Thou hast been the Giver of Laws, and the Mistress of Manners and Discipline. We have recourse to these, we implore thy Aid, we devote ourselves entirely to thee. One day spent well, and according to thy dictates, is to be preferred to a prevaricating immortality. Whose riches should we rather use than thine? Thou, I say, that hast granted us a *perfect Tranquillity of Life*, and has exempted us from the *Terrors of Death*!"

He detests, he avers, any sort of religion professed by man; nevertheless, he draws up a form of service for a new society whereby men are to become better and wiser, a society which will procure them perfect happiness and supreme content. His love of humanity prompts him to found a Socratic Society, of whose moral principles, objects and philosophy he gives us a broad idea. The members shall meet in secret; it shall have its chants, its libations, its love-feasts. There shall be a settled ritual; a President who shall recite verses, to which the faithful shall sing the responses. Let us accompany John Toland to the meeting house of these comrades, these brethren. What is this we hear?

The President: May all happiness attend our meeting.
The rest answer: We institute a Socratic Society.
The President: May Philosophy flourish.
Response: And the politer Arts.
The President: Attend with silence. Let this assembly, and all that is to be thought, spoke, and done therein, be consecrated to Truth, Liberty, Health, the triple wish of the wise.
Response: Both now and for evermore.
The President: Let us be called Equals and Brothers.
Response: Companions, too, and Friends.

Behold, then, the very man who, of all others, was most furiously bent on destroying the Church, building a chapel to his own design. We must not forget that the London Grand Lodge of Freemasons was opened in 1717; and that the first French Lodge was founded in 1725.

III

NATURAL LAW

DIVINE Right: here too, as with religion, the whole structure is as simple as it is grandiose. The Polity was based on words taken from Holy Writ and what foundation could be more firm than that? "Hearken, Israel, the Lord our God is the only God. Thou shalt love the Lord thy God with thy whole heart, with thy whole soul and with thy whole strength." The love of God bound men to love one another, and thus the social order came into being. The primary example of government is paternal authority. Monarchy, which derives from it, is the most general, the oldest, and the most natural form of government, for, by reason of their human state, men are all in the position of subjects; and paternal rule, which accustoms them to obey, accustoms them also to acknowledge one head. Monarchy is the best form of government and, of monarchies, the best is that in which the succession, confined to the heirs male, devolves upon the eldest son of each generation.[1]

Thus does the Bishop of Meaux, the Dauphin's tutor, rear the canopy which is to shelter the future King's royal person. His person is sacred, and no one on earth may dispute his authority. Not that the King's Majesty is exempt from all control. On the contrary, God's law lays upon the King obligations more strict and more onerous than any imposed on the humblest of mortals. The King's authority is absolute, but it is the authority of a father. It is absolute, but it must conform to reason. It operates through general ordinances, and not according to the caprice of the moment. If the man who is invested with enormous power makes an ill use of it, let him tremble and beware, for terrible is the account he

[1] *Politique tirée des propres paroles de l'Écriture Sainte*, 1709.

will be called upon to render on the Day of Judgment. Howbeit, though answerable to God, he is not answerable to his subjects. Not for him to seek counsel of them, or to act on their advice. And in truth, to give to those whose duty it is to render obedience, power to interfere with those appointed by God to command, would be to offend against God and logic. So strict is this law that, even if the King declared himself an infidel, were he even to persecute his people, it would still be their duty to submit. To the violence of their princes the people can but reply with respectful and dutiful remonstrance, while praying for their change of heart. God, in His heavenly abode, holds the reins of all kingdoms of the earth; kings rule their subjects in accordance with His inscrutable will; their subjects uncomplainingly obey; and such transitory events as seem to sound a discordant note will, when, ceasing to view them with the eyes of the flesh, we come at last to understand their mutual interaction, swell, and not mar, the universal harmony.

If, now, we look about us for a visible example which shall do justice to the pomp and splendour of this power, and soar to the height of this well-nigh superhuman majesty, the image of Louis XIV rises spontaneously to our eyes. It haunts us with its very splendour, this symbol of regal state; it pursues us across the gulf of time, it is with us, here and now; it is living still. There yet linger in our memory the famous words which the *Grand Monarque* —we can almost hear him saying them, as on the day he signalized the inauguration of his personal sway—*l'état, c'est moi*: I am the State. We know how he made up his mind to fulfil to the letter the motto: One King, One Faith, One Law; how he crushèd every attempt at resistance; how, in the presence of the Pope himself, the helmsman of Christ's Church, he upheld the rights of the captain who is responsible for the Ship of State; the captain being, of course, himself. He is the commanding exemplar, the hero, of the Monarchy. At Versailles we wait to see him pass through the halls and the courts, we follow him as he enters the Gallery of Mirrors surrounded by courtiers eager to interpret and obey his slightest gesture; and when, as the shades of evening begin to fall, we prepare to leave the groves and alley-ways laid out in accordance with his sovereign pleasure, we seem, as we retrace our steps towards the Château, to behold at one of the windows the figure called back for us by La Bruyère from the land of shadows: "He himself in a manner of speaking, is his own Prime Minister. His mind forever dwelling on his people's needs, there is for him no leisure time, no hours that he can call his own. Night draws on, the guards have been relieved at the approaches to his palace; the stars come out in the heavens, and proceed on their appointed way; all nature sleeps, buried deep in shadow, now that the day is done; and we too, take our rest; not so the King; quitting the balcony, he retires within his chamber, there, with sleepless eye, to watch over us and all his realm."

But from a very different source there came ideas favouring the doctrine that absolute power should be vested in the ruling prince, ideas, the reverse of religious, which were intended to prove that men could only be governed if they were treated as instruments, as tools. Machiavelli was a far-off figure, but the memory of him still survived. Nearer, in point of time, was Hobbes. As early as 1642, that keen and cynical philosopher had made a preliminary sketch of his theory. In 1651, in his *Leviathan*, he presented it in its finished and final form. Not a single European thinker but had been profoundly impressed by it, but had had to take it into account, were it but to refute it. How often, perusing some doctrinal work, one came across the name Hobbes at a turn of the page! What a profound commotion his ideas provoked! How they echoed and reverberated throughout the world!

You are by nature evil, said Hobbes, addressing mankind at large. There is no spiritual principle anywhere in all the world: pleasure is the one and only good; pain the one and only evil; self-interest the one and only aim; and freedom is but the absence of whatever hinders the indulgence of the passions. The principle of the conservation of life being selfishness, and everyone defending his right to live, man's natural state is a state of war; they live like wolves. Man's state, in this natural freedom, is a state of war, for war is none other than the time in which the will and the endeavour to attack and to resist, by word or deed, are made sufficiently evident. The time which is not war is called peace. Will the destruction of the species result therefrom? Assuredly; unless something is devised to remedy the evils of the natural state, unless equality among men is replaced by a régime of inequality, which alone can save them from themselves. Hence the institution of a body-politic under the authority of a monarch, who, from the nature of the case, must be a tyrant.

Pacts and pledges would be useless to maintain peace, for they would constantly be violated. Force alone can control men's savage instincts, force, and the fear which it inspires; therefore the King must wield the sword of war and the sword of justice. Power of every description, complete and absolute, must be concentrated in his person. To limit his authority by some democratic device, such as an assembly of the people, would be to invite anarchy and, very soon, to relapse again into the natural state of chaos. The King is answerable to no one; he cannot be called to account; he is all in all. No doubt this means surrender-- ing our freedom to him, and freedom is something to which we all cling more or less. But what would you? Since it is impossible to enjoy both freedom and life, better choose life. Man's ingenuity is astonishing. He has learnt to construct artificial animals, automata that can walk about, sit down, wag their heads, open their mouths, and wink their eyes. So also he has contrived to create an artificial society, a monstrous machine, a political automaton which, with the happiest results, takes the place of natural society. This automaton is called Leviathan. "That great Leviathan called the Commonwealth or State is but an artificial man, though of greater stature and strength than the natural, for whose protection and defence it was intended." But over against these theories, which, though they derive from such widely different sources, all combine to fortify the principle of authority, other, and contrary, theories were to arise. Another battle was to be joined, a battle of abstractions to begin with, but not without a certain pathetic beauty of its own. We see ideas coming to birth, timid, fragile and promptly opposed; we see them grow in stature. Not one of them is confined to its native soil. They take wing, they laugh at frontiers, for that is their nature, their very life. They seem to gather new strength in the lands to which they fare. Constantly attacked, they are as constantly on the defensive, and, refashioned and disciplined in the process, they gain ground, they seize the initiative. At last they feel powerful enough to supersede the ideas by which men were actuated of old, and to guide them towards what they hope will be a happier future. Natural law was the offspring of a philosophy which rejected the supernatural, the divine, and substituted, for the acts and purposes of a personal God, an immanent order of Nature. It further proceeded from a rational tendency which affirmed itself in the social order. To every human being certain inherent faculties are attached, and, with them, the duty of putting them to their natural use. Finally, it derived from a sentiment, a state of feeling: the authority which at home arbitrarily determines the relations between subject and ruler, and which, abroad, is the cause of nothing but wars, must be done away with, and replaced by a new law, from which happiness may perhaps result, a political law which shall regulate the relations of the various peoples imbued with the idea that they themselves are the architects of their own destiny. The law of the people. . . .

Law, philosophy of life, social values, practical values; law, a tree deep-rooted, with branches laden with foliage, does not change its character without much travail. Massive works of controversy stand out along the road. To take them in their due order, looking at each against the background of the period to which it belongs, all this is to take part in a prodigious effort, which, at every stage, increases its awareness of the object it pursues.

1625. Hugo de Groot, *De jure belli et pacis*. It was a Dutchman who had sought refuge in Paris who gave the first signal. A man of highly sensitive nature, rich in knowledge and in intellectual endowments, in the fore-front of the political disputes, in the very centre of the religious controversies of his time, he grew sick at heart as he contemplated the ceaseless strife by which Europe was laid waste. "I beheld throughout Christendom an orgy of bloodshed of which even the barbarian races would have been ashamed. For frivolous reasons, or for none at all, men flew to arms and, once those arms were in their hands, no heed was paid to any law of God or man, as though, in obedience to some universal urge, the Furies were rushing unchecked along the road to every crime." Grotius, who had suffered persecution for his opinions, made a romantic escape from the prison in which his enemies had confined him, and took refuge in France. It was to our King Louis XIII that he dedicated, in 1625, his treatise on the Law of War and Peace, a great work which passed unnoticed by the masses, the usual fate of authors who have had the profoundest influence on the people's destiny. Who pays any attention to that department of the law which concerns the mutual relationship of peoples and their rulers? In Grotius' opinion, no one. Nay, it is commonly held that war is something incompatible with law of any kind, and that by virtue of certain state reasons alleged by Machiavelli, perfidy and violence of every description should be recognized and excused. This is not true; there is a law which holds good even in time of war, a law which governs war, and that law is named Natural Law. The truth is that Nature has graven it on the hearts of men, whom it desired to live sociably together; nothing can prevail against this unwritten, but vital law. "In order that war should be a just war, it must not be carried on with less regard for religion than is usually observed in the administration of justice." "When war is being waged, the civil laws are silent, but not those unwritten laws which are laid down by Nature." But what of divine law? Grotius does his best to safeguard it. "What we have just said", he declares, "would hold good even if we were to agree (which we could not do without sinning) that there is no God, or that He is indifferent to the affairs of men. Since God and Providence are undoubted realities, we have in them a source of law other than that emanating from Nature, the source which derives from the will of God. Natural law itself may be attributed to God, since God it was who willed that such principles should exist in us."

The law of God, the law of Nature. . . . It was not Grotius who invented this twofold formula. It had done duty long before his time; the Middle Ages were acquainted with it. What then was it that was new about it? How came it to be criticized and condemned by the ecclesiastical authorities? Why did it create such a stir?

Its novelty lay in the patent separation of the two terms; in the no less evident tendency to stretch their opposition; and then in an attempt to reconcile the two, which of itself implied that the rift was a real one. Above all, it lay in an idea of which we have already made mention, an idea which, though not as yet clearly defined, was full of vigour: War, violence, disorder, which the law of God does not repress but suffers rather, and even justifies, as being part of an inscrutable design, all the ills which man is heir to—perhaps the day will come when some human law will bring about their mitigation, their abolition. Thus it is that we are invited, with manifold excuses for such boldness, to pass from the Order of Providence to the Order of Humanity. Throughout the century, translations of the book were constantly appearing; it was expounded and commented upon in every seat of learning.

1670. Spinoza, *Tractatus theologico-politicus.*

1677. *Ethic.*

The idea that kings are impostors, making use of religion to consolidate their unlawful power; and this other one, no less profound in its way, the idea that everything strives of necessity to persevere in its being:

Demonstration. Individual things are modes by which the attributes of God are expressed in a certain and determinate manner; that is to say, they are things which express in a certain and determinate manner the power of God, by which He is and acts. A thing, too, has nothing in itself by which it can be destroyed, or which can negate its existence, but, on the contrary, it is opposed to everything which could negate its existence. Therefore, in so far as it can and is in itself, it endeavours to persevere in its own being. Q.E.D.

1672. Samuel Pufendorf. *De jure naturae et gentium libri octo.*

1673. *De officio hominis et civis juxta legem naturalem libri duo.*

A German, engaged as a teacher in Sweden, took up the task, and set his indelible seal on the theories which were taking shape. Samuel Pufendorf was the first to occupy the chair of natural and international law at the University of Heidelberg. In 1670, he accepted a chair at the University of Lund offered him by Charles XI of Sweden. "The duty of the man and the citizen": strange to hear those words, at that early date! We seem to be at least a hundred years ahead of the times. If anyone had asked us to what era they appertained, we should unhesitatingly have answered that they belonged to the phraseology of the French Revolution; and it is a fact that the work did contain certain basic ideas which, handed on from one thinker to another, came finally to exert a decisive influence on the collective mentality of the ensuing century: philosophical abstraction taking the place of history, since we may look upon "the first man as having fallen from the clouds, so to speak, with the same inclinations as those possessed by men when they come into the world to-day"; social morality, duty, being human action precisely conforming to the

laws which command us to perform it; the political pact. Civil
society which succeeds the state of nature by way of marriage, the
family, the constitution of the body-politic, reposes of necessity
on agreements: the several individuals covenanting together to
unite in one body, and to regulate by common consent whatever
concerns the common safety, and the common weal; those to
whom the sovereign authority is entrusted pledge themselves to
do all that in them lies to preserve the security and welfare of all;
the rest promising them their loyal obedience.

Natural Law gains form and substance; it now not only asserts
its rights in war, it imperiously demands a place, and takes it,
in the political constitution of the different states; it plays a predominant part in social life: "the law of nature is one which is so
uniformly adapted to all that is sociable and reasonable in human
nature that, unless its dictates were obeyed, it would be impossible
for mankind to live together in peace and security." Pufendorf
does not deny the divine power, but he relegates it to another
plane: there is the plane of pure reason, and there is the plane of
Revelation; in the same manner, there is the plane of natural law
and the plane of moral theology; the plane of duties which
impose themselves upon us because the right use of our natural
reason makes us regard them as essential to the maintenance
of human society as a whole, and there is the plane of duties which
we are called upon to fulfil because God in Holy Writ has laid
them upon us. That said, he adduces arguments designed to show
that these two planes do not clash, that they may work together,
and only succeeds in demonstrating how profoundly they dis-
agree. Theology is concerned with Heaven; human reason, with
earth. Pufendorf confines himself to earth; Heaven seemed to
him altogether too remote.

The Swedish pastors saw only too plainly the dangers of this
divided, or rather, avowedly one-sided allegiance; and against
this exponent of the theory of natural law there arose such a
storm of indignation that he was compelled to call in the aid of
the secular arm to avoid being driven from his post. He was not
driven from it; on the contrary, he won the day.

1672.   Richard Cumberland, *De legibus naturae disquisitio
philosophica*.

Now it is England that brings her contribution: the Reverend
Richard Cumberland, Doctor of Divinity, and a future Bishop,

refutes the abominable ideas put forth by Hobbes. What is the backbone of his argument? Why, precisely that same natural law which is in direct opposition to the violence that loomed so large in the mind of the author of *Leviathan*: natural laws amount simply to this, that we should be well-disposed to every reasonable being.

But it was a different order of assistance that was to come from that ancient land in which politics have always entered into the intellectual, moral and religious life of the nation; in which the throne, in jeopardy all through the seventeenth century, overthrown, then restored, again overthrown, again restored, but essentially modified in character, was the centre of a passionate controversy in which the people, the nobility and gentry, poets and philosophers, and the kings themselves, were all anxious to play a part. But all in good time. For the moment things must needs wait a little.

1685. *The Revocation of the Edict of Nantes.*

From the France which had established itself outside the borders of the motherland, from France in exile under foreign skies, there arose the voice of revolt. True, not all the reformers, not all even of those who suffered persecution and exile, deemed themselves released from their oath of allegiance to the King; they did not all apply the same solution to the problem of conscience which confronted them, for some there were who still thought, obedience to the King being the due of his Divine Right, no faults he might commit could ever diminish the authority of one so appointed. But there were others, more vociferous, who loudly demanded that violence should be repaid with violence. From 1686 to 1689, Jurieu poured forth his *Lettres pastorales aux fidèles qui gémissent sous la captivité de Babylone*; letters in which he proclaims aloud the right to rebel. "The right of princes to use the sword does not extend to matters of conscience." Louis XIV, having used the sword to coerce men's consciences, had put himself outside the pale of the law: so now revolt is lawful.

Hearing such doctrine expounded, Bossuet was scandalized, and to refute it he devotes his *Fifth warning to Protestants concerning the letters of the minister Jurieu against the Histoire des Variations* (1690): *The foundations of empires undermined by the said minister.* M. Jurieu disseminates "seditious teachings which tend to the overthrow of all empires and to the degradation of all dominions set up by God". Eh, what! Shall the ancient Christian Church suffer persecution and not rise up against it? The Protestants themselves have long disclaimed ever having rebelled, whether in France or England, against the power of the Throne; yet now, to-day, Jurieu declares that men have the right to levy war on their own king, their own country! This spirit of rebellion is an abomination. "I undertake to prove to you that your Reformation is an unchristian thing, because it has failed in loyalty to King and country."

However, all this was not merely a case of Catholics *versus* Protestants, for now this matter of natural law comes into it. Jurieu had based his arguments on Grotius. Now, Bossuet knew all about Grotius, knew him for a learned man, indeed, and well-intentioned withal; but he knew him also for a Socinian, a man with dangerous ideas, who tended to confound things human and divine. What was he really driving at, with all this talk about the law of nature? The idea that the people are invested by nature with sovereignty implies no doubt that the human race had already, in its primitive state, an idea of the sovereignty which belonged to it of right, and of its power to delegate that sovereignty to whomsoever it thought fit. What a glaring mistake! Grotius, and Jurieu after him, err at the very outset; they fail to understand the terms of the discussion. Now, let there be no mistake; the earliest state of mankind was one of barbarous and ferocious anarchy, and if, as we have reason to suppose, the earliest tribes were not so much a people as a mob, how can we possibly imagine that they had any conception of sovereignty, for sovereignty in itself would involve a sort of government? "Far from the people in those primitive ages being sovereign, there was not, in the strict sense of the word, any such thing as a people at all. Families there may have been, but undisciplined and unstable; there may have been an agglomeration, a confused multitude, of human beings, but not a people, since the word implies a community amenable to definite rules and fixed laws; and that is something you only find among those who have already begun to emerge from the miserable state to which we have referred, in short, from anarchy." Bossuet could not see how sovereignty could possibly be delegated by anarchy.

Meanwhile, the case of Louis XIV, considered as an absolute

monarch, was over and done with; he stood for what, even at this stage, might be called the *Ancien Régime*—the Old Order. Even in his own realm, in France itself, what a flood of opinion there was against the idea of a ruling authority deriving its sanction solely from God. There were opponents of the doctrine who went rummaging about amongst ancient documents regarding the earliest beginnings of the monarchical power; they discovered that it had been unlawfully acquired; there were stubborn, self-opinionated parliament-men who wrangled endlessly about the rights and prerogatives of their own august body; there were the nobles, who jealously insisted on maintaining all the privileges to which they were entitled as peers of France; everyone—commoners and nobles, disaffected grumblers and red-hot rebels, the sane and the insane—all, in treatises printed in Holland, in hand-written documents circulating under the rose, all gave vent to their discontent, their wrath, their impatience of the yoke.

Abroad, as we have seen, Louis XIV was an object of detestation. Nevertheless, from the legal point of view, Bossuet's argument is sound enough. If, in their natural state, men were nothing but a disorganized mob, how could a law of any sort have been born of this primeval confusion?

1688. *The English Revolution.*

James II, by the grace of God King, is driven from his throne, and William of Orange takes his place. The historians inform us that the new King, crowned at Westminster on the 11th April, 1689, "reigns by virtue of a right which differs in no respect from the right by which any landowner chooses the representative of his county". He agrees to submit himself to the authority of the two Houses of Parliament, thus ensuring the triumph of constitutional government, in accordance with an unwritten pact between the monarch and his subjects.

And those ideas which learned professors had enunciated from their lofty academic chairs, which their students had duly assimilated, of which learned journals had treated, which had been maintained, contradicted, and yet again maintained, and which, since the time of Grotius, had formed the mental *pabulum* of two generations—were not these ideas to be thrown into the battle? And then those others which, expounded by the Doctors of the Church, enlarged upon by official jurists, had also had their pupils, and had the advantage of a long tradition behind them.

Were *they* going to remain aloof from the fray at the very moment when a practical example, in the shape of an event that was stirring Europe to its depths, offered them such an admirable opportunity to come out into the open and show their mettle at what promised to mark a decisive stage in the battle? To bolster up the tottering power of the Stuarts the theorists had been laid under heavy contribution. Among the works supporting absolute power which had been unearthed, were those of a sturdy disputant who, about the middle of the century, had struck a shrewd blow for the Royalist cause. Robert Filmer had gone about preaching submission and obedience far and wide, saying that a limited monarchy could result in nothing but disorder, that subjects had no right to rebel; that Hobbes had been wrong in his premises, but right in his conclusions; in a word, that the absolute power of kings in general was a necessity. Filmer became fashionable once more. In 1680, a new edition of the *magnum opus* of "this learned man", *Patriarcha*, was given to the world, and was several times reprinted in the course of the ensuing years. This work proved, as clear as daylight, that the kingly authority is the extension of paternal authority. Against his father, no son who had any respect for God or man would dare to rise up in revolt. However the facts belied the Jacobite claims. But a man was now about to come on the scene who would invest the facts with the dignity of a universal principle.

1689. John Locke, *Two Treatises of Government. In the former the false principles and foundation of Sir Robert Filmer and his followers are detected and overthrown. The latter is an essay concerning the true original, extent, and end of civil government.*

On the selfsame vessel that was bringing William of Orange from Holland to England and the Revolution, was John Locke, the philosopher of the New Age. He it was who, in these two treatises, was to take up the challenge of the monarchists.

What, in fact, Locke really does is to hark back to a set of ideas with which we are already tolerably familiar; but he carries them further than they had ever been carried before, and he makes them prove, by a series of logical deductions, the right of subjects to rebel. Like Pufendorf, and like everyone else at that time, he begins with the Natural Man. To do so was the fashion, we might almost call it the craze, of the day. The state of Nature was not, as Hobbes would have it, a state of violence and ferocity. But

neither was it perfect. To remedy the evils inherent in the natural
state, man sets up a social state, but not on the patriarchal pattern,
as Filmer depicted it. He sets it up, as Pufendorf shows, on the
basis of an understanding, a covenant. His readers should be
quite clear about it. "There, and there only", he says, "is political
society where every one of the members hath quitted this natural
power, resigned it up into the hands of the community in all
cases that exclude him not from appealing for protection to the
law established by it." Absolute power, which denies this right
of appeal, is purely and simply incompatible with a Civil Society;
and Divine Right, which Catholic teachers are always insisting
upon, entirely fails to justify the contention that any one man
may control the lives and destinies of all the rest. Power should
be controlled, and divided, as in Great Britain, into legislative
and executive. If the executive power failed to act in accordance
with the purposes for which it was set up, if it encroached upon
the liberties of the people, it must be taken out of the hands of
the person wielding it. Nay more; if the subjects perceive that
the tyrant is preparing the means to cast them into slavery, let
them steal a march on him, let them, by open rebellion, prevent
him from fulfilling his nefarious designs.

Locke's genius was of the practical order, and he set himself to
adjust matters: to the idea of Nature, he added another one, the
idea of Civilization. It looked as though he was answering
Bossuet in advance. No doubt this state of Nature idea involved
some perplexities. No doubt history, which, as regards the origin
of human societies, is neither as explicit nor as accurate as one
could desire, furnishes us with ground for plausible conjecture,
rather than with solid fact. The best we can do is to form a
reasonable notion of the circumstances which led men to delegate
their power. We may take it, then, that men, in the first place,
were naturally free; but as to the manner in which they were to
consolidate this freedom, they were divided in opinion. And as
to defending it, to whom should they appeal to do that? Men
were, by nature, equal; but what means had they of defending
this equality against possible encroachment? It would have meant
a state of perpetual warfare if they had not entrusted their power
to a government capable of preserving this primitive freedom
and equality. They were not a horde, but a horde they would have
become had they not taken due care. Natural law engenders

political law, the law which prevents natural qualities from being endangered in the rough and tumble of existence.

Whenever a difficulty presented itself, the sagacious Locke endeavoured to propound a considered solution. For example: there was some reluctance at parting with the idea of paternal authority, a sort of bridge between God and Man, the earliest foreshadowing of kingly power. Locke intervened, pointing out that children are not born *into* a state of complete freedom; although they are born *for* it; that the parents (the father and, equally, the mother) have a species of jurisdiction over them. The parents, in fact, are under an obligation to prepare their children for their freedom until they arrive at the age of reason. Paternal authority, paternal power, does, then, exist. It exists, but it is not absolute; it is a duty, rather than a prerogative; it cannot lay down laws; and if we may suppose in the earliest times the existence of a patriarchal state, such a state would have reposed solely on the tacit consent of the children.

Now let us consider the question of property; a question of some gravity. The ownership of property does not fit in very well with the idea of natural equality. By the light, not only of reason, but also of Revelation, we see that God gave the earth in common to the whole human race. That being so, how is it to be explained that individuals could lawfully appropriate to their own use a portion of this common property? Individual property, he tells us, comes about as the result of work: "Though the earth and all inferior creatures be common to all men, yet every man has a 'property' in his own 'person'. This nobody has any right to but himself. The 'labour' of his body and the 'work' of his hands, we may say, are properly his. Whatsoever, then, he removes out of the state that Nature hath provided and left it in, he hath mixed his labour with it, and joined to it something that is his own, and thereby makes it his property." The water which flows from this spring here may be made use of by all who pass by; but if I fill my pitcher with it, who shall tell me that the water in my pitcher is not mine?

Locke was busy with his notes and comments, acting as a sort of intermediary between the professional jurists on the one hand, and the general public on the other; as an intermediary, too, between ancient and modern, retaining, on the one hand, just enough of the old beliefs to avoid shocking the public conscience, and, on the other, producing a large assortment of novelties: No more Divine Right; no more Right of Conquest: "But conquest is just as far from setting up any government as demolishing a house is from building a new one in its place." The effect of his interpretation of things was that the light of the English constitution was reflected back on to Natural Law, while Natural Law shone forth as the foundation of the English constitution, complete with Parliament and King, a King called to the throne by the voice of the people. He integrated Natural Law into the political ideas of his time, of his country, of his race, and, further than that, he showed how it was connected with the reformed religion. When Divine Right went to the length of setting up an absolute monarchy, it was supernatural no more; it was contranatural. The justification of absolutism by those who claimed that it was based on the Divine Will was no more than a belated afterthought of the Catholic theologians: "Nothing of the kind had ever been heard of until this great mystery was revealed by the theology of this last century."

1699. *The Adventures of Telemachus.*

In point of fact, Fénelon does not contest the principle of Divine Right. However, amid all the various sentiments and ideas to which this long-famous book, circulating in its millions among young and old, gave currency, one sentiment, and one idea, we must not allow to escape us.

To begin with the sentiment: This was a horror and a detestation of Louis XIV. What we have here is something more than a mere intellectual disagreement; it is much more like unbridled passion, the indignation of a public accuser. "Have you sought out those who were the most disinterested, the most likely to contradict you? Have you preferred such as were least devoted to your pleasure and to their own interest? such as appeared most capable of opposing your passions when they were irregular, and your sentiments when they were unjust? When you detected a flatterer, did you banish him from your presence? Did you refuse to trust such people? No, no, you have not done what those do who love truth, and deserve to know it. While you had abroad so many enemies who threatened your still unstable kingdom, you thought of nothing but adorning your new city with magnificent buildings. You exhausted your wealth; you never thought to better your people, or to till the fertile soil. A vain ambition has driven you to the very brink of the precipice. By trying to appear great, you have all but destroyed the foundations of substantial greatness."

Now, for the idea: the worthiness of the people. "Not for himself did the gods make him king, but that he might give himself to his people. All his time, all his care, all his affection, he owes to his people, and he only merits the kingship in so far as he takes no thought for himself, but devotes himself to the service of his country." "Know that you are not a king save in so far as you have people to govern." Nay, more than that: An oppressed people has but one desire, and that is to be avenged on their kings: then sounds the hour of revolution. "Absolute power degrades every subject to the condition of a slave; the tyrant is flattered, even to the point of adoration, and everyone trembles at the glance of his eye, but at the least breath of revolt this monstrous power perishes by its own excess. It drew no strength from the love of the people; it wearied and provoked all that it could reach, and rendered every individual of the state impatient of its continuance. At the first stroke of opposition the idol is cast down, shattered into fragments, and trodden underfoot."[1]

Great was the want and misery in the kingdom of France. We all know La Bruyère's dramatic description of the state of the peasantry. Locke's account, which strains less after effect, is perhaps even more impressive. He states that the peasants live in hovels, that they are hardly able to clothe and feed themselves; yet, miserable as is their plight, the Treasury contrives to squeeze something more out of them. So the land is falling out of cultivation and lies fallow; and, seeing that the more they toil the more they are oppressed, men cease to do any work at all. Then, again, industries either decay, or try to establish themselves across the frontiers, endeavouring to find abroad the liberty which, in France, is denied them. Customs duties, exacted at every station, are ruining trade. The check to Colbert's policy, noticeable even in his lifetime, becomes conspicuously so after his death. In 1694 came the Great Famine, and utter bankruptcy. Oh, the pity of it!

However, a select few gave ear to these complaints and essayed to remove their cause. France's great sorrow came to be recorded in writings which the bare need of keeping body and soul together

[1] *Télémaque*, XIIIe.

seemed to dictate. Clumsily, without art, but with a grimness, a tenacity, which have something touching about them, Bois-guilbert shows how France, once the richest country in the world, had lost five or six millions of her annual revenue; a deficit which was daily increasing. Taxes were iniquitously levied, favouring the rich and inflicting a crushing burden on the poor; thus the poorer classes had been reduced to utter destitution, and the whole country was hurrying to its doom.[1] Something must be done, and that quickly, to readjust the incidence of taxation, said Vauban, in his turn. A system of tithes established on an equitable basis would bring in more and be cheaper to run. Now, Bois-guilbert and Vauban were anything but revolutionaries; their object was to put the national finances on a sound basis, and to furnish the King with the resources of which he was so desperately in need; however, they were looked upon as trespassing on ground hitherto regarded as a close preserve, and the *Dîme royale* was ordered to be publicly burnt.[2]

But how much bolder, how far more bitter is Fénelon. The questions which Telemachus puts to Idomeneus, those same questions, in the same sorrowing tone, Fénelon puts to his pupil, the Duc de Bourgogne, against the day when he will have to take over the royal power: Do you understand the constitution of kingship? Have you acquainted yourself with the moral obligations of Kings? Have you sought means of bringing comfort to the people? The evils that are engendered by absolute power, by incompetent administration, by war, how will you shield your subjects from them? And when, in 1711, the same Duc de Bourgogne became Dauphin of France, it was a whole string of reforms that Fénelon submitted to him in preparation for his accession.

Finally, to complete the credit items of Fénelon's account, we must put his defence of Human Rights. Thus he speaks: "A people is no less a member of the human race, which is society as a whole, than a family is a member of a particular nation. Each individual owes incomparably more to the human race, which is the great fatherland, than to the particular country into which he was born. As the family is to the nation, so is the nation to the universal commonweal; wherefore it is infinitely more harmful

[1] Pierre Le Pesant de Boisguilbert, *Le détail de la France*, 1695.
[2] *Projet d'une dîme royale . . .*, 1707.

for nation to wrong nation, than for family to wrong family. To abandon the sentiment of humanity is not merely to renounce civilization and to relapse into barbarism, it is to share in the blindness of the most brutish brigands and savages; it is to be a man no longer, but a cannibal."[1]

1705. Thomasius, *Fundamenta juris naturae et gentium ex sensu communi deducta.*

1708. Gravina, *Origines juris civilis, quibus ortus et progressus juris civilis, jus naturale gentium et XII Tabulae explicantur.*

It was Gian Vincenzo Gravina who introduced the concept of natural law into history. He also endeavoured to explain a contradiction which this elusive idea of Nature inevitably brings out. Natural law is reason, and reason demands virtue; virtue excludes vice; and yet we see that vice, too, is in Nature. To that objection, here is the answer: "Over and above the general law wherein the soul and the body, so long as they remain united, participate, man has a law which is proper to himself and which is often opposed to the other. The first I call the common law; the second, the law of the soul only. The common law covers all living beings, consequently man himself. But the law of the soul, the law of reason, which consists in thinking, is proper to man alone. By .the operation of this latter, man is subjected to his own reason, and, therefore, to the virtues, as though to magistrates created by reason to judge our actions and to keep watch and ward upon our senses. . . ."

Thinkers continued to work on these ideas, and their diffusion was destined to persist right down to our own day. But the end of the XVIIth century marks a decisive stage in the process, because it was then that the theory of Natural Law, the theory of the Law of Nations, and the facts were brought into juxtaposition. Incomparably less vigorous, less profound than either Grotius or Pufendorf, and often illogical, Locke, nevertheless, succeeded in bringing about the popularization of this law. Liberty, Equality! He might well have taken those words for his motto. "The state of Nature has a law of Nature to govern it, which obliges every one, and reason, which is that law, teaches all mankind who will but consult it, that being all equal and independent, no one ought to harm another in his life, health, liberty or possessions."[2]

[1] *Dialogues des Morts*, Socrate et Alcibiade (1718).
[2] Locke, *On Civil Government*, Bk. II, Chap. II.

IV

SOCIAL MORALITY

IF there was one man who, more clearly and more cogently than any of his predecessors, insisted that there was no necessary connection between morals and religion, that man was Pierre Bayle. Time after time, in his *Dictionnaire*, in his *Réponses aux Questions d'un provincial*, he returned to the charge. But it was in his *Pensées sur la Comète* that, taking his time, bringing all his powers into play, with great heat, yet with great lucidity, he drew up the *Magna Charta* of the Separation.

He began on a soft note. Atheists are no worse than idolaters, whether in heart or mind. Then, following up the train of thought thus suggested, he went on to insinuate that Atheists were no worse than Christians. Ah! if one were to say to a man from some other planet that there were people on earth endowed with reason and sound sense, God-fearing people, believing that Heaven would reward their merits and Hell their vices, the man from another world would expect to see them performing works of mercy, showing kindness to their neighbours, forgiving trespasses, and, in a word, striving to attain to an eternity of happiness. Alas! it is not thus that things happen in reality. We must needs see to believe what the spectacle of human life brings out into startling relief, namely, that between what people believe and what they do, the gulf is wide. Principles have no effect on our behaviour. Pious words are followed up by wicked deeds. We pretend to worship God, but we think only of ourselves, and of gratifying our own passions.

> I know and praise what's good, but still
> Whate'er I do, 'tis always ill.

There's nothing new about such an avowal as that. Take the Christians, look at their lives. They read devotional books, and forget them as soon as read. The soldiers of the most Christian armies are rakes and robbers. They sack and pillage the land of friend and foe alike. They don't stand on ceremony, and, if it suits their purpose, they give churches, and chapels, and monasteries indiscriminately to the flames. The Crusades; what a splendid enterprise! In theory, yes. But what a host of frauds, treacheries, betrayals and crimes accompanied and followed them! Women are particularly devout, but how many of them slip away to meet their lovers as soon as they are out of the confessional. There are courtezans, robbers, assassins who profess a special devotion to the Madonna, and many are the stories, professedly pious, that represent the Blessed Virgin as extending her protection to wantons and malefactors, provided they burn a taper and bend the knee before her statue. The Jansenists discourage frequent communion because they are well aware that a man may approach the Holy Table every day and still remain a criminal. In short, whatever faith a man professes, it does not affect his morals or his conduct. Nay, there are some passions to which devotion is a positive stimulus. For example, we show anger to persons who do not think as we do; a great outward show of piety may be but the mask of hypocrisy.

Bayle then invites the reader to look at the matter from the opposite standpoint. If we frequently see orthodox Christians living unedifying lives, we see, no less frequently, freethinkers whose lives are exemplary. We will not now dwell on the instances furnished by men of ancient times, on men like Diagoras, Theodorus, Nicanor, Euhemerus, Hippo; on Pliny, who never belied his reputation as an illustrious son of Rome; on Epicurus, whose life was stainless; we will turn rather to the Moderns: The Chancellor de l'Hôpital was believed to have no religion at all, yet nothing could have surpassed the noble austerity of his life. Everyone who had to do with Spinoza praised his affability, his integrity, his obliging nature, and his lofty moral character. Yet Spinoza was an Atheist.

An atheistic republic; why should there not be such a thing? A society without any religion at all would be like a pagan society; and Christians, so far as their practical, everyday lives are concerned, are no different from pagans. Atheists would be just as sensitive as Christians to praise or blame, to reward or punishment. To deny that the soul is immortal does not preclude the ambition to immortalize one's name. Finally, if a school of thought must have its martyrs in order to command respect, unbelief can boast of many; Vanini, for example, who did not shrink from dying for his atheism; and, more recently, a certain Mahomet Effendi, who was put to death at Constantinople for publicly denying the existence of God. He could have saved his life if only he had acknowledged his error and promised not to repeat it; but he preferred to persist in his impiety, declaring that, *although he had no reward to look for, his love of truth compelled him to lay down his life for its sake.*

The evidence being thus complete, Bayle now comes to his summing-up. "Morals and religion, far from being inseparable, are completely independent of each other. A man can be moral without being religious. An atheist who lives a virtuous life is not a creature of wonder, something outside the natural order, a freak.   There is nothing more extraordinary about an atheist living a virtuous life than there is about a Christian leading a wicked one." There are atheists in Turkey and in China who live purer lives than some Christians in Paris or Rome.

May it not be contended, indeed, that a non-religious morality is loftier than a religious morality, seeing that the former expects neither punishment nor reward, whereas the latter, with its fear of Hell and its hopes of Heaven, has always a selfish motive? Toland, as usual, goes one better: Atheism at its worst is less noxious to the State and to human society than the savage and barbarous superstition which rends asunder the most flourishing countries with division and sedition, which not only works havoc in the greatest of them, but often brings them to their ruin; which wrests children from their fathers, friends from friends, and sunders things which should be joined together by the most inviolable ties.[1]

But having destroyed morality on the divine plane, how were they going to rebuild it on the human? That was an awkward problem.

Would they have to retrace their steps? Would they have to

[1] *Adeisidaemon,* 1709.

turn back to antiquity, and take the pagans for their guides? And
if so, which of the pagans? Epicurus? Epictetus? They were
mutually contradictory. Or would they have recourse to a
philosopher who, though not setting forth any new or original
doctrine, endeavoured to show the world what was best in
ancient morality? Would they, in short, have to betake themselves
to that orator of old Rome, to the author of the *de Officiis*, to
Cicero, and demand of him the rule that should govern a purely
secular existence? Long ago, Erasmus had admired his noble life,
his saintly character; and it is true that "the pagan world never
left us anything which unfolds in such perfection and urges upon
us with such force, those generous principles from which human
nature derives its crowning glory, the love of virtue, of freedom,
of country and of all the human race."[1]

But the Christian moralists were not lacking in replies to
arguments like this. Those doctrines, which it was now proposed
to revive, Christianity had disposed of seventeen hundred years
ago. Sorry models to imitate were Brutus, Cato and the like.
They were too fond of fine words, imposing gestures,
and theatrical posturing. Their lives ended in bankruptcy.
From that bankruptcy Christianity had redeemed the human
race.

Then a wholly new brand, a wholly new pattern of morality
came upon the scene; the code of self-respect; a psychological
morality. It was not averse from drawing on the ancient world,
which, in truth, it vastly preferred to Christianity. Nevertheless,
its main appeal was to Reason. However, it was a polite, a
civilized reason, not the old austere, uncultured brand; it was a
reason that betrayed little or nothing of its erstwhile rigidity.
"Let us forget all about those days when to be harsh meant to be
virtuous. Polished manners, gallantry, the art of pleasing are
now all held in esteem. As for hatred of evil, that should last
as long as the world, but let us congratulate ourselves that people
now call pleasure what rude and untutored folk of old called vice.
Do not compose your stock of virtues from old notions which
uncouth and savage nature implanted in primeval man."[2] This
new morality did not exclude the pleasures of the senses, nor did

[1]We borrow these expressions from the *History of Cicero*, by C. Middleton (London,
1741), translated by the Abbé Prévost in 1743.
[2]Saint-Évremond: an article by Gustave Lanson, *La transformation des idées
morales* (*Revue du Mois*, 1910).

it banish the passions, provided they were regulated and kept within bounds. . . . Of course! However, this new code could not claim to have a binding, still less a universal, mandate. Duly to understand and practise it, one must be a Saint-Évremond, or a Sir William Temple, or a Lord Halifax. It was the code of the aristocrat, the exquisite, the disillusioned; its structure was frail; it meant making the best of both worlds; adaptation rather than domination was its note.

To adopt the lofty and austere metaphysical moral code propounded by Spinoza was, as we have seen, within the capacity only of the very few. How bewildering it was to contemplate the immense variety, the constant contradictions presented by the moral systems of mankind. How difficult to discover a common norm, a universal rule applicable to all men, in every time and in every place. Here, it is the custom to expose infants to be devoured by wild beasts, or to let them die of hunger. What boots it after that to prate about the universality of family ties? Here, by way of contrast, the children do not hesitate to kill off their parents in their old age. "In a part of Asia, the sick, when their case comes to be thought desperate, are carried out and laid on the earth before they are dead; and left there, exposed to wind and weather, to perish without assistance or pity. It is familiar among the Mingrelians, a people professing Christianity, to bury their children alive without scruple. There are places where they eat their own children. The Caribbees were wont to geld their children, on purpose to fat and eat them. And Garcilasso de la Vega tells us of a people in Peru which were wont to fat and eat the children they got on their female captives, whom they kept as concubines for that purpose, and when they were past breeding, the mothers themselves were killed too and eaten." We have but to look at the world to see that morals are essentially variable. "He that will carefully peruse the history of mankind, and look abroad into the several tribes of men, and with indifferency survey their actions, will be able to satisfy himself that there is scarce that principle of morality to be named, or rule of virtue to be thought on (those only excepted that are absolutely necessary to hold society together, which commonly too are neglected betwixt distinct societies), which is not, somewhere or other, slighted and condemned by the general fashion of whole societies of men, governed by practical opinions and rules of living quite opposite to others."[1]

Except only those that are absolutely necesary to hold society together. . . . Here there appears the possibility of a new morality; a morality with nothing innate in it, not even the idea of good and evil, but which was legitimate and necessary as carrying with it the duty of maintaining our collective existence. We are made to live in societies and we have a very proper fear of anarchy, which would bring about the destruction of our species; therefore we take the measures that are necessary to save us from mortal disorder; we embody in a system the counsels we derive from our instinct of self-preservation. For there is a lawful *amour-propre*, an *amour-propre* which maintains the life of the group. Consideration of self only becomes a vice when it threatens the group, and, with it, the individual himself, as being an entity inseparable from the whole. Moral good is not a matter of opinion like reputation, wealth, pleasures, but a vital necessity; on it depends the continued existence of the human race.

An admirable and unprecedented advantage of this system, say its partisans, is that it permits of demonstration. It is based, not on any *a priori* postulate, but on realities perfectly susceptible of analysis. Let us look within ourselves: whatever has an aptness to produce, to increase and to maintain our sensations of pleasure, we call *good*; on the other hand, whatever tends to produce, to increase and to prolong our sensations of pain, we call evil. Hence our own interest, of course, or it were better to say our very being, leads us to obey the civil laws, seeing that by observing them, we shall safeguard our property, our freedom, and, so doing, we shall be labouring for the continuity and the security of our own pleasure. If, on the other hand, we do not keep them, we incur the risk of punishment, and thence of the disorder and anarchy in which it is impossible to live without pain, or even to live at all. Similar considerations hold good in the matter of the laws governing opinion and reputation: virtue brings with it the esteem and love of those among whom we live and, therefore, increases our pleasure; vice brings with it blame, criticism, hostility, and therefore pain.[2]

[1] This quotation, like the preceding one, is taken from the *Essay concerning Human Understanding*, Book I, chap. II.
[2] *Essay concerning Human Understanding*, Book II, chap. XXVIII.

But can it be said that social well-being is a matter of pure
·virtue? Is a community that fulfils its duty to the letter likely to
prosper, or even to survive? About that, Locke had no doubts
whatever. Yet it was the very thing that was called in question
by an ignoble individual, a freethinker, a man who had been
exasperated beyond endurance by those moralists who would
insist on it that the heart of man was compounded of generosity,
kindliness, and solicitude for others. The person in question
was a Dutchman by birth who had settled in England, and who
called himself Bernard de Mandeville. He belonged to the new
school of philosophy, in that he spoke his mind freely, recking
nothing of the authorities, of custom, or of any other object of
respect. Daring, coarse, he specialized in the sort of startling
paradox that attracts popular attention and makes a noise in the
world. And a noise he *did* make when he began to narrate that
fable of his. He had already tried his hand at imitating Aesop
and La Fontaine; but this latest effort was no food for babes and
sucklings.

On the 2nd April, 1705, there appeared a pamphlet of some
twenty-six pages; author's name not stated. It was called *The
Grumbling Hive*, or *Knaves Turn'd Honest*. Once upon a time there
was a hive which bore a close resemblance to a well-ordered
human society. It lacked neither knaves nor swindlers. It had
plenty of bad doctors, bad priests, bad soldiers, bad ministers; it
also had a bad Queen. Every day, frauds were committed in this
hive; and justice, called upon to put down corruption, was itself
corruptible. In a word, every profession, every class was full
of vices; but the nation was none the less prosperous, none the
less strong on that account. In fact the vices of its individual
members contributed to the felicity of the state as a whole and,
vice versa, the felicity of the whole made for the well-being of the
individuals composing it. And having absorbed this fact, the
most rascally members of the tribe strove stout-heartedly for the
promotion of the common weal.

But now behold a change came over the mind of the bees.
They actually conceived the egregious notion of concentrating
henceforth on honesty and virtue. They clamoured for radical
reform, and it was the most slothful and the most knavish who
were the loudest in their vociferations.˙ Jupiter swore that this
noisy multitude should be freed from the vices it complained

about. He gave the word, and forthwith all were seized with a single-hearted longing for goodness; whence, in no long time, followed the utter ruin of the whole hive. No more excesses meant no more ailments; no more ailments, no more doctors. No more quarrels meant no more lawsuits, so no more need for lawyers and judges. The bees, now thrifty and sober, gave up squandering their money, and so, no more luxuries, no art, no more trade. The desolation was complete. Neighbouring bees now thought the time had come to attack. The hive defended itself and routed the invaders; but it paid dearly for its triumph. Thousands upon thousands of the bravest bees perished in the conflict. The survivors, to avoid relapsing into vice, flew away decorously to a hollow tree. There, all that the bees had left to them was their virtue, and their sorry plight:

> Then leave complaints, fools only strive
> To make a great an honest hive.
> T'enjoy the world's conveniencies,
> Be famed in war, yet live in ease
> Without great vices, is a vain
> Eutopia seated in the brain.
> Fraud, luxury and pride must live,
> Whilst we the benefits receive.

What a spate of angry comment this fable provoked! What endless disputes! Bernard de Mandeville was a hard-bitten customer, and gave as good as he got. He lived long, but his fable lived longer, and people talk about it to this very day.

V

HAPPINESS ON EARTH

AND happiness—must we still go on looking to the next world for that? Those adumbrations, those foreshadowings of the world to come, are altogether too vague, too hazy. Indeed, they are hardly even shadows now, but some sort of eternal substance of which no one can conceive the nature. Farewell to haloes, and harps and heavenly choirs! If we want happiness, we must get it in this world, and quickly. Time presses, and tomorrow—who knows what tomorrow has in store? Make the most of today. Only fools set their hopes on the time to come. Make the best of what our human state has to offer. Thus argued the apostles of the New Morality, who set out to seek happiness in the here and now.

To live a happy and contented life, one thing, and the first thing, we have to do, is to reason calmly about things like sensible beings, and put a curb on our imagination when it would magnify our ills. When we set out to create troubles for ourselves, there is no limit to our ingenuity. We exaggerate them, we regard them as unprecedented and beyond all consolation. We even cherish a kind of love for sorrow; we nurse our grief and make much of it. There's another awkward thing about this delusive imagination of ours: it tries to grasp at a heaven beyond its reach; it lures us on deceptively to mirage after mirage; we hasten to reach them, but always they elude us, and leave us with a sense of infinite frustration. Let us take life for what it really is, and not ask too much of it. We are dissatisfied with our humdrum, everyday existence, we call it dull; but suppose that, before we came into the world we were shown all the accidents, all the disasters, that might conceivably befall us, should we not recoil aghast? And considering the many perils we have escaped, ought we not to look on it as a mighty boon to have got off as cheaply as we have? "Slaves, unable to keep body and soul together, or who can only live by the sweat of their brow; others for whom life is one long malady—that is the fate of a great proportion of the human race. How came it that we were not one of these? Learn how dangerous it is to be a man, and count the misfortunes from which we are exempt as so many perils from which we have come off unscathed."[1]

And so, having thus adjusted our perspective, let us now apply ourselves to using what we have got to the best advantage: it is not much, but it is real. Let us give a wide berth to the passions; their violent motions do but end in sorrow and repining; let us study to be quiet. And if the people round about us say that that is a tame and insipid mode of life, shrug we our shoulders: "what sort of a notion has one of the human state who complains that his only boon is a holy calm?" Avoid attracting attention to ourselves, shun the limelight and ambition, all dangers which threaten the peaceful voyage of this humble barque of ours which we should gently steer towards the haven of rest. Let us come to an understanding with ourselves. A conscience that is sure of itself, that knows where it stands, is the best protection a man can have. Jealously, like a miser guarding his hoard, determined not to waste a jot or tittle of it, let us keep watch and ward over our humble treasure. True, a turn of fortune may always rob us of it, despite our most sedulous care. But if we take heed and keep a wary eye, the chances are we shall preserve it; for we are, in so far as we can keep within the bounds of reason, the artizans of our own lives.

Little windfalls of pleasure, the small change of that blissful state that lies beyond our reach; such things as an agreeable conversation, a shooting-party, an engrossing book, these and the like are the stuff of our daily lives. Such pleasures are within our compass; let us make the most of them and forbear to set our hearts on uncertainties. "We grasp the present in our hands, but the future is a sort of conjuror that dazzles us with brilliant promises and then cheats us of the prize." Let us then enjoy our simple pleasures like crumbs of contentment tossed to us by a

[1]Fontenelle, *Du bonheur*.

lordly master who tomorrow may change his mind, and take them from us. We must seize our opportunities as they occur, nor underrate our pleasures. "It's all a matter of calculation, and it is always wise to have the counters handy."

This metaphor of the accomplished card player who never loses interest in the game, who knows when to follow suit and when to pass, is rather an attractive one. All the same there is no doubt that it does not fit everybody; it needs an exceptionally clear head and a cool judgment. It looks on the passions as though all you had to do to control them was to argue with them; and, as for the imagination, that is a sort of obedient slave; further, it postulates easy circumstances, independence, leisure. The egoist's paradise!

But there was another one on offer. What we have to do if we want to be quite easy in our minds is to banish all sense of the tragedy of human life. If we let our minds dwell on that theme, we shall be miserable every hour of the day; and when the time for our own departure draws near, the pain becomes more intense than ever. Then the curtain goes up on yet another tragedy, the tragedy of eternity. Happy were they who set out for the farther shore with a jest and a smile on their lips.[1] They never knew that sombre enthusiasm which is the relentless foe of all inward peace, and which, not content with sowing unrest in the minds of its own victims, inspires them with a fanatical craving to torment the rest of mankind. Fanaticism, illuminism, endless mental torture, gloomy visions of hell and its torments—how could things like these be stamped out and done away with? The process was simple enough; it was to be done by cultivating an attitude of mind which goes by the name of good nature, good humour; you only had to put it to the test. Put a pair of benevolent spectacles, slightly rose-tinted, on your nose, and everything will take on a cheerful, smiling hue. If ever the human race were brought to be always ready with a smile, that day would mark the end of that sour and acrid state of mind which sharpens the edge of every woe. Do not underestimate the remedial effects of good humour; it does its work unfailingly and works a lasting cure. Mr. Spectator, who, as we are aware, undertook to administer a little mild corrective treatment to his contemporaries, dispenses a

[1]Deslandes, *Réflexions sur les grands hommes qui sont morts en plaisantant*, 1712.

friendly dose of moral counsel in each issue of his journal. He tells them that good humour is a garment we ought to put on every day. What a far better place the world would be, if we did. This rather vague and intangible sentiment was not unknown in France, but it was more pronounced in England, because it tended to counteract, not only those fits of spleen to which the English were notoriously prone, but also the excessive austerity of the over-zealous Puritans. It found a refined and graceful exponent in the person of Anthony Ashley Cooper, Earl of Shaftesbury. It would be agreeable to let our gaze dwell for a few moments on this delicate and engaging figure. Shaftesbury had, beyond question, many reasons for optimism. Of illustrious lineage, he was the son of the statesman who had taken Locke under his wing, and Locke himself had superintended his education. As he was ill-equipped for a political career, he devoted himself to the tranquil pursuit of intellectual and artistic interests. Being a man of wealth, he had been able to travel and to surround himself with fine pictures and rare works of literature. He was also in a position to alleviate the hardships of needy men of letters, such as Des Maizeaux, Bayle, or Le Clerc. Fortune had showered her gifts upon him; but she had forgotten one, and that was health. He was consumptive; so quitting his mansion, his estates, his friends, and his native land, he went abroad in search of a cure. His search was vain; he died at the age of forty-two. Thus he had many reasons to bless his stars, and only one—a decisive one— to curse them. However, he found life good and full of happiness, and his comments thereon, so cheerful and, despite his malady, so serene, have something strangely pathetic in their tone. Surrounded by the dignified amenities of a nobleman's park, with its groves of immemorial trees; or on the shores of the sunlit Mediterranean, Shaftesbury held converse with his peers. His conversation was easy and agreeable, never ponderous or stilted. If it had a fault, it was that of being a little desultory, a little too leisurely. Sometimes, it contained a graceful and unforced allusion to a fine flower of the Greek or Latin classics, some ancient poet or philosopher; sometimes, it conjured up some aspect of the present, some current event, some personage of the day; its graces varied. It did not disdain a touch of irony, or, to be more precise, of humour, which is not exactly the same thing. What irony is with the French, humour is with the English. But whatever the theme of his graceful discourse, one thing was always close to his heart and that was to gain his point by charm and by persuasion. How should we seek for happiness?

How, but by humanizing people, if one may be permitted the phrase, by divesting them of their affected gravity, their hypocrisy, of the sort of puffed-uppedness that blinded them to what their feelings really were. The enemy whom Shaftesbury attacks in a letter that has justly remained famous is Enthusiasm;[1] by which he meant not, of course, the creative impulse which leads to the birth of works of beauty and genius; but pious enthusiasm, the sort of thing that induces us to think that we have a spark of the divine in us, whereas, all the time, we are nourishing within us our worst defects: melancholy, mental inertia, morbid tastes, self-sufficiency, vainglory, and, over and above all that, a burning desire to interfere in other people's business; to disturb their consciences, and to indulge in hatred and cruelty. Against this enthusiasm we must arm ourselves with the weapons of sound sense, of freedom of ideas, and—this was somewhat unlooked-for —a timely dose of ridicule.

We must learn to laugh. There is no better moral remedy. What is the good of losing one's temper and slinging mud at the mud-slingers? No good at all. Far better laugh at them. Deflate the pompous, chaff the dismal, and as for the enthusiasts, treat them with derision.

Now, here come some poor devils of Frenchmen, Camisards from the Cévennes, who have fled for refuge to London. They are filled with a sort of sacred frenzy; they pour forth prophecies; they lie writhing on the ground in fanatical delirium. After a time, they come to be regarded as a public nuisance and the arm of the law takes them in hand. But what was to be done with them. Should they be flung into gaol? Or hauled off to the gallows? Were they to be made martyrs of? Or what? What *did* happen was that they were held up to ridicule in a puppet theatre; and that settled the business. Allowed to take its course, smiled at, laughed at, the eruptive malady with which they are afflicted will cure itself, of its own accord. So it was said, and that is what actually happened. Ah! if only people had taken that line from the first in these religious disputes, how many penal fires we should have been spared!

[1] *A Letter concerning Enthusiasm*, 1708.

Religion should be treated as something quite natural and ordinary. A good temper will bring you to sound religion; a bad one to atheism. If God is Love, as indeed He is, let us think on Him with peace in our hearts, not in fear and bitterness of mind. What strange aberration is it that leads us never to appeal to Heaven save when we are afflicted, anxious, or embittered?

"In short, my Lord, the melancholy way of treating Religion, is that which, according to my apprehension, renders it so tragical, and is the occasion of its acting in reality such dismal Tragedies in the World. And my notion is, that provided we treat Religion with good Manners, we can never use too much Humour, or examine it with too much Freedom and Familiarity. For, if it be genuine and sincere, it will not only stand the Proof, but thrive and gain advantage from thence: if it be spurious, or mix'd with any Imposture, it will be detected and expos'd."

It was natural, and in a sense inevitable, that Shaftesbury should come to grips with the one man who, above all others, was most deeply imbued with a sense of the tragic element in life, that is to say, with Pascal. He knew all about the wager argument, but he would have none of it. To put your money on religion because, if there *is* a God you win everything, and if there isn't, you lose nothing, is to copy those cunning beggar-men you see in the street who salute every passer-by as "Your Honour". If the person thus accosted happens in fact to be a lord, he would not have liked it had he not received his proper title; if he was not a lord, he would be only too flattered to have been taken for one. In either case, the beggar gets his alms.

About God Himself there is nothing of a tragic nature. Nor is God unjust, as those who believe in predestination would have Him to be. God does not harbour resentment, as those who fear eternal punishment aver that He does. God is not one who compels men to play the selfish hypocrite, as they who practise virtue with an eye on a future reward, suppose Him to be. God is all the goodness and charity that are scattered up and down the universe. Whoso is charitable and kindly disposed is united with Him.

"To love the public, to study universal good, and to promote the interest of the whole world, as far as lies within our power, is surely the height of goodness, and makes that temper which we call divine.*"*

Controversies, logomachies, quarrels, angry commotions, these, as we have frequently remarked, were the distinguishing characteristics of the period, for as yet men had not reached a state of boredom, or of weary disillusionment; indeed, they hated indifferentism, misdoubted scepticism and were perpetually seeking, seeking. Shaftesbury, while just as firm in his convictions as any of his contemporaries, struck a milder note in what he had to say. His urbanity, his gentleness, his air of well-bred refinement, his kindliness and warmth of feeling, his philosophy, which he thought based on reason but which was often enough the outpouring of a generous heart—all these things are comforting to note and awaken our affections. What is quite remarkable about this moralist is that he never came to hate his fellow-men or even to judge them harshly; nor did he regard the times in which he lived as evil. No doubt there were extravagances, follies, but these were duly condemned and pilloried. The critics were abroad and unmuzzled, and that was a step towards salvation. If his remedies were looked on as too simple by half, if his recipe for happiness was criticized as insufficient, his philosophy (this plain homespun philosophy of looking into ourselves, this plain honest morality, as he puts it in his Letter) as too ordinary, too homely, he was not going to be discouraged by a trifle like that. With his feet well planted on the solid earth, he tries to catch a glimpse of Heaven through Beauty.

Beauty and Good are one and the same, he tells us. Since the Universe is one great harmony, the idea that there are discords in it is inadmissible, and since our moral sense aims at realizing this harmony, it cannot but wish to make it complete. Vice is an aesthetic defect; wilfully to commit a sin is, in the first place, an offence against logic, in the next place against morals, and finally, against good taste. Just as art reproduces the splendours of the material world, splendours which are the outward and visible sign of the Idea which orders all things, so man cannot but seek to reproduce within his own being, that moral grace, that moral Beauty which is likewise a reflection of the same commanding Idea. He is the sculptor of his own statue. Out of himself he calls up true ideas, virtuous acts, and beautiful forms; and the union thus brought about by his creative will is what is termed happiness. The atheist voluntarily renounces this co-operation in the creation of order; he is in the wrong, he does harm, he propagates what is ugly, he is an object of pity.

Such is the philosophy of the man who has been rightly

surnamed "the virtuoso of humanity". To confirm him in his idea
that morality is essentially a social matter, he turns to Locke, who
was his tutor. For notions about happiness he consults Spinoza:
and he (Spinoza), wholly discarding the idea of sin, counsels the
wise man to enjoy the pleasures of life, the sweetness of perfumes,
the beauty of plants, of music, the attractions of games, of the
theatre: only a hostile divinity would take pleasure in the sorrows
of man. It is not merely that Spinoza is flooded with a joy both
secret and profound; joy, for him, was the feeling that he had
attained to a higher order of being; sadness was a sense of a
diminution of being, and he goes so far as to assign a high place
and a philosophic value to gaiety. Shaftesbury concurs with him;
but, always with an eye to the best, he takes good care not to
leave Plato out of the account. If the period in which he lived
was in more ways than one reminiscent of the Renaissance, how
should Plato fail to be remembered? The Cambridge professors
fostered his cult with pious zeal. Cudworth's explanation of the
world postulated the existence of certain plastic natures which
played the part of intermediaries between ideas and creation; and
Shaftesbury sped the hours gazing on the walls of our cavern and
watching the interplay of the mighty shadows. He fancied that
he had but to catch the harmony of the spheres to shut out the
sound of our complaints and moanings.

To sum up his message, happiness was to be sought no longer
in Stoicism, which bears and despises the ills which it cannot
avoid. Nor is happiness to be purchased at the price of asceticism
and the constant repression of our corrupt nature. This earth is
no longer a place of trial, where the ills that afflict us are
more precious than joys, because they that weep shall be
comforted.[1]

No more shall men gaze upon the sorrowing Christ, who had
died upon the Cross for the salvation of the world; no more shall
they heed the mute appeal of His arms. Happiness is the growth,
the upsurge, of a spontaneous force within us, which we have
but to direct. To resign ourselves to pain, to yearn for self-
sacrifice, to fight against our instincts, the wild idea of the Cross
—these things are now called errors of judgment, old habits that

[1]Bossuet, *Oraison funèbre de Marie Thérèse d'Autriche*: "A Christian is never alive
on earth because he is ever mortified there, and mortification is a trial and an
apprenticeship, a rehearsal for Death."

ought to be eradicated. The god Reason forbids us to regard
our mortal life as a preparation for a life to come.

In bringing about the reign of happiness on earth there was a
particular virtue that was called on to play its part; and it was a
new virtue.

Up to now, it had not been a virtue at all, but, on the contrary,
a sign of weakness, not to say of cowardice. To tolerate all sorts
of opinions; to tolerate my brother's ideas, even if he has gone
completely astray and is well on the road to perdition; to tolerate
false prophets and liars—you might as well confess straight out
that you are in league with error and deceit. . . . Is it not a man's
bounden duty to open the eyes of those who are walking in
wilful blindness; to bring back those who have wandered from
the path? No doubt we should not ride rough-shod over other
men's consciences; but ought we to leave them to their fate, we
who know that there is but one truth, and that upon the knowledge of it depends our eternal salvation? Duty and charity alike
forbid us to be tolerant. That being so, the tolerationists, as they
are called, must be none other than Socinians in disguise, the sort
of people who would obliterate the marks by which the True
Church is to be recognized, people who would admit all manner
of heretics into the true fold; sceptics who profess religious indifferentism, rebels, freethinkers. Tolerant, Bossuet and his like
could never be, nor yet a Pellisson, not even when he was discussing with Leibniz how to persuade the Protestants to turn
again towards Rome. "It is my belief", he said in-a letter he wrote
to Leibniz in 1692, "that these Socinians, as they are called, and,
with them, all who go by the name of Deists and Spinozists, are
largely responsible for spreading this idea, which we may describe
as the error of errors, since it accommodates itself to all the others.
Fearing that they would not be borne with, that the law of the
land would be set in motion against them, they tried to establish
the principle that everything should be put up with. Hence this
doctrine of toleration, as it is called; hence—and this is something
newer still—the intolerance of which they accuse the Church of
Rome."

Wasted words! A change was coming about; he knew it, he
felt it in his bones. And so, indeed, it was. Slowly, laboriously,
with efforts year after year continued, toleration contrived at last

to change its recognition-sign and, instead of a vice, became a virtue. It was a bone of contention in two different fields of debate, the political and the religious. Yes, said the one, the King of France is perfectly within his rights in using force to compel the recusants to abandon the error of their ways; the Dutch magistrates have a perfect right to dismiss and imprison all those who, refusing to recognize any authority in the sphere of ideas, disturb the peace and threaten the existence of the State. The King of England has the right to outlaw those terrible Catholics, who will always insist on upholding the supremacy of Rome over the civil power. No, said the other side; men cannot and should not interfere with the workings of conscience, because that is a matter which concerns man and his Maker alone. A genuinely Christian soul knows that persecution is as contrary to the true spirit of the Gospel, as darkness is to light. Therefore, a Christian monarch should show tolerance to all his subjects so long as they duly respect his political authority. Such a ruler, said the Protestant historians, was William of Orange. "Whereupon, he said that he was a Protestant, and that, as such, he could undertake to support none but the reformed religion; then he went on to say that he did not know what exactly was meant by the word heretic, nor how far its application was to be extended, but he added that, so far as he himself was concerned, he would never allow anyone to be persecuted for his religion, would never attempt to convert anyone otherwise than by persuasion, in accordance with the spirit of the Gospel."[1] To the Revocation of the Edict of Nantes he took care to reply, in 1690, with the Toleration Act.

In the religious field, the controversy was still more lively. As far back as 1670, the Pastor d'Huisseau raised the signal when he called on the sects to lay down their arms and agree on a creed so comprehensive that it would embrace all mankind. It was the occasion of one of Jurieu's earliest outbursts. He tells us that, to confute d'Huisseau, he wrote his *Examen du Livre de la Réunion ou Traité de la Tolérance en matière de religion*: "Clearly, hatred for this ignoble toleration of heresy is a long-standing disease with me, which time has aggravated still more." The struggle had

---

[1]David Durand in his continuation of the *Histoire d'Angleterre depuis l'établissement des Romains*, by Rapin Thoyras, 1724-1736. Vol. XI, p. 48: *Ses sentiments sur la tolérance.*

continued with added intensity in the land of the Refugees. Arguments were discharged from side to side, but they did not always hit the mark; treatise followed treatise in endless succession. The leading lights among the pastors, Henri Basnage de Beauval, Gédéon Huet, Élie Saurin were for showing that intolerance and not tolerance was the sin; and if they excluded the Catholics—as in fact they did—from their scheme of universal benevolence, even as William III had excluded them from his Toleration Act, they at least found allies among some Dutchmen of sagacity and learning, such as Gilbert Cuper, Adrian Paets, Noodt, all of them faithful to the free traditions of their country. Thus, one and all addressed themselves to the difficult task of bringing a new virtue to birth. Sometimes there were storms that threw everything into confusion. The publication of *A Word to the Refugees*, which, rightly or wrongly, was ascribed to Bayle, and which asserted that the Protestants were quite as intolerant as the Catholics, provoked an outburst of furious antagonism. However, once the storm had subsided, toleration, with its olive branch, was seen in clearer outline.

Locke was the one that had the most humanity about him. Among all that mountainous heap of writings, no appeal was more eloquent, more generous, than that of his *Epistola de Tolerantia*, which he brought out in 1689 and defended till his dying day. Do not forget, cried Locke, that tolerance is the very stuff of Christianity. For if a man have not charity, gentleness, kindliness, how dare he call himself a Christian? The instrument of Faith is charity, not fire and sword. For a few differences of opinion, the rights of which will never be known till the Day of Judgment, shall a man burn his brother? Let those furious zealots, if do something they must, fight against the crimes and vices of which their co-religionists are daily guilty. Such things are far worse than haggling with their conscience as to whether they should obey some ecclesiastical ordinance or not. The spiritual is one thing, the temporal another; a religious society is one thing; a secular society, another. A magistrate has no jurisdiction over the spirit; as a magistrate, he has no business in a place of worship. Toleration is so consonant with the Gospel of Jesus Christ, and with the common feelings of all mankind, that all who refuse to recognize its necessity and its benefits we may look upon as moral monstrosities. What matters it whether or not Latin is spoken in churches, whether you kneel down or stand up, whether a robe is longer or shorter? You who practise the Catholic ritual, and you, too, men of Geneva, and you Remonstrants and Counter-Remonstrants, Anabaptists, Arminians, Socinians, know that you will never take a soul by force: you have neither the power nor the right to do so. Bear ye one with another, and, united in the will to do good, love ye one another.

VI

SCIENCE AND PROGRESS

IN the solitudes of a great park, two figures are to be seen: a
dainty marquise and a gentleman of fashion, her friend, or,
perchance, her lover, who, amid the shades of night, is holding
long and earnest converse with her. What, you ask, is the subject
of his discourse? Astronomy! "Tell me," she says, "about these
stars of yours." Gallant, sophisticated, exquisite, thus does
Fontenelle portray them, not only because his own nature is like
that, but because it is part of his plan to present them in an
attractive light. He is particularly anxious that his book
should repel no one, that it should appeal to all, especially to the
unlearned, whom it was to fascinate at the very outset by its
charm and its lightness of touch. He came very near robbing his
theme of its grandeur; it came out, however, despite all these airs
and graces, in all its sovereign splendour. The man-about-town
and his marquise, enveloped in the shades of night, play over
again the part enacted by those ancient shepherds of Chaldea,
trying to read the secret of the heavens. Like the earliest inhabitants of the earth, they marvelled at the stars even as they had
marvelled at the sun; a pair of mortals pathetically trying to read
the secret of the skies.

The marquise knows nothing; but Fontenelle, _he_ knows, and
in the space of an evening or two, he will explain to her the
courses of the stars, at first sight so mysterious. There had been
errors enough in the past; long enough, indeed, had men misread
the motions of the heavenly bodies! Long enough had they
supposed it was the sun that hurtled round the earth; the prime
mistake from which innumerable others did proceed. However,
at last, that error had been dispelled. "There came on the scene a

certain German, one, Copernicus, who made short work of all those various circles, all those solid skies, which the ancients had pictured to themselves. The former he abolished; the latter, he broke in pieces. Fired with the noble zeal of a true astronomer, he took the earth and spun it very far away from the centre of the universe, where it had been installed, and in that centre he put the sun, which had a far better title to the honour." So once again the Ancients were at fault, and mankind had gone astray by following them. But now a new era was dawning. Reason and observation had given short shrift to those hoary old errors. Science speaks, and we must give heed to what she says. The heavens and the earth are changed.

This discovery might have been expected to fill the hearts of men with dread. After the manner of that demented Athenian, who thought that every ship which came to anchor in the Piraeus belonged to him, the marquise had believed that the universe had been constructed especially for her; and now, what a rude awakening! The earth, a place of toil, of wars, of endless excursions and alarms, was now like a silkworm's cocoon, so tiny, so fragile, so pitiable it seemed. She might well tremble at the infinite spaces that were now unfolded to her gaze.

She might have trembled, but she did not. On the contrary, she felt all the joy, all the pride, of the professed and initiated adept; she lent an attentive ear to this newly resurrected science. She became a member of a sort of sodality, breaking forever with the pagans that had never known the truth, and with those heretics that had ever misrepresented it. That was her position, and she was proud of it. Now, by one of those similes of which Fontenelle makes such frequent use, and which transform abstractions into something pleasing to the sight (like a boat gliding on a river, a vessel sailing the sea, or a bowl rolling along the green sward) we will imagine ourselves at the opera. Phaeton quits the earth, he is caught by the wind, and flies up to heaven. Let us suppose that Pythagoras, Aristotle, Plato, and all the sages we hear so much about are witnessing the performance: Phaeton, one of them will say, is composed of certain numbers which cause him to ascend. Another: it is a certain hidden virtue which raises Phaeton aloft. Another: Phaeton has a certain predilection for the upper part of the theatre; he is not happy when he is not there. Imagine all the fairy tales the ancients had in stock to explain things! Pitiable, was it not? Fortunately Descartes and some other modern thinkers arrive. They tell us: Phaeton ascends because he is pulled up by ropes, and because a weight, heavier than he, is let down. No one had thought of peeping behind the scenes. From the day the machines were discovered, men began to use their reason; they *knew*. How delightful is discovery! What bliss to know the truth!

Scientific knowledge has a beauty of its own, for the contemplation of a perfect piece of mechanism wherein the most complicated effects are produced by the simplest of devices, is a delight to the mind. Some people may not care over-much for a mechanical universe, but when the marquise learned that it resembled a watch, she liked it more than ever. Such regularity, such economy of means, such simplicity—what could be more admirable! In thus discovering the laws of nature, she was filled with a rapture rare and delicate, a rapture not of the senses, but of the intellect. "It is not the sort of pleasure you get from a comedy of Molière's, but something that has to do with your reason, and you laugh only with your mind." Science, as we have seen, is everywhere, and now we are about to make contact with a set regarded as the very last word in learning, with men who cover blackboards with figures that make your head swim, men who peer through telescopes, men who dissect bodies both animal and human; we are about to set foot on their special preserves. Fontenelle invites us to enter. In the matter of philosophy he takes his stand with the "restless"; in science, with the "enquirers"; they both amount to the same thing. Now may the general run of men draw near without apprehension to the Tree of the Knowledge of Good and Evil. Truth will come like a revelation enlightening the minds of all mankind. The *Entretiens sur la Pluralité des Mondes*, dated 1686, are an introduction, profound but engaging, to a new interpretation of the universe.

It is not only the geometrical way of thinking that caught on, but geometry itself. From the airy heights to which the preceding age had raised it, it now came down to the level of the ordinary educated public. In Paris, a mathematician, one Joseph Sauveur, made himself quite a name by giving a series of lectures to which gentlemen of the fashionable world came in crowds. Ladies stipulated that the solution of the problem of squaring the circle should be the passport, and the only one, to their favours. So, at least, the *Journal des Savants* gave out, quizzing the popular craze. "Ever since the mathematicians managed to penetrate into the innermost of feminine sanctuaries, and, with the aid of the *Mercure Galant*, to bring with them the terminology of a science as solid and serious as mathematics, we hear that Cupid's empire is rapidly crumbling, and that no one talks now of anything but problems, corollaries, theorems, right-angles, obtuse angles, rhomboids, and so on. It reports that quite recently there were two young ladies in Paris whose heads had been so turned by this branch of learning that one of them declined to listen to a proposal of marriage unless the candidate for her hand undertook to learn how to make telescopes, so often talked of in the *Mercure Galant*; while the other young lady positively refused a perfectly eligible suitor simply because he had been unable, within a given time, to produce any new idea about 'squaring the circle'" (4th March, 1686). Seeing that matter was nothing but extension, then physics was nothing but mathematics. The geometricians were to be thanked for enabling us to get a hold on matter and for substituting for such wordy vacuities as "Opium induces sleep by reason of its sleep-giving properties", the sure and solid method of mathematical calculation. Thanks to them, we hold the key to all the phenomena of the universe.

But, in point of fact, mathematics were not the only thing that occupied an important place in men's minds. There was another matter that clamoured for solution more peremptorily every day. Mathematics represented one form of knowledge, no doubt; but was it the only one? To reduce everything to an abstraction—was that the way to know all that there was to know? Perhaps geometry, in the flush of victory, had gone a little beyond its proper limits. What seems to prove it is that M. Descartes, excellent geometrician though he was, had gone very considerably astray in physics. Observation and experiment, those were the two things to which the new philosophy exhorted us. Was science bound to disdain them? Men heard the voice of Galileo, and, clearer still, the voice of Bacon. Bacon had never been forgotten. Bacon, men call to mind, had said that we must start with observation; that the human mind apprehended things by perceiving them through the senses; that the impressions made upon the senses, being transmitted to the brain, supplied matter

for the reason to examine and report upon; that the reason in its
turn gave back these impressions purified and sublimated; wherefore true philosophy should begin with the senses if it was to
provide the understanding with a direct and certain line of progress. The geometricians, starting with their definition of matter,
had asserted that space did not exist; whereupon other learned
men proceeded to show by experiment that space did exist, beyond all question. It was these latter who had discovered the real
truth merely by studying the actual facts. The fact: be guided by
the fact. That is the thing.

Here, then, was another task to shoulder, and a heavy one. Yet
once again the mind of man must needs start on a new trail,
work and toil unceasingly and get some tangible result. Avail
yourself, by all means, of such assistance as the mathematicians
can offer, for they can give you certitude in their own sphere; but
get hold of another way of acquiring knowledge, a way which will
not denude the living being of all its flesh, and which, realizing its
complexity, will master it. So a new collective effort was begun
by a Europe in its formative stage. Here we have the Italians,
grouped, to begin with, about the Academy of the *Cimento* at
Florence. In the eyes of its learned members, every natural
phenomenon is a thing to be enquired into: how do grubs get
into fruit? What are those excrescences which make their appearance on the twigs and leaves of trees? How is it that a fish
which is phosphorescent in water ceases to be so in air? The
quest begins. They have no laboratories, no apparatus; often
enough they don't trouble to doff their frock coats or their
imposing wigs before starting on their labours. Still the quest
goes on. They manufacture instruments. They are forever ex-
perimenting. No doubt, they say, geometry is the type of ideal
knowledge; but, then, geometry goes soaring off into boundless
space, and leaves us standing. Then we turn to the experimental
method which, by dint of proof and counter-proof, leads us on
to the truth. In 1667, the Academy of the *Cimento* came to an
end, but the Italian tradition did not die with it. It lived on, all
through the following century, fostered by such men as Marsigli,
Vallisnieri, Gualtieri, Clarici, Micheli, Ramazzini, Fortis; we do
not profess to name them all. In the *Gallery of Minerva*, 1704,
Giovanni Maria Lancisi printed a speech which he had delivered
on the method of applying philosophy to the art of medicine,

wherein it is shown that, for a medicine based on reason, it is better to have recourse to experimental philosophy than to any other.

The English school, of which Boyle was a leading light, displayed no less activity. The Royal Society was the admiration of Europe. The sagacious and gifted persons who compose it think much less about showing off their cleverness, or their remarkable memory, than they do of making a solid contribution to the arts and sciences. That being so, the propositions that engaged their attention, into the truth of which they are concerned to enquire, are, by preference, those to which a practical test can be applied; to the rest, they pay little or no heed. Then they seek out causes by a process of reasoning, combined with further experiments, which, one after another, take these eminent naturalists very far afield, as far, in point of fact, as the top of the peak of Teneriffe, where some of them have been to prosecute further researches, after conducting countless experiments at home, and inventing special apparatus for the work.[1]

The Dutch scientists were past masters in the method that was now coming into fashion; medical men, botanists, naturalists, all worked unsparingly: Swammerdam, Huygens, Boerhaave, Gravesande, and Leuwenhoeck. The last named, with deft fingers, searching eye, and a forward-looking mind, began by perfecting his technique, as we should say to-day. He spared himself no pains till he had manufactured with his own hands, and after innumerable experiments, a microscope more powerful than any which had served his predecessors. He made a success of it; the microscope which he at length contrived to construct, was capable of magnifying objects two hundred and seventy times their actual size. In a single drop of water he beheld a whole world; a world of tiny creatures moving about, struggling, seeking for food. Maybe that drop of water is as full of things as the ocean, palpitating with a whole world of life. He submits various liquids to a similar test, blood, and other fluids. However, his discoveries were contested and, as usual, arguments, rejoinders, *opuscula*, books and labour untold, were needed before public opinion would acknowledge the truth of what the eye had beheld.

[1]Sorbière, quoted by G. Ascoli, *La Grande Bretagne devant l'opinion française*, 1930, II, p. 42.

Then there were the Scandinavians, Olaus Roemer, Thomas Bartholin, Nils Stensen, whose anatomical discoveries gave new life to medical science. There were Germans, too, like Otto van Guericke, who busied himself with the nature and problems of space. Working as disciplined collaborators in a common task, the Germans brought out a specialist publication in the shape of a journal dealing with medico-physics which described the lines on which students of natural science were working. Bayle thought very highly of it, saying that its contributors were rendering most valuable service to scientific research, both by their indefatigable industry and their inventive genius.

The French also became smitten with natural science. Parisians went to the *jardin du Roi* to hear Duverney's lectures on anatomy. They boasted of possessing, in the person of Nicolas Lémery, who began as an apothecary, the man to whom Voltaire was later on to refer as the first intelligent chemist; as well as Mariotte, one of the most famous physicists of the day. "In Paris, a new Nature Office has been opened, for that is what I call the *Académie des Sciences*: M. l'abbé Bignon, who keeps the key of this office, has declared that nature would appear there quite unadorned, not having thought fit to borrow from the gentlemen of the *Académie française* any of the finery and bedizenments they have in stock. That was quite right."[1]

Spain itself took part in the research movement. A society of physics and experimental medicine was founded at Seville in 1697. Just as in literature, and just as in philosophy, though possibly more promptly, swarms of ideas began to germinate. An illustrious Etruscan doctor, Francesco Redi, published a treatise on *animalculae*. In it he demonstrated that substances do not go bad when they are kept away from flies, which, if they are not, lay eggs in them: all the learned folk in Europe were interested in his discovery; and, by way of setting a seal on this intellectual co-partnership, it was a Frenchman, Pierre Coste, who translated this work from the Italian and it was in Holland that the translation was published. A Venetian, Paolo Sarrotti, became acquainted with Robert Boyle in London and, fired with enthusiasm for scientific studies, took back with him to Venice, "A couple of young Englishmen who were very adept at handling mechanical appliances used in connection with scientific

[1] *L'Esprit des Cours de l'Europe*, 1699, p. 25.

experiments". When Père Tachard went on his second journey to Siam, M. Thévenot asked him to look into a matter which struck him as very remarkable, though he had been assured that it was perfectly true. It was that sea-shells were to be found on the top of Mount Sinai. Now was that really so? Greatly daring, Frs. Le Blanc and de Bèze undertook to make the ascent. The chief European journals gave a lot of space to problems in higher mathematics, but more still to the natural sciences. Often the reports sent in by readers do but indicate an inveterate taste for things out of the ordinary, unnatural: A hen that had never laid an egg, being startled by a loud noise, began to cackle in the most extraordinary fashion, and then laid an enormous egg, which was marked, not with a comet, as some people had got the story, but with a lot of stars. Someone caught a butterfly that had a head like a baby's. A girl vomited a quantity of spiders, caterpillars, slugs and other insects. Such were the sort of "strange events" that took the public fancy. But on the same pages, there were items that bore witness to genuine scientific work; learned men were busy in every country, all animated by a like spirit of en-quiry, by a like eagerness to get at the bottom of things: What is the function of sap in trees? What, precisely, are the effects of quinine? What causes fermentation? Then there was the ana-tomy of the eye; of the stomach; newly discovered tubes in the human heart. Someone comes across a monstrosity of a cat. Well; no use gaping and saying oh, how wonderful! Let's take and dissect it.

As with philosophy, as with criticism, when the time was ripe, there appeared on the scene one of those mighty figures for whom the great ages never call in vain: to wit, Newton.

Is it not clearly a sign of the times that the two men whom Vico described as the outstanding geniuses of the age, Leibniz and Newton, discovered well-nigh simultaneously the infinitesi-mal calculus. The application of this new method enables us to treat natural phenomena, not as discontinuous, which they generally are not, but as continuous, which they generally are. What an immensely important place in the evolution of human ideas was henceforth taken by science, science which men in those days quite honestly thought they could do without. It has been observed that whenever some great mathematical truth was discovered and brought out, it was made the basis of a theory by which the whole universe was to be explained. Pythagorism was based on arithmetic; Spinozism on geometry; similarly, it was on the infinitesimal calculus that the philosophy of Leibniz was founded.[1] In fact, Leibniz himself declared that mathematics were the main resource of the philosopher, and that he would never have discovered the theory of harmony had he not in the first place established the law of motion. Meanwhile, Newton, in the light of the infinitesimal calculus, was led to discover the law of gravitation.

It was, in fact, in the year 1687 that his great work, the *Principia mathematica philosophiae naturalis*, first saw the light. These principles were a long way from being understood when they first appeared. It was not till a generation or so later that their full importance was realized. As in philosophy, so in criticism, so, indeed, in all things, the XVIIIth century was to profit by the discoveries of the latter part of the XVIIth. Such potent substances have to be ingested slowly. Be it added that the *Principia* regard mathematics, not as the whole of physics, as Descartes would have them, but as the instrument to which physical science has recourse in order to make and verify its discoveries. And be it further added that the immortal book restores to observation and experiment their dignity and importance. Facts attentively observed; due submission to the facts; humble acceptance of the facts; an almost instinctive abhorrence of any theory that cannot stand the test of fact—such were some of the characteristics of Newton's genius, and his cosmic discovery is, as it were, the astounding illustration of his principles and the reward of his intellectual allegiance. The popular imagination, which pictures Newton sitting under a tree, observing the fall of an apple, and wondering what made it fall, is not so wide of the mark, not so trivial as it might seem, when we look on it as symbolizing the method of one who takes the real for his starting-point. He realized, in an eminent degree, the aim which inspired those bands of pioneers whose patient and zealous labours we have lately been reviewing. Begin with the concrete; interpret it in the light of reason; then verify your conclusion by again comparing it with the concrete—such, explicitly stated, is the rule of the science towards which these pioneers were dimly feeling their way.

[1]Léon Brunschvicg, *Les étapes de la philosophie mathématique*, 1912.

When Fontenelle, as Perpetual Secretary of the *Académie des Sciences*, came to write his panegyric of Sir Isaac Newton, his clear understanding enabling him to explain his discoveries with such lucidity that the man in the street could understand them, or thought he could; when his writing, while losing nothing of its precision or its elegance, took on an added glow and vivacity, as though warmed by the creative breath of the man whose genius he had set himself to extol; then, indeed, we were presented with a parallel that was no mere literary flight of fancy, something "to point a moral or adorn a tale", but a most accurate and faithful comparison of these two great men, Descartes and Newton. Despite his partiality for Descartes, his master, Fontenelle brings out with admirable clearness the difference in the intellectual attitudes of the two men, both of whom, in their respective ways, marked the limits to which the human mind can soar.

The two great men who stand forth in such marked contrast, one against the other, nevertheless, had many links between them. Both were geniuses of first order, born to hold sway over the minds of men, and to be the founders of Empires. Both of them, excellent geometricians themselves, saw the need to bring geometry into the domain of physics; both founded their physics on a system of geometry which they owed almost exclusively to their own intelligence. But one of them, soaring aloft in daring flight, sought to take his stand at the fountain-head of all things in the light of a few clear and fundamental ideas, so that when he came to deal with the phenomena of Nature he would be able to treat them as necessary consequences thereof. The other, less daring, or more modest, in his aims, beginning with phenomena as his starting point proceeded therefrom to unknown principles, resolved to treat them as the logic of the consequences might require. The one starts from a clearly formulated idea to ascertain the cause of what he sees; the other starts from what he sees, and goes on to seek out its cause. . . .

In like manner, when, proceeding with his discourse, he comes to deal with the subject of Optics, as set forth by Newton in the *Treatise of Light and Colours*, published in 1704, Fontenelle demonstrates the purpose, the difficulty, ay, and the beauty, of those experimental labours:

The art of experiment, when it is carried out with a certain degree of nicety, is by no means one that is commonly met with. The most trifling effect presented to our senses is complicated by so many others which constitute or modify it, that it is impossible, without the exercise of extraordinary skill, to disentangle all the various strands which compose it, and it requires the most acute understanding even to guess at the various elements which might conceivably enter into it. The sensible fact has to be resolved into other facts, themselves composite, and these in their turn, must be resolved into their constituents, and sometimes, if you chance to miss your way, you find yourself in a maze from which there is no visible issue. The primary and elementary facts seem to have been hidden by Nature from our sight with as much care as the causes thereof, and when we do succeed in catching a glimpse of them, they present an appearance as novel as it is startling.

We recognize in the coming of experimental physics the formal ratification of a process whose effects were to prove as varied as they were numerous. The brilliant genius of Newton marks the same transition from the transcendental to the positive as Pufendorf had essayed to achieve in the sphere of law, Richard Simon in Biblical exegesis, Locke in philosophy, and Shaftesbury in ethics. He dismissed with confidence any apprehensions that might be entertained about the possible abuse of reason, which, for the time being, seemed purely destructive. He brought about the union—a task so difficult as to be deemed impossible—between the strict demands of the critics and the facts of experience. So once again does man set forth to survey and subdue the universe.

On the 8th February, 1715, before the Leyden Academy, Boerhaave, a doctor of medicine, delivered a lecture entitled *De comparando certo in physicis,* in which he summarized the results achieved in the course of the last few years. All attempts to get at the essence of things had been unavailing. First causes, the nature of matter, eluded us. We invented words, we talked about atoms, monads and so forth; but all this got us no farther. We had to make up our minds to it, and recognize that all this talk was just so much guesswork which tomorrow would falsify. Newton himself was careful to state that when he spoke of attraction he had no intention of repeating the error of the schoolmen, who ascribed the action of mysterious properties to all such phenomena as they could not account for. It looked as if all bodies attracted one another; but as to why they did so he was careful not to commit himself. He observed and noted visible

and sensible phenomena; he compared and calculated effects; and
there he stopped. In consequence, we should consider as out of
bounds those metaphysical regions in which so many philosophers have lost their way. Let us be content with the things that
experience makes known and confirms. Leave metaphysics alone
and stick to physics. Only when we do that shall we begin to find
out the real facts about nature which, up to now, have eluded us.
So here again is another brand of Pyrrhonism, of defeatist
Pyrrhonism, *Pyrrhonismus physicus*, as Boerhaave himself denoted
it. He could never have taken the line he did had not those
changes in the intellectual outlook, whose progress we have been
endeavouring to trace, already taken place. The great Dutch
doctor was but summarizing the principles of a new school of
thought, of a general system of philosophy, whose essential
tenets had been expounded by Locke. Tired of trying to discover
the essential nature of matter, which they had now come to regard
as eternally beyond their reach, men addressed themselves to the
task of taking stock of the limited domain which they were still
able to call their own. To make the most of *that*; to put up a
comfortable abode there, to make work less of a drudgery and
more remunerative; to increase their well-being, to find themselves better off every day—this was now their aim in life. And
who was to be their guide in the prosecution of their task? Why,
the scientist. To him it belonged to instruct mankind in the
ordering of their lives. So, to the scientist went all the honours.
He is proclaimed as greater than princes, or military conquerors;
his praises are sounded in all the seats of learning, and to him
are addressed the eloquent tributes that used to be paid to the
masters of the pen. And why should he not also take the lead
in public affairs? If politics require the nicest calculations, the
utmost skill in planning, surely the scientist is the very man for
the job. Newton cut no indifferent figure as a Member of
Parliament. The historian prides himself on observing the winds
of destiny which sway the fate of nations, which call Empires
into being, and bring them to the dust. A paltry satisfaction,
that, compared with what the man of science can enjoy. "The
most striking pages of History could scarce surpass in interest
those phosphorescent substances, those cold liquids which, when
mixed together, burst into sudden flame, the almost magical
properties of the magnet, and all those countless wonders whose

secret Science, by a close and watchful scrutiny of Nature, has managed to unveil."[1]

What wonder, after that, that Poetry should sing the praises of the microscope, the pneumatic engine, the barometer? What wonder that it should hymn the circulation of the blood and the laws of respiration? The Muse was but paying homage to the Spirit of the Age.

Science never pauses in her onward march. Today, it is gravitation that has been revealed to us; tomorrow, other men of genius will arise, other secrets will be brought to light; and so, little by little, we shall come to know all the parts of that mighty machine of which, hitherto, we have known nought. And knowledge means power. Even if Science did no more for us, it would still be useful in that it would teach us how to think with accuracy and precision, and to shape our minds in conformity with her inexorable laws; an accomplishment not to be despised. But theory must needs find expression in practice: *theoriam cum praxi.*[2] "To know that in a parabola the subtangent is double the corresponding abscissa, is, in itself, a very barren piece of knowledge; nevertheless, it is one step towards acquiring the art of firing shells with precision which we now possess." "When the foremost geometricians of the seventeenth century addressed themselves to the study of a new curve which they called the cycloid, they had no practical object in view. . . . However, as a result of their continued investigations into the properties of the curve in question, it came to be applied to clocks, and brought measurement of time to its ultimate perfection." "The application of science to nature will constantly grow in scope and intensity, and we shall go on from one marvel to another; the day will come when man will be able to fly by fitting on wings to keep him in the air; the art will increase more and more till one day we shall be able to fly to the moon." In a word: "Here is a vast field of knowledge all adaptable to the use and well-being of humanity here below. We know, for example, how to invent new and swift machines that will add to the speed and comfort of

[1] These, and the phrases which follow, are borrowed from the Hymn to Science chanted by Fontenelle in his preface to *l'Histoire du renouvellement de l'Académie royale des Sciences,* 1702.

[2] A phrase from Leibniz's *Denkschrift über die Errichtung der Berliner Academie* (*Deutsche Schriften,* B.II, p. 268). See also his general scientific plan: "De utilitate scientiarum et verae euriditionis efficacia ad humanam felicitatem" (Unpublished *opuscula* and fragments, Couturat's edition, p. 218).

travel, how to blend a variety of agents, or materials, so as to obtain new and wholesome products which we can put to profitable use, thus augmenting the sum total of our riches, in other words of things which will add to the comfort and convenience of our daily lives." Earth will become a paradise. Already, thanks to the toil of that learned sisterhood, Mechanics, Geometry, Algebra, Anatomy, Botany, Chemistry—more potent than the old-fashioned Muses—Death has been forced to retreat.

> Savantes soeurs, soyez fidèles
> A ce que présagent mes vers:
> Par vous, de cent beautés nouvelles
> Les arts vont orner l'Univers.
> Par les soins que vous allez prendre
> Nous allons voir bientôt s'étendre
> Nos jours trop prompts à s'écouler;
> Et déjà sur la sombre rive
> Atropos en est plus oisive,
> Lachesis a plus à filer . . .[1]

What a sense of triumph, of joyous expectancy, in that one word, Progress! It brought with it a feeling of conscious pride, that feeling which makes life so much more easy to live; and it opened up vistas of a future which, instead of differing from the present, was to prove, rather, its complement and its crown. Progressive are our methods, progressive is our science; our potentialities in the sphere of action increase. The quality, the texture of our minds grows finer. "The various sciences, the various arts, whose progress has been almost completely interrupted for two centuries past, have drawn new vigour from this one, and have entered, so to speak, on a new career."[2] "We are now in an age which bids fair to become daily more and more enlightened, so much so that all preceding ages when compared with this will seem to be plunged in darkness . . ."[3] All anxieties, all agitations were to be removed. Man, weary of turning back,

---

[1] Houdar de la Motte, L'Académie des Sciences, *Ode à M. Bignon.* "Learned Sisters, be mindful of what my verses here foretell. With your aid the arts shall adorn the universe with countless new beauties; through you we shall soon see our days, now so few and fleeting, made many more. Even now, on the banks of the Dark River Atropos has longer leisure and Lachesis more to weave."

[2] Fontenelle, in the Preface already quoted.

[3] Pierre Bayle, *Nouvelles de la République des lettres*, Avril 1684. Article XI.

and looking behind him for some Golden Age in the distant past, man uncertain of the world to come, concentrates his hopes on a future less remote, a future which he himself may possibly live long enough to see, but which, at all events, his children will enjoy. . . .

Even now Science was becoming an idol, an object of worship. Science and happiness were coming to be looked upon as one and the same thing, as also, were moral and material progress. It looked as if Science were going to usurp the place of Philosophy, to supersede Religion, and that it would supply the answer to all the longings of the human heart. But by way of reaction, there were even then audible some voices from the opposing side, some voices raised in protest. Upbraiding Science with attempting to overstep the limits which it had itself scrupulously laid down, they spoke of its overweening arrogance, they even proclaimed, so great was the need promptly to crush this budding myth—they even proclaimed that Science was bankrupt.[1]

[1] Thomas Baker, *Reflections upon Learning, by a gentleman*, London, 1700.

VII

TOWARDS A NEW PATTERN OF HUMANITY

THE Italian Courtier, having played his part as master of the ceremonies, made his bow, and the Gentleman took his place. On an age that was still far from settled, he inculcated the importance of prudence and moderation, and the lesson went home. He told people they should accept the existing religious, social and political order, which, after manifold experiments and much toil and trouble, did seem the best there was to be had. He exhorted everyone to try and fit himself into that framework without demur, so that they might all settle down together as happily, or at least as contentedly, as possible. He himself was made up of contrasts, but so cunningly were the contrasts welded together that he presented what seemed a perfectly harmonious whole. The philosophy of the Ancients had to be reconciled with Christian morals, the claims of the intellect with the exigencies of ordinary life, the aspirations of the soul with the demands of the body, the workaday with the Sublime. He taught politeness, a difficult virtue, which consists in pleasing other people in order to please oneself; he preached the avoidance of excess, even in well-doing, and said no one should ever pride himself on anything save on being a man of honour. He trained himself by constant discipline and kept an unremitting watch on himself. It was no easy matter for a man to prevent the *ego* from getting out of hand, and to realize that his importance in the scheme of things was not that of an individual but as one of a community. To live up to a standard such as that calls for a sort of quiet heroism and the Gentleman appears to be compounded of all the graces merely because he is perpetually controlling the forces within him and dispensing them in little harmonious doses.

The century was drawing to a close, but a glow still lingered on the Gentleman's figure. There were people who still looked on him with marked respect, and held him up as an example for young men to follow. Writers there were who, exploiting the success of their predecessors, gave liberally of counsel that was fast becoming threadbare. For example they portrayed the Gentleman as one who has a taste for social gatherings, and looks forward to them with pleasurable anticipation. He is a good judge of works that appeal to the intellect, and discusses them without prejudice, captiousness, or jealousy. . . .

All this was behind the times; quite out of date. It was not a matter of accepting the *status quo*, and, having done so of your own free-will, of making the best of it. No; the business now was to reform things from top to bottom, and to do it quickly. The whole social and political structure needed overhauling. How could anyone possibly accept the idea of a State religion? The new men, the up-to-date men, like Lord Halifax in the maxims he gave his daughter for living a happy life, recommend the rising generation to make themselves a religion of their own; a kindly, easy-going, cheerful religion, free from fear and gloom. God rules His creatures no longer; it is they who have taken possession of Him. In a word, all the principles which made up the philosophy of the Gentleman have given way; the imposing statue is falling to pieces.

Time was, long ago, when the idea of the Gentleman had been regarded as the creation of Reason. But that was the whole point; Reason meant something different now from what it did in those days. Reason was now no longer a mediating power, imposing an order based on accommodations, compromises, give-and-take. It was a critical force whose main duty was to enquire, to examine, to question. To this sort of Reason, which was never satisfied with things as they were, the "Gentleman" was not *persona grata*.

He abdicated of his own accord. He had been reigning for a long time, and there had come to be a touch of the mechanical in the way people had of copying and obeying him. There were a good many people for whom the gentlemanly character had become, not so much a means to right living as an end in itself. It was now all a matter of elegant accomplishments, of intellectual adornment. So much was this the case, that such people travestied its very nature. "You know", says the Chevalier de Grammont to his friend Matta, describing the sort of instruction he had received at the academy where he had been taught to bear arms, "you know that I am the most adroit man in France, so that I soon learnt all that is taught at such places, and at the same time I also learnt that which gives the finishing stroke to a young fellow's education, and makes him a gentleman, viz: all sorts of games, both at cards and dice."[1] He takes the chaff for the grain, and imagines that gaming, a pleasant enough way of passing the time with one's acquaintances, makes up the whole outfit of the Gentleman. And when, a little later, we learn that he used his skill to fleece a too ingenuous opponent, the conclusion is forced upon us that, at the beginning of the eighteenth century, good manners and good morals were not necessarily concomitant any more. So now, the Gentleman had fallen from his high estate, and we must look elsewhere for our pattern of the good life.

Surprisingly enough it was Spain that suggested the man, and the surprise was the greater because this Spanish hero was nobody very new; he seemed, rather, like one called back from the dead. In the year 1637, Fr. Baltasar Gracián of the Company of Jesus brought out a book entitled *El Héroe*. This was followed, in 1640, by *El Político*; in 1644, by *El Discreto*; in 1647, by *El Oráculo manual*; in 1651, 1653, 1657, by *El Criticón*; all of them works devoted to the study of man, and to constructing from his various attributes a model for all to imitate. However, as is always the case, particularly at this time when ideas were changing so fast, these books appear to have fallen out of date. How was it, then, that towards the close of the seventeenth century Baltasar Gracián began to be so widely translated, and his merits so widely extolled? Certainly he was not an unknown writer; people had heard of him; but how came it that he was thus, after several years in a sort of dim twilight of approbation, suddenly transported to the very pinnacle of fame and popularity? Possibly because a French translation by Amelot de la Houssaye, a work notable for the distinction and grace of its style (though it may have robbed the original of some of its native savour), bestowed on it a European character it had not previously possessed. Or it may have been that the Society of Jesus, forgetting the quarrels it had once had with the author, not only buried the hatchet, but was largely responsible for the book's

[1]Hamilton, *Mémoires de la vie du Comte de Grammont*, 1713; chap. III.

posthumous success. Or, again, it may have been that there was a vast public whom the latest trend of ideas failed to satisfy, and in whose mouths the food that was offered them, of the earth earthy, left a bitter taste behind it; there is, as Stendhal once remarked, a touch of the Spaniard in every human heart. It may have been for any of these reasons, or it may have been for others beyond our ken. There are some things that defy explanation. Be that as it may, the fact remains that, between 1685 and 1716, as many as fifteen different versions of Gracián appeared in France alone. Germany went positively mad over the Spanish moralist. Thomasius, in that resounding inaugural address of his, the address in which he inveighed so vehemently against servile imitation of the French, cites him as one of the masters of whom the Germans should seek inspiration, if they would lend refinement to their way of life; he quotes him with a great flourish both at the beginning and the end of his discourse. In England, in Italy, nay, everywhere, Gracián is held in the highest esteem.

The ideal man, in his view of the matter, is not he who is content to exhibit a smooth blend of unexceptionable, middling, qualities. Middling virtues, however many you may have of them, never add up to anything but mediocrity. A loftier ambition than that kindles the ardour of the ideal man; his aim is to be greatest among the great. Endowed with brilliant intellectual gifts, with a firm and unerring judgment, with a fiery spirit and passionate ardour (for what avail brains, if the heart responds not?); making the utmost of his dominant faculty, trusting with instinctive intuition to the designs of Fortune, of Fortune that favours the brave; choosing for his models the loftiest exemplars in every field of action, not merely to rival, but to surpass them, the ideal man is he who would fain be unique and inaccessible in his solitary perfection. To that end, he must be secret, inscrutable, ready to bide his time, even to cloak and dissemble his actions, so important is it to reveal oneself by degrees, so that, at every successive stage, the common folk may look and marvel at the manifestation of powers that seem to have no limit. The Hero bears his tribulations like a Stoic; like a Stoic he endures humiliation; though there is but one real humiliation, and that is the humiliation he should inflict upon himself before the judgment-seat of his own conscience if, in his own eyes, he should chance to fall short. Victory is not an end in itself; the domination of the world is but a means to something beyond: the power and pride of his triumphant personality the Hero lays before God, in token of his homage; to Religion he consecrates the moral victory he has won. Greatly skilled is he, even to the point of using a little saintly *finesse*; he is proud, yet simple hearted; he reads in men's inmost hearts, and yet remains a romantic; he is practical, yet hungers for ideal beauty; imperious, yet devout; loving difficulties for what is hard and grim in them; in short, a marvellous and brilliant compendium of contradictions—such is his portrait. The Gentleman, who was made to harmonize with the sedate colouring, the soft greys of the Ile de France, seems a faint and faded figure in comparison. The Hero needs that same brilliant sun which, on the highways of Castile, beat down upon Don Quixote and made the vision of Justice, Generosity and Love to glitter enchantingly before his eyes.

He took the fancy of all Europe; but only for the moment. Europe might look on Gracián with interest, nay, with sympathy; Europe might read his books and derive profit and pleasure from the reading; but Europe was not going to take him for her guide. He came too late; her mind was made up now, and, for her, there was no turning back. If the Gentleman was no longer sufficiently up-to-date for her, how could she be expected to follow in the steps of the Hero, far less completely secularized than he?

Society had now arrived at one of those epochs which are peculiarly interesting to study; one of those epochs where the screen grows misty and confused as different pictures invade it, one growing fainter and fainter yet loth to disappear, another supplanting it but still lacking in clearness and precision of outline. The Gentleman was gradually fading out, the *Bourgeois* was slowly taking form and colour. Till now it was the aristocrat that had taken the upper hand; but now he was over and done with. Goodbye to the Warrior! Past and gone were the days when the exploits of gallant captains—cities taken by storm, battles won in glorious combat, the foe routed by a dashing charge, the victor crowned with laurels—were the things, the only things that had excited admiration. Saint-Évremond pokes fun at that mighty man of valour, Maréchal d'Hocquincourt; Fénelon urges Idomeneus to impress upon Telemachus that the wise, and not the warlike, king is the proper object of admiration.

Fontenelle, too, has his little jest: "Most fighting men perform their task with abundant courage, but few use their brains. Their arms work with all the vigour one could look for, the head remains dormant and gets caught out for nothing". Bayle, in the name of common sense condemns "as weakness, or rather as downright lunacy, the vanity of those ambitious fighting men who care for nothing but their own reputation." Jean-Baptiste Rousseau, when anything like that reached his ears, himself took up the strain: what are conquerors but Fortune's minions, Fortune that glorifies the most outrageous crimes?

> Mais de quelque superbe titre
> Que tes héros soient revêtus,
> Prenons la Raison pour arbitre,
> Et cherchons chez eux leurs vertus.
> Je n'y trouve qu'extravagance,
> Faiblesse, injustice, arrogance,
> Trahisons, fureurs, cruautés;
> Étrange vertu qui se forme
> Souvent de l'assemblage énorme
> Des vices les plus détestés . . .[1]

Even the mighty heroes of antiquity must be divested of the fame which they had so long, and so unjustly, enjoyed.

> Quoi! Rome, l'Italie en cendre,
> Me feront honorer Sylla!
> J'admirerais dans Alexandre
> Ce que j'abhorre en Attila!
> J'appellerais vertu guerrière
> Une vaillance meurtrière
> Qui dans mon sang trempe ses mains:
> Et je pourrais forcer ma bouche
> A louer un Héros farouche
> Né pour le malheur des humains![2]

[1]With whatever proud title your heroes may be invested, let us take Reason for Judge, and find out what their virtues really are. All I can find in them is extravagance, weakness, injustice, arrogance, treasons, furious anger, cruelties; a strange virtue which is often made up of an enormous assemblage of the most detested vices.

[2]What! Shall Rome and Italy in ashes make me honour Sylla? Am I to admire in Alexander the very things I abhor in Attila? Am I to call warlike courage a murderous valour that soaks its hands in my blood, and force my lips to sing the praises of a savage Hero born to bring disaster on the human race!

A conqueror is one whom the gods, enraged by the wickedness of man, send into the world to ravage kingdoms, to spread misery and terror far and wide around them, and to make slaves of all free men. Those conquerors who are portrayed for us as crowned with glory are like rivers that have overflowed their banks, majestic, indeed, but bringing ruin to the fertile lands they were to irrigate. Who is it that speaks these words? Again, they are Fénelon's, and they come from Book VIII of his *Telemachus*.

Then there is that matter of honour. On that point, what extravagant ideas have been entertained! It is one of those ingrained fetishistic notions which prompt men to fight duels, that most outrageous of follies. Against the sort of things that were supposed to be smart and dashing, the sort of thing the aristocracy thought rather a feather in their caps, such as moral laxity, the craze for gambling, strong language—against all this, British Puritanism and French moderation presented a united front. And so, under a shower of maledictions, the Gentleman disappears into the shadows. In his place, on struts the *Bourgeois*, the Business Man, beaming with smiles, and already highly pleased with himself. Steele and Addison were his sponsors, both of them acute and sagacious observers of morals, whose only lack was perhaps a certain degree of concentration, a little dash, a spice of daring. However, they had taken it upon them to delineate a brave new type of human, for the delectation of the numerous readers they already had in England and were soon to have all over Europe. If it be true that a sociological element of some sort or other plays a part in all great literary successes, the latest instance was no exception to the rule, and this was the manner of it: *The Tatler* and *The Spectator*, in friendly collaboration, presented to an age that was feeling about for a rule of life, a code of behaviour, what they considered a model, an exemplar, of the human character. If they looked closely into man, it was, no doubt, that they were portrait-painters, and liked their work; they wanted to portray him, but they also wanted to reform him. Every time a new number from their printing-press started to go the round of the London coffee-houses and, a little later, to cross the Channel, they conveyed in it to a public seeking for a social order, a rule of conduct, a message that should enlighten them as to the proprieties, the amenities, the duties of life; and every time they did something, as the *Tatler* put it, to restore humanity to its place of honour. With irony, or upbraiding, and very deliberately, they would refute a falsehood here, rectify an abuse there, and, more important still, tell us what we ought to do, after telling us what we ought *not*. They knew their Classics from A to Z, and they revered them; they were familiar with the French moralists, Montaigne, Saint-Évremond, La Bruyère; they were familiar, too, with the most up-to-date specimens of the species they were studying, the Gentleman, the Dashing Blade, the Man of Breeding, the Dandy, the Wit; but they knew, also, that the human heart is at once changeless and changeful, and that we must ever be fashioning it anew. So they addressed themselves to the task. Castiglione and Benincasa, Nicolas Faret and the Chevalier de Méré—these Latins had all had their turn; now it was for a couple of Englishmen to try their hand.

A lawyer; Freeport, the merchant; Sentry, the captain; Will Honeycomb, the man-about-town; a clergyman; such are the sort of people that make up Mr. Spectator's little group. They are all middle-class folk except Sir Roger de Coverley, the Baronet. But Sir Roger is so simple-hearted, so sensible and level-headed, so different in every way from his brethren of the nobility, and, withal, so contradictory and paradoxical, so sensi-tive and so benevolent that he bore not the slightest resemblance to those rascally specimens of the gentleman class that had flourished so plentifully in the literature of the previous genera-tion. Mr. Spectator is the most unassuming of men. His property consists solely of one modest country estate, which was just as it had been for six hundred years; he is a man of considerable know-ledge, which, however, he exhibits no anxiety to display. He has travelled a great deal about the world, but he makes no fuss about it. Sober-minded, a man of few words, with a taste for solitude, with but few intimates, seeing little of his relations, he suffered no one to get a hold on him, not even his landlady. People who saw him doing the round of the London theatres, coffee-houses and other places of public resort, studying the manners and customs of his contemporaries, did not know what to make of him. Some took him for a Jesuit, some for a spy, some for a conspirator and some for a madman. What consoled him for all his little set-backs was that he had the satisfaction of observing how men lived and behaved, with a serene and untroubled eye, quite without prejudice. Being quite free from the passions and ambitions by which they were enslaved, he was the better able to discern their talents and their vices. The simplicity of his character, his imperturbable good-sense themselves set us an example of a good and happy life, without any special exhortations on his part. He tells us, however, that because of their mistaken ideas about honour, which lead them to insist on fighting duels; because, too, they fail to understand what the word justice stands for; because they get playing with professional gamesters who are only waiting to fleece them of everything they've got, the aristocracy seems to be on the high road to ruin. He laughs at the sort of people who pride themselves tremendously on their titles, titles which are theirs by an accident of birth, not because they have done anything to deserve them. He stresses the importance of polite and refined behaviour, disapproves of people who make a noise in the theatre, and is very down on women who drink over much and go in for taking snuff. At the same time, he was careful to point out that mere outward politeness is not the only thing that matters in life. He would much rather a man should emphasize his individuality than obliterate all marks of character: fine speeches, grimaces, affected manners make him feel sick. A man's worth is gauged by his spontaneous nature, not by his artificial acquirements. It is a mistake to think that man's supreme virtue, and almost his only one, is valour, and that woman's is chastity: a prejudice which explains in either sex the anxiety to please the other, women esteeming courage in men above everything else, and man hating women who are faithless. As if morality, a kindly nature were not as estimable as the so-called social qualities which are those customarily held in honour. Similarly, the useful should take precedence over the agreeable; coquettes, whose only aim is to shine; loungers whose only aim is to please; clever folk who, refining upon everything, become indifferent to good and evil, are a pernicious species. The jests, the witty sayings, the pointed sallies which the world in general likes so much are often pure spitefulness. And what, after all, is this fashionable life? Is it man's business to cut a figure in public assemblies, at social gatherings? Is it in things like that that he finds real happiness? Happiness is the foe of pomp and noise; it seeks peace and seclusion; it comes from the enjoyment of its own resources, or from the society of a few chosen friends; it loves shade and solitude, it frequents woods and streams and meadows, and, finding within itself all that it needs, it dispenses with audiences and onlookers. In contrast with all this, spurious happiness likes to attract attention; it seeks only to excite admiration; it lives in palaces, in theatres, in assemblies and dies as soon as there are no longer eyes to behold it. As regards happiness, we should not ask too much of it. The quest of happiness is less necessary and less beneficial to the human race than the art of bearing up firmly in the midst of afflictions. Contentment is the utmost we can look for here below; as soon as our ambitions begin to grow, they encounter obstacles and vexations. Let us do all we can, let us use all our endeavours to secure for ourselves tranquillity on earth, and happiness in the world to come. We see how Mr. Spectator indulges in some variations on ancient themes; but we also see how, quite classical as he remains, he evidently dissociates himself from the type of the Gentleman, and how he passes, essaying to construct a loftier civilization, from the aristocracy to the *bourgeoisie*, from the external to the inward, from social pleasure to social welfare, from art to morals.

The merchant, says the *Tatler*, has a better right to be called a gentleman than the courtier, whose only coin is words, and the *savant* who jeers at the ignorant. The *Spectator* is of the same opinion. To the merchant all honour is due. Not only does he confer upon England power, wealth and renown; not only has he set the Bank of England, that temple of the New Age, on a glorious throne, but by his commerce he lays the foundation for all countries to work together and enables them to contribute to the general welfare; he is the friend of the human race. The hero is content with what he vaguely calls fame; the merchant has need of a more delicate, more sensitive and, in a way, more subtle reputation, which is summed up in the word *credit*. A casual word, a passing allusion, an unfounded rumour getting about will undermine a merchant's credit and bring about his ruin. A gentleman was remarking the other day that he spoke freely enough about other gentlemen, but that he was particularly careful not to say anything unflattering about merchants. That would have meant putting them on trial, or rather bringing them in guilty without a hearing. So here, in full pride of place, is a new brand of honour, the honour of the Business Man.

In the theatre, the tones are heightened, as we all know. Writers are obliged to intensify them a little so as to bring them into the necessary relief. It was not enough for Steele to draw out the contrast between the Gentleman and the Merchant in print; he depicted it on the stage. The play in which he did so, one of his best, was *The Conscious Lovers*. The aristocratic Sir John Bevil has given his consent to the marriage of his daughter with the son of a Mr. Sealand, a well-to-do merchant who has made a fortune in trading with the East Indies. They stand up and confront one another. The merchant has a dig or two at the gentleman; he, Sealand, has a splendid genealogy, Godfrey, father of Edward, father of Ptolemy, father of Crassus, father of Count Richard, father of Henry the Marquis, father of Duke John—all of them first-rate fighting-cocks.

In case Sir John Bevil is not sufficiently impressed, Mr. Sealand proceeds to give a precise account of the revolution that has taken place in England:

"*I know the town and the world—and give me leave to say that we merchants are a species of gentry, that have grown into the world this last century, and are as honourable, and almost as useful, as you landed folks, that have always thought yourselves so much above us; for your trading, forsooth! is extended no farther than a load of hay, or a fat ox—You are pleasant people, indeed, because you are generally bred to be lazy.*" Then he goes on to say still more proudly that an accomplished merchant is the best example of the gentleman in the country; and that in knowledge, good manners and judgment the merchant is superior to many of the nobility.

In short, a revolution has taken place, a revolution which literature records and propagates:

'*Tis the misfortune of many other gentlemen to turn out of the seats of their ancestors, to make way for such new Masters as have been more exact in their Accompts than themselves; and certainly he deserves the Estate a great deal better who has got it by his industry, than he who has lost it by his negligence.*[1]

The new English pattern-man which now took shape made a profound impression throughout Europe. Journals, travel-books, the stage, novels—all brought him in, and the smart set tried to copy him. A plain exterior, no adornments, ordinary

[1] *Spectator*, No. 174.

broadcloth, no silks, and a walking-stick instead of a sword. Plain without and plain within. Open-hearted, frank and free, he scorns a lie, and lets you know it bluntly; plenty of sound common sense, with a practical turn of mind. "Ought a man", to quote Mr. Spectator again, "ought a man to be always thinking about polite letters and the fine-arts? Good honest work, business, trade, saving, those useful arts that tend to make life easier— things like that should occupy us as much and more." In 1695, when Pierre Coste brought out his translation of Locke's *Thoughts on Education*, he had an explanation to make. The author, he said, had designed his book to apply to young *gentlemen*; but Coste warned his readers that they must not misinterpret that word; it did not refer to the nobility but to the class immediately below the rank of baron, that is to say, to the sort of people who in France would be called *de bons bourgeois*, the upper middle-class. "Therefore, we may take it that this work, intended for gentlemen, in the English sense of that word, is in fact of general application." Through the good offices of Pierre Coste, the English *bourgeoisie* holds out a friendly hand to all the *bourgeoisies* in Europe.

But the delineation of the type universal ceased to be the prerogative of any one nation. That meant it would be something more composite; less simple, less clearly-defined in form and outline. Never again would any model present the purity of outline with which Classic art had endowed the concrete embodiment of its spirit. France set to work on her own account. What she wanted, what her temperament and her aims demanded, was someone to guide her steps towards reason, towards intellectual emancipation. At last she brought forward as her chosen type someone to whom the intellectuals of the eighteenth century were to give their unqualified approval. He was a sort of amalgam of French and English, an abstract thinker, yet a practical guide: he was, in fact, the Philosopher.

What does he look like in the early days, when he was struggling into being? We will turn him up in the Academy's Dictionary for 1694: "Philosopher: one who devotes himself to research-work in connexion with the various sciences and who seeks from their effects to trace their causes and principles. A name applied to one who lives a quiet and secluded life remote from the stir and troubles of the world. It is occasionally used to denote someone of undisciplined mind who regards himself as above the responsibilities and duties of civil life."

In these days, these various ideas of the Philosopher got mixed up, superimposed one upon another. In the first place the Philosopher was not now the sort of pedant who swore by Plato and Aristotle and no one else; he was not the expert, the specialist, the professor. You could be completely innocent of metaphysics and still be a philosopher. Or, again, he is a man of learning who relies not on his memory, but on his reasoning powers. He may be a student of astronomy and hold forth about the plurality of worlds, explaining, if not why, at all events how, we know that the earth goes round the sun. Or, he is just a wise, sensible man whose wisdom tells him how to live a snug, cosy life, with his friends—including his lady-friends—around him, never aiming at being anything higher than keeper of the ducks in St. James's. He will indulge himself, but within reasonable limits, for he is a prudent voluptuary. Freedom to think what you like—that, of course, was essential. He looked at everything with a perfectly free and unbiased mind, and, as Mme. de Lambert was later to remark, he restored Reason to its pride of place. Where the gentlemen of the Academy went wrong was in saying in their dictionary that the philosopher placed himself above the responsibilities and obligations of civil life. On the contrary, what he wanted was to reform them. No philosophizing without a touch of preaching. Finally, he was to have a glowing heart; but that came later. We must wait half a century longer before we see him with all his fires ablaze.

From the outset, the philosopher is the foe of revealed religions. When you say that in China the Emperor's counsellors and favourites are all philosophers, what you mean is that all of them, like Confucius their master, are sage laymen. If you hear a philosopher discoursing about morals, or about learning, you may be quite sure that his morality has no connection with religion, nor his learning with the things that are God's. Very much the reverse. When you hear that a man has lived and died like a philosopher, you may be equally certain that he has died an unbeliever. The champions of tradition saw all that plainly enough. In 1696, Père Lejay wrote a play for his college theatre, which he called *Damocles sive philosophus regnans*. The gist of it was, "Be foolish enough to put a philosopher in power and he'll turn the world upside down for you in no time".

A philosophy which abandons metaphysics; a philosophy which purposely restricts itself to what can be directly apprehended in the human mind. An idea of nature which hesitates to recognize it as wholly good, but which regards it as powerful, regulated and consonant with reason: whence a natural religion, natural law, natural freedom and natural equality. A morality subdivided into a number of constituent moralities; recourse to social usefulness in order to know which one to choose. The right to happiness, to earthly happiness. A frontal attack on those foes to man's happiness in this world, namely, absolutism, superstition and war. Science, which will ensure the boundless progress of man, and therefore his happiness. Philosophy, the guide of life. Such, it would seem, are the changes which have been taking place before our eyes; such were the ideas and aims which, before the seventeenth century had come to an end, had become conscious of themselves and had combined to form the doctrine of the relative and the human. All is now ready. The stage is set for —Voltaire!

PART FOUR

The Feelings and the Imagination

I

THE MUSES ARE SILENT

THE rationalist movement may be traced, *via* the *Encyclo-pédie*, and the *Essai sur les Moeurs*, *via* the *Declaration of the Rights of Man*, down to our own times.

But Richardson, and Jean Jacques, and the *Sturm und Drang*, where do *they* come from? How are we to account for *them*? Even now there must have been some hidden springs somewhere for such floods of passion to have gushed forth later on. Up to this point we have allowed it to be inferred that the only actors to be seen on the World's Stage were the Rationalists, and, indeed, these were the times when they advanced to the foot-lights, played all the big parts, and were all very self-important, very declamatory. Well; that is true, but it is not true that they were the only ones; there were others, and it now behoves us to take a glance at them. However, we may as well admit at the outset that the task is none too easy. Appearances can be decep-tive, and we must confess that the results of our first line of enquiry were disappointing.

It was in the sphere of poetry that we decided to begin our investigations. Poetry, we thought, would surely prove to be the home of those imaginative and emotional qualities of whose source we were in search. However, it was essentially an age of prose. Where shall we find a prose style more rich, more firm and in every respect more admirable than Swift's? More sinuous than Saint-Evremond's? More subtle than Fontenelle's? More vehement than Bayle's? Bayle, that master of logic and dialectic, who, as Leibniz put it, cared only for incrimination and dis-crimination. Bayle is never cold. He grows indignant, he waxes wroth, and his pages still glow with the fires that first inspired them. When words in current use failed him, he coined new ones. He grips and squeezes his ideas till he has forced them to yield their last drop of meaning. There is none like him, none, and you would instantly recognize anything he had written, even if he had not put his name to it.

Everybody alike, the English no less than the French, made prose their medium for the communication of ideas, and, with them, it became a weapon, challenging and aggressive. Essays, letters, dialogues of the dead and living, imaginative travel-tales— all became the repositories of their moral and religious ideas, of their philosophy.

Poets, however, they were not. To the rich music, the soothing caress that may be born of words, they were wholly insensitive, and all sense of mystery had vanished from their souls. They floodlit the world with the pitiless glare of realism, and they took care that even their most unpremeditated effusions should lack neither clarity of meaning, nor symmetry of form. If poetry is prayer, they never prayed; if it is a reaching out towards the ineffable, they would not hear of the ineffable; if it is to hesitate on the delicate line betwixt music and meaning; they never hesitated; no, not they! They aimed at being just so many proofs and theorems. When they did write verse, it was merely a vehicle for their ideas on geometry.[1]

And so poetry died; or at least seemed to die. Strictly logical and matter-of-fact, machine-made, sapless, it lost sight of its true mission. Versifiers there were in plenty in those days, but, after La Fontaine had gone, no more poets in France. And when the marvellous efflorescence of the classical school burst forth in England, it was the true poets that were the hardest to discover.

Then, the creative spirit met with another balk, and that, paradoxical as it sounds, was the excessive admiration paid to the masterpieces which the preceding age had produced in such profusion. Men like Corneille, Racine, Molière, had too many friends, too many disciples. These great men, it was considered,

---

[1][Limajon de Saint-Didier], *Le Voyage au Parnasse*, 1716, p. 258: "All at once a loud noise was heard. A hundred poets suddenly lifted up their voices to Apollo, beseeching him to give ear to their Odes. O God of might, cried one, I have written an ode about the motion of the globe; I, shouted another, have composed an ode to algebra. . . ."—For England, see Georges Ascoli, *La Grande-Bretagne devant l'opinion française au XVIIe siècle*, 1930, Tome II, p. 119.

had for ever to be imitated, for ever to be copied. They were regarded as having made use of some sort of secret formula, or technical device, and it was held that if this was mastered and put to account, that was all that was needed to produce works of unfading beauty, just like theirs. Those bold intellects whose boast it was that they stood in awe of nothing and nobody, the sworn enemies of prejudice and superstition, turned out, when it came to literature, to be as mild as sheep. They bowed down to the idols, they regarded as sacrosanct the law of the three unities, and the distinction of *genres*. They refused to believe in demons or angels, but they *did* believe in Pindar and Anacreon and Theocritus, interpreted according to their own ideas. They even believed in Aristotle; not, indeed, in the philosopher, but in the author of the *Poetics*, regarding him, in that capacity, as nothing short of a demigod.

For such a one as Racine, Greece was a heart-moving poetic reality, Phèdre would have suffered less grievously had she not been a child of the gods:

> J'ai pour ayeul le Père et le Maître des Dieux.
> Le Ciel, tout l'Univers, est plein de mes ayeux.
> Où me cacher? Fuyons dans la Nuit infernale.
> Mais que dis-je? Mon père y tient l'urne fatale.
> Le Sort, dit-on, l'a mise en ses sévères mains.
> Minos juge aux enfers tous les pâles humains.
> Ah! combien frémira son ombre épouvantée,
> Lorsqu'il verra sa fille à ses yeux présentée,
> Contrainte d'avouer mille forfaits divers
> Et des crimes peut-être inconnus aux Enfers?
> Que diras-tu, mon Père, à ce spectacle horrible?[1]

But this very triumph of hers procured her own undoing, and Greece, thus misconstrued, ere long was Greece no more. Her

[1] My grandsire is the Father and Ruler of the Gods. Heaven, the whole Universe, is thronged with my ancestors. Where can I hide me? Let me flee to the darkness of the underworld. But what am I saying? My father holds there the fatal urn. Fate, they say, placed it in his stern hands. Minos, in the realms below, sits in judgment on every pallid human ghost. Ah, what a thrill of anguish would pass through his horror-stricken shade when he saw his daughter brought before his sight constrained to confess to countless different crimes, crimes perchance unheard of in the World below. What wilt thou say, my Sire, at a sight so terrible?

spontaneity, her bloom, her very life—all these she lost, and came to resemble a burial-ground peopled only with statues. Her great original works of genius had dwindled to mere products of a code of rules, masterpieces manufactured according to plan. Greece was brought up to date. Instead of setting themselves to study the characters of Ajax or Ulysses, they applauded them, thought them fine fellows, because they wore a wig and sported a small-sword.

When, somewhat about 1715, Homer was exalted to the skies and the Ancients thought to be revenged upon the Moderns; when Pope brought out his *Iliad* with a preface that was rendered into French and German, what exactly was it that people saw in the Greek epic? Homer, his happy translator declared, had more invention than any other writer whatever. Invention it is that supplies Art with all her materials, for Art is like a prudent steward that lives on managing the riches of Nature. Homer, thanks to this faculty, was able to devise those fables which Aristotle calls the soul of epic poetry and which may be divided into three classes: the probable; the allegorical, which enable the poet to wrap up the secrets of nature and physical philosophy; the marvellous, which includes whatever is supernatural, and especially the machines of the gods. "Homer seems to have been the first who brought the gods into a system of machinery for poetry, and that is what gives it its greatest importance and dignity." This invention, useful as it is in speeches, descriptions, images, similes, as well as in style and versification, is not without its drawbacks; its marvels come to lack verisimilitude, its metaphors are exaggerated and its repetitions wearisome. . . .

When she read those words, the impetuous Mme. Dacier scarcely knew how to contain herself. What does he say, this English person who has translated Homer, and doesn't understand him in the least? According to him, the *Iliad* is "a wild paradise of beauties without order or symmetry, a place where only seeds are to be found, but nothing that has reached perfection or maturity, a work overladen with much superfluous growth which ought to be cut away, and which stifles or deforms the things which are worth preserving. Even the enemies of Homer never said anything more mischievous or more unjust. So far from the *Iliad* being an untended wilderness, it is the best laid out and most symmetrical garden that ever was. M. Le. Nostre, who led the world in his particular art, never achieved a more consummate regularity in his gardens than did Homer in his poetry."

Those words mark the final stage of the down-slide: Ithaca has become Versailles!

Poetry—how cruelly it was mishandled! No one any longer knew the meaning of the word. No more now did those airs from heaven steal softly over the heart. Poetry was fast coming to be looked on as a branch of rhetoric; which was its worst foe. Instead of searching the depths of the soul, it was content, in a manner quite contrary to its real nature, to look at things from the outside, insisting on arguing, proving and concluding. The imagination was looked on as one of the lower faculties; poetic images, carefully filed and indexed, were so much tinsel frippery. Versification, monotonous and hollow, merely showed how skilfully the craftsman could mould his material. That is what poetry had come to. As Valincourt said in reply to the speech in which M. de Fleury welcomed him to membership of the Academy in 1717, the Muses had forsaken Parnassus, they were divinities no longer, they were but divers manifestations of the expedient Reason had always employed to find a way into the mind of man.

To get a just idea of the distance such aberrations could lead people in those days, we should read again what Fontenelle said about the Eclogue, and Houdar de la Motte about the Ode. The latter was the more logical of the two, for he had the courage of his opinions, and followed fearlessly whithersoever his principles led him: verse he said is a hindrance, an encumbrance; we should keep to prose. Prose is quite able to express anything you can say in verse; it is more precise, more to the point, and it takes less time. You do not have to rack your brains to discover rhymes, or to make your verses scan. Let us take a new line and give the public odes in prose instead of verse. . . . Do not imagine, however, that what he had in mind was anything in the nature of *vers libre*, or the idea that inspiration is entitled to create its form of expression according to its own good pleasure. *Vers libre!* No, he was a long way from that. Harmony, he said, was of no importance; and he gloried in the statement.

If, throughout its history, poetry has always had a deadly foe in rhetoric, there is no denying that rhetoric never scored a greater or more ruthless victory than when Houdar de la Motte composed that ode of his called *La libre éloquence*, on the theme, "Away with rhyme and metre!"

Rhyme, as fantastical as thou art imperious! Metre, thou tyrant! Shall my thoughts always remain your bond-slaves? How much longer will ye withhold from them the empire of the mind, their birthright? At the bidding of scansion and rhythm, accuracy, precision, clarity must needs be sacrificed upon your altars. Or, if I strive to retain them in spite of you, what tortures you inflict on me, in punishment for my resistance! Thou alone, O Eloquence free and independent, thou alone canst set me free from a bondage so inimical to Reason.

This Houdar de la Motte was the man who re-moulded the *Iliad*, cut it down to a dozen cantos, and then composed an ode in which the Bard himself is depicted as congratulating him on his good work; he it was who turned whole scenes from Racine into prose, and rubbed his hands with gleeful satisfaction. His friends and fellow-sympathizers looked forward to the day when everyone would recognize that a clear presentment of the facts was the only thing that mattered, and when these figures of speech, these figments of the imagination, would be abandoned in favour of the plain unvarnished truth; when language would no more be tortured and twisted just to titillate the ear; when poets would become philosophers; and what better use could they be put to![1] "The more perfect the reasoning faculty becomes, the more will judgment take precedence over imagination, and the less, in consequence, will poets be held in honour. The earliest writers, we are told, were poets. That I can well believe; they could not very well have been anything else. But the latest will be philosophers."[2]

But until that day, as yet far-off, arrived, a wary eye must be kept on the useless, persistent and deceitful tribe. Jean Le Clerc defines a poet as one who invents, in whole or in part, whatever he chooses for his theme, who puts his ideas in a way best calculated to cause surprise in the reader, so as to sustain his attention, and who employs a phraseology very unlike the ordinary, not only in the way he arranges his words, but in his choice of the words themselves. "When you begin reading a piece of poetry,

[1] Fontenelle, *Sur la poésie en général, Œuvres diverses*, VIII, 1751.
[2] Abbé Trublet, *Essais sur divers sujets de littérature et de morale*, 1735.

remember you are reading the work of a purveyor of lies, whose aim it is to feed us on chimaeras, or on truths so twisted and distorted that we are hard put to it to disentangle fact from fiction. We must always bear in mind that the resounding phrases he employs are intended to bemuse our judgment, and that his mellifluous cadences are designed so to charm our ears as to attract us to the theme, and give us an exalted notion of the writer. If we remember this, we shall have an antidote to writings of this kind, not that they too may not have their advantages for strong-minded people, however misleading they may be for those whose tendency to be carried away by their feelings is not balanced by a sound judgment."[1] Whence comes this hostility on the part of one of the most representative of the rationalists? It comes from the conviction, firmly implanted, that poetry is just another name for falsehood. And, after all, that was the view held, albeit unconsciously, by the great majority of people in those days. The great thing, they thought, was to produce odes like Pindar's, or like the *Ode on the Fall of Namur*, which was for them a particularly unfortunate model. "It has always been my belief", said Jean Baptiste Rousseau, who was regarded as the foremost lyric poet of his time, "that one of the surest ways of attaining the sublime is to imitate the illustrious writers who have preceded us." So sublimity for him meant a shower of notes of interrogation, or exclamation, and simulated emotional transports. He will start by referring to some wonderful, some unspeakably marvellous thing that has happened. What is this I see before me? What is this I hear? Why are the heavens thus riven asunder? The reason is that some princess or other is about to be married, some prince has been born, or some king has died. Then come some strophes, tricked out with a brave display of mythological trappings, with a simile, a purple patch, a vivid touch of some kind to finish up with. And there you have it, the ode, the finished article; yet not quite perfect, unless its logical structure, its mechanism, is concealed by a studiously calculated artlessness. "This artlessness has its rules, its method; it is indeed an art in itself, and the more this artlessness conceals the framework of the thing the better; just as our conversation flows on more naturally when a sort of intellectual intoxication keeps it from languishing: The fact of the matter is that this so-called artlessness

[1] Jean Le Clerc, *Parrhasiana*, 1699. *Début*.

is really wisdom masquerading as folly, and disencumbered of the geometrical shackles that weigh it down and take the life out of it."[1]

One could, at a pinch, adduce a few extenuating circumstances. In the ledger containing the profit-and-loss account, there are a few items to be put on the credit side, against all the things written off as gone with the wind.

People who talk about *poésie pure*, "absolute" poetry, are simply dreaming: there is no such thing; but only *relative* poetry; relative, that is to say, to each successive age. For poetry to keep alive, it suffices that the age, given over though it be to "abstract reasoning", should yet find a certain charm in what it is pleased to call "a false deceiver"; it suffices that, however inconsistently with its theories, it should refuse to concur with a man who, in the plainest terms, would reduce verse to the level of prose, it suffices that for poetry to be kept alive there should still be left a few practitioners of the art capable of imparting to their work, however feebly, some faint and far-off echo of a loftier harmony. *Poésie pure*, there is not; but there is an everlasting craving for poetry. Pope seemed a poet of genius, and such he was. He satisfied, and more than satisfied, the modest demand of his generation. Therefore it would not be wholly beside the mark to say that, even in this arid age, there was, for those who lived in it, such a thing as poetry. For the Germans, Canitz was a poet; and not only for the Germans, but for the French as well, since, later on, he was included among the models brought to their notice to show them how simple and natural the Germans could be. The Italians offered a whole tribe of poets for Europe to admire; and the extraordinary thing was that, despite all the causes they had to write ill, they wrote some things which lived for more than a day, more than a year, ay, and more than a century, things that still retain a charm for us today. They were fettered by the traditions of Marini and his school, which led them to sing of things like frozen fire, of scorching ice, of cruel kindness, of sweet asperity and the like; still more were they burdened by memories and echoes of the classic past. Whenever they did not think it their duty to copy Anacreon, they did their best to copy Pindar. Nor was that all; there was another encumbrance, and

[1]Apropos de *l'Ode sur la naissance du duc de Bretagne*, 1707.

that was Science, a newcomer, which they took to their bosoms and must needs drag into their poetry at all costs. Overloaded with high-sounding words, trying to display that engaging artlessness which is born of the highest art, their odes, for all that, were laboured and ponderous. But one fine day, aping Pindar though he was, it occurred to Francesco Redi to invite Bacchus to visit the Tuscan hills, there to regale him with, one after another, the famous vintages yielded by their fertile vineyards, and then to portray him staggering, stammering, getting more and more fuddled till at last he was reeling ripe:

> Chi la squallida cergovia
> Alle labbra sue congiugne,
> Presto muore, o rado giugne
> All'età vecchia e barbogia:
> Beva il sidro d'Inghilterra
> Chi vuol gir presto sotterra:
> Chi vuol gir presto alla morte,
> Le bevande usi del Norte . . .

By merely uttering the names of those unholy beverages, Bacchus has spoken blasphemy; needs must his erring lips

> Si purifichi, s'immerga,
> Si sommerga
> Dentro un pecchero indorato,
> Colmo in giro di quel vino
> Del vitigno
> Si benigno
> Che fiammeggia in Sansovino.[1]

That day a poetry, with plenty of "body" in it, rich in savour, original despite its pretence of echoing the dithyrambs of ancient days, was garnered in. And one day, Vincenzo da Filicaja,

[1] *Bacco in Toscana*, 1685.

He who carries to his lips pale and melancholy beer dies soon, or seldom attains to babbling old age. Let him drink the cider of England whoso wants to go quickly underground, whoso wishes for a quick death, let him drink the beverages of the North. . . .

Let him purify himself, let him immerse, nay, submerge himself in a golden cup filled to overflowing with the vine so benign that flames at Sansovino.

lamenting his country's servitude gave utterance to his grief in melodious and moving plaints:

> E t'armi, o Francia? e stringi il ferro ignudo
> Contra a me, che a tuoi colpi armi ho vi vetro,
> Nè a me la gloria de l'antico scetro,
> Nè l'antica grandezza a me fa scudo?[1]

But now, enough of this sort of thing; enough of quaint conceits, of absurdly exaggerated metaphors, of affected figures of speech, complicated, refined upon, twisted and tortured—enough of all this! The Italians would banish the *secentismo*, and all its trappings, from their poetry. They are up in arms against it all. No more, for them, of these poetical high-flights! Give us simplicity, they cried. Nature plain and unadorned. The house is cluttered up with knick-knacks. We must have a thorough turn-out, make a clean sweep of the place. But what am I saying? The house, the house itself is not wanted. No more walls! No more roofs! What real poetry needs is the open-air. At Rome, in 1690, poets and sages met together. It was decided that they should hold their future meetings in the woodlands, under the open sky. They would fain bring back the days of ancient Arcady, when men breathed poetry in the wind's soft sighs, when shepherds wooed celestial airs from their rustic pipes. An alluring idea, but when they tried to put it into effect, it all turned out to be just make-believe and masquerade. These Arcadians draw up a code of rules for themselves; that was their first concern; they called themselves by the names of Greek shepherds; there were whole colonies of them all over Italy. They were more anxious about being "correct" in all the details than Roman Arcady itself. Their rustic groves echoed to verses just as indifferent as those they were so eager to banish. They were, indeed, the very same. They had had them stowed away in albums, and now they brought them forth again, not a whit changed. The enterprise ended in failure. It is the failure that is usually emphasized; yet something might be said about the beauty, the nobility of the enterprise.

[1] *L'Italia alla Francia*, 1700.
You take up arms, O France? You grasp your naked sword—against me who can but oppose your blows with arms of glass? Against me, whom neither the glory of my ancient sceptre, nor my former greatness can protect?

There were some gleanings, too, to be gathered from English fields. Prior may not give you broad frescoes and vivid colouring, nevertheless, in his dainty little sketches, he portrays the picturesque with charm. Not his the swelling tones of great symphonies; yet he sings sweetly and melodiously, and, if the studied graces he got from the Greeks and the Romans sat on him with the ease of a second nature, they did not wholly overlay the original beneath. Anacreon and his beloved Horace lent a polish to his talent; they did not create it. There is an undeniable grace about his numbers as he sings the charms of quiet leisure, the trials of life, our dread of mortality, the flight of time, Chloe in tears because her flowers have withered. Not his the tones of anger, scorn, or gnawing grief; yet, ever and anon, there steals into his song a note of sadness that stirs a deeper echo in our hearts. Matthew is travelling in old England with his friend, John. He comes to an inn which he had known long ago:

> Come here, my sweet landlady, pray how d'ye do?
> Where is Cicely so cleanly, and Prudence, and Sue?
> And where is the widow that dwelt here below?
> And the hostler that sung, about eight years ago?
> And where is your sister, so mild and so dear,
> Whose voice to her maid like a trumpet was clear?[1]

It recalls some old-fashioned English print: the guest seated at table, the landlady:

> By my troth! she replies, you grow younger, I think.
> And pray, Sir, what wine does the gentleman drink?
> Why now let me die, Sir, or live upon trust,
> If I know to which question to answer you first.

The whole thing is natural, homely; then, without any noticeable heightening of the tone, the answer comes, and, with it, the emotion which every mortal feels when he summons up remembrance of bygone days:

> Why, things, since I saw you, most strangely have varied,
> And the hostler is hanged, and the widow is married.
> And Prue left a child to the parish to nurse:

[1]Matthew Prior, *Down Hall, a Ballad*; first published 1723.

And Cicely went off with a gentleman's purse;
And as to my sister, so mild and so dear,
She has lain in the churchyard full many a year.

There are other singers, too, in whom it would not be difficult
to detect a strain of poetry; whether it be poetry that appealed to
people when first they read it, or whether it be, that, time-
mellowed after all these years, it wears for us an old-world and
touching grace.

This notwithstanding, we would still revert to our plea of
extenuating circumstances; renouncing the absolute, and making
the best of the relative, and agreeing with Carducci that there
was never a period less poetical than the first fifty years of the
eighteenth century, and that here was the starting-point of an age
of sterility, and, finally, confessing that, compared with Dante
or Shakespeare, the best of the poets we have mentioned are but
pallid lay-figures, indeed.

Nor can it be denied that in most other departments of literature
a similar change took place. The notion of creative inspiration
was completely lost. Literary composition, it was considered, was
a matter of imitating, of conforming to pattern, that and nothing
more.

At all the crossroads critics were invariably found to police
and regulate the traffic. Their duties were to see that authors
kept to the right road, or to put them on it if they had gone
astray. As Thomas Rymer—who achieved fame for discovering
that Shakespeare knew nothing about tragedy—as Thomas Rymer
remarked, the poets would fall into some pretty bad ways, if they
did not know that the critics were there to keep an eye on
them.

Ah, those critics, what a tribe of them there were! The dead
ones stood firm in their places, Aristotle, Horace, and Longinus,
who had never been so fêted before. The living ones—what a host
of them! Père Bouhours, Père Rapin, Père Le Bossu, learned pundits
who taught you how to bring your mind to bear on intellectual
matters, how speeches should be made, and poetry written, strictly
according to rule, and they told you how to lay out the plan for an
epic. Then came a string of English carpers and cavillers, Gerard
Langbaine, Edward Bysshe, Leonard Welsted, John Dennis and

a number of even smaller fry. In Italy, there was Muratori, and Crescimbeni, and Gravina, all analysing the nature and workmanship of the perfect poem, the perfect tragedy. In Germany, we have Christian Wernicke explaining that the reason why literature had attained such a high degree of perfection in France was that, in Paris, every work, no matter how distinguished its author, was immediately subjected to criticism. What zeal! What stern lawgivers! What scoldings! What wrangles! And those writers, poor browbeaten fellows, so mercilessly rated, don't *they* deserve a tear? As a matter of fact, they accommodated themselves to the times tolerably well; they had a twofold satisfaction to choose from; they could hold up their heads and give their critics as good as they got, or they could hold their peace and quietly do as they were told.

Boileau was growing old. In the preface to the 1701 edition of his works, he summed up his literary creed with a vigour that betrayed no sign of declining strength, and in these words he took his leave: "As the present edition will probably be the last I shall be able to revise, and since in all likelihood—I am now sixty-three and oppressed with many infirmities—I have not much longer to live, my readers will deem it fitting that I should take formal leave of them, thanking them for the generosity they have shown in purchasing so many volumes with such a slender title to their approbation". The public showed no sign of getting tired of him. In that same farewell, Boileau includes an expression of thanks to M. le Comte d'Eryceira, in connection with "his translation into Portuguese verse of my *Art Poétique*, which he was so kind as to send me from Lisbon, together with a letter, and some French verses of his own composition". In what country is the *Art Poétique* not read, discussed and translated? In what country is it not looked upon as a standard work? Boalo, the fellow that dared to talk about Tasso's tawdry tinsel, may get roughly handled; Boileau, that vainglorious Frenchman who never knew anything, or cared about anything, outside his own country, this same Boileau is still the lawgiver of Parnassus, the one authority who stands his ground, when, everywhere else, authority is going by the board.

He was more than a personage now; he was an institution. People went to Auteuil on purpose to get a sight of him, just as they went to the Louvre to look at the Colonnade, just as they went to look at the "chevaux de Marly". Listen now to what a well-known woman of letters, Lady Mary Wortley Montagu, has to say. She is about to join her husband, England's ambassador at Constantinople. Someone puts into her hands a translation of a Turkish poem, and of whom should it make her think? Of Boileau! "In my opinion", she writes, "there is a good deal of beauty in them. The epithet of *stag-ey'd* (though the sound is not very agreeable in English) pleases me extremely: and is I think a very lively image of the fire and indifference in his mistress's eyes. Monsieur Boileau has very justly observed, we are never to judge of the elevation of an expression in an ancient author by the sound it carries with us: which may be extremely fine with them, at the same time, it looks low and uncouth to us."[1]

Boileau had never believed that a writer could do without genius. Not so his successors. They considered method more important than genius; they even went so far as to say that in order to write good verse one thing only is necessary and that is to have a most scrupulous regard for the rules. Boileau had emphasized the importance of the differentiation of *genres*, but to what finicking distinctions, divisions, sub-divisions, and double sub-divisions his precept was to lead! The Classic spirit had a living soul, a living purpose; pseudo-classicism was a mere formula, a recipe. That is the difference between them.

Morals; that was what these poverty-stricken successors of the old classical school determined to take up, apparently by way of consoling themselves. The epic should have a moral purpose; its aim should be moral reform; it should impart religious truths; it is an ethical instrument; you might almost say it was a branch of theology. A good poet is described as one who so blends usefulness with pleasure that he entertains when he instructs and instructs when he entertains. Poetry is a witch, but a kindly one, a fine frenzy that puts folly to flight. The theatre, above all, should be a school. Shame on the playwright who should belittle virtue and dissemble vice. Comedy, in England, had taken on a character of its own. For its plots, it had recourse to French models, chiefly Molière; but by the way they mixed and spiced their ingredients, these playwrights contrived to give their work a flavour all its own. They went in for naughty speeches and risky situations, and their comedies were a combination of the immoral

[1] Letter to A. Pope from Adrianople, April, 1717.

and the scandalous, of gaiety and charm. Such was the material with which a Congreve or a Vanbrugh scored such brilliant successes on the London stage. But lo, one of the cloth, Jeremy Collier, pours forth the vials of his wrath upon them. It was in 1698 that his *Short View of the Immorality and Profaneness of the English Stage* appeared. Morality, sound morals, that is what we want. The theatre, look you, should display the frailty of human greatness, the fickleness of fortune, the grievous consequences of violence and injustice, the folly of pride, and the sinfulness of hypocrisy. But instead of this, what does it do? Honesty is held up to ridicule. On the English stage, blasphemy, impiety, indecency are the order of the day; even the ministers of religion are made objects of derision. The shame of the thing! The scandal of it! The strange thing is that, after the fierce disputes to which Jeremy Collier's outburst gave rise, an alliance between the Puritanic spirit and pseudo-classic morality did in fact succeed in reforming the character of Comedy, which, having shone forth with a last frail and delicate lustre in the plays of Richard Steele, decided, since to live on in the form she loved was denied her, that the best thing was to die. It was about this time that the *commedia dell' arte* came in for some severe reprobation in Italy. What was wanted was a form of comedy that should comply at once with the demands of good sense and good morals. Now, it was not in Florence, not in Rome that a writer—Niccolo Amenta was his name—appeared, who turned his back on sprightliness, wit, buffoonery, extravagances—he also turned it on pleasure and gaiety: no more licentious characters, no more coarse language, no more abandoned love-making, no more immodest serving-wenches, or rapacious lacqueys, no more wild intrigues, but, in their stead, perfect correctitude and impeccable morality.

To possess an official government department whose main office it should be to adjudicate on matters concerned with maintaining the purity of the language, to arbitrate on matters of taste in literature—this was an idea that had occurred to no country except France, an idea she had conceived when her heart was passionately set on discipline and order. But now her neighbours were beginning to grow envious of this *Académie française*, whose labours had, little by little, come to assume a quasi-hieratic character. That society had acquired a prestige which no other society could boast, a distinction which no other society could bestow, and every one of its acts, the awarding of a prize, a reception, an official oration, took on the importance of a public event. The English, the most freedom-loving people in the world, ardently desired to have an Academy of their own. Among its members would be numbered Mr. Prior, England's La Fontaine he might be called; and Mr. Pope, its Boileau, Mr. Congreve, who might be dubbed its Molière.[1] Then there was Mr. Swift, who, impatient though he was of rules in general, was willing enough to bow to an Academy.[2] The project, discussed at great length, eventually fell through. However, in 1700, the Berlin Academy did get founded, and so, later on, in 1713, did the Royal Academy of Spain; while even far-off Russia had an Academy of her own.

The critics, who had been all for making a clean sweep of tradition where politics and religion were concerned, here showed themselves conspicuously conservative. The Ancients, they had said, had stood in the way of progress and enlightenment, but now they invoked them as tutelary deities. In all other matters, free, unfettered, individual judgment had been what they had clamoured for; but here the strict observance of authoritative rule was the only way of salvation. Instead of the freedom to experiment at large, you were confronted with rules and regulations and told to obey them. If you would write a tragedy, the action must last twenty-four hours, you must have a state apartment in a palace, the passion of love, the call of duty and a few stately heroes.

In 1711, the English had the joy of hailing the birth, on their own soil, of another *Ars Poetica*; the work of a lawgiver of Parnassus. Of frail and slender build, highly strung, incredibly sensitive to the sound and scent of every breeze that blew, he was, despite these differences and a few others, a worthy successor of Boileau. His reign promised to be a lengthy one, for when he brought out his *Essay on Criticism*, Alexander Pope was not yet twenty-two. Reading this work, which soon became one of the most famous of its day, we seem to be witnessing the finish of a fight. In the author of the *Essay on Criticism*, two men co-exist

[1]Voltaire, *Lettres philosophiques*, XXIV. Sur Les Académies.
[2]Swift, *A Proposal for Correcting, Improving and ascertaining the English Tongue*, London, 1712.

side by side, but the two do not always see eye to eye. Indeed, they often contradict each other. One displays the dash and impetuosity of a strongly individualistic character, the other stands for law and order; and law and order are certainly going to carry the day. The first of these two personalities gives full rein to his youthful ardour, and expresses a feeling which exists, avowedly or not, in many an author's bosom, the feeling, that is to say, of irritation, of impatience with the critics. Writers, we know, court their praises, but hotly resent their disapproval. Pope handles them very roughly: these people who find fault with my work, who hold me up to judgment and to censure—what right have they to do so? They gave out, one fine day, that they were going to set up as critics; that that was the calling they had chosen. But with what qualification does this choice of theirs endow them? What! Is the first fool that comes along to give himself airs, and presume to lord it over me? Is the first addled poet that comes my way, to lecture me about the quality of my verse? Shall the playwright whose work has been hissed off the stage come and tell me how to write a comedy? Now let them hear a few home truths. For one bad poet there are ten bad critics. Arrogance is no guarantee of worth; before we condemn, we should at least understand the thing we are condemning. A narrow mind, incapable of seeing with the author's eye, only writes, can only write, in vain. What a store of qualifications we have a right to demand of those who would play the Aristarchus. Is their judgment firmly based on experience and honest work? Have they supple minds and the gift of intuition? Are they modest enough not to be jealous? Are they capable of ignoring minor defects in a work and stressing its larger merits? Do they dispense their praises with a free hand, instead of eking them out with the niggard fingers of a miser? Are they impartial? Alas, they are the hirelings of the great, the mouthpieces of political parties, and religious factions.

These outbursts, which betoken a spirit anything but *blasé*, a temperament for which the worst storms are those in an inkpot, are vastly entertaining. But it is still more diverting to observe how the second Mr. Pope lays down the law to the first. The first, however, is a little too easily convinced and the fact of the matter is that he only found fault with the critics because he wanted to see them in a position of greater eminence and dignity.

Pope the disputant, but a disputant ready to listen to reason, sets forth precepts, enunciates dogmas:

> First follow Nature, and your judgment frame
> By her just standard, which is still the same:
> Unerring Nature, still divinely bright,
> One clear, unchang'd, and universal light,
> Life, force, and beauty, must to all impart,
> At once the source, and end, and test of art.

But it must be Nature guided by Reason:

> 'Tis more to guide, than spur the Muse's steed;
> Restrain his fury, than provoke his speed.
> The winged courser, like a gen'rous horse,
> Shows most true mettle when you check his course.

Art is Nature still, but Nature methodized, contentedly obedient to the laws of her own devising. Therefore, let the poets conform to the laws which the Ancients derived from Nature, let them acquaint themselves with those salutary precepts which Greece, enlightened Greece, bequeathed to us:

> Hear how learn'd Greece her useful rules indites,
> When to repress, and when indulge our flights . . .
> When first young Maro in his boundless mind
> A work t'outlast immortal Rome design'd,
> Perhaps he seem'd above the Critic's law,
> And but from Nature's fountains scorn'd to draw:
> But when t'examine ev'ry part he came,
> Nature and Homer were, he found, the same.
> Convinc'd, amaz'd, he checks the bold design,
> And rules as strict his labour'd work confine,
> As if the Stagirite o'erlook'd each line.
> Learn hence for ancient rules a just esteem;
> To copy nature is to copy them.

Let the poets polish their work, and repolish it again, and yet again. A truly natural style is the outcome of art, not of chance:

> True ease in writing comes from art, not chance,
> As those move easiest who have learn'd to dance.

Thus speaks Pope, the lover of the classics, one nourished on the works of those whom he salutes as his illustrious predecessors: Aristotle, Horace, Dionysius of Halicarnassus, Petronius, Quintilian, Longinus, Erasmus who triumphed over Gothic superstition, Vida who brought back Italian supremacy in the days of Pope Leo X, and, finally, Boileau. Then, filled with pride at this gallery of ancestors to whom he has rendered reverential homage, Pope turns to the writers of his own day, and takes it upon himself to give rules and directions, in his turn, to them.

Obviously, it would be no bad thing to have a few works with which to give a practical demonstration of the soundness of his theories. As it turned out, this was an easy matter. Knowing to perfection how to construct an epic, what more could the poets ask:

> Excelling that of Mantua, that of Greece,
> A wond'rous, unexampled Epick Song,
> Where all is just, and beautiful, and strong,
> Worthy of Anna's arms, of Marlbro's Fire,
> Does our best Bard united strength require . . .

Richard Blackmore, who thus exhorted his compatriots, had already set an example. The aim of poetry is to enrich the mind, to regulate morals. Of the various kinds of poetry, the epic is the foremost in dignity, as it is as an instrument of morality. The great characters which it presents for our contemplation teach us religion, virtue, the control of the passions, and wisdom. It is, therefore, to the epic that the poets should direct their efforts. It is true that since the days of Homer and Virgil no one has achieved any success in this department, but this is due not so much to any lack of poets of genius as to ignorance of the necessary rules. To-day, in addition to Aristotle and Horace, we have Rapin, Dacier, Le Bossu and Rymer to guide us. Now we know everything that is necessary to command success. Let us, therefore, make a start.

And a start he makes. He invokes the Muse, and the Muse inspires him with *Prince Arthur*, an heroic poem; with *King Arthur*, an heroic poem; with *Eliza*, an epic; with *The Creation*, a philosophical poem; with *Alfred*, an epic. Of cantos there were dozens and dozens, of lines thousands upon thousands. But Richard Blackmore preached better than he practised. To-day, his epics are quite forgotten.

And now, what about tragedy? A man of first-rate intellect, a lawyer of renown, Gian Vincenzo Gravina, was to lead the way. He made an intensive study of the various treatises on the subject, the various "poetics", and, not content with the French classical school and the works of the Renaissance, he betook himself to the true, the earliest source of all, to Greek tragedy. He gripped it firmly, never to relax his hold. In 1712, at Naples, Gravina published a group of five plays. There is a Prologue, and in it Tragedy, in person, speaks these words: "Behold, I come!" she cries. "After lingering on forgotten for so many centuries, I now appear again at last, and in my pristine form. Guided by a man of law, an orator, a philosopher, escorted by poetic Reason and the rules inspired by her, lighted on my way by the torch of criticism, at last I come." The Muse spoke well; but Gravina's tragedies are none the less detestable.

And now a sort of international tragedy-competition was set on foot for Europe as a whole. The several countries set to work to try and win the palm. Everywhere the gentlemen of the buskin were getting busy. Crébillon sets up as a rival to Racine; but he is entirely given up to niggers and people of colour. Other countries enter the lists with France. Ah, if only they could outdo *her*. At all events they spared themselves neither time nor trouble. The air was thick with tragedies, and still the rivalry went on. An epoch-making day was that—it was the 12th June, 1713—when the Marchese Scipione Maffei put on for the first time at Verona a somewhat fleshless but exceedingly correct *Merope*, more correct, indeed, than the strictest examples of the French classical school. The applause that greeted it! It spread from province to province, throughout the whole of Italy. What a triumph it was; what delighted admiration greeted those swelling phrases, those bombastic tirades, those lines that ran with the regularity of clockwork! The play achieved a world-wide reputation. It was everywhere translated, everywhere mouthed and discussed. It was talked about by Voltaire and by Lessing and at last it got as far as Goethe. The English, too, had come to the conclusion that their ideas about drama needed overhauling. They would have to do away with the preposterous liberties that

Shakespeare and his school indulged in. Tragi-comedy must be kept in its place, and not allowed to intrude into the sphere of tragedy proper. And those battle-scenes, those tumultuous crowds, those processions marching across the stage, those drums and trumpets, those murder-scenes, too ghastly to look upon, at least for anyone with a spark of taste about him. What they aimed at was that marvellously smooth and symmetrical pattern, cunningly made to measure, where horror and pity are administered in scrupulously graduated doses—heroic, but soberly so; sublime, but within reasonable limits. They worked with a will. There is Nathaniel Lee, who produces a *Nero*, a *Sophonisba*, a *Gloriana*, *The Rival Queens*, a *Mithridates*, an *Oedipus*, a *Theodosius*, a *Lucius Junius Brutus*, not to mention some others; plays in which his genius, though little conspicuous for order and clarity, studiously avoided having two actions going on at one and the same time. No irrelevant episodes for him; unity of time must be scrupulously observed, so must dignity; his characters must speak in accents of the loftiest grandiloquence. And it must be confessed that, now and again, he all but achieved his aim. Otway's *Venice Preserved*, a striking success, had already shown the world that English drama could be both moving and correct. But it was the year 1713 that brought the crowning victory, the year that witnessed the birth of Addison's *Cato*, a play judged worthy of being translated straightway into French. London, which already had a second Boileau, now boasted a second Racine. Thus did the noble Cato set forth upon his progress through all the lands of Europe. It was the fruit of well-nigh half a century of effort. It took the English all that time to subdue the uncouth element in their genius and to bring forth the perfect specimen of literary law and order.

The Germans still lagged behind. But patience! They would come along in their own good time. It pained Gottsched to see the German stage in such a state of chaos. He sets to work, masters Aristotle's *Poetics*, studies the commentators thereon, and the classical drama, the French poets, not forgetting their prefaces. It opened his eyes to discover that dramatic art is governed by laws so firmly based on reason, laws so absolute, so urgently compelling, that clearly Germany would never emerge from barbarism so long as she refused to observe them. So Gottsched set to work to master the secrets of the art, and, at last, in 1732, came out triumphantly with his *Dying Cato*. He might almost have been satisfied with just translating Addison's *Cato* into German. But somehow even that play fell short of perfect regularity, it still needed lopping and pruning. There were still some irrelevant episodes, some redundant ornaments that marred the architecture of the whole. But, the gods and his own craftmanship be praised! all the scenes of the German *Cato* take place in one room in the castle at Utica, and the action "extends from somewhere about noon until close on sunset".

It is a strange thing that even such a man as Voltaire, when he came to write a tragedy or an ode, adopted a manner completely foreign to his genius, though neither he nor his contemporaries suspected it. His idea was to imitate Corneille, and Racine, and Boileau, and do what they had done over again. Before the coming of the neo-classical period, which took longer to develop than did any other school of modern times, before all that, it is a melancholy sight that is offered to our contemplation, all this rubble-heap of fables without the bloom on them, tragedies without truth and verses without poetry; a dead-weight of lifeless lumber. Such was the price of the benefits which the classical spirit conferred upon the world. Because the writers of the French classical school attained a degree of lofty perfection which so dazzled their obscurer descendants as to make them think there was nothing to be done save copy them; because second-rate writers, taking the line of least resistance, preferred to do over again what their predecessors had succeeded in doing before them; because the mathematical spirit involved the suppression of all non-rigid forms, of all living hues; because the tyrant Reason would not tolerate flowers that were content to be just flowers and nothing more, the power of song withered away and the springs of Helicon ran dry.

II

PICTURES, STRANGE OR BEAUTIFUL

SINCE these fields of artificial flowers have no charm for us, let us seek elsewhere. . . .

Mr. Spectator, holding forth to his readers on the need for wisdom and moderation, interrupts his moralizing to extol the delights of the imagination, affirming that the pleasures we derive from the faculty of sight are in no way inferior to those we owe to the mind; he even permits himself to belaud the noble exuberances of Shakespeare: *Juvat integros accedere fontes*. The Italian theorizers insisted on obedience to rule, yet, contrary to rule, they admitted that a creative fancy of some kind had its rights and its merits. Thus it was that they came to enjoy the flattering, the rather too flattering, reputation of being the forerunners of the Romantics. These alluring contradictions! Look at the French; they would be submitting everything to rule and compass, if only the Fairies didn't come and play the dickens with their geometrical designs. The end of the century was marked by gloom and austerity, conscious as it was of a great falling-off. In the wake of the majestic creations of the masters, came the works of the critics, but now, all of a sudden, what is this that the latest twist of fashion demands? What books are these that are making so brave a show in the booksellers' windows? Fairy tales!

The contemporaries of the now rapidly ageing Louis XIV, and of the devout and sober-minded Mme. de Maintenon beguile themselves with the stories that Old Mother Goose used to tell the little ones. Admittedly, Descartes was not discarded holus-bolus. When a golden pumpkin was turned into a coach, the coach was a golden one; when lizards were turned into footmen, the footmen were attired in gaudy liveries, whiskered rats were metamorphosed into mustachioed coachmen, and in this way the logical connexions, so dear to our race, were, in a measure, preserved. But what a mass of improbabilities, too, there were! Gorgeous palaces spring up out of nothing, all built of gold and rubies; the gate is studded with carbuncles, and, to gain admittance, you pull at a deer's foot attached to a chain made wholly of diamonds. Animals talk; the roe that grazes in the wood, the female cat that lives in its lair, are really women that have been bewitched. Every Blue Bird is a Prince Charming. Marvels, marvels everywhere, everywhere flowers, jewels, all the adornments of fairyland. A strip of linen four hundred ells in length is contained in a single millet seed, and when unwound goes through the eye of a needle. All living things, on earth, in the sea and in the air are depicted on it, together with the sun and the stars. You may ride on wooden steeds that race like the wind, and jump more nimbly than the horses in a riding-school; you may drive in a cabriolet drawn by a fat sheep that always knows the road, or in a little sleigh smartly painted and gilded and drawn by a pair of stags prodigiously fleet of foot; or in a flying chaise drawn by winged frogs; in chariots of fire which dragons sweep athwart the sky. The world has no longer any recognizable laws; the powers of fairyland bemock them as they will. No more do solid things have weight; dreams come true; virtue is rewarded, vice punished. When at last you lay aside these tales of wonder, how grey and bleak the world appears, and life how great a burden!

It was the women who were the first to revive these tales that come down to us from the distant past, so distant as to be beyond all human ken; stirrings, promptings of the primeval spirit that saw in all things, in the whispering of the wind, in the darkness of the night, in blossoming time, in winter, only the works of the fairies—women, more instinctive, more alive to the past than men; women, the guardians of the imagination. And then Charles Perrault arrived upon the scene; and behold, this ex-superintendent of the royal palaces, taking a few butterflies' wings, a few threads of gossamer, a few beams of moonlight, wove for us his tales of fairyland, masterpieces fragile but immortal. Beauty lay sleeping in the wood; all things, even dreams, were stayed in their course; goblins played their pranks no more, and fairies ceased their frolics. Over Versailles, over the Court, over the city, brooded the sadness that comes of a task that is done, of a tale that is told. Then, on a sudden, the enchanter waves his wand, and lo! everything awakes. The kitchen-knaves begin to stir their stumps, the lacqueys dance a jig, the horses neigh, the birds of the forest call to one another from their branches, the Princess opens her eyes and smiles, and tells the Prince he has been long away, that she has long awaited his arrival.

The actual travellers did not bring back with them all the things we expect from them to-day; those subjective developments were to come later, and gradually. They did not project their *ego* into the far off beyond, if haply they might learn what would befall it there, or feel their spirit mysteriously stirred at the breath of winds from the unknown. Yet, have we said all that is to be said about them when we have spoken merely of their intellectual impressions? Were they just intellect, and nothing more? Were not their eyes beginning to take in something of the picturesque wonders of the world? Did not these travellers unfold to an age that was steeped in intellectualism, pictures and scenes that laid a magic spell upon it?

Even as fresh islands strangely uprising from some familiar sea, so, in this old Europe, did lands of marvel begin to heave in sight. Such a land was Lapland, which, little by little, was beginning to emerge from its Cimmerian darkness. Queer folk, as François Bernier the explorer noted, "those Laplanders, squat, dumpy, with fat legs, broad shoulders, bull-necks, faces like fiddles, ugly as sin, somewhat resembling bears, and disgustingly addicted to fish-oil". And a strange country too, where, in summer, the sun never sets, and, in winter, never rises; where reindeer take the place of horses, where men slide along on the snow on wooden lathes buckled to their feet; where wizards go off into a trance at a mere word. So strange is it all, that the travellers seemed "to be bringing back accounts of another planet rather than of somewhere on this old continent of ours".

Of barbarous lands, there came a constant stream of amazing narratives; thrilling adventures by sea, travellers made captive, escapes and rescues, lovers sundered and reunited, tales of martyrs and renegades; glimpses of pashas and janissaries, of beautiful women bathed in tears, unwilling inmates of the *seraglio*; of infidels moved to compassion by their weeping, of prison-warders, and galley-slaves bending over their oars, of missionaries striving heroically to collect enormous ransoms in Spanish doubloons or French *écus*. Repeated over and over again, constantly embellished, such stories never lost their popularity. There was the theatre—comedies with elaborate plots, tales where the course of true love was anything but smooth, fiction which was strange enough, and truth which was still stranger.

From Jerusalem, from the Holy Sepulchre, there arose, at least once, a cry of melodious lamentation. O Jerusalem! O hapless city! O city of tombs! The skeletons, the bones, scattered and broken, which are to be seen in the cemeteries, fill one with sombre reflections, and the poet breathes them forth in verses he entitles *Contemplation*:

> Is this, alas! our boasted mortal State?
> Is it for this, we covet to be great?
> What Happiness from envied Grandeur springs,
> When these poor Reliques once were mighty kings?
> O frail uncertainty of human Power,
> While Graves can Majesty itself devour!

Who is he that voices this lament? Not Young in his *Night Thoughts*, not Hervey in his *Meditations among the Tombs*; no, it is Aaron Hill the romantic, Aaron Hill the traveller in the Holy Land.

If Louis XIV read the letters which Père de Prémare sent home from Canton to Père de La Chaise, he must have realized that there were stranger beings in the world than ever a Dutch painter committed to canvas. Canton! What an amazing place! Whole tribes of mortals swarming in the narrow streets. Porters going about with nothing on their feet, wearing extraordinary-looking straw headgear proof alike against sun and rain. No wheeled carriages; only chairs. Père Prémare goes about in a huge one, lavishly gilded, borne on the shoulders of six or eight men. Then the military processions. The Tsong-Tou, that is to say the Governor of two provinces, never goes abroad without an escort at least a hundred strong. "I imagine that what I have told you will conjure up a city very different from anything Paris has to show.

Take the houses for example. Imagine whole streets without a
single window, all shops, poor ones too for the most part, often
with nothing but a bamboo hurdle to do duty for a door."[1] And
the pagodas, served by *bonzes*, as the Buddhist priests are called;
the street gates closed at evening; on the river, a floating city,
each boat housing a complete family; paddy fields stretching far
and wide in the country round about.

From the West Indies come accounts of the most daring
adventurers that ever were on sea or land. With their headquarters
on the island of Tortuga close to San Domingo, these despera-
does, drawn from every race and country, had a code of honour
peculiar to themselves and a very different one from that of
other folk. These men were the buccaneers or filibusters. They
hunted the buffalo for its hide, and the boar for its flesh. Armed
with long sporting guns manufactured expressly for them at
Dieppe and Nantes, with their dogs at their heels, attended by
serving men whom they take on for three years and then put on
the strength if they prove satisfactory, they went forth in pursuit
of their prey. When a beast was brought down, the leader of the
party took out the four big bones, broke them and sucked out
the marrow while it was warm. That was his breakfast. They
were splendid shots, and one of their ways of passing the time
was to shoot at oranges and sever the stem without touching the
fruit. Some of them were such doughty fellows that they would
race along after the bulls, catch them up, and slit their hamstrings
in full career. Rude, violent, intractable, fierce, always ready to
spill blood, they were as brave as lions and strangely loyal to the
bonds of friendship. The filibusters were the huntsmen of the
sea. Speeding along on the ocean billows, they would swoop
down on some large vessel, usually a Spaniard, as she was sailing
on laden with gold from the Indies. Scrambling aboard, they put
the crew to the sword, and took possession of the ship. From
fight after fight, prize upon prize, they piled up the spoils till,
putting one day into some port or other, they squandered the
whole lot like madmen, as witness those specimens who, having
taken some magnificent prizes, at last reached Bordeaux, where
they paraded the place in sedan-chairs, preceded by men bearing

[1]Letter from le P. de Prémare to R. P. de la Chaise, confesseur du Roi,
Canton, 17 February, 1699. (*Lettres édifiantes et curieuses écrites des missions
étrangères*, tome I, 1703.)

lighted torches, in broad daylight. The courage and ferocity of the filibusters became legendary. They used to call themselves by fanciful names, such as "Alexander Strong i'th'arm, so called from the power behind his fist"; a man who made his name as famous among gentlemen of fortune as did Alexander of old among the conquerors of nations. Then there was "Peter the Great" who hailed from Dieppe; Roc, commonly called the Brazilian, from Groningen; Morgan, the Welshman; Captain Montauban, who, for upwards of twenty years, harried the coasts of New Spain, Carthagena, Mexico, Florida, New York, the Canaries and Cape Verde. L'Olonois, a native of Poitou, with a crew of one and twenty, came one day and hove-to off Cuba. He fought and captured the vessel which had been ordered to pursue him, and was told that the Spanish governor had had a hangman put aboard with orders to string up the pirate crew. "L'Olonois, when he heard the words 'hang' and 'hangman' flew into a mighty rage. He ordered the hatches to be opened, and commanded the Spaniards to come up one at a time. Every time a head appeared above deck he struck it off with his sabre. This butchery he carried out alone, and to the very last man." L'Olonois seized Macaraibo and Gibraltar in the province of Venezuela. When all the loot was collected together, it was found that, what with the jewels, and the various coins, calculated at ten crowns the pound, they had got the equivalent of about two hundred and sixty thousand crowns all told; apart from the rest of the plunder, which was worth at least a hundred thousand more. This is leaving out of the account all the damage they had wrought. This must have amounted to a good million, seeing the churches that had been despoiled, the furniture that had been destroyed and the ships that had been set on fire. One vessel, laden with tobacco, they towed away with them. It must have been worth at least a thousand livres. L'Olonois was less fortunate in his end. He had the ill-luck to fall into the hands of some savages belonging to the tribe which the Spaniards call Indian Braves. They cut him up into quarters, roasted, and then devoured him.[1]

It was from the East that the most wonderful stories came, "for we all know that where tales of the marvellous are concerned

[1] A. O. Oexmelin, *De Americaensche Zee-Rovers*, Amsterdam, 1678. French translation, 1686.

the Oriental races surpass all others." During the period 1704 to 1711, Antoine Galland brought out his translation of the Arabian Nights. When Scheherazade began to recount her stories of the night, to unfold the infinite wealth of an imagination enriched with all the dreams of Araby, of Syria and the great Levant; when she began to tell of the manners and customs of the peoples of the East, their religious ceremonies, their domestic habits, the details of their dazzling and colourful existence; when she showed how mankind could be held and enthralled, not by abstruse intellectual ideas, not by recondite reasoning, but by the charm of colours and the lure of fairy tales, all Europe was fain to stop and listen. Then did the fairies Carabosse and Aurora make way for the throng of Sultanas, Viziers, Dervishes, Greek doctors, negro slaves. Light, fairylike edifices, fountains, pools guarded by lions of massy gold, spacious chambers hung with silks and tapestries from Mecca—all these replaced the palaces where the Beast had waited for Beauty to open her loving eyes. All this merely meant that a new fashion was ousting an older one, but amid the ebb and flow, the ceaseless change, there was one thing that did not change, one thing that remained constant, and that was the inexhaustible craving of the human heart for dreams and tales.

And pictures, too! Travellers embellished their narratives with drawings of their own, Chinese pagodas, African serpents, Siamese priests, the wondrous plants that grow in the gardens of Malabar. Père Bouvet had a number of plates drawn in order that the French, who were amazed at the sight, might see how the Mandarins attired themselves. M. de Fériol, French ambassador at the court of the Grand Turk, ordered a hundred prints to be executed to give the Parisians an idea of the rich costumes worn by the people of the Levant. There were some who entertained the reader with stories and incidents by means of actual pictures of these different exotic types; we see a savage setting fire to the couch on which his mistress is lying; explorers groping their way into one of the Egyptian pyramids, their torches flinging weird lights and shadows over the tombs that have lain there for thousands of years. Often enough they have great charm, these pictures of far-off, unfamiliar lands. It seemed as though their novelty were giving back to artists something of the spontaneity they had lost through their prolonged subservience to antique models. Sometimes a traveller, realizing that pictures speak louder than words, turns artist himself. Cornelius Van Bruyn confronts his models with the high seriousness of one performing a sacred office. His mission is to convey the truth.

But books were not everything. Visitors from divers lands, from the West Indies, from Bangkok, from Peking came and thronged the familiar places in their unfamiliar garb. The Flemish weavers became more and more eager to introduce into their tapestries scenes and subjects from the utmost ends of the earth. Chinamen, who had already played a part in Opera, and in the booths of country fairs, were now delineated on walls and screens. China-ware and lacquer-work come crowding hither no less speedily than the tenets of Confucius.

Spinoza, Malebranche, Leibniz, ah, yes; important names, those; but do not overlook Alexander Strong-i'th'arm, and Scheherazade. There were the great metaphysical systems based on philosophy, on reason; but there was also the imagination to reckon with, the fancy flitting from fairy tale to fairy tale; the eye that takes on a far-off look as it calmly surveys the picture of a rhinoceros or a sea-calf. Many were the efforts to probe the mysteries that lay hid beneath the surface of life, but many were the pretty toys and glittering gewgaws that sparkled on its surface.

The roysterers, the rakes, the toss-pots and rapscallions, precious little they trouble their heads about Spinoza and his philosophy; about as much as a fish might fancy a fig. The only pre-established harmony that interests these merry fellows is the harmony between their gullets and a bottle of good, sound wine. On they go, never caring whence they come, or whither they are going. Why trouble? To be alive is the main thing; a live dog is better than a dead sage, any day. The concrete, the tangible, that's their bit of country, and with carefree hearts they go roaming about it far and wide, whistling, singing, making merry, and trading on the simplicity and innocence of any nincompoops they chance to meet on their way. As for death, and what comes after it, why worry?

There must be something inherently attractive about your rogue, your vagabond, your scallywag—there must be something with an irresistibly human appeal about him, or else he must be a prodigiously entertaining fellow, thus, under various guises, to go on giving pleasure to generation after generation of human-kind. Immortal *picaro*! The sons and grandsons of Guzman d'Alfarache and of Lazarillo de Tormes still roam the world, arm-in-arm with the descendants of Panurge, and Meriton Latroon their English cousin. But this indefatigable band of brothers was not without some fresh recruits. In London, Ned Ward, the innkeeper, quits his tavern, not, however, before he has sat down to table with a few sound cronies and discussed with them a brace of roast geese, a couple of calves' heads and an enormous hunk of Cheddar; the whole washed down with liberal draughts of ale, and port to finish up with. Leaving his tavern, and running into Locke, maybe, or Samuel Clarke, or Boyle, or Newton, on his way, he sauntered down one street after another, putting his head into taverns, houses, churches, banks, museums, wherever, in short, you might expect to come up against amusing specimens of that queer species that goes by the name of Man. These he tells us about with immense gusto, a vivid pen, and a vocabulary of rich savour. With unflagging vivacity, bubbling over with humour and irony, he makes every page of his *London Spy* a bit of real life. Reality and laughter, of such was the miracle he accomplished, and continued to accomplish, day after day. Not far from him, Tom Brown, a bohemian of bohemians, a satirist if ever there was one, always ready and willing to sell his pen for money, always prompt to squander the money he made by his pen, was another who observed and noted the follies of the great city. How say you? What is life but a pastime, a way of amusing ourselves? One man finds amusement in ambition, another in money-making, another in that altogether preposterous thing they call love. Little things amuse little minds. Great ones find amusement in trying to cover themselves with glory. As for myself, I find entertainment in the reflection that the whole business is just a way of passing the time, just another game.

Thus spoke our moralist in reverse, who, having drunk deep, made love, borrowed money, and slept in prison cells beyond all reasonable limits, died when he was but one and forty. Meanwhile, in Paris and Madrid, the Diable Boiteux was entertaining himself in like manner. Instead, however, of going in at the front door when he went a visiting, he preferred to lift up the roof. No matter; he discovered, just the same, anti-metaphysicians, anti-heroes, people steeped in materialism and thinking none the worse of themselves for that, that is if they ever thought at all. They were content just to exist. "The pother, the peregrinations, the pains poor mortals take to fill up as agreeably as may be the brief interval betwixt the cradle and the grave."[1] That was about the sum of their aspirations, just that and nothing more. About higher things, about the Beyond, not a word, it would seem not a qualm, not a spark of curiosity. Reality, here, spells ugliness, unloveliness of soul, unloveliness of body. Rub the surface a little and that is what you always find, and that is all you find. "I see in the house next door a couple of rather amusing pictures: one is an elderly coquette who is just getting into bed, having deposited her hair, her eyebrows and her teeth on the dressing table. The other is a sexagenarian *beau*, just back from a love affair. He has already removed his glass eye, his moustache and the wig that covered his bald pate. He is waiting for his man to come and take off his wooden arm and leg, so that what is left of him may get into bed." Is beauty non-existent, then? Can we not hope to find it anywhere? "If I can trust my own eyesight", says Zambullo, "I perceive, in this house here, a regular picture of a girl." "Oh, you do, do you?" replies the cripple. "Well, the young beauty you fancy so is the elder sister of this dashing gentleman who is just about to get into bed. You might well say that she and the old battleaxe she lodges with are a proper pair. Her waist, which you so much admire, is the latest thing in mechanical devices. Her bust and her hips are artificial. Nevertheless, she puts on the airs of a bread-and-butter miss. And look! There, I see, are two young gallants competing for her favours. They have come to fisticuffs about her. They are pounding into each other like mad. They look to me for all the world like a couple of dogs fighting over a bone." You won't find ideas in the *Diable Boiteux*, but rather the workings of a grotesque or sombre imagination. Lesage achieved perfection in this particular line with his *Gil Blas*, the first part of which appeared in 1715; the hero is more subtle, more mercurial, more complex; the observation is more penetrating, more comprehensive; the *tempo* is easy and natural. But we are still worlds away from the Tragedy of Ideas.

Finally, bringing up the rear, trying to look unconcerned, as

[1] Alain René Lesage, *Le Diable Boiteux*, 1707.

if they didn't belong to the main body, here come some gentlemen of rather imposing mien who, however, have this defect about them; they never tackle the moral question, or, if they do, tackle it as an afterthought. We might very well say of these gentlemen what the Amiens innkeeper said of Manon Lescaut and Des Grieux, that they are charming, but a wee bit on the shady side. They are all for a life of adventure, a roving life, for dicing, for making love. They like to score off people, to pull off a bit of sharp practice, to sail as near the wind as possible, to whip out their swords and hit freely, sometimes getting hit back themselves, but never mortally. Their wounds attended to, they are duly put to bed, only to be up again a week or so later and carrying on as lawlessly as ever. Merely to hear about their doings is enough to make any decent citizen's head turn. They could all appropriately bear the name which Gatien de Courtilz, who let loose so many rogues disguised as aristocrats on the world, bestowed on one of his heroes, they could all be dubbed le Chevalier Hasard, Sir Chance-my-Luck. How they went the pace! The Chevalier Hasard never knew either father or mother; he was found in his swaddling-clouts on the steps of a church and was brought up by the parish. He quitted his foster-parents in order to go and try his luck in the world. Some well-to-do lady apprenticed him to a goldsmith, whom he shortly abandons and enlists in the army, joining Mylord S. T.'s regiment of marines. The vessel on which he embarks is shipwrecked. By a miracle he manages to reach the shore with another member of the crew with whom he sails for Boston. His friend is killed in a gambling brawl. He avenges his death and gets into hot water with his mistress. He is accused of getting a girl into trouble. On the point of marrying another one, he is attacked in the street, and wounded with a pistol shot. The wound grows dangerous. Meanwhile there are troubles about his marriage. The girl he has wronged wants him to marry her. Her brother vows he will kill him. He is again attacked and wounded four times. On his recovery, his mistress gets smallpox and dies. . . .[1] With all these things on his hands and living at the pace he does, how should such a restless soul find time to think?

The most engaging of these illustrious adventurers is not the

---

[1] *Mémoires du chevalier Hasard*, translated from the English of the original manuscript. Cologne, Pierre le Sincère, 1703. *Argument.*

Marquis de Montbrun; nor that ill-starred prince, the Chevalier de Rohan; nor even M. d'Artagnan, who was completely unaware of the brilliant career that was awaiting him after he had been wrapt in slumber for a hundred and fifty years. No; it was the Comte de Grammont, whose life story Anthony Hamilton diverted himself by giving to the world.[1] Who is unacquainted with the brilliant piece of portraiture with which an Englishman enriched the literature of France? Who has not followed the Comte de Grammont through his 'prentice years, through his Piedmontese campaigns, in exile at the English court of which he was so scandalous an adornment? Who has not delighted in those entertaining pen-portraits, as that of Matta, his gossip, of Mlle. de Saint-Germain, or the Marquise de Sénantes? Who has not admired his free and flowing narrative, his eye for the picturesque, his full-blooded, and incisive, pregnant style, his vigour, his sense of humour? Hamilton himself shall tell us of his concern, not with morals, but with character; not with good or evil but with the contrast between the two. His aim is to portray life, not to philosophize about it. "It is my part", he says, "to describe a man, whose inimitable character casts a veil over those faults which I shall neither palliate nor disguise; a man distinguished by a mixture of virtues and vices so closely linked together as in appearance to form a necessary dependence, glowing with the greatest beauty when united, shining with the brightest lustre when opposed. It is indefinable brilliancy which, in war, in love, in gaming and in the various stages of a long life, has rendered the Comte de Grammont the admiration of his age." Vital force: it is that whereof Grammont is the living symbol, and that it is which Hamilton has portrayed.

It would argue some degree of *naïveté* to betray astonishment at the multi-coloured swarms of humanity portrayed in literature. But by fixing our gaze too exclusively on the loftier peaks, we had almost forgotten them.

[1]*Mémoires de la vie du Comte de Grammont*, Cologne, Pierre Marteau, 1713.

III

LAUGHTER AND TEARS:
OPERA TRIUMPHANT

Je chante les combats, et ce prélat terrible
Qui, par ses longs travaux et sa force invincible,
Dans une illustre église exerçant son grand coeur,
Fit placer à la fin un lutrin dans le choeur.[1]

INSTEAD of parodying the *Aeneid*, how about taking some
quite trivial theme and treating it in the "Grand Manner"?
Say, the quarrels and squabbles of a treasurer of the Sainte
Chapelle and some member of the choir with whom he was at
loggerheads, and, with this as the subject, to burlesque the various
stock ingredients and embellishments of the great poetic masterpieces, the descriptions, the battles, the tumults, the prophecies,
the dreams, and so forth; is this the right recipe for provoking
laughter?

Be that as it may, *le Lutrin* (the Lectern) did make us laugh when
we were schoolboys, and had nothing much else to feed upon. It
made all Europe laugh, when Europe was two hundred years
younger than it is today. But that was a Europe that had not lost
its enthusiasms; a classical Europe, a gentleman's Europe. We
may say that it appealed to the flower of Europe as a whole, since
there was hardly a country in which this amusing skit of M.
Boileau's, that prince of satirists, was not admired, translated and
copied. Samuel Garth, one of London's leading physicians,
established a reputation as a poet merely by borrowing the theme,

---

[1]Of battles and that prelate terrible I sing
Who after many toils by power invincible
Wielding his mighty force in a most famous church
At last a lectern in the choir caused to be placed.

turning the Lectern into a Dispensary, canons into doctors, and choristers into apothecaries, complete with syringes, pestles and mortars.

> Muse, raconte-moi les débats salutaires
> Des médecins de Londre et des apothicaires
> Contre le genre humain si longtemps réunis:
> Quel Dieu, pour nous sauver, les rendit ennemis?
> Comment laissèrent-ils respirer leurs malades,
> Pour frapper à grands coups sur leurs chers camarades?
> Comment changèrent-ils leur coiffure en armet,
> La seringue en canon, la pilule en boulet?
> Ils connurent la gloire: acharnés l'un sur l'autre,
> Ils prodiguaient leur vie et nous laissaient la nôtre . . .[1]

So, take a line or two from Milton, and then flop suddenly into the ludicrous:

> Sing, Heavenly Muse,
> Things unattempted yet in Prose or Rhyme,
> A shilling . . .[2]

Having thus set the tone, chant, in pseudo-heroic verse, the blissful state of the man who owns a shilling, a splendid new shilling, gleaming, glittering. He fears no more the pallid face of poverty; he can go into a tavern, call for a pot of foaming ale and oysters of the very best; never allowing melancholy to show its ugly shape; chasing it away, when it looks as if it had come to stay, with a facetious turn of the tongue—is this the comic spirit? It looked as if it was, for the *Tatler* declared that the finest English parody in verse was *The Splendid Shilling*, by John Philips.

Then there is Pope, who sits down at his writing-desk and with consummate skill composes his *Rape of the Lock*. He prides himself on striking out quite a new line, even as Boileau prided himself on producing a work which had no counterpart in

---

[1]Sing, O muse, the salutary quarrels of the London doctors and apothecaries, long since united together against the human race. What God, for our salvation, made them enemies; how came they to let their patients go on breathing while they left them to go and fight with their dear comrades? How came they to exchange their head-gear for an iron helm, syringes for guns and pills for bullets? Glory was theirs. Fiercely they fought each other, losing their lives and leaving us our own. Voltaire, in reference to *The Dispensary*, by Samuel Garth, 1699.

[2]J. Philips, *The Splendid Shilling*, 1701 and 1705.

French. No heroi-comic work is complete without its "machines", that being the term invented by the *cognoscenti* for the gods and goddesses who superintend the action. The supernatural is all a matter of machinery. This being so, it occurred to him to re-place the angels and demons, who were a little tired of being so long in harness, with sylphs, gnomes and salamanders. These were all borrowed from the occultists, for there was not the least need to be shy of borrowing; the difficulty was to find someone new to borrow from. Then he bethought him of a new device; supposing he brought in things not generally regarded as suitable for poetic treatment, like a game of cards, shall we say? What a feather in his cap! To subdue recalcitrant material to his purpose—therein lies the artist's crowning triumph. A noble lord very much in love snips off a tress from a fair lady's head. The lady is sore indignant. Whereupon there is a terrific com-motion among the men and among the goblins. The flimsy web of an ancient poem, a few flowerets cunningly embroidered on it, a *quantum sufficit* of verbal wit, and the interplay of dazzling colours—is this comedy? Is this the genuine article?

More sonorous, if nothing more, was the laughter of Italy. In that Tuscan countryside, the Muse was more at her ease, more light-hearted. She did not stand on ceremony:

> Non è figlia del Sol la Musa mia,
> Nè ha cetra d'oro o d'ebano contesta
> E rozza villanella, e si trastulla
> Cantando in aria . . .[1]

This is not to say that she, too, was not bent on caricaturing the heroic tales of bygone days; but she did it with a care-free, happy-go-lucky sort of air. If she found herself in a quandary, like those ants that came upon plaster or flour—they knew not which—in their path, she thought it a joke, and treated it as such:

> Ma canta per istar allegramente,
> E acciò che si rallegri ancor chi l'ode;
> Nè sa, nè bada a regole niente . . .[2]

[1] This Muse of mine is no daughter of the Sun; no lyre of gold adorned with ebony is hers. She is but a rude country wench and likes to go about flinging up her songs into the air.
[2] She sings only but to put herself in joyous trim and to gladden those who hear her song; she knows no rules and cares nought for them.

No qualms about her; no die-away vapourings; no swelling phrases about shining honour; no more chivalry. Instead of doughty knights, she gives us country bumpkins, lewd fellows, toss-pots—

> E Rinaldo ed Orlando in compagnia
> S'ubbriacano ben bene all'osteria . . .[1]

This Muse, so sportive, and at times so coarse, mocked at all such old-fashioned paraphernalia as magic, enchantment, knightly cavalcades, pursuits, ambushes, duels, haunted inns, prisons, heroic deaths. She took one tale after another, mocking, burlesque-ing, never heeding where she was going, with no definite end in view, but trying all the time to show how easy it is to laugh and to make the world laugh with you, and be hanged to prigs and pedants!

The Italian actors of the *Commedia dell'arte* were expelled from Paris in 1697; they were too daring, too brilliant, too gay. Their theatre was closed down. However, Regnard was there still, and everybody liked Regnard. Paris folk were not a dismal set, and they were quite content with the most threadbare plots, the same old tales—impersonations, recognitions, "surprises" you could see coming a mile off, old stock-characters trotted out again, usurers fleecing wealthy heirs, widows cheated of their money, domineer-ing matriarchs, love-lorn damsels, youthful rakes; and a whole crowd of lacqueys and serving-wenches to help carry on the game. Now, by some miracle, or, it may be, by reason of his exuberant vitality, his dexterity, his unfailing dash, his instinct for dramatic situations and effective dialogue, his irrepressible good humour, Regnard contrived to construct, out of this well-worn material, comedies that had all the air of novelty. What could run more easily than his *Distrait*, in which the wool-gathering Leander who loses one of his boots on the road, who sets out for Picardy by way of Rouen, who dips his finger into a boiled egg and chews it till he draws blood, who blunders into someone else's bedroom, who dashes his watch to the ground, who makes love to the girl he detests, and abuses the girl he adores, who, after countless similar exploits, forgets on his wedding-night that he has been married at all—what could be

[1] Reynaldo and Roland, arm linked in arm, get as drunk as they can at the inn.

more familiar than all this sort of thing? What could have done duty more often? What, in a way, could be more trite, more hackneyed? The whole thing is just one of La Bruyère's "Characters", spun out to fill up five acts. Well, have it so if you like. All the same, you come under the spell of the thing; you roar with laughter, just like the children, every time someone goes and puts his foot in it.

Now and again, we have a scene, sometimes a whole play, that has a touch of sadness about it, though not the deeper sadness of Molière, for there is nothing very profound in his psychology. Nevertheless, Regnard is not blind to the foibles and faults of his fellow-men. He knows the influence that money wields over a society that is beginning to disintegrate; he makes no bones about portraying broken-down, unhealthy, epileptic, paralytic, diseased, asthmatic, dropsical old men, with a single tooth left in their head which will drop out the next time they cough, but who cast lecherous eyes on any specimen of fresh young womanhood they happen to see. There is something definitely *macabre* about *Le Légataire Universel*. No matter; it is not the gloomy side of the thing that strikes the eye, but its gaiety. The characters only come to provide us with a little temporary diversion, and to make a few sparks fly. They are nimble and sprightly, they frisk and frolic, for they have convinced themselves once and for all that every ill can be cured with a modicum of folly. When the play is over; when the envious and the miserly have got what they deserve, when the Crispins and the Lisettes have been duly pardoned and absolved, when the lovers have been wedded, when the actors make their bow, and the curtain comes down, the spectator will bring but one thought away with him from the evening's entertainment:

Il faut bien que je rie
De tout ce que je vois tous les jours de la vie. . . .[1]

Something new in the way of accompaniment, brought in on the quiet, secretly running counter to the dominant. Toland was not much given to laughter; nor was Collins. As for Fontenelle, you could barely get a smile out of him, and that rather a faint and ironic one. Jean Le Clerc was grave, and Jurieu tragic. Bossuet in his old age had grown austere; woe unto you that laugh, for

[1] *Le Distrait*, act 1, scene 6.

ye shall shed tears. Fénelon considered that laughter had something indecorous about it.   Louis XIV, now in the sere and
yellow, laughed no more. But these people were not all the world;
there were others. . . .

And now, like the Diable Boiteux, let us go and take a peep at
some other houses. We will say goodbye to the jesters, the toss-
pots, the crooks, the scallywags and all that happy-go-lucky crew.
And the merry and bright ones—of those too we will take our
leave.   We will now turn our attention to the sentimental,
emotional people for whom melancholy and despair are the
breath of life. Let us consider those mortals who look on reason,
on the intellect, as an inhuman thing. What we have to do is to
find out, not whether man ever gave up shedding tears here
below, but when it came to be thought that he could decently
shed them in public.

Here, now, we have the stage in a theatre. One hero, wearing a
plumed helmet, a grandiloquent, pompous personage, is unburdening to another hero, no less an antique Roman in appearance, all
the sorrows of his tender heart:

SERVILIUS.

Mais quand je songe, hélas! que l'état où je suis
Va bientôt exposer aux plus mortels ennuis
Une jeune beauté, dont la foi, la constance,
Ne peut trop exiger de ma reconnaissance,
Je perds à cet objet toute ma fermeté.
Eh! pardonne, de grâce à cette lâcheté,
Qui, me faisant prévoir tant d'affreuses alarmes
Dans ton sein généreux me fait verser des larmes.

What is this? Tears? A gallant knight, in armour dight, blubber-
ing like a booby on the stage? His interlocutor is moved to rage
much rather than to pity:

MANLIUS.

Des larmes! Ah! plutôt, par tes vaillantes mains,
Soient noyés dans leur sang ces perfides Romains.
Des larmes! Jusque-là la douleur te possède![1]

---

[1]Servilius: When, alas, I bethink me that my present plight will expose to the
most mortal distress a beautiful maiden whose trust and constancy has a greater
claim on my gratitude than words can tell, all my strength deserts me. Pardon, I
beseech you this poltroonery of mine, which disclosing to me all the dread things

The audience are puzzled. They would like to know for what mysterious reason it is no disgrace to laugh as much as you want to on the stage, but very definitely a disgrace to weep there.[1]

In this room Pierre Bayle is inditing a letter to his brother Jacob; their mother has recently died. He agrees that it is permissible to shed tears on such an occasion:

"I quite understand your floods of tears, and I see nothing amiss in your urging me to let mine flow unstintingly. We should turn a deaf ear to the Stoics. The tears we shed when our hearts are wrung by the trials heaven lays upon us will not be unrequited. Wherefore we should pray for a tender rather than a stern and rock-like heart. God will turn our tears and mourning into blessings."

But here Bayle seems to hesitate, to hedge, a little. We may weep, yes; but we must not keep on weeping,

"In saying that, however", he goes on, *"I don't at all approve of the sort of temperament you refer to when you say in so many words that you are so soft-hearted that you cannot see or think of anything at all distressing without being moved to a terrible flood of tears. Such weakness ill becomes a man; it would be hardly excusable in a woman. Whatever trials life may hold in store for us, men should never forget that they are men."*

But was that a little unkind, the least bit wounding? Again he modifies his statement. If his brother must weep, then let him weep.

"But just as, while recognizing the grounds of your own excessive grief, I nevertheless cannot feel any sympathy with this great and universal fund of tenderness of yours, I am far from wishing to animadvert on the tears which you have shed and are still shedding. One may give way to one's feelings thus unrestrainedly without detriment to the strength of mind which should mark our sex; and, since the mightiest heroes and the greatest saints have shed them, tears should not be looked on as a womanish display of weakness."[2]

A woman's tears . . . Here, in this handsome, middle-class residence, one of the weaker sex is writing a love-letter, and

---

that lie ahead compels me to fall weeping on thy manly breast. Manlius: What, tears? Ah! Better these traitorous Romans should by thy valiant hands die bathed in their own blood. Tears! Is this the extremity to which thy grief hath driven thee?

Manlius Capitolinus, a Tragedy by La Fosse d'Aubigny, first presented by the players in ordinary to the King, on Saturday, 18 January, 1698.

[1] La Bruyère, *Caractères. Des Ouvrages de l'Esprit.*
[2] *Unpublished Letters of Pierre Bayle*, by J. L. Gerig and G. L. van Roosbroeck (*The Romantic Review*, July-September, 1932).

weeping as she writes. In her young days she had fallen in love with the Baron de Breteuil whom she believed to be the handsomest man in all the world. Plunged in despair when she discovered that he was not free to marry, she fled one day from her father's house, intending to betake herself to a nunnery. She was pursued and overtaken. In order to bring her to her senses, she was compelled to marry against her will; Anne de Bellinzani became the wife of President Ferrand. But the lady met the Baron again. She surrendered to him in a tempest of passionate ecstasy. Hence these letters of hers, some of the most beautiful ever penned by a woman in love, throbbing with the whole gamut of emotions: joy in a love which the world knows not of, a love all the more precious because it is secret; sadness, because her love cannot expand freely and triumphantly; anger at the obstacles which accumulate little by little in her path; a tenderness that is almost maternal in its tone; outbursts of passionate love; disgust at the thought of quitting her lover and returning to a husband whom her flesh abhors; insight—"Yes, my dear one, you love me, and I worship you" . . .; disesteem, which, however, does not kill her love: "I have lost the good opinion of my people, I have turned my own home into a hell, and all for a lover who only deserves my hate. But, God knows, my crowning misery is that hate him I cannot. I despise him, I shrink from him, but I cannot hate him." This woman, thus born for love, exhibits some of the traits that were to be the pride of the heroines of romance a century and a half later on. She deems that a cheerful temperament is apt to be too volatile; that sadness adds a deeper tenderness to love; she is the unhappiest of women; melancholy has marked her for its own; from her childhood upwards, Love has looked on her as its destined victim, doomed to endure its torments. She weeps in torrents.[1]

Society was disintegrating, it is true. Slowly but surely the contagion of luxury was gaining ground. Luxury must have money, must have it quickly, and plenty of it. So speculation, lotteries, the tontine, card-playing became the order of the day. *Turcaret* dates back to 1709, and Turcaret the ex-footman, now a bloated millionaire, thinks money will buy anything, good manners, wit, the female heart. True, Lesage shows him

---

[1] *Histoire nouvelle des amours de la jeune Bélise et de Cléante*, 1689. *Lettres de la Présidente Ferrand au Baron de Breteuil*, Eugène Asse, 1880.

bemocked, taken in, reduced to beggary in the end, and that is the moral which Frontin, the manservant, draws from it all, as he talks things over with Lisette, the maid. Life is a rum go, we bleed some pretty lady or other; the pretty lady bleeds a business man; the business man takes it out of another business man and it's all like a jolly old game of battledore and shuttlecock played by crooks and swindlers. In Dancourt's comedies, which are little mirrors of the age, with some engaging facets, the most hypocritical, corrupt, tuft-hunting, money-grubbing characters are the women.

Of course it is also true that women were encouraged to take up philosophy and science. Now, it is Lord Halifax that urges them on; now Fontenelle. Some there were who said that it was high time that women kicked over the traces. They had been slaves long enough, and men, taking a mean advantage of their own strength, had framed the laws so as to keep them slaves, assigning them the meanest and most trivial occupations. Custom had ratified the injustice, education had increased it. It was time the whole thing was changed. Women ought to be on an equality with men; it was only just and reasonable that they should be. They should be educated on the same lines and fulfil the same duties. They should be magistrates, teachers, and so on. Even the Army, nay, the Church itself, should be open to them. Boileau, who is mindful of *les Femmes Savantes*, is not at all of this opinion; the wanton, the flirt, the female gambler, the blue-stocking, the fly-by-night, all come in for the rough side of his tongue. He has some ironical things to say about the blessedness of the married state. Whereupon, Perrault at once springs to arms to defend the sex. Boileau, he says, is old-fashioned, out of date; he satirizes women simply because Horace and Juvenal did, and he thinks he's got to say "ditto" to everything the Ancients said. But the Moderns know better; they know that life is very different now from what it used to be. Three cheers for the women! An Italian philosopher, Paolo Mattia Doria, chimes in, showing that "in pretty well everything that matters most, women are not a whit inferior to men."

All that is true enough, no doubt. People who have kept their eyes open, report that young girls are throwing off all restraint, forgetting their manners and rapidly becoming a scandal; that grown women are brazen, grasping and selfish. But let some great love affair come along, one whose course is anything but smooth, and, in a flash, passion will blaze forth and reassert its rights with heart-rending appeals and choking sobs; a sort of call to a new era, an era now close at hand, whose dominant, whose one and only note is—passion!

How cunningly that "sensibility", which some people wanted to banish altogether from the world, managed to find its way in. And now from England a signal was seen. It was an actor, Colley Cibber, who gave it. He had divined what the age was secretly longing for. Enough of those licentious plays! Enough of those lordly debauchees strutting and swaggering up and down the stage! Jeremy Collier was right; it was high time that English drama was recalled to a sense of decency and moral rectitude. Thus did morals link arms with feeling.

Now take the case of the faithless husband who has deserted his wife and gone off to roam the world. Having, as he confesses, wasted all his substance on old wine and young women, he returns to England without a penny to bless himself with, but just as heartless a rogue as ever. Not to put too much of a strain on our powers of invention, let us call the gentleman Loveless. But now, on the other side, behold Amanda, his wife, a perfect model. She has never ceased to dote on that rascally husband of hers, poor soul, and has made up her mind to win him back again. How will she set to work? A curtain lecture? Not on your life! The very thing to choke him off again. No; sentiment, the appeal to the heart, that's the thing. She will appeal to his feelings; she will make him feel sorry for being so cruel to her. He still has a spark of affection for her; she will kindle it into flame. And more than that, she'll see that he has a good time. Well, the up-shot is that Loveless realizes what a wicked brute he has been and becomes the meekest of penitents: "Oh thou hast rouz'd me from my deep Lethargy of Vice! For hitherto my Soul has been enslav'd to loose Desires, to vain deluding Follies, and shadows of substantial bliss: but now I wake with joy to find my Rapture Real.—Thus let me kneel and pay my thanks to her whose conquering Virtue has at last subdu'd me. Here will I fix, thus prostrate sigh my shame, and wash my Crimes in never ceasing tears of Penitence." Evidently this gentleman has graduated in the School for Sentiment.

This highly decorous play of Colley Cibber's, *Love's Last Shift*, was put on at the Theatre Royal, London, in the year 1696, and scored an immense success. Thereafter followed a number of comedies of mixed ingredients, grave, gay, homely, moral but with a few faint whiffs of the old licentiousness here and there; for, now and again, one of the old stock characters would be trotted out, and of course he would not have forgotten how to swallow his liquor, dangle after petticoats, and break out into obscenity, no matter what chaste ears were there to hear. There were tales, stories, sometimes new enough in parts but always freely introducing the old threadbare devices—disguises, masquerades, letters going to the wrong person, mystifications, misunderstandings. Colley Cibber set the example when he made Loveless fail to recognize his wife, because, he explained, her face had been slightly disfigured by smallpox. Ill-constructed, encumbered at the end of every act, sometimes of every scene, with homilies that were not very good and were certainly not spontaneous, however, they all bore witness to the same quickening of the conscience, the same psychological truth. It was that no moral reform can be effected from without, at the dictate of force or authority. The soul, the spirit, must be moved; before any attempt at regeneration is made, the spirit must be first aroused, and then guided, by the feelings. The husband who has become aware that his wife has wandered from the path will be powerless to influence her unless he can awaken in her heart the pangs of contrition and remorse. So to bring this about, what he does is to stage a sort of play; he gets someone to pretend to make up to her, a hireling lover; then, when she has been brought to within an inch of the precipice, she will have a sudden pang of loathing for the deceit and the treachery of which she was all but guilty, and this loathing for vice is the pathway that will bring her back to virtue.

Tenderness, compassion—these are now the things; aged domestics, like faithful hounds, grateful for all the benefits their masters have bestowed on them, display, in the latters' hour of need, a devotion truly admirable. A few disreputable women, definitely past praying for, will be left to their miserable fate, but, for the most part, the women will be tender and gentle, and, if their hearts lead them astray, means will be found to bring them back to the right path before it is too late. As for the men, constancy in love will never go unrewarded, though, of course, it will have to be put to the proof by a few searching tests. Then, a father who would spare his son the slightest pain will be held up to our admiration; so will the son, who is no less tender, no less affectionate. Yes; the best and most loving of fathers, the best and most loving of sons! Yet, like a pair of sensitive plants, they shrink into themselves the moment they are touched. In the same play, we meet a pure and charming *ingénue* who refuses to believe in the existence of evil, despite all that is said to the contrary. Even the characters that are least engaging will be nothing more than just a trifle rough in manner, or a little bit jealous. However, the jealous fits will be dispelled, rough ways will soften into tenderness, everyone will kiss and be friends amid universal tears of joy. Such is the kind of thing we get in Steele's *The Conscious Lovers* which was produced in 1772 and carried off the palm in its particular line. One department of literature is becoming "an obliging service to human society."[1]

Opera!—What an insult to human intelligence! Please the eye, please the ear, and revolt the reason. The thing is an outrage against common sense. Fancy singing everything from start to finish! not only declarations of love, but speeches, messages, orders, curses, confidences, secrets! The thing is too absurd. Just imagine a master singing to call his servant; singing when he is sending the man on an errand; fancy singing when you have a secret to tell a friend, singing when you are addressing a meeting; singing when you are giving an order; singing when you are in a fight and melodiously slaying your man with sword or spear. "You want to know what opera is like?" Well, I'll tell you. It's a queer mix-up of poetry and music, in which the poet and the composer keep getting in each other's way, and put themselves to no end of trouble to produce a very mediocre result.

That's saying nothing about the scene-painter, another offender. To go and clutter up the stage with a lot of wonderful scenes all made of cardboard, to substitute for the intellectual or psychological interest, a lot of elaborate devices to amaze and astound, to contrive machines of extraordinary complexity—winged chariots,

---

[1]Richard Steele, *The Tender Husband*, a comedy, 1705. To Mr. Addison, "Poetry . . . is an obliging service to human society".

gods and goddesses mounting up to heaven, live monsters and so on—what a preposterous idea! In short, in the opinion of sensible people, people that have some respect for truth, who like things to have at least a semblance of probability about them, logical, level-headed people, like Saint-Évremond, say, or Boileau, or La Bruyère, Addison, Steele, Gravina, Crescimbeni, Maffei, Muratori—people like that all say that opera is an absurd thing, utterly puerile and irrational. For, say what you will, "an absurdity served up with music, and dancing, and complicated stage devices and elaborate scenery is no doubt a magnificent absurdity, but an absurdity none the less."[1]

Precisely; opera was absurd, but opera caught on. That was a fact, and there was no getting away from it. This new departure, which enraged everyone with a grain of common sense about them, was a success. Everywhere it triumphed; Florence, Venice, Rome, Naples, not a city in the whole of Italy but had come under the spell. It had made itself at home in the leading musical centres of Germany, at Dresden and Leipzig. In Vienna, which became a sort of second home to it, people simply raved about it. Not a Prince, or a Grand Duke but must have his theatre, his scenic artist, his composers, and must needs engage the finest *maestro*, the finest ballet-master, the finest *prima donna* to be had. In Paris, Lulli and Quintault were the lions of the hour. London had its Handel, and meant to keep him. Madrid was not up to date; Mme. d'Aulnay in her *Relation du Voyage d'Espagne*, which appeared in 1691, says with a smile: "There never was such pitiable stagecraft; the gods came down astride a plank which reached from one side of the theatre to the other; the effect of sunlight was produced by a dozen or so oiled-paper lanterns each with a lamp inside it. When it was Alcine's turn to do her witchcraft business, and she called up her demons, they obligingly climbed up from the infernal regions on ladders." But help was coming. In 1703, an Italian company came and took up its quarters in Madrid.

How is the *furore* to be accounted for? The fact is, the human heart has an incurable craving for the pathetic; it loves to be moved. Tragedy, which from about the end of the last century had been a purely imitative, a wholly mechanical affair, failed now to satisfy this craving. Music, then, should do what the drama could not do. It was this spiritual, this psychological need that

[1]Saint-Évremond, *Lettre sur les opéras*.

resulted in the emergence of something quite unfamiliar in art,
a completely new form of artistic expression.

A vast assemblage of beautiful things; a pattern to which every
art made its contribution, a feast of sound, colour and rhythmic
motion; enchantment both for eye and ear, a completely and
definitely novel kind of emotional appeal, defying analysis since
its effect was physical, so that one's bodily substance seemed to
melt and dissolve under its influence: a delight born of magic
and enchantment; a sensation inexplicable, unfathomable and in-
communicable.   Such was opera.   You might condemn it a
hundred, nay, a thousand times over, you would be but a voice
crying in the wilderness. The critics were all on a false scent.
They did not understand that a new want had arisen, a craving
that *would be* satisfied, the craving for the breath-taking, the heart-
rending, for floods of compassionate tears. Such were the things
that people demanded now. They cared no more about being
convinced; what they wanted was to be thrilled.[1] Therein lay the
key to the whole matter. Let us consider the question a little
more closely. What Europe was so enthusiastically taking to its
bosom was opera, the *Italian* opera. Italy, which had provided
the pattern of the thing, was the source, the inexhaustible source,
whence flowed these endless waves of sound. She furnished
Europe not only with the music, but with the musicians to perform it. Italy was but another name for Music. Thus it came to
pass that these music-dramas made their way into all the neighbouring lands. However, Paris, too, wanted to have a finger in
the pie; but the genius she chose to pit against the Italians was
himself an Italian. Moreover, we must bear in mind that it was
only one half of France that tried to resist the invasion. The
other half had surrendered already. Hamburg for a long time
remained loyal to German music; but Hamburg, too, at last gave
in. The operatic world was one Italian colony; no more and
no less.

How are we to account for the favour it thus received, for the
leading position thus accorded to it? The Italian librettists, for
their part, were as anxious as anybody to render fealty to the
sovereign rights of Reason. By so doing they would cease to
expose themselves to the scornful judgment of the critics; they
would yield nothing in dignity to the great tragic poets. What

[1]Mme. de Sévigné, *Lettre du 8 janvier*, 1674.

Benedetto Marcello, and what Apostolo Zeno, master of music to His Imperial Majesty, and a would-be Pierre Corneille of Opera, both wanted to do was to give the *libretto* an organic shape, to do away with its customary inconsistencies, to compress and simplify it, in a word to bring it closer to the tragic model. Finally, sometime later, we find Metastasio appealing to Aristotle's *Poetics*, in order to establish the title of music-drama to be classed as a legitimate form of art.

Vain attempts. Misled by the literary fallacy that still prevailed around them, and which would have men believe that the works of the great epic and tragic poets were the choicest flowers of the human spirit, they failed to see, these obstinate librettists, that the literary part of the thing was of very minor importance, that literature, so far as opera was concerned, was a mere hand-maid, whose business it was to do whatever the music required of her. If the music wanted a solo here, a duet there, and somewhere else a chorus; if it demanded that so many lines, in such and such a metre, were to be assigned to the tenor or the bass, as the case might be, the music had to be obeyed. The music decided every-thing, even the librettist's vocabulary, which must consist of words that were harmonious and easy to sing. All it required of the writer was that he should be adaptable, endowed with the will and the skill to do what was required of him. His was the art of accommodation, of doing what the composer, the conductor, the *prima donna* wanted him to do. And then the language, the Italian language, richer, more sonorous, more harmonious and more varied, than any other European tongue! It now began to recover some of the prestige it had lost when it tried to act as a vehicle of ideas.

Ah, this Italian music, how delightful it was! How it soared heavenwards like a fountain of melody, free and unfettered! How rich, how warm, how copious! And what triumphant ease! Generous, inexhaustible, it gave to a people to whom music was the breath of life, something which French music could not give; no, nor the music of any other country; it gave fire, and spirit and a style all its own. Yes; a style that was always characteristic, whatever the theme, gay or sad. Gentle, smooth-flowing numbers were not what it aimed at; nor rigidly correct transitions; it had little respect for rule, it took hazards, it would do and dare, and the very recklessness of it held you spellbound.

There were people, even in those days, who realized this, some Frenchmen among them. "French composers would be terrified that disaster would follow if they ventured on the slightest deviation from the rules. They were all for soothing and caressing the ear; the ear was their god, and, even when they had done their utmost to obey the rules, they were still haunted by the fear that, for all their care, they might have done something amiss. The Italians are bolder than that. They will make abrupt changes of key and time, give the most numerous and complicated trills to notes we should think incapable of sustaining the slightest shake. They will sustain one single note for such a time that people not used to it get impatient at what they first think an outrage, but afterwards cannot sufficiently admire." In short, "they cause mingled surprise and alarm to the hearer. He gets it into his head that the whole composition is about to crash in hopeless chaos; and then, when all his thoughts are centred on the ruin which he supposes to be imminent, his calm is restored by cadences so regular that he is lost in wonder as he sees harmony reborn from the very soul of discord, and drawing its crowning beauty from the very irregularities which, a moment ago, seemed destined to destroy it".[1]

The pleasure that is born of audacity, the pleasure that even the appearance of violating the sacred canon can procure, a pleasure which is really physical, a pleasure which makes our flesh creep and our nerves thrill like a violin beneath the bow of a master; that was the nature of the pleasure for which all these Italian composers were responsible, men whose very names had music in them, men "whose excellent productions laid all Europe under a spell". When some pupils of Scarlatti, the most illustrious of them all, asked him why he wrote this rather than that, or why he told them to do so and so, he always made the same reply, "Because it makes one feel better".

---

[1] Raguenet, *Parallèle des Italiens et des Français en ce qui regarde la musique et les opéras*, 1702.

IV

INFLUENCES, NATIONAL, POPULAR AND INSTINCTIVE

WE have examined a few of the forces which, confusedly, instinctively, were tending to prevent Europe from becoming the exclusive domain of critics, analysts, logicians, and philosophers. These forces, which were to come into full operation later on, were, in a vague sort of way, preparing for the time, still far distant, when they might strike a blow in behalf of the feelings and the imagination. We have looked at these forces objectively, as it were, recording their visible manifestations in all their complex variety. What it now behoves us to do is to look at them from a higher plane, to examine them from some more elevated vantage point, so that we may discover, at least some of the guiding principles from which these various forces of resistance were accustomed to draw their inspiration.

Nationalism: the consciousness of the differences which separate nation from nation—who shall eliminate nationalism? It goes down to the very bedrock of ideas; it derives from causes some of which Reason recognizes, some of which it does not.

There was at this time a tendency for a uniform mode of thought, a uniform mode of expression, to establish itself in every country; order, precision, disciplined lines of thought, beauty, the solid and enduring fruit of prolonged patience and enduring toil. That was all very well as a general principle, but was there not a secondary aspect of the matter to take into account, were there not subsidiary details which each nation interpreted in its own manner, so that differences, sometimes downright clashes, occurred to disturb the general uniformity? Here is an example: England had embraced the classical ideal, partly as a result of French influence, partly because she needed some inwardly stabilizing principle to regulate and discipline her material power. But her attitude towards the classics was always a distinctively British attitude.[1] Here, ready to hand, is a striking example: In England Swift figures among the classics, and it is a fact that he played an important part in fixing a standard for English prose. He is read and commented upon in school class-rooms, and no doubt he will continue to be so studied and expounded. There is a firmness, a solid quality in his work, and that unquestionable hall-mark of genius which entitles him to a place in the foremost rank of his country's men of letters. But what a strange sort of classic he would seem to a Frenchman today! And how much stranger still to a Frenchman who took Boileau for his guiding light. Let us take a glance at the *Tale of a Tub*; let us look at it with the eyes of a continental reader of 1704, we will say. Imagine his stupefaction, his bewilderment! What a hopeless jumble! The man hasn't got even the most elementary idea of composition. Off he goes at a tangent on whatever trail happens to strike his fancy, leaves that, and starts on something else, only to leave it and begin on something else again; apparently completely ignorant of that artistic device which goes by the name of transition. He obeys nothing but his own caprice. His introductions are longer than the things they introduce; for logic he doesn't care a fig; and he seems to be laughing at us all the time. "After so wide a compass as I have wandered, I do now gladly overtake and close in with my subject, and shall henceforth hold on with it an even pace to the end of my journey, except some beautiful prospect appears within sight of my way." What are we to think of an author who writes a digression in praise of digressions? And what extraordinary similes; what extravagant ideas! what a frenzied imagination! "Wisdom is a fox, who, after long hunting, will at last cost you the pains to dig out; it is a cheese, which, by how much the richer, has the thicker, the homelier, and the coarser coat; and whereof, to a judicious palate, the maggots are the best: it is a sack-posset, wherein the deeper you go, you will find it the sweeter. Wisdom is a hen, whose cackling we must value and consider, because it is attended with an egg; but then

[1]With regard to this matter, we refer the reader to some penetrating remarks by Louis Cazamian, in the *Histoire de la littérature anglaise*, by E. Legouis and L. Cazamian, 1924, p. 694.

lastly, it is a nut, which, unless you choose with judgment, may cost you a tooth, and pay you with nothing but a worm."

This mania of his for attacking and demolishing! First of all he falls out with the Catholics; but he is also at odds with the Lutherans, the Calvinists, indeed with enthusiasts of every kidney. You can never be sure whether, when he has done soothing and caressing, he won't suddenly begin to bite. He flies into tempestuous passions, he rages at this, he rages at that, he insults, he reviles. The man is a sort of Aristophanes gone mad. And those everlasting allegories, and irony, there's no end to it. And, oh, those appalling jokes! "Last week I saw a woman flayed, and you will hardly believe how it altered her person for the worse."

How many an Englishman, while freely admitting the value of classical rule, and even endeavouring to conform to it, nourished in his heart a secret longing for his vanished freedom! Think how many of them deemed that Aristotle, and Horace, were quite enough for them to be guided by, and that there was really no reason why they should submit to that inflexible French discipline. "It is as if, to make excellent honey, you should cut off the wings of your bees, confine them to their hive or their stands, and lay flowers before them, such as you think the sweetest, and like to yield the finest extraction; you had as good pull out their stings, and make arrant drones of them. They must range through fields, as well as gardens, choose such flowers as they please."[1]

The resistance is more pronounced, it displays more tenacity, more violence even, when, instead of letters, it is manners and customs that are in question, when, that is to say, it comes to defending something that is more inbred, more instinctive, like a people's own particular way of life. When we read the novels or the comedies of an age which, after all, did accept, more or less, the French mode of living, the French ideas of social behaviour, we cannot help being struck by the vigour of the national reaction. France is represented as a shameless creature that sends over to London her dancing masters, her rascally lacqueys, her disreputable serving wenches, her fashion-merchants, her adventuresses, her coxcomb marquises, her fops and popinjays, who go about showing off their fine manners and are but a pack of rogues

[1] William Temple, *Upon Poetry*, 1692.

and runagates. What a contrast to the straightforward Englishman, simple of heart and bluff of speech, whose very lack of polish is accounted a virtue. Better keep his bluntness of speech, his uncouth manners and his native vigour, than be softened and spoiled by foreign ways that would turn a man into a tailor's dummy, a hypocrite, a strutting coxcomb. There are plenty of plays in which French men and French women are brought on in this way, merely to serve as foils, to tickle the ears of the groundlings, but also to serve the additional purpose of bringing the virtues, the indomitable virtues, of the British national character into stronger relief.

Italy's complaint was that she was France's slave; and, to a certain extent, she was in a fair way to becoming so. But here again we must beware of rash generalizations. For not only were there poets beyond the Alps who kept the idea of Roman unity very much alive, the idea that Gaul was after all one of the late-comers to civilization, and looked forward to the day when Italy, the rightful sovereign, should resume the sceptre, but, since classi-cal ideas were the order of the day, the champions of Italy declared that there had been a classical school in Italy long before there had been one in France, and that the Italian model was not only the original, but the only genuinely authentic one. They kept harping doggedly on the Renaissance, *their* Renaissance they were pleased to call it; who would dare to dispute their title? While the poets do their best to copy Corneille and Racine, with the object, openly avowed, of outdoing their masters, they keep repeating, over and over again, that they are, and intend to remain, faithful to the spirit and letter of Greek Tragedy, which is the only form that counts, and which is theirs in a special sense, for it was they who first discovered it and made it bear fruit. What, after all, had the French done? Tragedy, the antique model, they had converted into an effeminate, pretty-pretty thing, a love-story with protestations of inordinate prolixity on the theme of love. Sophocles was the great master of tragedy, and to the Sophoclean model they must return.

Every country wanted to prove that it had a longer pedigree than any of its rivals, and delved back as far as it could into the past to see what titles to nobility it could unearth. Each boasted that it had a language, a poetry, a prose tradition, a civilization older than any of the rest, and each haughtily declared that its neighbours were nothing but pretentious upstarts.

In this connection, no country displayed a bolder front than Germany. Crushed and humbled to the dust as she was, swept and swayed by every wind that blew, she wielded no influence of her own, and was to all outward seeming a moral force completely spent. Howbeit, she was struggling manfully all the while to keep alive her inward spirit, and on every front she was striving to hold her own. There was the question of her unity. She would soon recover that if she could but put her house in order; so said Pufendorf, so said Leibniz. And law? Was there not a Germanic law, an older, and a better, than Roman law, than Canon law. Roman law and Canon law—none but these were taught in the universities. That was all wrong. The time had come to restore the national, autochthonous law to its rightful place. And then there was the language question. Why, the German language was as ancient, ay, and as beautiful as the Latin, or the Greek, or as any other language that could be named. The German tongue went back to the beginning of the world. And literature—what of that? The answer was that German literature was second to none. That was clearly established by the learned Morhofius in 1682. How he threw himself into his task! What mountains of evidence he brought together! How his love of the fatherland shines through every page of his turgid and ponderous work! He asserted that Germany had had some glorious, but unjustly forgotten, poets, like Hans Sachs, and others older still, whom Olaus Rudbeck had claimed for Scandinavia. His zeal prompted him to advance a strange argument indeed. He insisted that Germany had had poets who had left no trace behind them, but that the fact that they had left no trace did not prove that they had never existed. On the contrary, they must have existed, because in every nation poetry is in the primitive form of literary expression. Therefore they had existed, albeit they were now unknown and undiscoverable.

The German language, which possesses the rotundity of the Greek, the majesty of the Latin, the flexibility of the French, the graces of the Italian, the richness of the English, the dignity of the Flemish—this age-old tongue would bring forth, its zealous champions hoped, masterpieces that should compel a jealous Europe to acknowledge its worth. So when, in 1689, Caspers von Lohenstein's *Arminius und Thusnelda* appeared, what a shout of triumph rent the air! At last a great writer, *patriae amantissimus*, had sought and found a subject worthy of the German race; had sung the praise of that Arminius who had confronted Rome, not in her early, puny days, but in the fullness of her might, and given back to Germany the crown of oak and laurel. Hence these huzzahs of joy, these shouts of triumph.

The appeal of the *Sehnsucht*, what more generally recognized feature is there in the psychology of the eternal Germany? It was not lacking in an age when knowledge was claiming to dispel all the darkness of the soul and to cast a light even on the sub-conscious. Christian Weise, poet and pedagogue, who, in all his work betrayed a moving desire for the simple and the natural, wrote a play every year for the school theatre. This was highly diverting for the pupils, turned actors for the nonce, and some-thing to make the parents feel proud of their offspring. All the torment of a yearning but unrequited spirit was made manifest in one of these plays called *Die unvergnugte Seele*, which was produced in the year 1688. Vertumnus, a young man of good family, well disposed, should, logically speaking, have been happy, but he is not; he is unhappy. He feels unable to enjoy the worldly blessings that are his, yet he cannot even put in words what it is he lacks. He does his best to fill up the void in his being by female society, by joining in the carousals of his boon companions, by the pursuit of worldly honours, by frequenting the society of the Parnassians—all in vain. He falls into a state of utter des-pair; he is on the point of putting an end to his life. Is there, then, no peace anywhere but in the grave? At this point the play takes on a moralizing tone and loses its psychological interest. There happen to pass by a couple of peasants, Contento and Quiete. They have had their misfortunes, and pretty cruel ones, but they have not lost their zest for life, of which they ask no more than it can give. Such is the lesson they give Vertumnus; he takes it to heart, and turns over a new leaf.

So far, the yearning soul is, as we see, timid and modest. It is not puffed up; it does not look on itself as something apart; it does not despair of a cure. But we know that Vertumnus will have successors who will carry their despair beyond all reasonable limits, who will call the world, and God Himself, to witness to their misfortunes, and that no Contento, no Quiete will come to save them when they resolve to quit a world that is unworthy of them.

Little did they dream, the critics who admired *Arminius und Thusnelda* and the numerous poetical effusions of Christian Weise, little did they dream that Germany had already produced one of the finest romances in which the idea of the collective spirit ever found expression, the *Simplicissimus* of Grimmelshausen. Picaresque, if you will, considering the number of adventures which befall the hero, but savouring so richly of its native soil that it defied translation, and for some countries, France included, defies it still. A tale composed of memories of the Thirty Years War, of crops laid waste, villages plundered, peasants put to the sword, fire and slaughter on every hand; a tale of a simple, upright soul flung into the midst of a corrupt civilization, tempted and impaired thereby, who rises above it at last and proves its conqueror in the end. It is the tale of a creed which girdles the earth like a forest of symbols, which, while conscious that it is living in the midst of a host of transient illusions, never ceases to reach out towards the eternal verities; the tale of a Christian who, struggling heavenward through many tribulations, through ignorance, sin, remorse, clings to the hope that promises eternal joy, and attains his goal at last. These various themes develop, interlace, coalesce, separate anew, following one upon another with unexampled richness and splendour, sounding the glories of a race which their neighbours deemed on the point of extinction, but which manifested, notwithstanding, its invincible resolution to survive.

The theory of racial superiority had not yet come to the fore. The profound significance of the expression "native land" had not been fully gauged. No notion had been formed as yet of the dynamic potentialities of the idea of nationality. The feelings awakened in a man's breast by the thought of his countryside, of his village church, had not as yet been analysed and philosophized upon. But they were no less operative for all that, and no sooner did an Italian of dismembered Italy, a German of disrupted Germany, a Pole of riven Poland, a Spaniard of sleepy Spain, get it into his head that a slight had been offered, not merely to the inner spirit of his country but to the outward symbol of it, than complaints and protests filled the air. Against the nationalistic prejudices of the various peoples, the idea of universal egalitarianism could make no headway.

Sometimes a song broke forth; not an ode by some accomplished bard, not a madrigal, not a piece of subtle verbal artistry, but a sort of semi-barbaric chant. The story is told how, in the Middle Ages, a certain Scandinavian king, Regner Ladbrog, was bitten by a deadly serpent, and how, before the poison reached his heart, he sang a kind of runic chant;[1] a chant so weird and strange as to cast a spell upon the contemporaries of William of Orange and Louis XIV. And besides things of that kind folk sang snatches of melodious lamentations that came from very far indeed, from the home of those outlandish denizens of the frozen north, the Laplanders, such as the Song of the Moors of Orra:

> Thou rising Sun, whose gladsome ray
> Invites my Fair to rural Play,
> Dispel the Mist, and clear the Skies,
> And bring my Orra to my Eyes.
>
> Oh! were I sure my Dear to view,
> I'd climb that Pine-Tree's topmost Bough;
> Aloft in Air that quivering plays,
> And round and round for ever gaze.

Or, maybe, the Song of the Reindeer:

> Haste, my Rain-Deer, and let us nimbly go
>   Our am'rous Journey through this dreary waste,
> Haste, my Rain-Deer, still thou art too slow,
> Impetuous Love demands the Lightning's Haste.[2]

No great things, in comparison with poems composed on the grand pattern; their significance would have been slighter still if Addison had not taken it into his head to draw attention to these rude compositions and to protest that there was something in them that strangely took his fancy. There was the old ballad of Chevy Chase, the touching song about the Babes in the Wood. He loved to listen as he travelled about England to songs that had been handed down from father to son, songs that were so dear to the hearts of the country folk.[3] It is true that to justify

[1] W. Temple, *Essay upon Heroic Virtue. Miscellanea*, Part II.
[2] *Spectator*, Nos. 366 and 406.
[3] *Spectator*, Nos. 70, 74, 85.

his taste Addison brought in Homer and Virgil and would have it that these rude rustic measures had qualities in common with the *Odyssey* and the *Aeneid*. It is as well that he did not pursue that line, and came back to belauding the artlessness, the spontaneity, of some such outpouring of the spirit as the song of a countryman returning home from his labours in the field. "This is a plain simple copy of Nature, destitute of all the Helps and Ornaments of Art . . . and pleases for no other reason but because it is a copy of Nature."

At the very opposite end of the scale there prevailed, or at least showed signs of growing influence, the idea that power rightly belonged to the people and that the powers wielded by a king were his only by delegation. Even in France there were people who recalled that Gaul had been conquered by the Franks; that the Frankish people, assembling on the Campus Martius, used to choose their own leaders; that, in consequence, sovereign power did not derive from God, nor was it connected in any way with any Roman tradition; it was conferred upon one of their number by the whole assembly of fighting men freely exercising their right of election. The people had not yet taken on the shape of a democracy, but the conception of popular power was beginning to emerge, fraught with significance for the future.

And now, as touching instinct. It cannot be said that as yet it was not looked on askance. Christians regarded it with mingled repulsion and alarm. As for the philosophers, they were unable to make up their minds as to whether it was an unmixed good. They would like to bring it under the controlling influence of reason. However, it can at least be said that it was not excluded from the topics of current speculation. For example, a medical practitioner might take it into his head to say something uncomplimentary about the Faculty and their precepts, explaining how a man can treat himself, that keeping well was a matter of instinct. Or again, some eccentric individual, referring to the idea of poetic inspiration, would declare that it was a sort of maniacal frenzy, an exalted madness, and that it was born of instinct. And, incidentally, there was another awkward customer that, by eluding logical analysis, by refusing all intellectual discipline, caused the rationalists, who wanted to bring it under their jurisdiction, no slight inconvenience. That was the Sublime. It was all very well to say that it was something new and something true embodied in one grand idea, expressed with elegance and precision; all very well to say that if a thing were not true it could not attain to the highest beauty nor reach the altitudes of the Sublime; that was all very sound, but it was felt that there was more in the matter than that. So, with a longing still unsatisfied, the question was put to Longinus, for he had not shrunk from giving a definition of this difficult word, and his was the prestige which attaches to a classic of ancient times. Well then, the Sublime—is it not, when all is said and done, a quality which, at least to some extent, lies outside the domain of Reason?

The controversy which was afoot concerning the souls of animals had been going on since the days of Descartes, and still showed no signs of reaching a conclusion. That dialectical tilting-ground, where champions of every shade of opinion cantered up to try a fall with somebody—what was it in reality but a thing that told, often obscurely enough, in favour of instinct?

In singing the praises of a favourite horse or a faithful dog, there was no implication that animals had souls like the souls of men and women; a modicum of the reasoning faculty, that was all that was claimed for them. But anyone could see that they loved and suffered, that they were not mere machines, for machines don't have feelings. Said La Fontaine, in his Address to Mme. de la Sablière, I ascribe to animals:

> Non point une raison suivant notre manière,
> Mais beaucoup plus aussi qu'un aveugle ressort:
> Je subtiliserais un morceau de matière
> Que l'on ne pourrait plus concevoir sans effort,
> Quintessence d'atome, extrait de la lumière,
> Je ne sais quoi plus vif et plus mobile encor
> Que la flamme. . . . .
>   Je rendrais mon ouvrage
> Capable de sentir, juger, rien davantage,
> Et juger imparfaitement. . . .[1]

[1]Not reason after our manner of thinking, but, nevertheless, much more than a mere blind impulse. Suppose I were to take a piece of matter and divide it up into fragments so small you could hardly conceive them, the quintessence of an atom, of light something livelier and more mobile than a flame. . . and then made it capable of feeling and judging, no more, and judging imperfectly.

Magalotti, the Florentine naturalist, the moving spirit of the Academy of the *Cimento*, took a bolder line, instancing, in opposition to Descartes, our love of animals, and referring to "the very great, very tender, and, often enough, very stupid and absurd affection we show for a dog, or a cat, or a horse, or a parrot, or a sparrow".

Dante said:

Amor, ch'a nullo amato amar perdona. . . .

And Tasso, too:
amiamo or quando
Esser si puote riamati amando;

—"we only love when we can be loved in return". Therefore, if we love animals, the reason is that they love us; and therefore they are not devoid of feeling. In these scattered utterances, pronounced in such a variety of circumstances, we detect that part of the consciousness which inclines towards the feelings, the emotions, making itself audible: bubbles, if you like, rising from the bottom of a pond, and breaking, as often as not, as soon as they reach the air.

Happy nymphs and happy shepherds, what blissful days were yours, beside the murmuring brook or in lonely forest glade, and how folk envied you in those hard and arid days! Oh, happy denizens of Betica, Oh, happy simple-hearted folk, able to dispense with all the complex apparatus of civilization, how men sang the praises of your happy happy lot, a happiness unknown to those who have ceased to live in accordance with the laws of Nature! "Oh, how far removed are those ways of life from the vain ambitions of those who are deemed to be gifted with superior wisdom! So warped are our notions that we can hardly bring ourselves to believe in the reality of such simplicity. We look on what we hear about their life as just a pretty fairytale; they must look on ours as a sort of nightmare." Happy Wild Man of the Woods, what a revolutionary zeal rings in the cry that proclaims you the model of the perfect life, exhorting every son of Europe to turn himself into a Huron!

The wittiest and most gifted minds of the day proclaimed the bankruptcy of the intellect:

Source intarissable d'erreurs
Poison qui corromps la droiture
Des sentiments de la nature,
Et la vérité de nos coeurs;
Feu follet, qui brilles pour nuire,
Charme des mortels insensés,
Esprit, je viens ici détruire
Les autels que l'on t'a dressés. . . .

Esprit! tu séduis, on t'admire,
Mais rarement on t'aimera;
Ce qui sûrement touchera
C'est ce que le coeur nous fait dire;
C'est ce langage de nos coeurs
Qui saisit l'âme et qui l'agite;
Et de faire couler nos pleurs
Tu n'auras jamais le mérite. . . .[1]

People who were anything but soft-hearted or sentimental, but who sensed which way the wind was veering, had some hard words to say about the thinking apparatus:

C'est elle qui nous fait accroire
Que tout cède à notre pouvoir;
Qui nourrit notre folle gloire
De l'ivresse d'un faux savoir;
Qui par cent nouveaux stratagèmes
Nous masquant sans cesse à nous-mêmes
Parmi les vices nous endort:
Du Furieux fait un Achille,
Du Fourbe un Politique habile,
Et de l'athée un Esprit fort.

---

[1]Inexhaustible source of errors, poison that corrupts the natural feelings, and the true promptings of the heart. Will o' the wisp which shines but to betray, charm of witless mortals, spirit, I come to destroy the altars which have been raised to thee.
Spirit that leadest astray, people admire but seldom love thee. What is really touching is what the heart bids us say. 'Tis the language of our hearts which takes hold of the soul and moves it; and to awaken our tears will never be yours.
Chaulieu, *Ode contre l'esprit*, 1708.

Mais vous, mortels, qui dans le monde
Croyant tenir les premiers rangs
Plaignez l'ignorance profonde
De tant de peuples différents,
Qui confondez avec la brute
Ce Huron caché sous sa hutte
Au seul instinct presque réduit:
Parlez: quel est le moins barbare
D'une raison qui vous égare
Ou d'un instinct qui le conduit?[1]

A little later, we encounter an arresting expression of that same sentiment, that is to say of the longing to get rid of all the artificialities, of the age-old burden under which we bow, and particularly of that kind of hypocrisy which, without in the least believing in it, we call morality. Once upon a time, there was an Englishman named Thomas Inkle, the third son of a well-to-do London citizen, who set sail for foreign parts in order to improve his fortune by trade and merchandise. At one place where they went ashore the greater number of the party he was with were captured and put to death by Indians. He, however, escaped and hid himself. An Indian maid discovered him. She was young and beautiful, and her name was Yarico. She fell in love with the stranger and was moved to pity by his hapless plight. She gave herself to him, body and soul, fed and protected him. He vowed that he would take her back to England, if he ever got the chance. One day they caught sight of a sail, and made signals. The ship drew near; some of her crew came ashore and in the end took them on board. Here, then, was safety at last. But as they voyaged on, Thomas Inkle began to think. What was he going to do with this woman? He had wasted his time, and all his money was gone. He decided he would sell her as a slave at the next port they touched at. The Indian woman wept

[1]She it is that makes us think that all things yield to our power; which feeds our mad pride with the intoxication of false knowledge, which by a hundred new stratagems, continually masking us from ourselves, makes us sleep in the midst of vice; calls the madman an Achilles, and the cheat an able politician, and the Atheist a clever fellow.
But you, ye mortals, who thinking you hold the first place in the world pity the profound ignorance of so many different people, who regard as a brute beast this Huron in his hut, with nothing to guide him but his instinct, say, which is the least barbarous, reason which leads you astray, or instinct which guides him truly?
Jean Baptiste Rousseau. *Ode IX, à M. le marquis de la Fare.*

and wailed and vainly entreated him to have pity on her. She told him she was with child by him, but he only made use of that information to raise his price. Such are the ways of civilized folk.[1]

One fine day Fontenelle came up against Instinct. He was taken aback, and, indeed, annoyed at the apparition. "This word 'instinct' is supposed to stand for something over and above my reasoning faculty, something which works in such a manner as to assist the preservation of my being, something that tells me to do this or that without my knowing why, but which nevertheless is highly beneficial; and that is the wonderful part about instinct." As he could not admit anything so derogatory to his reason, and as he considered that the marvellous had no business to exist, he went through the most complicated mental acrobatics, performed the most intricate feats of argumentation, in order to show that what is called "instinct" is nothing more nor less than reason in a hesitant mood, reason, which, confronted by a number of possible courses of action, has not yet consciously decided which one it will adopt. Having come to that conclusion, he is quite easy in his mind again. We are, it would appear, a long way from that "divine instinct" of which Rousseau will one day be singing the praises. Yet, perhaps, it will not seem so long after all, if we leave those who find it impossible to exist without the refinements of modern life, and turn our attention to less sophisticated circles, to a certain Switzer, one Béat de Muralt, for example, who presents us with a sort of foreshadowing of the famous apostrophe of Jean Jacques:

Man having lost his proper occupation and his dignity, the sense of what concerns him has likewise disappeared in the disorder in which we now find ourselves, and we no longer recognize those things wherein our dignity and our buisness consist. Since order alone is capable of giving us this knowledge, I believe there is but one way of abiding therein and that is by obeying the instinct within us, that divine instinct which is perhaps all that remains to us of man's primeval state, and which has been left with us as the means of restoring us thereto. All the living creatures we know of have their own particular instinct, and it never misleads them. How then should man, the noblest of all creatures, be lacking in the instinct proper to himself, an instinct which should permeate his whole being, an instinct, as sure as it is all-embracing? Doubtless, he does have it, and

[1]*Spectator*, No. 11.

in him, instinct is the voice of conscience by which God speaks and makes Himself known to us.[1]

"Divine instinct which is perhaps all that is left to us of man in his primeval state, and which has been left to us as the means of restoring us thereto": could the return to Nature be sounded in clearer or more peremptory tones than those?

[1] *Lettre sur les voyages*, written between 1698 and 1700. *Vide* Ch. Gould's edition, 1933, p. 288.

V

THE PSYCHOLOGY OF UNEASINESS, THE AESTHETICS OF SENTIMENT, THE METAPHYSICS OF SUBSTANCE AND THE NEW SCIENCE

THE PSYCHOLOGY OF UNEASINESS

JOHN LOCKE, as we have said, indulged in no soaring flights. Content with more modest aims, he made no attempt to scale the mountain tops of truth, satisfied with such relative verities as our puny hands can grasp. If you expect high imaginative flights from him, you have come to the wrong address. The prudent Locke will do no more than put you on a quiet road leading to the foothills of certitude, a smooth and level road, without any sudden twists or turns.

All the same, what a profound effect the principle he laid down was to have on generations to come; the principle, namely, that the *primum mobile* of the soul is sensation. Such a theory, when one comes to think of it, involves a complete revolution in the hitherto universally accepted hierarchy of values. The noblest, the fairest, the purest of ideas; moral teaching; the promptings of the spirit— all derived from the senses! Our mind, which functions at the call of sensation, is merely a servant, a labourer. So there is no rational life without an emotional life to give it its orders! The handmaid is now the mistress; she has settled herself in; she has the rights and privileges of seniority; the patent of nobility; her titles are inscribed in the pages of the *Essay concerning Human Understanding*.

Sensation is not the soul's essence; not the soul itself, for the soul cannot be taken and isolated. Nevertheless, this much is certain, namely, that on no conceivable hypothesis can the mind be regarded as its seat. If the soul were essentially intelligence, we should not see it swing (as we do) by degrees which vary between the most vigorous and determined activity and quiescence hardly distinguishable from self-effacement. The understanding is in complete abeyance when we are asleep; even when we are awake it has phases of ineffectiveness and obscurity which reduce it to something like nullity. Now, such vicissitudes, such waxing and waning, are not the normal manifestations of an essence, but rather of a function, for a function can be interrupted, or brought to a complete standstill.

Further than that: the psychology of desire and uneasiness follows directly from this re-assessment of values.

What is this? Are we to understand that Locke paved the way for the coming of the Yearning Spirit—for Saint-Preux? for Werther? and for René? They are not all his immediate lineal descendants but, in the multifarious causes which were to transform the mentality of the succeeding generations, and in the evolution of a psychology which was to lead men to demand of the heart the satisfaction which the intellect denied them, we must certainly include Locke and his philosophy. Listen to what he was saying before the seventeenth century had come to an end:

"The uneasiness a man finds in himself upon the absence of anything whose present enjoyment carries the idea of delight with it, is what we call desire; which is greater or less as that uneasiness is more or less vehement. Where, by the by, it may be of some use to remark, that the chief, if not the only spur to human industry and action is uneasiness."[1]

Uneasiness: such is the word in the English original, and Pierre Coste, Locke's translator, was not a little perplexed by this word, for which he could find no exact French equivalent. *Inquiètude* is as near as he can get, and he prints it in italics to indicate that he is using the word in a special and unfamiliar sense. This he does several times, for Locke returns to his theme again and again:

"That desire is a state of uneasiness, every one who reflects on himself will quickly find. Who is there who has not felt in desire what the wise man says of hope (which is not so much different from it), that it being deferred makes the heart sick (Proverbs XIII, 12); and that still proportionable to the greatness of the desire, which sometimes raises the

[1] *Essay concerning Human Understanding*, 1690, Book II, ch. 20.

*uneasiness to that pitch, that it makes people cry out, 'Give me children',
give me the thing desired, 'or I die'.*[1]

It is not what we have got that prompts us to act; it is what
we lack. What we do depends on the will, and the spur of the
will is uneasiness. If it were not for this uneasiness we should
continue in a state of listlessness and apathy. From it come our
hopes, our fears, our fits of depression; from it are born our
passions; it is the mainspring of our lives. Locke's disciples
were in due time to take up this theme and to push it to its ultimate
conclusion. Condillac, paying due tribute to his master (Condillac
maintained that between Aristotle and Locke there were no
philosophers worth mentioning), said that it now remained to
show that uneasiness is the exciting cause of our habits of touching,
seeing, hearing, feeling, tasting, comparing, judging, reflecting,
as well as of desiring, loving, hating, fearing, hoping and resolv-
ing; in a word, that all our habitual activities, whether of mind
or body, proceeded from uneasiness. He magnified the part
played by desire, and defined *ennui* as a malady of the soul. Helvetius went farther than Condillac, laying emphasis on the power
of the passions and the distress that comes of *ennui*, declaring that
people of a passionate nature are of a higher order than those of
equable and placid disposition, and that when our passions decline,
we grow dull of understanding. Many attempts were made to
account for the spread of romanticism, without its ever occurring
to anyone to cast a glance in Locke's direction. Locke led straight
to the *Encyclopaedia*; Locke was the father of the ideologists.
Well and good, and that is not a little. But it is not all; Locke
was also the man who noted, and drew attention to, the uneasiness
which goads us on, the uneasiness which accounts, alike for what
we do and for what we desire to do, for our actions and for our
aspirations.

And when he takes up the question of education; when,
combining his experiences as a teacher with his philosophic
theories, he sets to work to mould the human creature, what is it
he seeks above all to elicit and develop if not the spontaneity of
Nature? He is for revolutionizing existing methods, and inveighs
against the manner in which the children about him are brought
up. To start with, children are not shadows; they have arms and
legs, a chest and a stomach; a body which must be hardened by

[1]*Ibid.,* Book II, ch. 21. Pierre Coste's translation.

all sorts of exercises to make it healthy and strong. As to their mind, that should be governed by reason but not by routine; still less by an authority applied from without, indiscriminately to all alike, which would only obtain a superficial obedience. For there is in every child a natural genius which must be duly considered. "Every one's natural Genius should be carry'd as far as it could; but to attempt the putting another upon him, will be but Labour in vain; and what is so plaistered on, will at best sit but untowardly, and have always hanging to it the Ungracefulness of Constraint and Affectation." "Plain and rough Nature, left to itself, is much better than an artificial Ungracefulness, and such study'd Ways of being Illfashion'd." Virtue must come before learning, for the important thing in life is not to know a lot of things, but to be upright and good. Further, in order to inculcate into the child the necessary minimum of knowledge, we must bear in mind the spontaneity of which Locke is so constantly thinking. The time and the place, the disposition of the moment, a passing curiosity, these should be watched for and taken advantage of. Lessons represented as a piece of task-work, as a burden that has to be shouldered, are wearisome and repugnant. Take advantage of the humour, the disposition, of the moment, and you will see how much more pleasant the task becomes. Nature must be aided, corrected, guided, but without her being aware of it. A little play-acting may not come amiss to make things seem more natural.

The individual; that, at bottom, is Locke's main concern. No public schools. A good tutor, who should take the father's place and devote himself entirely to his pupil. No corporal punishment, for that degrades and humiliates. As little restraint as possible, except in the very earliest years. As the child grows older, he should be allowed more and more freedom. Endless precautions should be taken to protect the growing plant, and every explanation ingenuity can suggest should be employed to justify the lessons it is desired to inculcate upon him. In this system of education, which fancies itself so simple, and is in fact so complicated and so commanding, sometimes stoical to the point of harshness, but more often swayed by the dictates of the heart; which talks of realities and feeds on dreams, which is at once the pupil's syllabus and the master's romance, wherein are written his revolts, his regrets, his longings, his desires—in all this we catch a glimpse of the man who, seventy years later, will be openly proclaiming his admiration for Locke; and the name of that man is Jean Jacques Rousseau.

THE AESTHETICS OF SENTIMENT

"This philosophical spirit, which transforms men into such reasonable, such logical beings, bids fair to turn a large part of Europe into what the Goths and Vandals made of it in days gone by. I see the essential arts neglected; customs that contributed most usefully to the preservation of society done away with, and speculative reasoning taking the place of practical work. We order our lives without any regard to the dictates of experience, the best teacher the human race can possibly have. Solicitude for posterity is completely set aside. All the energies our forefathers expended on buildings and their furniture, would be lost to us, we should find no wood in the forests to build with, or even to light a fire to keep out the cold, if they had been as 'reasonable' as we are today." He who spoke those bold words was the Abbé Dubos. His *Critical Reflections on Poetry and Painting*, which appeared in 1719, was the result of prolonged and careful excogitation.

There were two opposing camps: to begin with, there was the school that aimed at subjecting art itself to the rules of logic. What is Beauty? What is Good Taste? How are we to recognize the beautiful when we see it? What do we mean by the Sublime? Difficult questions, these. There were the philosophers, and not only the philosophers, but all who, quite apart from philosophy, but because they were used to it, or because it pleased them, or because it was the fashion, relied solely on geometry to supply the answer. They said—we have already heard them saying it— that beauty was truth, or at all events what looked like truth; that, being truth, it played its part in morals, in virtue; that good taste was based on settled principles, on recognized models, and that consequently it could pronounce infallible judgments, infallible because they were in accordance with firmly established rules.

Transpose this theory of art into the practical sphere, give practical effect to this theorizing, and you get the idea of an Academy: the imitation of the Classics; the acquisition of a

technique to which every individual talent must be made to conform; the study of Nature, yes; but also the control and regimen-
tation of Nature, for, in matters of detail, Nature is given to
indulging in plenty of whims and fancies. Le Brun, the famous
painter of Louis XIV's day, who, rendered august by success,
by Time, and by royal decree, became, like Boileau in another
sphere, a sort of public institution—this same Le Brun, whose
name calls up a whole procession of stiff and solemn portraits in
great gilt frames, gave his disciples a number of instructions as to
how to portray various different expressions—wrath, surprise,
terror, or what was harder still, esteem, admiration, veneration.
"In rising from esteem to admiration, there is little or no change
in any particular feature; if there *is* a change, it is in the elevation
of the eyebrows, but both sides will be level, the eye being a
little wider open than usual. The pupils will be equidistant
between the two lids; they will be motionless, fixed on the object
that has excited the admiration; the lips should be slightly parted,
but neither here, nor in any other part of the face, should anything
be noticeably altered . . ." and so on and so forth. Everything is
regulated, prescribed, classified, all according to rule. Beauty is
Reason neatly dispensed in little recipes.

The other group is not so numerous; it consists of artists who
had got tired of Le Brun; of sculptors who were ceasing to be
influenced by Bernini and his school, aiming rather at grace and
elegance than at the noble and imposing; of architects who,
instead of building churches like the Gesu, or palaces like
Versailles, went in for designing attractive-looking residences,
where gentlemen of lax morality could carry on their clandestine
love-affairs; then there were the young folk, the rising generation,
who had small regard for their elders, or for the authorities in
general; yet again, there were the non-professionals, the amateurs,
who weren't going to be talked to by a parcel of professors, who
snapped their fingers at academies and academicians, declaring
that they had a perfect right to like the things that pleased them,
men like Roger de Piles who preferred Rembrandt, and especially
Rubens, to any artists of the Bologna school, and was not afraid
to say so. He was not exactly a revolutionary in the sense of one
who is systematically opposed to the whole established order of
things; he was a man who was merely determined to be himself,
and that, according to circumstances, may mean a little less, or a

great deal more, than a revolutionary. His very independence of party ties lent a sort of racy, devil-may-care note of freedom to anything he happened to say. Take this, for example: "Genius is the first thing we must require in a painter, and genius is a thing that no amount of study or hard work can supply". "Lawlessness is so essential that you find it in every branch of art. Such licences are against the rules taken according to the letter, but, judged according to the spirit, they, too, become rules when circumstances render them appropriate."[1]

Among this crowd of defiers of the law, the Abbé Dubos stands out in conspicuous relief. He does so because he unites in his person some rare qualities seldom found in combination, being at once a man of the world, and a man of learning. He was as much at home studying ancient coins in a museum as he was in the wings at the Opera; his intellectual powers were as subtle as they were vigorous; he was French to the backbone, yet a thorough citizen of the world; a man of action, and a man of ideas. Then, again, his association with Locke (he came to know him in London, where he had come to check Coste's translation with the original) led him towards that well-spring of sensibility which the great Englishman had revealed; and Dubos realized that it might well appease the strange heart-hunger of his contemporaries. From the heart comes the sense of the Beautiful, the Sublime, nay, Art itself. That it was so, he took it upon him to prove to mankind at large.

The *Réflexions critiques sur la poésie et la peinture* is packed full of ideas. The Abbé Dubos was so rich in experience, he had seen so many pictures, had witnessed so many comedies, tragedies and operas; he took such delight in conversation—not idle chatter, but thought-inspiring talk—his cleverness is so dazzling that, even when he falls short of the truth, his book still gives us the impression of being an inexhaustible treasure house. With a view to proceeding on methodical lines, he divides his work into sections; some of them short, some of them long. Some of his expositions stop short of the mark, some extend inordinately beyond it; he will start a theme, and drop it abruptly, or return to it again and again. There is nothing of the grand classical composition about this book. It comes much nearer the lines of the *Esprit des lois*, only it is not so brilliant. The sensibility which

---

[1] *Abrégé de la Vie des peintres*, 1699.

emerges, not without a struggle, from the analytical mind, does so through the medium of a lively understanding that gives chapter and verse to support its conclusions.

How profound is the effect of the pathetic on the human heart! Is it not strange to note that poems and paintings never afford us deeper pleasure than when they succeed in moving us to tears? In a room where the furnishings are designed to minister to our pleasure, a picture portraying the ghastly sacrifice of Jeptha's daughter detains us longer, and fascinates us more completely, than pictures of a specifically cheerful character. A poem describing the tragic death of an ill-fated princess may be included without incongruity in the programme of some festive entertainment, and charm the minds of people gathered together for the sole purpose of enjoying themselves. "I make so bold as to undertake the elucidation of this paradox and to explain the origin of the pleasure we derive from poetry and pictures. . . ."

The truth is that man's greatest enemy is *ennui*. People endeavour to escape from it by way either of the senses or of the intellect. The first-named is the more potent; the force of the passions is overwhelming. So great is the tumult they excite in us, that any other state of mind seems pale and languid in comparison. Only the real, genuine passions are fraught with perilous consequences, as we know to our cost. Well, that being so, we imitate things which, had they been real, would have excited our passions in good earnest. Such is the office of Art. "Pictures and poetry excite factitious passions in us by representing things which, when real, do arouse them in very truth."

Henceforth, the generally accepted formula, "Art means Reason" was no longer valid. Now, it was "Art means Passion". But it was passion at once sublimated and intensified. The degree of intensification determines the relative status of the several *genres* of poetry; tragedy, for example, moves us more deeply than comedy. "Any given kind of poetry affects us more or less deeply, according as the theme which it is its province to portray and imitate has greater or less power to excite our emotions. This is why the elegiac and bucolic forms are more attractive to us than the dramatic." So the upshot was that everybody, critics and creators alike, had to readjust their attitude. The great thing now was the portrayal of the passions, to portray them effectively, and to be able to say whether that aim had been successfully accomplished. The Abbé Dubos sets out to discover the secret of Art, and, probing down to the very depths of our being, finally arrives at the *substratum*, at sensation, the most potent factor of all. Things apprehended through the medium of the understanding seem pale, insipid, artificial in comparison with those apprehended by the senses. "I think", he says, "that pictures affect people more deeply than poetry, and I think so for two reasons. To begin with, a picture acts upon us directly, through the organ of sight; secondly, the painter does not employ artificial signs to convey his effect, but natural ones. It is by nature's means that painting achieves its imitations. The pleasure we derive from style is a physical pleasure; physical, too, is the pleasure we get from the music of poetry. Genius, so far from being something that may be increased and fortified by practice, is a natural endowment, an innate force, which nothing can arrest; a power which transcends all rules and conventions. It is, we may safely assume, a power of a physical nature. Genius is a divine rage, an enthusiasm which without doubt arises from physical causes, some peculiar state or quality of the blood, combined with a propitious organic constitution." We shall be told more about this sort of thing later on, when these physical explanations, for the moment inchoate and tentative, have established themselves more securely. But even now, with the limited knowledge at our command, we may well ask whether physical causes do not play some part in the astonishing progress in literature and the arts; whether sun, air, climate do not influence the productiveness of painters and poets, nay, whether these climatic conditions do not affect the human mechanism as a whole. Our intellectual outlook, no less than our tastes and inclinations, are dependent in large measure on the quality of our bloodstream, and that, in turn, is determined by the air we breathe, particularly in our earlier and formative years. This no doubt explains how it is that people living in different climates vary so widely in their tastes and tone of mind.

Dubos stops there. But what a distance he has travelled, and how clear is the signal he gives of the coming revolt! It is a dual revolt, an uprising against academic dogmatism on the one hand, and rationalistic theorizing on the other. In the days when the Abbé was committing his ideas to paper, the word aesthetic had not yet been invented. It did not appear till 1735, when it occurred in a thesis which a young German, Alexander Amadeus Baumgarten, composed for his doctorate. Nevertheless, we shall find in the *Réflexions critiques* an attempt to construct a system of aesthetics based on the feelings. It is in effect a protest in behalf of the world of sounds and colours, of earth and sky and water, of everything we see and hear and touch, of everything that impinges on us through the senses, of all we have in our composition of the emotional, the animal, and I had almost said, the material, against the neglect and disdain they had suffered at the hands of pure reason.

THE METAPHYSICS OF SUBSTANCE

In the philosophy of Leibniz we may discern another claim demanding consideration, that is, a system of metaphysics based on the infinitely little, the imperceptible, the inapprehensible, the obscure; on psychic force; on the existence of simple substances which are as it were the essence of the vital instinct, the essence of the *Ego*.

Leibniz found it impossible to admit that geometry could furnish the final and conclusive explanation of things. For Descartes he evinced at once a sincere admiration and a repugnance to which he gave expression in pamphlet after pamphlet, as his manner was. At last, in 1714, two years before he died, he drew up his last philosophical will and testament, his *Monadologie*. It was not published straightway. Prince Eugène of Savoy directed that it should be preserved in a casket. Only the privileged few were allowed to see the secret treasure. But the day was to come when letters and treatises would emerge from the shades, when the casket would be opened, and when its spiritual contents, at last set free, would begin to work like a leaven.

It seemed to Leibniz that Descartes tended to simplify things too much, confounding, as he did, extent and substance, motion and vital force. He considered, also, that his way of dividing things into two parts, without regard to the gradations by which we come down to the infinitely minute, of ignoring the hidden, unconscious perceptions of mind, was too rough and ready. To treat perceptions which we cannot apprehend as if they were simply non-existent, was, as he expressly stated in his *Monadologie*, precisely where the Cartesians made their fundamental error. As he had pointed out ten years earlier, in his *Nouveaux essais sur l'entendement humain*, there are an infinite number of changes taking place within us to which we pay no heed because our im pressions are either too faint, or too numerous, or too uniform. Most of us cease to notice the noise of a mill or a waterfall when we have been living near it for a certain time, yet the sound still impinges on our *sensorium*. When we stand on the sea-shore, we hear the sound of the sea; it follows, then, that we must perceive the sound of every drop and trickle of every wave, yet we are unaware that we perceive them. Those unconscious perceptions, which are the very stuff our psychological life is made of, were not taken into account by Descartes. "It must be confessed that *Perception*, and all that it implies, does not admit of a purely mechanical explanation, that is to say, one of figures and diagrams. Let us imagine a machine so constructed as to produce thought, feeling, the power of perception; then let us imagine this machine to be so enlarged in all its parts that we are able to get inside it; as we explore its interior, we shall find nothing save the various parts interacting one upon another, but nothing at all that would account for perception. Therefore, it is in the substance itself, and not in the thing made from it, not in the machine, that we must look to find it."

This primary substance is the Monad, nature's true atom. What strikes us, as we note how Leibniz explains the properties of the Monad, which was to transfer the possession of the secret of life from physics to metaphysics, is his care, his anxiety to safeguard the theory of individual psychic force. Whereas Spinoza proceeds from the particular to the general, Leibniz seeks a synthesis which will admit the universal, but, without detriment to the claims of the particular. The Monad cannot be changed or modified in its inner nature by any other created thing; it has no windows affording ingress or egress. Any given Monad has, in comparison with the other Monads around it, specific qualities of its own, since in Nature, no two things are ever identical. The Monad, like every other created thing, is liable to change, but this change takes place within the Monad itself and does not result from any action brought to bear upon it from outside.

This very marked characteristic of the Monad gives rise to a difficulty. Since it is simple substance and is unaffected by any-thing outside itself, is it not necessarily doomed to perpetual isolation? It is not so doomed, and that by reason of a pre-established harmony.

How Leibniz explains the nature of this wonderful harmony is not a matter into which we need enter here. Any history of philosophy will explain it far better than we could possibly do. But we have all we need to make good our case, we have the unconscious. "Every mind being, as it were, a world in itself, sufficient unto itself, independent of every other creature, comprehending the infinite, expressing the universe, is as lasting, as self-subsisting, and as absolute as is the universe of created things itself." And here is a poetic vision of life multiplied *ad infinitum*:

Every portion of matter may be regarded as a garden full of plants, and as a pond full of fish. But every branch of the plant, every member of the animal, every drop of animal fluid, is likewise such a garden, such a pond.

And although the earth and air that are implicated in the garden plants, or the water about the fish in the pond, are themselves neither plant nor fish, they nevertheless contain them though generally in forms so minute as to be imperceptible by our senses.

Therefore nothing in the whole universe is barren, or sterile or devoid of life; there is no chaos, no confusion, save to the outward view. . . .[1]

There we have the affirmation of a sovereign harmony of such a nature, that drinking deep thereof, we find ourselves within the realms of perfect love.

THE NEW SCIENCE

Naples! the sun! what joy to be alive! Hark to the shouting and the tumult! See, in the narrow, winding streets, what swarms of people, the most mercurial people in the world! What vivacity! What zest! Where shall we find their like? And how keen they are to learn, to improve their minds! How animated they are! How eagerly they converse! Look at their assemblies, their salons, where men, carrying the burden of profound learning with graceful ease, discuss the various questions that engage the attention of philosophers and men of science, consider the various schools of thought and weigh the facts. At Naples, which receives, because it always keeps its ears open, the latest tidings of all that

[1]*Monadologie*, §§ 67, 68, 69.

is being said and thought in Europe, at Naples, the old, original, tumultuous Naples, which stands forth as the very embodiment of force and vitality, there was born into the world on the 23rd June, 1668, a certain Giambattista Vico.

Every sort of hindrance that fetters the spirit, he knew; yet he managed to evade them all. He might, for example, have been an infant prodigy—he escaped. He might have been one of those too docile disciples who meekly lap up everything their masters tell them; he escaped. He might have become a slave to his profession; he escaped. Finally, he might have become prosperous, one of the greatest perils a man of ideas can be threatened by. That, too, he escaped. He read Aristotle and all the Greeks, St. Augustine, St. Thomas, Gassendi, Locke, Descartes, Spinoza, Malebranche and Leibniz without surrendering himself to any of them. He took four models as his guides. They were Plato, Tacitus, Bacon (who realized "that the sciences, both human and divine, had a lot further to go, and that such few discoveries as they had made still had need of correction"), and Grotius who "brought together under a single code of law the whole province of philosophy, and who based his theology on the history of facts, whether fabled or authentic, as recorded in three languages— Hebrew, Greek and Latin, the only learned languages of antiquity which have been handed down to us by the Christian religion". However, the influence of these geniuses did not deter him from criticizing them very thoroughly. Solitary, majestic, melancholy, he determined to be himself; himself and none other.

There are two sorts of intelligence, the intelligence which absorbs, and the intelligence which creates. Vico possessed them both. He would plan out a route for himself, and then incontinently abandon it, from sheer impulsiveness. He revelled in metaphor and imagery. He would tell himself that he would proceed in his analysis step by step, and then suddenly, off he would go, up into the skies, on the wings of some inward intuition! He will begin to demonstrate something in the most approved logical manner, and then, because he is in such a tearing hurry, he will forsake the line he has chosen, not because he sees some obstacle ahead of him, but simply because it is his nature so to do. He is persistent, and will tell you the same thing over and over again; he is impatient, he outstrips himself, and tells you his conclusion before he is done with his preliminaries. He hankers after

the novel, the daring, the paradoxical. He loves disentangling a
thread of truth from a skein of error, and then, holding it up for
all to see, cries, " 'Tis I did it, I, Giambattista Vico! " There is
no suggestion of classical restraint about him; fiery, intense, to an
almost insane degree, he is the very personification of the Soul
Unsatisfied. He is never tired of proving things, of re-shaping
his text, of clarifying his ideas, of impressing on his readers the
marvellous nature of his discoveries. He was a tenacious
customer, not easy to get on with; in fact, quite the reverse.
Overbearing, irascible, he persuaded himself that he was endowed with superior intellectual gifts which his contemporaries
failed to recognize, and their blindness gave him pain. Therefore,
he redoubled his efforts to bring them to see things in his light.
He battled with them; he battled with himself. What he felt he
absolutely must do, sooner or later, was to initiate them into his
great secret, the secret of the New Science.

New, indeed, it was; in the first place by reason of the faculty
it liked best to employ, the faculty that went by the name of the
creative imagination. No doubt criticism has a part to play, and a
useful part, but it is out of touch with the deeper significance of
life, which is no mere abstract thing, but perpetual creation.
Again, there was novelty in his method, which was precisely the
one with which the people about him would have nothing to do;
it was the historical method; only, in his view of it, history was
to be read not merely in books, but also in the countless traces
man had left behind him in his pilgrimage down the ages, in the
poetry of the primitive peoples, in their languages, their laws,
and their public institutions; in everything, in short, that had to
do with their way of life. Then, again, his line of approach was
new. Instead of peering into the distant future for the object of
his quest, he turned his gaze backwards down the aisles of time, to
the very origins of our kind. Finally, his philosophy was new in
its essence. It was concerned with the idea of collective evolution,
of being which creates itself and is at the same time conscious of
itself, finding the guarantee of its certitude in the identification of
subject and object: Science is the creation of humanity by humanity,
and recorded by humanity. "In the midst of that night of darkness
and shadow in which antiquity lies enwrapt, antiquity from
which we are so far removed, we discern an everlasting light
which never wanes, a truth which none can call in question.

Therefore it is possible—it is also both profitable and necessary—to discover its principles by tracing the changes which our ideas have undergone."

Poor Vico! so forlorn and yet so great. No one could make out what he was talking about; they hardly took the trouble to listen. His ideas were too novel. They clashed too violently with what was generally received and approved of. The majority of people kept prosing on about the abstract, the rational, and blushed at the very thought of the past, which seemed to them something that enlightened and civilized people like themselves ought to be ashamed of. History, they took to be a lot of fairy tales, and poetry mere verbal jugglery. As for sentiment, the silly stuff, they would have none of it, and imagination, which was equally crazy, they sent to the right-about. But Vico, with the invincible obstinacy of genius, refused to treat humanity as though it were an anatomical specimen; he insisted on discerning in it the pulsation of the living thing. With jurisprudence and philology, and pictures, and symbols, and fables, to help him, gradually acquiring an intimate knowledge of the past, he plunged into the remotest depths of antiquity; to discover at once the history of our evolution and the ideal form of the human mind.

The golden branch which he brought with him made no impression. This accounts for the cry which we can still hear in the *Scienza Nuova*[1], the cry of a wronged soul. Passion, with him, tries desperately hard to lend wings to sentences too heavily laden with thought to take the air with ease, and Vico, eager to prove all things at once, in constant apprehension lest he has insufficiently explained himself, always in a hurry, puffing and panting and floundering along, presents his public with his *magnum opus*, and his *magnum opus* falls completely flat. Three quarters of a century were to elapse before this admirable work at last began to fling a shaft of light athwart the European sky-line.

---

[1] *Principii di una Scienza Nuova intorno alla comune natura delle nazioni* (Première édition 1725: *Prima Scienza Nuova*. Deuxième édition 1730: *Seconda Scienza Nuova*).

VI

SOULS OF FIRE

THOSE towers that crown the landscape in the green
countryside, and, in the cities, the cathedrals with the
houses clustering round them, to which they seem to be
pointing the way to Heaven; the golden glory of the tapers
lighting up the tabernacles with their tremulous beams; the in-
toning of the priests, the chanting choirs, the *Credo*, the *Magnificat*,
the sound of bells, the teeming censers, the countless churches,
conventicles, synagogues, mosques, all the various places where
people congregate to confess the mystery that enshrouds their
birth, their life, their death, leaving it to God to reveal the secret
to which their own unaided reason finds no key.

The need for religion abides eternally in the human breast.

Now, it was, that religious folk began to feel alarm at the
activities of the freethinkers and atheists. Many were the
Christian apologists who gave warning of the growing danger.
Though there were some who did not hesitate to engage the
terrorists on their own ground, others sought for different
weapons to repel the foe. The wolves were ravening in ever-
growing numbers round the fold; new methods must be found
to keep them at bay. If the voice of the ungodly was loud in the
land, let religion make answer with an ever swelling diapason,
with an ever livelier faith. Against those who watch and pray,
and slumber not, the enemy shall not prevail.

"This sublime age, which may be called the age of the spirit,
or, more than that, the age of perfect love . . ." Thus speaks
Henri Bremond, reviewing the Christian life under the *Ancien
Régime*; and he showed that the spread of Cartesianism in no way
diminished, among religious folk, the keenness of their devotion

to the fundamentals of the faith, or discouraged the practice of religious exercises and observances. Among the books of devotion quoted by him in support of his statement, one in particular, so noble is its simplicity, remains fixed in our recollection; it is called *L'Horloge pour l'adoration perpetuelle du Saint Sacrement*, and the date of it is 1674; "a Clock for the perpetual adoration of the Blessed Sacrament." This sacred timepiece gives warning of the hours of pressing danger. The faithful, when they hear it strike, may imagine they see the enemy hosts, with Satan at their head, launching an assault upon religion, in an attempt to compass its destruction. Every hour, as it strikes, calls up some vision of terror. Midnight: the Powers of Darkness, in the murky deeps of Night, which is their empire's chief domain, come forth from their cavernous dens armed with the instruments of torture, and the fires which they take with them wherever they go, up and down the world, to gather their tools and agents about them. Five in the morning: the Sacred Elements cast to the dogs. But each offence is answered by a healing litany. The ticking of this solemn clock awakens "a new instinct", "a latent ardour", such as nothing availed to arouse in the tranquil days of peace.

A life richer in sensibility; here, it may be, is the crucial point; here we may discern, albeit still faint and evanescent, the beginnings of an apologetic which it took a whole century to develop. Knowledge, certainly: no church is opposed to knowledge. And Reason, too, of course. No Church can afford to dispense with Reason. Nevertheless, disregarding the extremer forms of atheism, and taking account only of the effect observable in the general run of people, religion undoubtedly did lose the support of a certain section of the thoughtful public, the section that wanted to be independent of religion, to by-pass it, and to set up a humanistic ideal of their own. "No one can deny that this is a learned and enlightened age. Great progress has been made in all branches of Science and Art, whether by way of giving them sounder principles to work on, or supplying them with a firmer basis of proof and demonstration. What a number of discoveries have been made, what a number of experiments have seen the light, which have enabled us to penetrate beyond those limits in which, all through the dark ages, the mind of man was so narrowly confined. Nevertheless, it is greatly to be doubted whether the

cause of religion has benefited by all this laudable quest for
knowledge, whether, indeed, it has not lost, rather than gained,
because of it."[1]

Well, but religion can recover the lost ground by calling in
other spiritual values to its aid, values which its adversaries either
deride or deny.

The best proofs of the existence of God are, no doubt, the
metaphysical ones; but metaphysics are "caviare to the general".
With the vast majority, the feelings are the main guides and, by
availing himself of them, the Christian apologist can arrive at a
proof not a whit less cogent. Do not the wonders of Nature
reveal His existence, His power, His loving foresight? The
argument may not be new, but it can take on fresh power if it is
presented with appropriate emphasis, if logic is heightened with
emotion. A state of admiration and wonderment is thus created,
in which all is made clear, a lyrical state which carries all before it.
Look at the woods: "In summertime, these branches shield us
with their shade from the sun's hot rays; in winter they feed the
fire which enables us to maintain our bodily warmth. Nor is
wood useful only as fuel; it is of a tractable consistency, though
solid and durable, and can be fashioned by man into whatsoever
shape he pleases, great architectural structures, and ships that
sail the sea. Then, again, the fruit trees, with their branches
bending low towards the ground—with what gracious con-
descension they seem to proffer their fruits to man!" And then
of water: "If water were by a shade less dense, it would be something akin to air. The whole face of the earth would be parched
and sterile; there would be no winged creatures; no animal of any
kind would be able to swim; no fish could live; there would be no
sea-borne merchandise. If water was a little more rarefied, it
could not sustain those prodigious floating edifices we call ships;
the lightest bodies would straightway sink to the bottom."
Look at the air, at fire, at the stars, at the dawn, which "for
thousands upon thousands of years has never failed to usher in
the day; punctually, to the very second, she comes, and at her
appointed place". And the animals. "The elephant, whose neck
would be too heavy for its body were it as long as the camel's, is
furnished with a trunk."[2]

[1]Isaac Jaquelot, *Dissertations sur l'existence de Dieu*, The Hague, 1697. Preface.
[2]Fénelon, *Démonstration de l'existence de Dieu tirée de la connaissance de la nature*, 1713.

A little while, and we shall have Nieuwentijit, and the Abbé Pluche, proving to innumerable disciples how God's existence may be inferred from the wonders of Nature; then will come Bernardin de Saint-Pierre; and, after him, Chateaubriand.

Having arrived thus far on our journey, having reached the threshold of the retreat where the Man of Feeling proudly makes his final stand, we will next call up Gottfried Arnold from the shades.   Behold him standing with his *Histoire impartiale des églises et des hérésies* in his hand!   He claims impartiality for it because it is the work of a man who owes allegiance to no sect in particular, and because he has treated his subject as a historian, not as a theologian.   Furthermore, he claims for it a general appeal, because, refusing to admit that there is one Church, and one only, it addresses itself to all who profess to believe in God and in Jesus Christ.   What it really amounts to is a glorification of heresy.

The truth is, he alleges, that people have made a great mistake about heretics, who, according to him, are a grossly misunderstood and maligned body of people.   Heretics is the description applied by people in power to such as might stand in their way, or diminish their influence.   They refer with ostentatious pride to their own orthodoxy.   But orthodoxy is not religion, it is not faith.   To swallow a lot of dogmas and formulas with your eyes shut; blindly to believe whatever the authorities tell you; to imagine that belief is a mere *opus operatum*—that is what orthodoxy amounts to.   In short, it is nothing but a sort of barren rationalism that knows nothing of religious experiences, of spiritual awakenings, of being born anew.

Heretics proper are not to be identified with those who, for sound motives, take the risk of wandering a little from the path of strict orthodoxy; they are much rather the sort of people who live like pagans, recking nothing of God, self-opinionated people, doctrinaires, intolerant bigots. . . . Thus, in the year 1699, spoke Gottfried Arnold, scholar, rebel and mystic: those who are commonly called heretics are your true Christians, sanctified by suffering, and glorified by love.   Those who commonly go by the name of orthodox, whose hearts are dry and withered—those are your true heretics.

And now, with Gottfried Arnold for our guide, let us make our way into the circle of the religious enthusiasts.

The year 1709 witnessed the expulsion of the last few nuns who had stayed on at Port Royal. In 1710, the buildings were themselves demolished. Jansenism was to be suppressed; the sect which for so many years had been a thorn in the Church's side, was to be exterminated at last; *ubi solitudinem faciunt, pacem appellant*. But no; it was not to be. The Jansenists began to open up new ground, to make progress abroad. Little by little, they forged ahead. There were still a few hot-beds of Jansenism left in Louvain; and at Utrecht, where, in defiance of authority, a church opened its arms to the exiles, the outlaws; in a number of German towns; in Vienna, the very heart of the Imperial Court; in Piedmont, in Lombardy, in Liguria, in Tuscany, and even in Rome itself. And Jansenist propagandists were busy in Spain. In France, the quarrel broke out afresh, and as violently as ever, with the promulgation, in 1713, of the Bull *Unigenitus*. Quesnel, an Oratorian, brought out a book on the *Morality of the Gospel* in which a hundred and one passages were condemned by the Pope. It seemed as though a signal had gone up, as though someone had given the word. The commotion began all over again: objectors; defenders; trimmers—all fell to arguing again, and to argue they were to continue for many a day to come. Soon, now, the *Convulsionnaires* were to appear on the scene; processions, miracles wrought upon the graves of the chosen ones. This time, the disturbances reached the proportions of a public scandal. If Jansenism contained two elements, the one theological, the other moral, it was the latter that grew stronger at the expense of the former. Spiritual anxiety, hopes and fears about salvation, bitter memories of persecution, the belief that miracles of divine vengeance were at hand—things like these are not to be done away with by royal decree, or on orders from Rome. In the long run Jansenism came to be, not so much a doctrine as a spirit; a spirit harsh, forbidding, austere, sternly opposing the progressive dulcification of faith and morals.

The Camisards of the Cévennes, hounded and hunted by a ruthless soldiery, tortured and martyred for their faith, had even more excuse for displaying an emotionalism that grew and grew in intensity till it reached the point of hallucination, of insane delusion. Take, for instance, the case of one of their leaders, Abraham Mazel,

who has left us his life story, or perhaps we should call it his confession: "A few months before I took up arms, before I even
dreamt of doing so, I had a vision in which I saw a number of
black oxen in a garden. They were very fat, and were devouring
the cabbages that were growing there. Someone whom I did not
know bade me drive them from the garden, but I refused. Then,
seeing that he grew more and more insistent, I did his bidding
and drove the beasts from the garden. Thereupon, the spirit of
the Lord descended upon me and seized hold of me as a strong
man might have done, and, unsealing my lips, caused me to
declare, among other things, that the garden I had seen was
really the Church, and that the fat, black beeves were the priests
who were devouring her, and that I had been called to complete
the moral of the picture. I was visited many times by the spirit
which made known to me that I was to make ready to take up
arms so that I might fight side by side with the brethren against
my persecutors, that I must assail the priests of the Romish
Church with fire and sword, and burn down their altars." The
spirit it was that bade them hold their meetings in the woods,
and the spirit came upon them in so terrible a manner that they
were seized with trembling in all their limbs, a trembling so
violent that all who beheld it were overcome with fear. It was in
obedience to the spirit that they took up arms, the spirit it was
that told them when to set out on the march, when to attack, and
when to scatter. It was the spirit that ordered them to set fire to
the presbyteries and to slaughter the priests. Taken prisoner at
length, Mazel was shut up in the Tower of Constance at Aigues-
Mortes. He began to saw through one of the stones of the tower
in order to escape, and "every time he set to work he felt that he
was filled with the Holy Ghost".

Élie Marion's case was more perplexing still. "On the first
day of this year, 1703, God honoured me with a visit from His
Spirit, and in the first words which my lips uttered under the
influence of that inspiration, it was made known to me among
other things that God had chosen me, while I was yet in my
mother's womb, to serve Him for the advancement of His glory."
Élie Marion is the Chosen One, the forerunner of Christ's
glorious reign. Without going into the details of his various
conflicts and his ultimate undoing, we will give a brief account of
his behaviour in London when he sought refuge there in 1706.

He saw visions; he gave utterance to prophecies; the spirit of
God descended upon him and sent him into a trance; he hurled
his thunders, not so much at the heathen, at the unbelievers, as
at the lukewarm, and at the pastors. He had already castigated
the Genevans because they would not believe that the coming of
Christ was at hand. "For them, this Second Advent is like a sun
whose face they are unable to look upon, whose brightness makes
them blind. Let them take heed that they be not cast aside, even
as the Jews." In London he fulminates against the pastors, both
French and Anglican, against everything and everyone; whereby
hangs a strange and lamentable story. With the doors of all the
various churches shut in their faces, mocked and booed at by the
rabble, taken into custody, haled before the magistrate and
branded as criminals, these prophesying Camisards seem to feel
as if they were surrounded by a ring of fire that kept growing
fiercer and fiercer. They gained some adherents among the
English, for the disease was catching, and one of their acquisitions
was a crack-brained Englishwoman. At last they gave out that
the fateful day was at hand, that fire and brimstone were about to
consume the city and all the ungodly ones within it; only those
who believed would escape the doom; and, in order that the
Destroying Angel might recognize them when he saw them, they
were recommended to wear a strip of green ribbon, either as an
armlet, or as a fillet round their brows. Another time they
declared that before six months were past and gone, the persecution of the prophets would cease, and that the truth of their
teaching would be made manifest. Six months went by, and
nothing happened. On another occasion, they boasted that they
had power to bring back the dead to life. The great majority of
the English people thought they were lunatics, and looked on
them with amazement. At first they merely showed annoyance,
but after a time they set the machinery of the law to work. Élie
Marion was put in the pillory with a placard above his head,
which read: "Élie Marion found guilty of attempting to pass
himself off as a prophet, the same being a blasphemous lie, and
of printing and uttering divers statements, which he alleges were
dictated and revealed to him by the spirit of God, with intent to
spread alarm among the Queen's subjects." At last, however,
Élie Marion took his departure, and with him went a few disciples who refused to quit his side. From country to country, the

little band of companions journeyed on, even to Constantinople, and, farther still, to Asia Minor, for ever preaching, prophesying, and foretelling woe; persecuted, sometimes cast into prison, but carrying with them that fantastic light of theirs with which, they said, they would lighten all nations: the Beam of Light coming down from Heaven to illumine the night of the peoples of the earth, and show them the corruption that was concealed in their dark places.

Up to a point, Spinoza's fatalism is in a line with the inflexible character of reason. But logic apart, there is an undeniable attraction in feeling oneself merging into, and becoming one with Universal Being. In order to be fully effective, integration into the order which governs the world, which is the world, which is God, which is the All in All, should proceed from a conscious act of the will. Nevertheless, it is possible, by an easy transition, to decline from an active and intentional, into a merely passive acquiescence, which is but another name for surrender. It need cause us therefore no surprise to see the *Ethics* engendering a mysticism of a kind that gained considerable ground both in Holland and Germany. Nevertheless, it is a far cry from these Spinozists to mysticism in its later and most ardent manifestations.

Since the Lutheran pastors were reproached for the very faults they had imputed to the Catholics; since they were slaves to the letter and careless of the spirit; since they had not charity, and the faith was not in them; since they took payment for performing the offices of religion, and even allowed penitents to redeem their sins with money; since their sermons, so far from being fountains of living truth, were but homilies learned by rote and spiced with popular pleasantries, having nothing to do with spreading the Word of God, there came into being, to combat all these things, what is known as pietism, or the religion of the heart. Piety; the heart; these words recur again and again in the writings and in the speeches of the man through whose influence German sensibility, so long repressed, was enabled to emerge into the light of day. His name was Philip Jacob Spener. It was in 1670, when he was a pastor at Frankfort, that he conceived the idea of instituting Colleges of Piety. The work of ministers of religion had nothing to do with polemics, with bawling and

bluster. But theirs it was to kindle and to foster the inward life.
Of an evening, therefore, twice a week, he gathered round him
a number of earnest, god-fearing men to read the Bible, to join
together in prayer, and to suffer the divine spirit to work within
them. That was the first step; the second he accomplished in
1675 when he published his *Pia desideria oder herzliches Verlangen
nach gottgefälliger Besserung der wahren evangelischen Kirche.* Thereafter his influence extended to the pastorate as a whole, and to
religious folk in general, whom he exhorted to return to a lively
and active faith, a faith founded on love. In 1688, he went to
Dresden, in the capacity of select preacher and chaplain to the
Elector of Saxony, and as a member of the Higher Consistory.
The significance of these honours lies in the light they throw on
the measure of his influence and success. Students and women
listened enraptured to his grave and ardent words. At his
instigation, groups were formed for the purpose of Bible study.
The name "pietist", once a term of derision, became an appellation to be proud of. A pietist was that August Hermann Francke
who, just as he was about to hold forth on the subject of faith,
realized suddenly that the faith was not in him. He was overwhelmed with despair, and falling on his knees implored the
Almighty to help him in his desperate extremity. God suffered
His light to shine upon him and from that day forth he resolved
to do all that in him lay to pass on that light to others. Pietists
were those princesses and nobles who sought by their own
efforts to find the way of salvation; of pietists, too, there were
many among the middle and the lower classes; Germany was
once more awakening to the faith. Pietism, contagion-like,
spread far and wide. In due time, Spener left Dresden and went
to Berlin, where he won over the Elector of Brandenburg; and
when, in 1694, the latter promoted the Halle Academy to the
status of a University, it was Spener who became its moving
spirit. Thus arose the Citadel of Pietism, girt about with works
of Christian charity. What did they stand for, these zealots, so
fiery and, here, so triumphant? What was it that moved them?
In the first place it was something they inherited. That was
Boehme's mysticism, which was still alive within them. In the
second place, it was a denial, a revolt against the tendency to
crystallize, to freeze the current of the inward religious life. Or,
to go a little deeper, they maintained that the analytical and

rationalistic approach was not the only way of arriving at knowledge; they held by intuition; they maintained that it was possible to enjoy immediate and absolute communion with the Eternal Source of Life—The *Ego*; and, within the *Ego*, the force of the emotive faculties, faculties more personal, more individual than any others. Lastly, there was the belief in a primary, underlying bond, which the customary forms of religious civilization threatened to destroy.

Countless *nuances* of sentiment go to the enrichment of their lives. They feel withered, sterile, cast aside; they feel the agony of one vainly crying in the wilderness; what can be more grievous than this long waiting for grace? Then comes the time for confession, for unburdening the heart—and now, behold a miracle! The light! An instantaneous revelation! And then the infinite sweetness of a more than earthly love, the losing of Self in the Being who knows all things, wills all things, and imparts to life a foretaste of Eternity. After that, what more is there to seek? What can philosophers avail? Or theologians? Or Biblical exegetists, seeing that the Word is plainly writ for all to read? *Unum est necessarium*: to do everything in God. But that carries the implication of action, of doing. And that, too, the quietists will eliminate.

How are we to explain the quarrel which set at odds the two most illustrious prelates of the Church of France, leading them to hurl reproaches and accusations one against the other, and ending in an appeal to Rome, and the condemnation of one of them—how are we to explain it all, unless we recognize in this great combat a particular manifestation of a general tendency. Quietism was but one example of the many forms of the flowing tide of mysticism, which, in the name of the emancipation of the feelings, was sapping the foundations of organized religion. With what dreams did Fénelon not beguile himself? Behold him about to set forth on a journey. The whole of Greece lies open before him; the Sultan recoils in terror. Already he sees—these are his own words—the end of the Great Schism and the reconciliation of East and West. "Asia I behold, the sound of her sighs reaching even to the far-off Euphrates, as she sees the day dawning again now that the long night is over." Or else he imagines, and portrays in glowing language, a land of dreams, an ideally beautiful Boetica, where the winters are always mild and the summers never torrid, so that Spring and Autumn, wedded one to the other, walk hand in hand through all the year. So rich and fertile is the soil that it yields a double harvest. Pomegranates, laurels, jasmines and other flowering trees befringe the scented highways. Or he sets to work to build with his own hands the ideal city, Salentum. There vice and misfortune shall be no more. Not even the boon countries of the South offer such happiness to the sons of men. At Salentum, peace shall reign, and justice, and social order, and abundance. Riches shall be borne in upon a flowing tide, and, as the tide recedes, it will leave other riches behind it. Every problem finds a ready solution. At a wave of the magic wand, everything is transformed, the town-dwellers are happy, the peasants, the women, the little children and the old men—all are happy. "The old men, amazed to behold what they had never dared to hope for all through their long life, wept for very joy and tenderness, and lifted up their trembling hands to heaven." Abroad, there will be peace. To halt the advancing foe, it will suffice to stand in their midst and hold discourse with them. The warriors will fling away their arms, and they will all embrace with tears.

Fénelon has a liking for tears; the heroes of his *Télémaque* shed tears in abundance. The whole book is bathed in them. Calypso, Eucharis and Venus; Telemachus, Mentor, Philocles, Idomeneus, shed oceans of these precious tears. He must needs be amiable, gentle, tender. "I prefer the agreeable, to the startling, to the breath-taking", he says in his *Lettre sur les occupations de l'Académie*; he also declared that he would willingly agree to admit into the language any term that it lacked, provided it did not sin against euphony. He was charitable and generous; he knew, and freely practised, all the divers ways of winning hearts, coy, or willing.

But he knew, also, perfectly well that he had ambitious and exacting ideas; he was not content to live in the clouds. He knew he had it in him to be haughty and abrupt; that he had no inconsiderable capacity for downright hatred. Ah, how far he was from perfection. What misery the thought of these incongruous shortcomings made him feel. This tortured soul, this heart so prone to weariness and sadness brooded with sorrow on something he could not explain, deep down in his moral nature.

The sight turned him sick, for what he saw was a swarm of reptiles.

How he longed for some clear spring to relieve his thirst; he longed for the grace that should cleanse him from his worldliness, his scheming, his ambitions and his play-acting. But the perfection which he aspired to he could not reach unaided. The thought of his anxiety made him more anxious still. This no doubt explains the power that Mme. Guyon wielded over him. The reason, the sole reason, of her great ascendancy was the crying need he felt within him to melt and destroy in the fires of mysticism the chains which dragged him down. Madame Guyon had won over the young ladies of Saint-Cyr, the great ladies of the Court, aye, and Madame de Maintenon herself. A short-lived triumph, for it took but little to make them slip back again. She had also tried to add Bossuet to her conquests, but he had not been in the least impressed; his religious faith had no need of such a dubious ally. This woman, this quite ordinary woman, who had such a great idea of herself, who boasted of her prophesyings, her visions, her miraculous powers, made his gorge rise. When she persisted in saying that prayer should involve a total annihilation of self, that she could ask nothing of God, not even the forgiveness of her sins, that was enough for him; Madame Guyon was a heretic, and not another word from her would he consent to listen to. But to Fénelon, that tortured, anxious heart, to that spirit great and lofty enough to read its own defects, yet too deeply committed to the world to have courage enough to forsake it—to Fénelon came Madame Guyon with her doctrine of perfect love, and did not come in vain.

Those intermediaries between man and his Creator, those channels, some of them solid and material, others refined and well-nigh insubstantial, are hindrances none the less, hindrances that become the more wearisome the nearer we get to our goal and never so wearisome as when we are within an ace of our heart's desire and all that is asked of us is a sigh or a prayer—these barriers betwixt God and His creature, Madame Guyon would do away with, one and all. Herself a proselyte, fired with a passionate desire to give spiritual help to others, she tells us what we must do to gain the highest peaks of the spiritual life. Learn to pray, she cries; you should live in prayer, even as you should live in love. Come, famished hearts, come poor suffering ones; come,

ye sick and ailing; ye sinners, come and draw near to God; if
you have hearts, come, oh, come!

You bring yourself into God's presence by a fervent act of
faith; you begin by reading a few lines of some devotional book,
not to reason thereon, but simply to keep your mind from
wandering. Then withdraw deep down into yourself, gathering
all your senses within you. When affection is awakened, suffer it
to remain at rest, and in peace. To move it still further at this
point would be to deprive the soul of its nourishment. It must
assimilate, in a brief period of repose, loving and full of trust,
that whereof it has tasted.

When you have grown used to this, the second degree of
intuition begins: the prayer of simplicity. Less effort is required;
the end grows more attainable, the presence of God is more easy
to feel, and seems to be more intense. Above all, let the soul
bring to its prayer love in all its purity, love that is freed from
everything other than love itself, and is therefore wholly un-
selfish. Let the soul ask nothing for itself; let it pray, not in order
that it may obtain something from God, for a servant who
measures his service to his master by the recompense he receives
from him is not worthy to be rewarded. Implore not, but wait.
Let it suffice that your prayer should bring you into a state of
recollection, for prayer is none other than the warmth of love
which melts and dissolves the soul.

The Christian that climbs the sacred mountain thus arrives
at complete self-surrender, the putting off of every thought of
self, resigning himself wholly to God's guidance. No more
reasoning; no more excogitating. Renouncement of the will, of
desire, however good the object. Indifference to all things,
whether of the body or the soul; indifference to our welfare,
whether temporal or eternal. Resign the past to Oblivion, the
future to Providence, but the present give to God. Whoso has
learnt the secret of complete surrender to God, will soon reach
perfection.

Thus disappears the distinct and specific character of the
individual, which is the source of all malice. The Almighty sends
His own Wisdom before Him, even as fire will be sent upon the
earth, to consume whatsoever is impure in man. The fire consumes all things, and whatsoever resists it, that, too, is consumed.
It is even so with Wisdom, it consumes whatsoever is impure in

the creature, so as to prepare it for union with the Divine. Such union is ineffable. If, however, one were to attempt to express it in words, we might say that we experience an inrush of love which fills us with a flood of happiness. There is, in this abandonment of self, in this possession of the infinite, a degree of bliss of which no human happiness can afford a notion. It is not emptiness, but abundance. To renounce is gain; to surrender all, is to abound in all. Love is all in all.

Thus does Madame Guyon, condensing for the nonce her overwordy explanations, furnish all who are interested enough to listen, with a *Moyen court et facile pour l'oraison, que tous peuvent pratiquer très aisément et arriver par là en peu à une haute perfection* (1685). Combining boldness of design with shrewdness in practice, she conceived a plan for bringing about a wholesale religious revival. Never, when she was journeying along the highways of Piedmont with her henchman Père Lacombe, preaching and spreading abroad the teaching of Molinos, nor, yet, in Paris, had she encountered a man capable of giving her quietist ideas the necessary scope and publicity. But now Fénelon should be the shining light that was to illumine the reawakened Church. He would show how to do battle with the Evil One; in a word, he it was who would usher in, under her guidance, the reign of Divine Love.

Others might say she was a mere adventuress; to him she was the guide that was to lead him along the road to perfection. How hard he found it to jettison those intellectual faculties of his, at once so delicate and so shrewd; to bid farewell to his worldly wisdom, to all those intrusive elements which vitiated and retarded the fulfilment of his good intentions. But the mystical ardour which emanated from her was gradually consuming these baser elements. "Yours ever more and more unreservedly in Our Lord, and with a gratitude which He alone can measure." He had his relapses, his distractions, his fits of wilfulness, his dislikes, his moments of impatience, of arrogance, of barrenness both inward and outward; inward because he could not pray as he longed to pray; outward as touching his intercourse with his fellows. But Madame Guyon told him where he went wrong, helped him along and cleared away all his stumbling blocks. He felt that the days of candour, of innocence were coming back to him once more: "O bliss ineffable that flows from lowliness," and he felt that he was becoming that which he longed to be, a thing of nought, bereft of everything, even as a little child. And he took to writing verses to the tune of well-known songs:

> O pur amour, achève de détruire
> Ce qu'à tes yeux il reste encor de moi.
> Divin vouloir daigne seul me conduire,
> Je m'abandonne à ton obscure foi . . .[1]

And again,

> C'est peu pour toi que n'avoir plus de vie,
> Et qu'abîmer ce moi jadis si cher.[2]

But even that was not enough. In those lines there still remained a trace of design, of something that could be understood. What he aimed at was the inconsequent, unintelligible murmuring of the helpless babe. He was continually harping on that theme. "Oh, when one has been a self-sufficient creature, full of guile, a restless, miserable tormented creature—oh, the bliss of being like a little child, asleep in his Father's arms." And she: "Some day you must become as simple-hearted as I am. The greater your wisdom now, the more innocent and childlike you will become, provided you sincerely desire to lay aside your greatness and become even as a little babe." And he to her: "I open all my heart to God, so that I may receive within me that spirit of child-like helplessness of which you speak"—"It seems to me as if God would carry me like a little child in His arms; as though I could not move a step by myself without falling. If only He will work His will in me, and through me, all will be well."

All would be well. Even the persecution, even the false interpretations that were put upon Madame Guyon's teaching; for false he considered them, seeing in her, as he did, only what we find in the greatest mystics, such as are recognized by the Church, like Saint Teresa of Jesus, Saint John of the Cross. It was only people who were incapable of enjoying the sweetness of pure love, who, bruising this delicate flower of sublime devotion with

[1] O pure love, destroy in me whatever, in your eyes, remains of self. O Will Divine, only deign to be my guide, I resign myself to thy secret guidance.
[2] It is a small thing for thee to have done with life
And to sink that "self" which once thou lovedst so dear.

their clumsy hands, declared that she was unworthy to approach the altar. Even the condemnation that came from Rome at the end of that long-protracted controversy, was for him but yet another test. To humble himself, to accept the verdict, to publish it in a pastoral letter addressed to the faithful of his diocese, all this was but a means vouchsafed him of mortifying the Old Adam, of submitting to the supreme sacrifice, of sweeping away the final barrier of human pride and of triumphing in God at last. *Inveni portum*: he had found peace, a peace such as, before his meeting with Madame Guyon, he had never known, a peace which he resolved never to forgo till his dying day. He recognized her errors, if errors they must be called; he would humbly submit to doing penance, if he himself had gone astray: but in his mind there was no room now for error, and his heart was incapable of sin. He was veritably nothing; a cinder; the relic of a love so vehement that it could find requital only in the death of him whom it had chosen to contain its fires. The drama of his soul's long journey towards the goal of perfect love was of far greater moment to Fénelon than those aspects of the matter which usually engage attention—the quarrel with Bossuet, the letters, the polemical prints, the rejoinders, the counter-rejoinders, the examinations, the speeches for and against, and then the verdict. That other drama was a hidden one, a drama of which the multitude had not an inkling. Could they even faintly guess at the pathos, at the awe-inspiring character of that transmutation of the human essence into the divine, of that purification by fire? "When I speak of pure love, I do not mean that fervour whose sole aim is to lend beauty to the possessor of it, and which seems to appertain to that person alone. The only love which I regard as pure, is love which relentlessly destroys, which, far from embellishing and adorning its subject, tears from it everything it has, so that when at last nothing remains to be taken, it will pass without hindrance to its destined end. For, apart from that end, it can in no wise endure. Its sole aim is to deface, to rend asunder, to destroy, to bring to nought; it lives only to destroy; it is even as the beast which the prophet Daniel saw, and which rends, crushes and devours all."

Madame Guyon had disciples all over Europe; Poiret published her writings, Poiret who was by no means the least considerable

of those who professed the theology of the heart. It was useless
to try to put down these Enthusiasts; useless to attempt to
repress them by force. As for appealing to reason, what was the
use of that with people who declined to recognize that reason
had any jurisdiction in the matter? They multiplied; they
swarmed like ants; hungry-hearted, passionate, sick in mind, for,
at last, out Heroding Herod, they came to seeking God in their
own pathological disorders, their mental aberrations, in stark
lunacy. Impatient of all order and discipline, they turned their
backs on the National Churches, which they compared to prisons;
on the ministers of religion, whom they called tyrants; and even
on society, for society persecuted them. Progress they called
corruption; science, perversion. They admitted, for the most
part, the doctrine of the Fall and the Redemption. But the
benefits that flowed from that first redemption being exhausted, a
second was needed, and it would come. The days were accomplished; Antichrist was reigning over a world where true
Christians were no more.

> Cet Antéchrist est né
> Ja plus d'un an passé
> Le temps est arrivé
> Qu'il soit manifesté.
> Je l'ai vu en esprit
> Par une claire nuit,
> Sur un théâtre grand
> Riche et resplendissant,
> Couvert d'un pavillon
> Bordé à l'environ,
> Tout tendu de velours
> Incarnat à l'entour.
> Dessus un lit mollet
> Demi couché il est,
> Il n'est plus en bas âge
> Ains un grand personnage.
> Sa gloire est sans pareille;
> On l'estime a merveille;
> Fait paraître son train
> De nuit, en grand festin;
> Il a valets en nombre,

Comme une armée innombre
Du peuple aux environs
De toute nation . . . .[1]

The first of the plagues had begun—War! The rest would
follow: Pestilence, Fire, Famine. But God would not suffer His
faithful to perish. Christ would come in all the glory of His God-
head. Then would begin the age of true happiness. Often they
formed communities, as, for instance, Johann Georg Gichtel,
who founded the confraternity of Angelic Brethren: abstaining
from all labour or business of whatever kind, devoting themselves wholly to contemplation and to the abandonment of self,
his disciples were to transform men into angels. Then there was
Jane Lead who established the cult of the mystical Sophy, and
founded the sect of the Philadelphians. Gichtel, however, looked
on her as somewhat limited in outlook, and rather too moderate
for his taste. She was satisfied with having frequent visions and
with foretelling things to come, as this, for example: the mystic
seals of the Book of the Lamb shall be opened, the great Attila
shall put the Dragon to flight, the Philadelphians shall raise on
high the banner of Love, embroidered with the royal name, the
Gospel shall be spread over the whole world and the remotest
nations of the earth shall belong to Christ the Saviour. . . .

Not content with spiritual self-abandonment, they had their
miraculous visions, their raptures, their ecstasies. Nor were
their experiences confined to spiritual delights. The senses also
played their part. They fought with the Evil One, who appeared
before them in hideous shapes, and they emerged triumphant
from these exhausting combats. They were prophets, healers,
wonder-workers. Alas, those poor hapless wonder-workers,
flung into prison, stoned, wandering from town to town, from
country to country, driven along by the authorities and the
tempest of their own frenzy. They soothed their tortured spirits
by telling themselves that it was Satan who was thus tormenting

[1]This Antichrist was born more than a year ago. It is now time for him to be
made manifest. I beheld the vision of him one moonlight night on a great stage
rich and resplendent, covered with an awning fringed all round with crimson velvet.
On a soft couch he was half reclining; he is no longer young this great personage;
his glory is unrivalled and he is held in wondrous great esteem. He comes forth
with all his train by night and holds high festival; he has numerous lacqueys and a
vast army of people of every nation.... Antoinette Bourignon, L'Antéchrist
découvert, Amsterdam, 1681, chap. XXIII.

them, because he beheld in them the destroyers of his kingdom and the chosen instruments of God. They died miserable deaths in hospital or poorhouse. Sometimes they met their end by torture, like Quirinus Kuhlmann, who journeyed all over Germany, Holland, England, France, Italy and Turkey, casting his seed on stony ground, trying to found communities as he went along, proclaiming that Babel was about to fall, and that the advent of the Fifth Kingdom of the Just was at hand. Finally, he went to Moscow and was burnt at the stake in 1689.

Think what a number of them there were; bear in mind the relationships between them, their different branches, the correspondence exchanged between them; think of the writings which they disseminated in such profusion, and which, wherever they originated, never failed to find translators, thus forming a vast network of theosophical ideas covering the whole of Europe. Then let us consider another category of people, people whose ideas were of a totally different order; people like the mysterious Rosicrucians, members of secret societies, adepts in search of the philosopher's stone, dimly fancying it possible to transmute from one to another the various outward manifestations of the one, solitary, Universal Substance. All this will at least give us the notion of a vast and ceaseless fermentation of ideas.

Sentiment is conquered by reason; but sentiment declines to accept defeat. As compared with knowledge, as the philosophers understand it, the *illuminati* laid claim to a fire which at once enlightened and inflamed them. Science, in the commonly accepted sense of the term, is progressive, it advances step by step, it is a matter of indefinite future development. In contrast with this, the theosophists claim that their science is immediate, intuitive, and, according to them, it alone is real and authentic. The majority of the thinkers of the period laid emphasis on the word *know*; but some, and they were a minority, put the stress on *love*. There was Antoinette Bourignon, a strange, aggressive and much persecuted woman who, at the end of an adventurous career, became purely a creature of the emotions; she held direct communication with God; she despised worldly knowledge, because it merely darkened the light of the wisdom within her, a wisdom which satisfied all her needs. She declared that, even if the Gospel itself were to perish, the created being would find within itself a guiding law that would suffice to lead it to the goal of truth and happiness.[1] On one occasion Antoinette did battle with some Dutch disciples of Descartes. "She had some conferences with the Cartesians and formed a sorry notion of their principles. They, for their part, were as little pleased with her as she with them. The Cartesian method did not suit her at all. She was against judging things in the light of reason, whereas their guiding principle is that everything should be submitted to that tribunal. She assured them that God had shown her and expressly declared that Cartesianism was the worst of all errors and the most accursed heresy the world had ever seen, being a formal declaration of atheism or rejection of God, for whom corrupt human reason was to be substituted." This is of a piece with what she used to tell the philosophers, namely, "that their malady arose from their trying to understand things in the light of human reason without preparing for the illumination of divine faith which required that we should abrogate our reason, our intellect, our feeble understanding so that God might kindle and diffuse His divine light within us. Unless this be done not only is God imperfectly recognized, but He and His truth are excluded from the soul by this activity of our reason, and the workings of our corrupt intelligence; and that, in itself, is a kind of atheism and denial of God. . . ."[2]

"When, after long and arduous toil, the eighteenth century had abolished or—which amounts to the same thing—believed it had abolished, the idea of God as an old man with a white beard gazing down upon all mankind and protecting them with His right hand, it had not, *ipso facto*, finally disposed of the religious problem. Mystical aspiration is one thing; the symbol offered for its satisfaction is another. We may destroy the symbol, but the aspiration remains. Man is eager to find above him something, somewhere, whereunto he may pour forth the inarticulate prayer which, do what he will, never ceases to well up from the depths of his being."[3]

[1]*La lumière née en ténèbres*, Antwerp, 1669. 2nd edn., Amsterdam, 1684.
[2]Pierre Bayle, *Dictionnaire*, art. Bourignon, note K.
[3]Pierre Abraham, *Créatures chez Balzac*, 1931, p. 15.

CONCLUSION

WHAT, then, is Europe? A cockpit, a seething cauldron of neighbours fighting one against another. There is England at grips with France, and France with Austria. There is the war of the League of Augsburg; the war of the Spanish Succession. War everywhere, say the history books, hard put to it to follow all the ramifications of the universal *mêlée*. Rulers may sign treaties, but the treaties do not last. Peace is what everyone is longing for and no one ever gets. The nations are sick to death of the interminable strife, but still the wars go on. Year by year, as Spring returns, the armies take the field again.

Leibniz, seeing it was useless to try to keep the Europeans from fighting one another, suggested that it would be a good thing to divert their bellicose activities to places beyond the European continent. Sweden and Poland might overrun Siberia and Russia; England and Denmark could have each their slice of North America; Spain would come in for South America, and Holland for the East Indies. France had Africa before her very eyes; let her seize it, then, and push right on to Egypt, let the *fleur de lys* advance in triumph to the very fringes of the desert. In this way, all those soldiers, all those firearms, all those guns, if busy they must be, would at all events have savages and heathens for their victims. National ambitions and interests, with plenty of elbow room in distant quarters of the earth, would never again come into conflict.

The Abbé de Saint-Pierre did not deem it sufficient merely to extra-domiciliate war. "When I came to ponder on the cruelties, the bloodshed, the outrages, the conflagrations, and all the havoc and destruction to which wars give rise, I asked myself whether war really was an evil beyond all cure, whether it was indeed impossible to bring about a lasting peace."[1] Yes, by all means let us have a lasting, nay, an ever-lasting peace. This was the plan: the rulers of the different countries were to sign a pact undertaking, for themselves and their successors, to renounce all existing claims against one another. What they then held was to be considered theirs in perpetuity. In order that no single power should have more men under arms than any of the others, military establishments were to be strictly limited; the number of troops should be definitely fixed, twelve thousand dragoons at the most. If, in spite of these measures, hostilities were to break out somewhere, the matter in dispute was to be referred to the Union for arbitration. If necessary, force was to be brought to bear on any sovereign who refused to abide by the ruling of that body. A permanent council of plenipotentiaries should function in some free and neutral city, such as Utrecht, Cologne, Geneva, Aix-la-Chapelle. . . . Like all Utopians, the Abbé de Saint-Pierre was marvellously precise in filling in the details of his visionary scheme; however, there was one word beyond all others which intoxicated him like some heady wine, a word on which, it seemed to him, all hopes were founded, and that was the word European: a European Court of Justice, a European military force, a European republic. If only people would listen to his words and act on them, Europe, instead of a battle-ground, a shambles, would become a friendly association of law-abiding, peace-loving nations.

When, however, in 1672, Leibniz attempted to secure the adherence of France to his great design, war had lately broken out with Holland, and it cannot be stated with certainty whether Louis XIV ever actually saw the philosopher, who was to have come from Germany to put his views before him. When, forty years later, the Abbé de Saint-Pierre began to pile up, one upon another, his cloud-girt castles in the air, his contemporaries just let him go on dreaming his untimely dreams in undisturbed tranquillity. The Abbé de Saint-Pierre, fired with redoubled ardour, and looking about him for support, expounded his ideas to Leibniz, the ageing champion of the great cause of peace, and

[1]Ch. Castel de Saint-Pierre, *Mémoires pour rendre la paix perpétuelle en Europe*, Cologne, 1712, Preface.

Leibniz replied a little sadly. He told him that what men chiefly needed, if they were to obtain deliverance from the evils that oppressed them, was will, determination. At a pinch, a resolute ruler might keep pestilence or famine away from his borders, but the prevention of war was a far more difficult matter, for it depended, not on the will of one man alone, but on the unanimous concurrence of all Kings and Emperors. There was not a minister, he declared, who would feel like taking it upon himself to advise the Emperor to renounce his claim to Spain or the Indies. The hope that the Spanish monarchy might be won for the French royal house had been the cause of fifty years of war; and it looked as if the hope of recovering it was going to account for fifty more. Look where you would, it seemed as though "some sinister fate was always interposing betwixt man and the attainment of his happiness".[1]

What, once more, is this Europe? A living paradox, something at once rigid and fluctuating; a jig-saw of barriers, and at each barrier, a body of officials whose business it is to exact all manner of dues and tolls: every imaginable obstacle to hinder man's free intercourse with his brother man. . . . There are tracts of country round which their proprietors are so busy putting up fences that they have no time left to till them. Not an acre but has been a bone of contention for ages past, and every time a new owner gets possession, he too must put a rampart round his property. The wide open spaces are things of the past. Every scrap of land is meted, delimited, parcelled out. "I've come into the world so late, I've hardly found room enough to dig myself a grave, let alone build a house."[2] These frontiers are rigidly defined, yet you cannot rely on them. Conquests change them; treaties change them; a piece of barefaced land-grabbing changes them. They are shifted forwards, they are shifted back; they are done away with altogether, and then put up anew.

[1]Leibniz to the Abbé de Saint-Pierre, from Hanover, 7 February, 1715. See, by the same author, *Observations sur le projet d'une paix perpétuelle, de M. l'abbé de Saint-Pierre* (*Oeuvres*, ed. Foucher de Careil, vol. IV).

[2]Marana, *Entretiens d'un philosophe avec un solitaire sur plusieurs matières de morale et d'erudition*, 1696, p. 29. See also p. 28. "People try to settle disputes by force, or by sudden attack; the strongest will always get the better of those who are unprepared to defend themselves; and so long as there are different Provinces, Kingdoms and Peoples, there will be hostile clashes and wars; just as there will always be vice, so long as men walk the earth."

Geographers, just putting the finishing touches to the latest maps, look up to find they are already out of date.[1] Some people would like to see whole kingdoms welded into one, and to treat the Pyrenees as non-existent. Hence this inveterate instability. Europe claims to be completely patterned out, and says that no one must meddle with that pattern; yet she herself is always meddling with it.

On the West, the state of affairs is quieter. No more will fleets of hostile barbarians come sailing over the sea; no invaders from alien lands will lay waste those ancient villages. If there is fighting, it will, thank God, be among brothers—English, French, Portuguese, Spanish. In the Mediterranean, the Turks are making trouble for travellers and the people along their borders, but there is at least this to be thankful for, they do not constitute a vital danger. But to the East—ah! that is another matter. In the old days, the great thing was to defend the Cross against the Crescent, whose forces were planted on the very border-line of civilization. But to-day the problem was not so simple. Now, at the gateway of the East, are gathered millions who, obedient to the orders of their Czar, are demanding to be integrated into Europe, to be looked on as Europeans. They must needs have goods sent them from Amsterdam, from London, from Paris; they clamour for models to copy from, and for people to instruct them how to do it. They trim their beards and cut their hair; they change their style of dress; they learn to speak German. So much for the outward man; but what of the inward one? Will that be changed as readily? Will they be like backward schoolchildren and tamely swallow whatever their teachers tell them. If their petition is granted (and how can that be avoided?), won't they insist on our importing their ideas in exchange for ours? Ideas, shall we call them? Or rampant madness? That is the question we shall have to face one of these days. Even now, Europe is a little uncomfortable, a little shaken in the saddle, by this competitor, this rival, this *simulacrum*, this spurious imitation of the real Europe, which is now raising its head on the confines of the East.

Europe, land of envy, hatred, and strife, of feuds and rancours! The Latins despise the Germans for their loutish bodies, coarse

[1] *Journal des Savants*, 13 April, 1693. *Apropos* of the present state of affairs in Europe, 1693; "hardly a day goes by but some fresh change or other takes place".

behaviour and dull wits. The Germans despise the Latins, calling them effete, worn out, corrupt in mind and body. The Latins wrangle among themselves. You would think it positively pained them to be forced to recognize any decent qualities in their neighbours, and that they only had an eye for defects. One cannot help being reminded of the cloak of Asmodeus, *le Diable Boiteux*, with its host of portraits done in Indian ink. There's not an honest face among them. All of them are smirking, putting on some expression or other: a Spanish *donna* wrapt in her mantilla ogling some foreigner who is walking at her side; a French lady practising some new-fangled airs and graces before a pier-glass, while a young abbé stands at the door holding some patches and a pot of rouge; some rough-looking German fellows, their doublets all unbraced, reeking of wine and stained with tobacco-juice, sprawling round a table befouled with the remnants of their late debauch; an Englishman gallantly proffering his lady-love a pipe and a mug of beer.[1]

Now glance at the garden of Mr. Spectator. When the flowers are looked on as the symbols of the different countries they lose all their scent and beauty. "The scent of Italian flowers is observed to be too strong, and to hurt the brain, that of the French with glaring, gaudy colours, yet faint and languid, German and Northern flowers have little or no smell, or sometimes an unpleasant one."[2]

But wait. After a time, as we listen to the plaints and laments that rise up from these tormented lands, we catch, amid the confused clamour, strains of loftier tone, strains of pride and glory. Listen attentively, and you will gradually recognize the sound of voices hymning the praises of a Europe whose strength, and intelligence and charm and splendour no other region in the world can rival.

True, Europe is the smallest of all the four divisions of the globe; but she is the fairest, the most fertile and the most richly cultivated, without deserts or barren tracts. In Europe the liberal and the useful arts flourish with incomparable splendour. People may say what they like about China and the marvels to be seen there, the fact remains that "there is a certain specific quality of mind or genius which you meet with nowhere but in

[1]Lesage, *Le Diable Boiteux*, chap. I.
[2]*Spectator*, No. 455.

Europe, or at any rate not far beyond it. It may be that it cannot, from its very nature, expand at once over an extended area, and that some decree of fate compels it to keep within a more or less restricted sphere. Be that as it may, let us make the most of it while it is ours. The great thing is, it is not confined to matters of science and arid philosophical speculation, it embraces art, and taste, and beauty, in which spheres I doubt if there is any race in the world to equal us."[1] Divided against herself she may be, nay, she is, but Europe always closes her ranks and stands four-square when she has to confront continents she has brought beneath her sway before, and which she would subdue again, if the need should arise. In the minds of her people there ever lives on the tradition of heroic voyages, of new discoveries, of galleons laden with gold, of glorious banners floating proudly over the ruins of barbaric empires. And they feel that they are still a power to be reckoned with, that they still have plenty of spirit left in them. "If Europe wanted to overawe East and West, it were no sooner said than done. Let the rulers but give the word, they would find more men ready and eager to fly to arms for the mere glory of the thing, than the Asiatics or the Africans could get together by lavish bribes of gold and silver."[2] Torn asunder, indeed, she is, and pierced with the poignant consciousness, not of her misfortunes alone, but of her faults, and of all her deprivations lamenting most bitterly the loss of that unity of faith that once was hers, realizing as she does that now no more, as of old, can she refer to herself as Christendom. Nevertheless, in spite of all, Europe prides herself that she still retains a privilege which is hers of right, a distinction, an originality that comparison with other peoples brings out into stronger relief, a noble heritage at once inalienable and unique.

And now, yet once again, what is this Europe? A spirit that is for ever seeking. Unsparing of herself, she is ceaselessly pursuing two goals: one of them is Happiness; the other—and this she holds the more vital and more dear—is Truth. No sooner does she make some discovery that seems to her to satisfy her twofold need, than she suspects, nay, she knows, that what

---

[1] Fontenelle, *Entretiens sur la pluralité des mondes*, Sixième soir.
[2] Louis du May, *Le prudent voyageur*, Génève, 1681. Discours IV. *De l'Europe en général.*

she grasps, all too precariously, is, after all, but a temporary, an imperfect thing. And so she sets forth once more on her unending quest, at once her pride and her enduring pain.

Beyond her borders, untouched by her civilizing graces, whole masses of the human race live on from day to day, never bestirring themselves to think, satisfied simply to be. Others, weighed down by the heaviness of age, turning a deaf ear to all importunate questionings, shut themselves up in a passive immobility which they call wisdom, in a self-centred calm which they call perfection. Yet others, tired of thinking for themselves, are satisfied to continue for all time doing as they have done hitherto. Not so in Europe. There the web that is woven by day is unravelled again at night. New threads are discovered and tested on a different woof. Every morning the air resounds with the hum of looms vibrating and trembling as they turn out the latest pattern.

If ever there was a time when the seeker deemed for once in a way that she might cease from her quest because she had reached her goal at last it was at the classical age. Could she hope to create forms more beautiful, more time-defying; things so perennially fair that we admire them to this day, so eternally beautiful that they will remain as models for our children and our children's children and for generations yet undreamt of. But this same beauty postulates a pre-existing peace of mind in those who created it. In this cult of the classic spirit it was found possible to live in accordance with the precepts of Christianity without forgoing the wisdom of the ancients, of duly balancing the several functions of the mind, of establishing an order based on civilization and culture and of bringing to pass countless other marvellous things all of which, summed up in a single word, meant putting up before mankind a pattern of life bordering on perfection, and on the peace that comes of it.

And so it came to pass that Europe, lost in contemplation of this wonder, did in fact pause for a moment. For a moment the illusion possessed her that she could cease her toil as she looked on a creation so graceful and so stately that anything more noble in concept, more exquisite in execution she could never hope to behold.

The illusion was short-lived, and very soon belied. Perhaps, after all, it had been a temptation to stop, rather than an actual standstill, for Europe can scarcely be said, even for a moment, to have eluded her ineluctable destiny. Before ever the philosophers of a school whose system was based on a free acceptance of Authority had had time so much as to adumbrate their doctrines, a rival school was already denouncing the perils, the abuses, the defects of that same Authority, and, pointing out what they considered excessive in the idea, finally came to the conclusion that it had no validity at all. And so, beneath the surface, beneath the illusory semblance of tranquillity, the quest began again. A start was made towards a different kind of happiness, a different brand of truth. The restless ones, the seekers, once scorned, persecuted, driven underground, now began to show themselves in broad daylight, pushing their way to the fore, making a name for themselves, demanding to be recognized as guides and leaders. That is the crisis, moral and spiritual, which we have seen developing between the 17th and the 18th centuries.

But this critical urge, whence came it? Who fostered it? What made it at once so daring and so strong? Where, in a word, did it originate? The answer is that it came from afar, from very far indeed: it came from ancient Greece; from this, that or another heretical doctor of the Middle Age; from many another distant source, but beyond all doubt or question, it came from the Renaissance. Between the Renaissance and the period we have just been studying, the family likeness is unmistakable. There is the same refusal on the part of the more daring spirits to subordinate the human to the divine. In both cases a like importance is assigned to man, to man who has no rival, man who limits the boundary of the knowable, resolves all problems that admit of solution, regarding the rest as null and void, man the source and centre of the hopes of the world. Now and then, Nature comes in, not very clearly defined, but powerful, Nature no longer regarded as the work of a Creator, but as the upsurge of life as a whole, and of human life in particular. And there are the same cleavages; the abortive attempt to unite the Churches which marked the end of the seventeenth century did but set the seal on the schism of the century before, whose finality some tried, and tried in vain, to contest. There were the same endless disputes concerning matters of chronology, about soothsayers and witchcraft. Rugged, strenuous, forthright age, when men

turned their eyes into their very souls, when assailants and
defenders alike felt they were fighting for their dearest convictions; when sceptics still resembled proselytes; when everyone
felt that the real point at issue was to seek, and find, the key to the
enigma of life—this age bears upon it all the characteristics of a
second Renaissance but a Renaissance sterner, more austere, and,
in a measure, disillusioned, a Renaissance without a Rabelais, a
Renaissance without a smile.

It is no vague similitude which we are here suggesting, but
a very definite and easily recognizable historical parallel. These
furious toilers, these patient compilers of huge folios, these indefatigable and insatiable bookworms may have had scant
respect for the poets, to whom the Renaissance owes its grace
and charm, but, if they neglected the poets, they at least studied
the philosophers who moulded its daring and adventurous
intellect, and made it free of the delights and despairs of limitless
speculation. To them they gave ear, them they admired, and in
their footsteps they followed. Bayle is the heir of the freethinking
brood who carried the sixteenth century well on into the seventeenth. He speaks with approval of La Mothe Le Vayer whose
Dialogues "contain a number of extremely bold statements about
religion and the existence of God". He refers to Lucilio Vanini
as the glorious martyr of scepticism. Further on in time, he makes
acquaintance with Jean Bodin, Charron, Michel de L'Hospital,
and, needless to say, with Montaigne; who gave him to understand in his old-style manner of putting it that there are a lot of
folk who let go their hold on *things* to go running after *causes*;
a true saying which was conspicuously exemplified in the matter
of the comets. He knew, as did most of his principal contemporaries, Giordano Bruno, who "was a man with plenty of brains
which, however, he misapplied because not only did he attack
Aristotle's philosophy at a time when to do so was to gather a
hornets' nest about you, but he also attacked the most fundamental truths of the Christian faith". He knew Cardan, "one of
the foremost thinkers of his age", "a man of curious mentality",
"who says that those who hold that the soul dies with the body
are, so far as their principles are concerned, much better people
than the others". He knew Pomponazzi—heavens, whom did
he not know! He knew Palingenius the Heretic, the Sieur
Naudé's favourite author. Speaking generally, he knew all the

people who declined to acknowledge any other guide than Reason.[1]

On a par with him, there was Richard Simon, who was not unacquainted with any of those who, before him, had pored upon the Scriptures, and who, as he said of Guillaume Postel, had but one aim, and that was "to measure the whole universe by the yard-stick of reason". Textual criticism, familiarity with the learned tongues, new developments in philology—all the writers who lighted him on his way were connected with the Renaissance. Going back a considerable distance in time, he took a leaf out of the book of the Collège Royal. "I have here", he writes, "the official report of an action at law which the Theological Faculty in Paris brought against the royal professors of Hebrew and Greek, four years after their appointment".[2]

This very evident alliance was noted and commented upon at the time. Bossuet involves in one sweeping condemnation "Erasmus and Simon, who, on the pretext of some alleged superiority possessed by them in the sphere of languages and polite letters, presume to pronounce judgment between St. Jerome and St. Augustine";[3] while Bayle's admirers consider that a statue ought to be put up in his honour at Rotterdam, alongside the statue of Erasmus.[4]

The opponents of the philosophical school include in one wholesale condemnation Spinoza, Bruno, Cardan, and the Italian Renaissance, which had revived the errors of the Pagan world and assisted the world-wide dissemination of atheism.[5] Its friends, on the other hand, looked with admiration on the end of the fifteenth century and the beginning of the sixteenth, whence a new source of light sent out its rays.[6]

And so the trend of modern thought can be charted more or less accurately as follows: starting from the Renaissance, an eagerness for invention, a passion for discovery, an urge to play the critic, traits all so manifest that we may call them the dominant

---

[1] *Pensées sur la Comète, passim*; and *Dictionnaire.*
[2] *Lettres choisies*, Letters, 5, 9, 23.
[3] *Défense de la tradition et des Saints Pères*, chap. XX, livre III. Part I: *Audacieuse critique d'Érasme sur saint Augustin, soutenue par M. Simon.*
[4] See Bayle, *Correspondance.* Pierre Jurieu, *Le philosophe de Rotterdam accusé, atteint et convaincu*, 1706, p. 2.
[5] See John Evelyn, *The History of Religion*, London, 1850, Preface. Ch. Korholt, *De tribus impostoribus magnis liber*, Kilonii, 1680.
[6] L. P. *Two Essays sent in a letter from Oxford to a nobleman in London*, London, 1695.

elements in the European mentality. Somewhere about the middle of the seventeenth century, there was a temporary pause, when a truce, wholly unlooked for, was entered into by the opposing forces, an entirely unpredictable reconciliation. This phenomenon, which was nothing short of miraculous, was what is called the Revival of Learning, the revival of the classical spirit, and the fruit of it was peace and tranquil strength. It was an example of an equilibrium deliberately pursued and consciously agreed upon by men who, though acquainted with the passions and uncertainties which are the common lot of human kind, were but too mindful of the tribulations that had afflicted the preceding generation, and therefore sought some sort of *modus vivendi*, that should fend off a return of them. Not that the spirit of enquiry was extinguished. It persisted among the partisans of the classics themselves, so disciplined, so regulated, whose aim was to put the finishing touch of perfection on works which demanded untiring patience in the making if they were to win the crown of immortality. It endured among the rebels, quietly biding their time; and among certain people who, while secretly sapping their foundations, paid eloquent lip-service to the political and social institutions to which they were indebted for all that contributed to the comfort and adornment of their lives; men like Saint-Évremond and Fontenelle, those aristocrats of revolution.

So it came about that, as soon as the classical ideal ceased to be a thing to aim at, a deliberate goal, a conscious choice, and began to degenerate into a mere habit, and an irksome one at that, the innovators, all ready for action, set to work with all the old zest and energy. And so, yet once again, the mind of Europe set out on the unending quest. Then came a crisis so swift and so sudden, so at least it seemed, that it took men completely by surprise; yet had it long been stirring in the womb of Time, and, so far from being a new thing, was in reality a very old one.

All-embracing, imperious, profound, it, too, in its turn, though born of the seventeenth century, was destined to leave its impress on virtually the whole of the eighteenth. The great clash of ideals occurred before 1715, indeed, before 1700. The daring utterances of the *Aufklärung*, of the age of light, pale into insignificance before the aggressive audacities of the *Tractatus theologico-politicus*, the amazing declarations of the *Ethics*. Neither

Voltaire nor Frederick II ever came near the ungovernable anti-clerical, anti-religious frenzy of Toland and his like. Had Locke never been born, d'Alembert would never have penned the *Discours préliminaire* to the Encyclopaedia: the quarrel over the philosophers and their ideas was not a whit more bitter than those which, later on, created such an uproar in Holland and England. Even Rousseau's "Back to Nature" ideas were not more revolutionary than those of Adario the Savage, as described by Lahontan the Rebel. In this era, so turbid, so crowded with events that it seems at first sight a mere welter of confusion, there took their rise two great streams which were to flow on through the whole of the century: one is the river of rationalism; the other, a mere trickle to begin with, but, later on, to overflow its banks, was the river of feeling, of sentiment. And since, all through this conflict of ideas, the aim was to extend the discussion beyond the sphere of the intellectual few and to get at the masses, since the basic principles of government and the very conception of right and wrong were at issue, since the principle of equality and individual freedom had been publicly proclaimed; since the rights of the individual as man and citizen had been openly canvassed, let it be recognized once more that virtually all the intellectual views and ideas which as a whole were to culminate in the French Revolution had already taken shape, even before the reign of Louis XIV had ended. The *Social Contract*, the principle of the delegation of power, the right of subjects to rebel against their rulers—all these things were ancient history by 1760. For three-quarters of a century and more they had been freely and openly discussed. Everything that is, is a microcosm of the whole. We know that. We know, too, that there is nothing new under the sun, for have we not been trying all along to trace relationships and construct genealogies? But if we are to give the name "novelty", "new" (and that seems the nearest the intellectual department is able to supply)—if we are to apply the word "new" to something which, after a long period of germination, comes finally to birth, or to a fresh manifestation of eternal forces which, long dormant, burst forth anew and with a blaze so sudden and so dazzling as to seem new to ignorant or forgetful men; or if, again, we apply the term "new" to a particular tone, a particular way of saying things; or to a resolve to look forward rather than back, to discard the past after winning from it all we can; if, finally, we call "new" an intellectual movement so dynamic as notably to influence our everyday lives, then something new indeed, a change whose effects have lasted right down to our times, was wrought during those years when certain men of genius—Spinoza, Bayle, Locke, Newton, Bossuet, Fénelon, to name only the most illustrious—addressed themselves to the task of exploring the whole field of knowledge in order to bring out anew the verities which govern and condition the life of man. Applying to the moral sphere what one of them, Leibniz, said of the political, we, too, may say: *Finis saeculi novam rerum faciem aperuit*:[1] in the closing years of the XVIIth century a new order of things began its course.

END

---

[1] *Works,* Ed. Foucher de Careil, Vol. III. *Status Europae incipiente novo saeculo.*

INDEX

François, Ier, 31-3
Franklin, Benjamin, 83
Frederick I of Prussia, 77
Frederick II of Prussia, 446
Frederick III, Elector of Brandenburg, 77, 175

Gale, Thomas, 49
Galland, Antoine, 16, 363
Garcilaso de la Vega, 288
Garofalo, Biagio, 196
Garth, Samuel, 369
Gassendi, Pierre, 106-7, 120, 241, 263, 412
Gassendists, 119
Gay, John, 65
Gemelli, Carreri, G. F., 9
George, Elector of Hanover (George I of England), 234
Gichtel, J. G., 432
Glanvil, Joseph, 168
Goethe, 354
Gomarians, 94
Gosse, Edmund, 65
Gottsched, J. C., 355
Gracián, Baltasar, 174-5, 321-2
Grammont, Comte de, 320, 368
Gravesande, G. J., 309
Gravina, G. V., 283, 347, 354, 381
Gregory the Great, St., 82
Grimmelshausen, H. J. C. von, 391
Gronovius, Jacob, 39
Groot, Hugo de, *see* Grotius
Grotius (Hugo de Groot), 87, 183, 209, 263, 270-1, 275-6, 283, 412
Gualtieri, Fr. Giovanni Antonio, 308
Guericke, Otto von, 310
Guyon, Jeanne Bouvier de la Mothe, 426-30

Haendel, G. F., 381
Halifax, George Savile, Marquis of, 288, 320, 377
Hamilton, Anthony, 368
Hanover, Duchess of, 226
Heinsius, Daniel, 127
Helvetius, C. A., 402
Henrietta of England, 138
Herbelot, Barthélemy d', 16-7
Herbert, Edward, Lord Cherbury, 141, 252, 263
Herodotus, 14
Hill, Aaron, 360
Hippo, 285
Hobbes, Thomas, 141, 148, 263, 268, 274, 277
Hochstetter, A. A., 67
Hocquincourt, Charles de Monchy, Maréchal d', 323
Homer, 338-9, 353

Horace, 346, 353
Huet, Gédéon, 302
Huet, Pierre Daniel, Bishop of Avranches, 45-6, 205
Huisseau, Pastor d', 95, 301
Huygens, Christian, 309
Hyde, Edward, Earl of Clarendon, 30

Irenaeus, St., 189

James II of England, 62-3, 276
Jaquelot, I., 85, 113-4
Jerome, St., 161, 192, 202, 444
Jérôme Acosta (Richard Simon), 194
Jérôme le Camus (Richard Simon), 194
Jérôme de Sainte-Foi (Richard Simon), 194
John of the Cross, St., 429
Josephus, 263
Julius Caesar, 33
Jurieu, Pierre, 85, 89, 104, 113, 147, 208, 274-5, 301, 373
Justin, Saint and Martyr, 161
Juvenal, 377

King, William, 111, 113
Knutsen, Matthias, 147
Kuhlmann, Quirinus, 433

La Bruyère, 12, 71, 162, 267, 281, 326, 373, 381
La Chaise, Père, 203, 360
Lacombe, Père, 428
La Fare, Charles Auguste, Marquis de, 129
La Fontaine, Jean de, xvi, 58, 64, 71, 290, 336, 350, 394
Lahontan, Baron de, 13, 258, 446
Lama, Bernardo, 134
La Mothe Le Vayer, François de, 23, 106, 443
La Motte, Antoine Houdar de, 54, 339-40
Lambert, Thérèse de Marguenat de Courcelles, Marquise de, 331
Lamy, Père François, 87, 147
Lancisi, Giovanni Maria, 308
Langbaine, Gerard, 346
La Roque, Abbé de, 185
Launoy, Jean de, 182
Lead, Jane, 432
Le Blanc, Père, 311
Le Bossu, Père, 346, 353
Le Brun, Charles, 405
Le Clerc, Jean, 75-6, 87, 97, 113, 145, 196, 210, 249, 295, 340, 373
Le Comte, Père, 11, 22
Le Dieu, Bossuet's secretary, 200
Lee, Nathaniel, 355
Le Gobien, Père, 22, 24

TITLES IN SERIES

For a complete list of titles, visit www.nyrb.com or write to:
Catalog Requests, NYRB, 435 Hudson Street, New York, NY 10014

J.R. ACKERLEY Hindoo Holiday*
J.R. ACKERLEY My Dog Tulip*
J.R. ACKERLEY My Father and Myself*
J.R. ACKERLEY We Think the World of You*
HENRY ADAMS The Jeffersonian Transformation
RENATA ADLER Pitch Dark*
RENATA ADLER Speedboat*
CÉLESTE ALBARET Monsieur Proust
DANTE ALIGHIERI The Inferno
DANTE ALIGHIERI The New Life
KINGSLEY AMIS Lucky Jim*
KINGSLEY AMIS The Old Devils*
WILLIAM ATTAWAY Blood on the Forge
W.H. AUDEN (EDITOR) The Living Thoughts of Kierkegaard
W.H. AUDEN W.H. Auden's Book of Light Verse
ERICH AUERBACH Dante: Poet of the Secular World
DOROTHY BAKER Cassandra at the Wedding*
DOROTHY BAKER Young Man with a Horn*
J.A. BAKER The Peregrine
HONORÉ DE BALZAC The Unknown Masterpiece *and* Gambara*
MAX BEERBOHM Seven Men
STEPHEN BENATAR Wish Her Safe at Home*
FRANS G. BENGTSSON The Long Ships*
ALEXANDER BERKMAN Prison Memoirs of an Anarchist
GEORGES BERNANOS Mouchette
ADOLFO BIOY CASARES Asleep in the Sun
ADOLFO BIOY CASARES The Invention of Morel
CAROLINE BLACKWOOD Corrigan*
CAROLINE BLACKWOOD Great Granny Webster*
NICOLAS BOUVIER The Way of the World
MALCOLM BRALY On the Yard*
MILLEN BRAND The Outward Room*
SIR THOMAS BROWNE Religio Medici *and* Urne-Buriall*
JOHN HORNE BURNS The Gallery
ROBERT BURTON The Anatomy of Melancholy
CAMARA LAYE The Radiance of the King
GIROLAMO CARDANO The Book of My Life
DON CARPENTER Hard Rain Falling*
J.L. CARR A Month in the Country
BLAISE CENDRARS Moravagine
EILEEN CHANG Love in a Fallen City
UPAMANYU CHATTERJEE English, August: An Indian Story
NIRAD C. CHAUDHURI The Autobiography of an Unknown Indian
ANTON CHEKHOV Peasants and Other Stories
RICHARD COBB Paris and Elsewhere
COLETTE The Pure and the Impure
JOHN COLLIER Fancies and Goodnights
CARLO COLLODI The Adventures of Pinocchio*

* *Also available as an electronic book.*

VASILY GROSSMAN An Armenian Sketchbook*
VASILY GROSSMAN Everything Flows*
VASILY GROSSMAN Life and Fate*
VASILY GROSSMAN The Road*
OAKLEY HALL Warlock
PATRICK HAMILTON The Slaves of Solitude
PATRICK HAMILTON Twenty Thousand Streets Under the Sky
PETER HANDKE Short Letter, Long Farewell
PETER HANDKE Slow Homecoming
ELIZABETH HARDWICK Seduction and Betrayal*
ELIZABETH HARDWICK Sleepless Nights*
L.P. HARTLEY The Go-Between*
NATHANIEL HAWTHORNE Twenty Days with Julian & Little Bunny by Papa
GILBERT HIGHET Poets in a Landscape
JANET HOBHOUSE The Furies
HUGO VON HOFMANNSTHAL The Lord Chandos Letter*
JAMES HOGG The Private Memoirs and Confessions of a Justified Sinner
RICHARD HOLMES Shelley: The Pursuit*
ALISTAIR HORNE A Savage War of Peace: Algeria 1954–1962*
GEOFFREY HOUSEHOLD Rogue Male*
WILLIAM DEAN HOWELLS Indian Summer
BOHUMIL HRABAL Dancing Lessons for the Advanced in Age*
DOROTHY B. HUGHES The Expendable Man*
RICHARD HUGHES A High Wind in Jamaica*
RICHARD HUGHES In Hazard*
RICHARD HUGHES The Fox in the Attic (The Human Predicament, Vol. 1)*
RICHARD HUGHES The Wooden Shepherdess (The Human Predicament, Vol. 2)*
INTIZAR HUSAIN Basti*
MAUDE HUTCHINS Victorine
YASUSHI INOUE Tun-huang*
HENRY JAMES The Ivory Tower
HENRY JAMES The New York Stories of Henry James*
HENRY JAMES The Other House
HENRY JAMES The Outcry
TOVE JANSSON Fair Play *
TOVE JANSSON The Summer Book*
TOVE JANSSON The True Deceiver*
RANDALL JARRELL (EDITOR) Randall Jarrell's Book of Stories
KABIR Songs of Kabir; translated by Arvind Krishna Mehrotra*
FRIGYES KARINTHY A Journey Round My Skull
ERICH KÄSTNER Going to the Dogs: The Story of a Moralist*
HELEN KELLER The World I Live In
YASHAR KEMAL Memed, My Hawk
YASHAR KEMAL They Burn the Thistles
MURRAY KEMPTON Part of Our Time: Some Ruins and Monuments of the Thirties*
RAYMOND KENNEDY Ride a Cockhorse*
DAVID KIDD Peking Story*
ROBERT KIRK The Secret Commonwealth of Elves, Fauns, and Fairies
DEZSŐ KOSZTOLÁNYI Skylark*
TÉTÉ-MICHEL KPOMASSIE An African in Greenland
GYULA KRÚDY The Adventures of Sindbad*
GYULA KRÚDY Sunflower*
SIGIZMUND KRZHIZHANOVSKY The Letter Killers Club*